THE COMIC BOOK FILM ADAPTATION

THE
COMIC BOOK
FILM ADAPTATION

Exploring Modern Hollywood's Leading Genre

LIAM BURKE

University Press of Mississippi / Jackson

www.upress.state.ms.us

The University Press of Mississippi is a member
of the Association of American University Presses.

First printing 2015

∞

Library of Congress Cataloging-in-Publication Data

Burke, Liam (Liam P.)
The comic book film adaptation : exploring modern
Hollywood's leading genre / Liam Burke.
pages cm
Includes bibliographical references and index.
ISBN 978-1-62846-203-6 (hardback) — ISBN 978-1-62674-515-5 (ebook)
1. Film adaptations—History and criticism. 2. Motion pictures and
comic books. 3. Superhero films. 4. Comic strip characters in motion
pictures. 5. Motion picture production and direction—United States.
6. Motion picture industry—United States. I. Title.
PN1997.85B87 2015

791.43'6—dc23   2014042191

British Library Cataloging-in-Publication Data available

CONTENTS

ACKNOWLEDGMENTS

With many solitary evenings spent pursuing an ever-receding goal, there are more than a few parallels between researching a book and the exploits of comic book loners. However, in compiling these acknowledgments I was reminded of the hero's epiphany in the final panels of Grant Morrison's *The Return of Bruce Wayne*, "The first truth of Batman . . . I was never alone. I had help." I would like to recognize the contributions of the many groups and individuals who guided this book to publication.

Firstly, I want to thank Leila Salisbury and the team at the University Press of Mississippi for taking on this project, and all the care and patience they demonstrated. Much of this research was carried out during my time at the Huston School of Film & Digital Media at the National University of Ireland, Galway, and I would like to acknowledge my former colleagues Seán Crosson, Sean Ryder, Tony Tracy, Dee Quinn, Conn Holohan, and Rod Stoneman for their advice and support. Equally, I must recognize my colleagues at Swinburne University of Technology, in particular Carolyn Beasley for her diligent proofreading and Jason Bainbridge for applying the keen eye of a fan and a scholar. I was fortunate to be funded by the Irish Research Council during the earliest stages of this research, support for which I am very grateful.

I would like to thank the industry professionals who took the time to discuss their work, including Evan Goldberg, Kevin Grevioux, Joe Kelly, Paul Levitz, Steve Niles, Dennis O'Neil, Scott Mitchell Rosenberg, Michael E. Uslan, and Mark Waid. These interviews provided insights that greatly enriched this study. Special thanks must go to Will Sliney, whose dynamic cover leaves little doubt as to why he is quickly becoming one of Marvel Comics most popular artists.

Over the course of my research, this book has consistently been reworked. Much of this refinement can be attributed to the scholars I have met on the long road to publication. Firstly, I would like to thank Will Brooker for his detailed feedback and guidance. I want to recognize Peter Coogan, Randy Duncan, and Kathleen McClancy of the Comics Arts Conference, and Imelda Whelehan and Deborah Cartmell of the Association of Adaptation Studies for the many opportunities to present my research and receive crucial advice. I would also like to thank Martin Barker for important pointers, as well as the opportunity to publish early findings in *Participations: Journal of Audience and Reception Studies.* Furthermore, I must acknowledge the "anonymous" readers who provided essential feedback.

A sincere thank-you to Neasa Glynn and the staff of the Eye Cinema, Galway, for allowing me to carry out important audience research, as well as the many filmgoers who graciously filled out surveys. I would like to acknowledge my friends who lent their support and expertise. From helping out with surveys to proofreading drafts, I am indebted to Dave Coyne, Veronica Johnson, Gar O'Brien, Siobhan O'Gorman, Barry Ryan, Adam Scott, and Maura Stewart. Graph-Man Andrew Rea deserves particular credit for his enthusiasm and essential design skills. I would, of course, like to thank my family for their unwavering encouragement. Finally, and most importantly, I need to express my heartfelt appreciation to my wife, Helen, who has endured too many hours of comics and films, incalculable dog-eared drafts, and holidays annexed by conferences. Her support is unconditional, and it is to Helen that I dedicate this book.

THE COMIC BOOK FILM ADAPTATION

INTRODUCTION

A gardener is innocently watering flowers when a mischievous young boy steps on the hose. When the man inspects the nozzle, the boy releases the flow, soaking him. Not to be outdone, the gardener catches the boy, and, after ensuring they are both in frame, reprimands him with a few vigorous slaps across the backside. This is the basic, but effective, setup of Louis Lumière's *L'Arroseur Arrosé* (1895). The staged comedy, a novelty in an era of slice-of-life *actualités*, is often celebrated as the first narrative film. However, what is often overlooked is that *L'Arroseur Arrosé* is also cinema's first adaptation of a comic.[1]

Throughout the early days of cinema, this emerging entertainment looked to other media to confer artistic credibility and narrative stability. Although novels and plays were the most adapted materials, films based on comics maintained an important presence. Georges Sadoul argues that *L'Arroseur Arrosé* borrowed its premise from a nine-image comic, *L'Arroseur*, by artist Hermann Vogle (1887), while Lance Rickman identifies variants on this gag in a number of comics in the years leading up to Lumière's innovation.[2] More explicit examples of comic book adaptations during this time included G. A. Smith's film version of British comic *Ally Sloper* (1898), eleven *Happy Hooligan*

FIG. I.1 A panel from "Un Arroseur Public (A Public Waterer)" by Christophe (3 August 1889), one of the many widely available comics that used the waterer premise in the years before cinema's first narrative film *L'Arroseur Arrosé* (Lumière 1895).

short films (J. Stuart Blackton 1900–1903), and, in 1906, Edwin S. Porter's live-action adaptation of Winsor McCay's *Dreams of the Rarebit Fiend*.[3] Today, it is impossible to ignore cinema's heavy reliance on comics. From superheroes to Spartan warriors, comics have moved from the fringes of pop culture to the center of mainstream film production.

Prior to this modern trend, comic book adaptations received little attention from scholars publishing in the English language.[4] Nonetheless, even with the high number of films produced since 2000, this area remains relatively underexplored. Most analyses appear as contributions to anthologies (e.g., Brooker "Batman"; Ecke; Loucks), journal articles (Becker; Ioannidou; Jones), or as chapters in monographs meeting wider remits (Lichtenfeld, Bukatman *Poetics of Slumberland*), with the collection *Film and Comic Books* edited by Ian Gordon, Mark Jancovich, and Matthew P. McAllister perhaps the only dedicated book.

Comics scholars are among those that one might expect to give this area sustained academic attention. Yet, motivated by a desire to maintain the boundaries of their nascent field, these academics have largely ignored the topic, with Greg M. Smith explaining: "Dealing with comics alone is hard enough without compounding the difficulty by studying two different objects" ("Studying Comics" 111).[5] Similarly, adaptations studies, which recently widened its view beyond the novel-to-film debate, has only made tentative steps in this area, with Thomas Leitch suggesting this reluctance may stem from a belief that "adapting texts that are largely visual to begin with seems so easy, simple, or natural that the process has limited theoretical interest" (*Film Adaptation* 180). However, the study of the modern comic book film adaptation does raise important questions about production in an era of filmmaking characterized by conglomerate strategies, transmedia ties, and seemingly limitless technological possibilities. This study is pitched as an opening salvo in that overdue debate.

To be specific, the book's five chapters each take a different perspective on the comic book film adaptation. The study begins, logically, by asking *why*. Why, after more than a century of coexistence, have comics and cinema recently become so entwined? It will argue that at the start of the twenty-first century Hollywood faced certain cultural, technological, and industrial challenges that comics were uniquely equipped to surmount, thereby facilitating their ascendency from subculture to mainstream fodder. However, modern comic book film adaptations were not merely symptomatic of these filmmaking practices, but proved influential in their development.

After considering the cause, the book next turns to the effect that this trend has had on film production. Chapter Two will chart how the success of comic book adaptations saw the films channeled through production, promotion, and reception into a group that displayed the shared attributes of a single genre, the comic book movie. Focusing on the fan audience, Chapter Three will first examine how the participatory practices of comic book fans found them ideally positioned at the start of the twenty-first century to take advantage of the Web, before considering the impact that this newly empowered group had on film production. Whether motivated by generic expectations or fidelity, many adaptations have strived for a comic aesthetic. The strategies filmmakers have used to engage with the language of comics will be the focus of Chapter Four. Expanding on that topic, the final chapter, Chapter Five, will explore how cinema's storytelling devices have been tailored to evoke comic book conventions in adaptations and related films. Through these various approaches, a rounded picture of this important and under-analyzed trend in Hollywood filmmaking will emerge.

The remaining sections in this introduction will outline the scope of this research, establish key terms, and describe where this project fits in the field of adaptation studies. Any reader eager to delve straight into the topic might be better served by moving directly to Chapter One.

Scope of Research

It is prudent at this early stage to outline the study's scope, boundaries, and key terms. When *X-Men* (Singer) opened to a $54 million weekend in the summer of 2000, it ushered in an era of unprecedented comic book adaptation production by Hollywood studios.[6] This post-2000 trend, which continues to dominate Hollywood cinema, will be the focus of this study. This should not suggest that comic book adaptations were not produced in other countries and at other times. Important examples from early cinema have already been identified, and adaptations produced by international filmmakers such as *Oldboy* (Park 2003), *Persepolis* (Satrapi and Paronnaud 2008), and *Blue Is the Warmest Color* (Kechiche 2013) have enjoyed wide acclaim. Rather, by narrowing the scope to modern Hollywood productions, the analysis will be more focused, reaching conclusions that should prove relevant to the study of films from other periods and national cinemas.

Additionally, while the adaptation of comics to television will be discussed as part of wider trends, they are not the focus of this research. With the success of *Smallville* (Gough and Miller 2001), *The Walking Dead* (Darabont 2010), *Arrow* (Berlanti, Guggenheim, and Kreisberg 2012), and *Agents of S.H.I.E.L.D* (Whedon, Whedon, and Tancharoen 2013), I anticipate and look forward to a detailed study of this stream of adaptation, particularly as television's serialized narratives are arguably better suited to most mainstream comics.

Occasionally, comics will make their way to the screen via another medium. For instance, the promotional material for the Adam West-starring feature-length film *Batman* (Martinson 1966) made many references to the popular television series, but there was no mention of the comics—"Soon, very soon, Batman and I will be Bat-apulting right out of your TV sets and on to your theatre screens." Similarly, the urtext for the musical *Annie* (Huston 1982) may have been Harold Gray's comic strip *Little Orphan Annie*, which was first published in 1924, but the film is essentially an adaptation of the 1977 stage musical. *Teenage Mutant Ninja Turtles* (Barron 1990) might also be considered another example of a "comic book" adaptation that is more greatly indebted to an intermediary version, with the film's poster promising "Hey Dude, this is *no* cartoon" in an overt reference to the successful animated series. Thus, as these films are more beholden to another form, they tend to garner less attention in this study than more direct adaptations.

Although the term "comic book film adaptation" seems self-explanatory, it requires clarification as the comic book has many sister forms and antecedents. *The Spirit* creator Will Eisner adopted the term "sequential art" to describe "an art and literary form that deals with the arrangement of pictures or images and words to narrate a story or dramatize an idea" (*Comics & Sequential Art* 5). Historical examples of this form include Paleolithic cave paintings, as well as the military campaigns chronicled on Trajan's Column and the Bayeux Tapestry.

With the advent of printing, sequential art could be reproduced, and in formats more mobile than lengthy scrolls or cave walls. Roger Sabin describes how in the seventeenth and eighteenth century sequential art, produced using woodcuts and later copperplate engravings, became a "mass medium" in Britain (11). Improvements in printing during the mid-1800s found an ever-increasing number of publications eager for material to fill their pages. While in Britain, sequential art more often appeared in satirical magazines like *Punch* (1841) and factual publications like the *Illustrated London News* (1842), in the United States graphic narratives were more commonly found in newspapers where they pandered to the country's growing immigrant population. Newspaper magnates William Randolph Hearst and Joseph Pulitzer, quickly realizing the potential of graphic narratives to boost circulation, began vying for the most popular comics. Pulitzer had the earliest success when he printed *Hogan's Alley* (Outcault 1894), a satire of slum life in the big city that was quickly dominated by its most popular character, the Yellow Kid. *Hogan's Alley* is widely cited as the first strip to include all the elements synonymous with modern comics (speech balloons, encapsulation, recurring characters, et cetera), an orthodoxy Duncan and Smith term the "Yellow Kid thesis" (14).

Commentators writing on the relationship between comics and cinema often subscribe to the Yellow Kid thesis as it suggests the forms were twinned from birth (Bukatman *Poetics of Slumberland* 2). However, such a stance would relegate earlier examples, including *L'Arroseur* and its variants, to the status of proto-comics. In a section of *The System of Comics* titled "The Impossible Definition," comics scholar Thierry Groensteen criticizes the US-centric Yellow Kid thesis as "an arbitrary slice of history" (13) summarizing that it is "almost impossible to retain any definitive criteria that is universally held to be true" (14). Thus, while an agreed definition (and therefore first example) of comics is elusive, this study is content to recognize the Yellow Kid as an important step in codifying the medium's language.

Another watershed moment came in 1933 when comics finally made the move from the pages of newspapers and magazines to their own format with the publication of *Famous Funnies: A Carnival of Comics*—a repackaging of popular newspaper strips (Goulart 4). The success and proliferation of this format soon necessitated the production of original material, a demand that was met by collections such as the appropriately titled *New Comics* (1935). Other genres soon followed, including in 1938 the industry mainstay, the superhero adventure.[7]

Providing a more specific umbrella term than "sequential art," cartoonist and comics theorist Scott McCloud defines "comics" as "the medium itself," and not a specific object such as comic book or comic strip (*Understanding Comics* 4). This study will use the term "comics" as McCloud suggests, to describe the medium, whereas "comic book" will be used as it was understood in 1938—a serialized publication reliant on the language of comics. Comic strips and their adaptations (e.g., *Dick Tracy*, *Garfield: The Movie*, and *Marmaduke*) will be acknowledged as part of wider discussions, such as Chapter Four's semiotic analysis. However, the focus will remain on comic books, as, despite the parallels, there are a number of qualities that distinguish comic books from strips, including: length, layout, mode of presentation, and readership. Similarly, satirical cartoons are outside the scope of this research, as they do not contain the deliberate sequence that many consider fundamental to comics (Saraceni 5). Equally, adaptations of illustrated books such as *The Grinch* (Howard 2000), *The Polar Express* (Zemeckis 2004), and *Alice in Wonderland* (Burton 2010) will not be considered.

Graphic novels, however, are central to this study. Although the "graphic novel" as a concept has a long history (Harvey 106), from the late 1970s the term was used to describe a comic that contains a complete story, has a comparatively realistic tone, is printed on higher quality material, and is longer than the average comic book. Will Eisner's 1978 portmanteau account of life in a Bronx tenement, *A Contract with God*, is often cited as the first modern "graphic novel." This term was frequently used throughout the 1980s and 1990s to confer credibility on works such as *Watchmen* (Moore and Gibbons 1987), *Our Cancer Year* (Brabner, Pekar, and Stack 1994), and *Ghost World* (Clowes 1997). As Art Spiegelman, whose Pulitzer Prize-winning *Maus* (1986) was part of the graphic novel boom, noted in his introduction to *City of Glass* (Karasik, Mazzucchelli, and Auster 2004) "the new label stuck in my craw as a mere cosmetic bid for respectability. Since 'graphics' were respectable and 'novels' were respectable . . . surely 'graphic novels' must be doubly respectable!"

The term "graphic novel" was diluted over time as the major publishers, realizing the esteem it implied, began collecting their periodicals in anthologies that, on the surface at least, mirrored the books being produced.[8] Many comics scholars agree that the "graphic novel" is today, and perhaps always was, a marketing strategy (McCloud *Reinventing Comics* 28; Saraceni 4; Hatfield 30; Sabin 165; Duncan and Smith 70), with Frank Miller concluding, "I think 'graphic novel' is a very pretentious term to describe something that has no good name" ("Miller on Miller"). The boundaries between the graphic novel and comic book are now so unclear that the greatest, and perhaps only, difference between them is the creator's intentions. Comic book creators tend to be interested in serialized, high-concept storytelling, while the graphic novelist aspires to produce a work that has a greater depth and permanency. This book will recognize those distinctions and apply the terms accordingly.

Implicit in any discussion of the graphic novel's relationship to comic books is the distinction between mainstream and alternative comics. When a redesigned Flash sped across the cover of *Showcase* #4 in 1956, the spandex-clad hero ushered in the so-called "Silver Age of Comic Books." Following that early success, the "Big Two" publishers (Marvel and DC Comics) increasingly focused on superhero titles to the point that any books that did not feature a mask or a cape were branded "alternative." As *Watchmen* artist Dave Gibbons noted in 2000, "superheroes are a genre that has overtaken a medium" ("Comics and Superheroes"). This ready association continued into cinema with the term "comic book adaptation" becoming synonymous with "superhero movie." However, as will be more fully explored in Chapter Two, in recent years the traditional boundaries between alternative and mainstream comics have become more diffuse with a number of "alternative" creators (e.g., Brian Michael Bendis, Robert Kirkman, and Matt Fraction) moving into mainstream comics, and non-superhero titles such as *The Walking Dead*, *Saga*, and *Fables* becoming bestselling books.

Similarly, it is the contention of this study that superhero movies have been subsumed into a larger genre that is most often termed the "comic book movie." This genre includes films based on "alternative" titles such as *Sin City* (Rodriguez 2005), *30 Days of Night* (Slade 2007), and *Scott Pilgrim vs. the*

World (Wright 2010). How the industry and audience corralled these films into a more cohesive genre will be explored in Chapter Two. Furthermore, it will be argued that the genre's boundaries have widened to include films with no recognized source text, but which have adopted characteristics of the comic book form and its film adaptations (e.g., *Creepshow*, *The Matrix*, and *Hancock*). Accordingly, this study is concerned with the larger comic book movie genre, which includes, but is not limited to, the superhero movie.

A final term that should be established before moving forward is "creator." There are many skills (writing, drawing, inking, coloring, and lettering) required to produce a comic book. These various roles can be filled by one skilled person, which Duncan and Smith, citing Mark Rogers, categorize as the "artisan process" (88), or, as is more commonly found, the tasks will be carried out by a number of professionals—the "industrial" process. In recognition of these various tasks, and the differing number of professionals involved, Joseph Witek puts forward the wider term "creator" ("Genre to Medium" 75). This is often a more appropriate term than artist or writer to describe the producer of a comic, and hence "creator" will also be used here.

Research Subjects

The films, and the comics that inspired them, will be this study's main focus. However, these primary sources will be supported by an examination of industrial relays and paratextual materials. A number of interviews with industry professionals have also been carried out, including those with screenwriter Evan Goldberg (*Green Hornet*); former president of DC Comics, Paul Levitz; the executive producer of *Batman*, Michael E. Uslan; Marvel Comics senior vice president of publishing, Tom Brevoort; celebrated comic creator Mark Waid (*Kingdom Come*); and writer Steve Niles (*30 Days of Night*). Interviews were also carried out with creators who have played an active role in the adaptation of their own comics, such as Kevin Grevioux (*I, Frankenstein*); Scott Mitchell Rosenberg (*Cowboys & Aliens*); and Joe Kelly ("What's So Funny About Truth, Justice & the American Way?"/*Superman vs. The Elite*). Following correspondence with former Batman writer Dennis O'Neil, this study also gained access to the Bat-bible—a guide introduced by O'Neil in 1986 to ensure continuity when he became editor of DC Comics' Batman titles. O'Neil's guide is a fascinating and as yet unpublished document that offers a rare insight into the editorial process.

Nonetheless, the films, comics, and even their creators could not address every question posed by this study, and thus it was essential to engage with the audience. While the ready availability of online comments allows one to scour discussion boards and Twitter feeds for evidence to support any number of arguments, a more targeted engagement with the wider comic book adaptation audience was needed. Accordingly, I carried out paper surveys at cinema screenings of the high-profile comic book adaptations *Thor* (Branagh 2011), *Green Lantern* (Campbell 2011), and *The Adventures of Tintin: The Secret of the Unicorn* (Spielberg 2011). Some findings and conclusions from the *Thor* and *Green Lantern* screenings have been published in *Participations: Journal of Audience and Reception Studies* ("Superman in Green"). This article also contains a detailed methodology, but it is important to briefly summarize my approach here.

Studies of comic book adaptation audiences have been carried out in the past, but most have tended to focus on the enthusiastic, readily available fan. For instance, Bacon-Smith and Yarbrough observed cinema screenings of *Batman* (Burton 1989), while Barker and Brooks attempted to interview filmgoers leaving *Judge Dredd* (Canon 1995). However, they were only able to make general conclusions—"the batmobile drew a favorable response, but the batwing did not" (Bacon-Smith and Yarborough 98)—or grab single respondents exiting via the foyer (Barker and Brooks 21). Ultimately both studies found more respondents via fan forums such as comic stores and conventions.

More recent fan studies have taken advantage of the Web—a methodology recently termed "netnography" (Kozinets). For instance, in his latest work on Batman's most "dedicated audience," *Hunting the Dark Knight*, Will Brooker surveyed "75 individuals . . . using an online questionnaire that [he] promoted through *Batman on Film: The Dark Knight Fansite*" (*Dark Knight* 35). Brooker employed a similar approach for his earlier study of *Star Wars* fans, *Using the Force*. In 2012, William Proctor, citing Brooker, used the same methodology to gauge fan response to Disney's acquisition of Lucasfilm, distributing 100 questionnaires to visitors of the fan site *TheForce.net*. It transpired that one of Proctor's respondents had participated in Brooker's study a decade earlier. Despite the potential reach of the Web, this repetition of respondent points to an inherent risk in relying on fan forums, as these studies tend to draw enthusiasts, resulting in a more homogenized response—a limitation Proctor acknowledged.[9] Accordingly, this audience research strived to gain a more balanced understanding of the comic book adaptation audience by including those with no particular devotion to the source.

Identifying a similar space in such studies, Neil Rae and Jonathan Gray adopted a dualistic strategy "to answer a question that is often overlooked in reception studies focusing solely on fans: how do viewers read and make sense of comic book movies differently when they have and have not read the original material being adapted?" (86). Rae and Gray used qualitative interviews with different combinations of readers and non-readers, but as their central research question was posed in relation to adaptation it seemed destined to fall under the yoke of fidelity, with non-readers considered "intertextually poor" because they "watch the films as films, and largely as distinct texts" while "readers, predictably looked at any adaptation as part of an episodic text" (99). However, as will be discussed in Chapter Two, these non-readers are not textually poor, but often compare these films to other entries in the comic book movie genre.

Like Rae and Gray, this study also sought to engage the non-readers ignored in most studies of comic book adaptation audiences. The methodology was adapted from the international research project to explore responses to *The Lord of the Rings: The Return of the King* (Jackson 2003). The project, and its methodology, is explained in detail in the edited collection *Watching The Lord of the Rings*. Building on this earlier study a quali-quantitative approach was applied. Furthermore, Internet sampling was avoided, as it tends to favor younger enthusiasts (Barker, Mathijs, and Trobia 222–23). The study took place at regularly scheduled screenings of *Thor*, *Green Lantern*, and *The Adventures of Tintin: The Secret of the Unicorn* (hereafter abbreviated to *The Adventures of Tintin*) at the Eye Cinema in Galway, Ireland.

Filmgoers were asked to complete a three-page questionnaire, two pages before the screening and one after. The quali-quantitative approach included multiple-choice responses and self-allocation scales, with follow-on spaces to allow participants to qualify their responses. In all, participants were asked to respond to fifteen questions before the screening and to eight after. To avoid influencing the participants, questions started generally—"Q1. List (1–3) the top three sources from which you find out about upcoming films— and became more specific—"Q11. Did you know *Thor* was based on a comic book?"

Unlike the difficulties Barker and Brooks recount, because this survey was distributed in the screening theatre (as opposed to the foyer) it had a more captive audience. However, despite the benefits of the cinema setting, it did not ensure a balanced mass audience. Surveys were distributed as audience members took their seats. As the cinema did not operate allocated seating, enthusiasts were likely to attend earlier, which may have skewed the number of fans that responded at a given screening.[10] Nonetheless, wide representation was sought where possible. In total, nine screenings were surveyed, and, after spoiled surveys were discounted, there were 113 respondents. The screenings included the first scheduled showing, and then a later 2D and 3D screening.[11]

By eschewing fan forums, this survey encountered a more diverse group of respondents than similar studies. For instance, Brooker found that of the seventy-five individuals who responded to the online questionnaire he distributed through *Batman on Film: The Dark Knight Fansite*, "sixty-eight per cent of respondents were aged between 20 and 30, while 93 per cent were male . . . one-hundred per cent identified themselves as Batman fans" (*Dark Knight* 35). Contrastingly, in this study only 47 percent of participants were aged between twenty-one and thirty, with respondents in all age sectors represented.[12] Furthermore, only 34 percent of participants identified themselves as fans, and while men still dominated, women made up 38 percent of total respondents.

Despite the balance this survey achieved, its scale was modest, especially when compared to the 25,000-plus respondents Barker et al. describe (19). Nonetheless, the results provided this study with an outline of the wider comic book film adaptation audience, which was further developed through an analysis of paratextual materials and industrial relays. By triangulating these methods, a more rounded understanding of the comic book film adaptation and its audience(s) emerged.

Adaptation Studies and the Comic Book Movie

While this study will apply a number of approaches to better understand the comic book film adaptation, this research is framed within adaptation studies. This methodology might seem so obvious that it does not warrant further explanation, but adaptation studies has traditionally lacked a clear methodological center. This vacuum most likely stems from the field's transdisciplinary position, which has given rise to a certain amount of redundancy and opportunism, with new procedures regularly suggested by scholars who ignore earlier approaches or hope to correct them. This condition has prompted leading scholars Deborah Cartmell and Imelda Whelehan to recently suggest that "the correctives have gone as far as they can for the time being; maybe it would be useful to declare a moratorium on some features of key debates, or curb the will to taxonomize just for long enough to observe what taxonomies give us" (*Screen Adaptation* 10–11). Following on from Cartmell and Whelehan's sensible proposition, this study will reapply the terms and taxonomies of earlier scholarship to this exciting area.

Many theorists have attempted to categorize adaptation. One of the first was Geoffrey Wagner who suggested three modes of adaptation in 1975: "Analogy," where elements of the original are used while the majority of the source is significantly altered to have no specific resemblance to the original; "Commentary," the original is altered, sometimes intentionally, but in a self-reflexive way; and "Transposition," where no overt attempt is made to alter the original (219–31).[13] A number of other scholars have put forward similar frameworks, including Michael Klein and Gillian Parker, John M. Desmond and Peter Hawkes, Linda Costanzo Cahir, Kamilla Elliott, and Thomas Leitch.[14]

These categories have proven useful as they delineate the nature of film adaptation, and suggest the approach a critic should adopt when analyzing a text. This study will make use of perhaps the most cited taxonomy, Dudley Andrew's three categories from *Concepts in Film Theory*. Andrew, with no reference to Wagner's earlier work, proposed his own "modes of relation between the film and the text . . . borrowing, intersection, and fidelity of transformation" (98), which closely correspond to Wagner's categories. Applying Andrew's terminology we can see how comic book adaptations might be separated into these three spheres, categorizations that will prove useful in later discussions.

Andrew contends that "borrowing" is the largest category of film adaptation, adding that "the main concern is the generality of the original, its potential for wide and varied appeal—in short, its existence as a continuing form or archetype in culture. This is especially true of that adapted material which, because of its frequent reappearance, claims the status of myth" (98). Traditionally, most comic book adaptations by Hollywood studios could be categorized as "borrowings." "Mythic" characters such as Batman and Superman have enjoyed non-stop publication since the late 1930s, undergoing a series of tonal shifts and story additions that have become character mainstays. Consequently, the choice to borrow only the characters and setup, and not a particular story, allows for a more all-encompassing adaptation, as former president of DC Comics Paul Levitz explained when interviewed for this study:

> If you make the decision that you want to do a Batman movie, OK, but there are 4,000 Batman stories: which one, or ones, am I going to do? Which are going to be my ideal version? Is this going to be more Denny O'Neil and Neal Adams, more Jeph Loeb and Tim Sale, more Frank Miller, more Bill Finger and Dick Spring? What do I want to do here? By virtue of there being 4,000 stories, I am implicitly given greater license to come up with brand new ones, for better or worse.

As Levitz suggests, if one were to faithfully adapt an early Batman comic it might contain the hero's familiar vigilantism, but it would not include recognized elements such as Alfred, the Batcave, or costumed villains.[15] Consequently, in adapting the myth of Batman rather than one specific comic book, borrowings such as Tim Burton's *Batman* maintain those staples that have reappeared in the character's many incarnations and have become his most identifiable traits.[16]

As will be more fully explored in Chapter Three, many comic book adaptations today could still be considered borrowings, particularly films such as *The Amazing Spider-Man* (Webb 2012), *The Dark Knight Rises* (Nolan 2012), and *The Avengers* (Whedon 2012) that rely on the mythic status that their characters have accrued through decades of adaptation. However, it will be argued that even within these borrowings greater fidelity can be detected.

Furthermore, in the post-*X-Men* boom, there was a discernible shift from generalized interpretations to more faithful films, with an increasing number of adaptations that could be categorized as "intersections" and "transformations."

Andrew defines "intersection" as when "the uniqueness of the original text is preserved to such an extent that it is intentionally left unassimilated in adaptation" (99). These films maintain the "otherness" of the original, thereby allowing one text to comment on the other.[17] Although entries to this category are limited, examples might include *American Splendor* (Springer Berman and Pulcini 2003), which was adapted from Harvey Pekar's autobiographical comic book series. The film is littered with self-reflexive moments, most notably in the narration by the real-life Pekar. Typically self-aware observations include: "Here's me. Well, the guy playin' me anyway. Even though he don't look nothin' like me. But, whatever" and "If you think reading comics about your life seems strange, try watching a play about it. God only knows how I'll feel when I see this movie." These moments critique the adaptation process from casting through to its effect on the creator, thereby placing *American Splendor* firmly in the mode of adaptation that Andrew calls "intersection" and Wagner labels "commentary."

While intersections often interrogate the source, transformations hold the original material up as the ultimate goal of the adaptation. Films in this category endeavor to make the smallest number of changes necessary to bring the source to the screen in an attempt to present it in a new form. Andrew describes this mode: "Here it is assumed that the task of adaptation is the reproduction in cinema of something essential about an original text" (100).

Many adaptations of novels could be categorized as "transformations." Such fidelity was made possible, in part, because of the inherent ambiguities of the written text, which allowed adapters a degree of latitude in "faithfully" recreating the world of the original. Traditionally, such freedom was not afforded to those adapting comic books, where, in order to make a film that could be considered a transformation, the often unachievable images of the comic would need to be recreated. However, as will be illustrated throughout this study, many adaptations have recently attempted to recreate more than just the source's characters, but also its aesthetic tropes. Among these transformations one might include *Sin City*, *300* (Snyder 2007), *Watchmen* (Snyder 2009), *Kick-Ass* (Vaughn 2010), *The Losers* (White 2010), *Scott Pilgrim vs. The World* (hereafter abbreviated to *Scott Pilgrim*), and *The Adventures of Tintin*. This expanding mode of comic book adaptation demonstrates the increased importance of the source material in film production, a development that will be explored in Chapter Three.

Although a useful system for exploring adaptation, these categories are not concrete. Neither Andrew nor Wagner address how these three modes often

FIG. I.2 A regularly cited panel from *The Amazing Spider-Man* #50 (July 1967), "Spider-Man No More," alongside its "transformation" in *Spider-Man 2*.

coalesce in the same film. For instance, although the original Spider-Man trilogy, like most traditional superhero adaptations, would fall within the sphere of borrowing, it does contain overt moments of intersection, with the comic's co-creator Stan Lee making a cameo in all three films, and even stopping in the trilogy-closer to utter the line, "I guess one person can make a difference, nuff said."[18] Furthermore, while the script for *Spider-Man 2* (Raimi 2004) is original, it is indebted to the storyline "Spider-Man No More!" from *The Amazing Spider-Man* #50, including a shot designed to mirror the oft-cited panel in which the hero dumps his costume in a trashcan. Scenes such as this move the film from the mode of borrowing and into transformation. The shortcomings of Wagner and Andrew's taxonomies have been pointed out in the past, with Deborah Cartmell noting that films such as *Schindler's List* (Spielberg 1993) avoid convenient categorization (24). Nonetheless, these categories provide an effective critical shorthand that will be relied on across this study.

This research will also make use of Brian McFarlane's narratological approach to adaptation. McFarlane prefaces his 1996 book *Novel to Film* by stating: "I shall set up procedures for distinguishing between that which can be transferred from one medium to another (essentially, narrative) and that which, being dependent on different signifying systems, cannot be transferred (essentially, enunciation)" (vii). Citing Barthes, McFarlane divides narrative functions into "distributional" and "integrational" functions (14). Within distributional functions McFarlane describes "cardinal functions or nuclei" and "catalyzers." Cardinal functions are the hinge-points of a story; deletion or augmentation of these functions in an adaptation is likely to evoke reader discontent, such as the amended ending of *Watchmen*. Catalyzers modify the nuclei and are more susceptible to change, such as the murder of the Waynes following the opera in *Batman Begins* (Nolan 2005), as opposed to the cinema in comics like Frank Miller's *The Dark Knight Returns*. Within integrational functions, McFarlane discusses "informants" (e.g., names, jobs, et cetera) and "indices proper." With the exception of "indices proper," McFarlane believes that all other functions can be transferred from novel to film, but as indices proper are tied to enunciation (i.e., a medium's unique means of expression), they cannot be easily transferred to other media. McFarlane argues that indices proper require the identification of medium specific equivalents, a process he terms "adaptation proper" (26). Here, McFarlane furnishes this study with a useful concept. Adaptation proper is a creative way of distinguishing between the source's transferable elements (narrative) and those necessitating equivalents (signifying systems). In particular, Chapter Four considers the medium specificities of comics and cinema, and how filmmakers often strive to achieve a comic aesthetic.

■ ■ ■

These useful concepts notwithstanding, scholarly analysis of adaptation has traditionally been quite rigid, prompting Dudley Andrew to suggest in 1984 that "frequently the most narrow and provincial area of film theory, discourse about adaptation, is potentially as far-reaching as you like" (*Film Theory* 96). More recent assessments have been equally damning, with James Naremore opening his 2000 collection, *Film Adaptation*, by describing the subject of adaptation "as one of the most jejune areas of scholarly writing about the cinema" (1). Encouragingly, the research quagmires of the past have been identified and there has been a concerted effort by those working within the field to surmount these obstacles.[19] A study of the comic book film adaptation is well positioned to traverse these pitfalls and move debate onto new and more productive ground.

(A) An Overemphasis on Literature

An oft-criticized feature of traditional adaptation studies is the disproportionate attention literary adaptation has received. It is an issue that pervades academia, with Naremore pointing out that in universities, "the theme of adaptation is often used as a way of teaching celebrated literature by another means" ("Introduction" 1). A more inclusive approach to adaptation was suggested as far back as 1948 when André Bazin noted that the "problem of digests and adaptations is usually posed within the framework of literature. Yet literature only partakes of a phenomenon whose amplitude is much larger" ("Cinema as Digest" 19). Nonetheless, decades later much of adaptation theory is still viewed from the perspective of literature.

However, more recent theorists have begun to consider a wide variety of sources and a plethora of possibilities under the banner of adaptation. This transition was heralded by critics such as Imelda Whelehan, who called for "an extension of the debate . . . [to] move from a consideration of 'literary' adaptations . . . to a focus on adaptation more broadly" (3–4). Whelehan's proposal was echoed in Linda Hutcheon's argument that "adaptation has run amok. That's why we can't understand its appeal and even its nature if we only consider novels and films" (xi), with Hutcheon suggesting cover songs, video games, theme park rides, and museum exhibits as possible examples in her book *A Theory of Adaptation.*[20]

This in-depth study of the comic book adaptation is in keeping with the goals of contemporary adaptation studies. As discussed, in the past, comic book film adaptations garnered little scholarly attention within adaptation studies, or beyond. Now, as theorists are shifting their gaze beyond the once dominant novel to film debate, the comic book film adaptation emerges as one of the next logical steps, as it allows for considerations that a study of text-based sources often precludes. For instance, Timothy Corrigan, who identified comic book adaptations as one of the most distinctive trends in modern film adaptations during his keynote address at the 2009 Association of Adaptation Studies Conference, suggested these films have become "repositories themselves for adaptations that respond to the unique representational overlap between source and adaptation, as they recycle both visual images and graphic *mise-en-scènes*" (Burke "Adaptation Studies Conference" 55). This fertile area will be the focus of Chapters Four and Five, testifying to the importance of this research within adaptation studies.

(B) A Line of Inquiry Mired in Fidelity

Fidelity criticism is regularly cited as the greatest impediment to the analysis of adaptation, with McFarlane concluding that the "insistence on fidelity has led to a suppression of potentially more rewarding approaches to the phenomenon of adaptation" (*Novel to Film* 10). Many other prominent scholars have also criticized this orthodoxy and suggested a move away from fidelity criticism (Andrew *Film Theory* 100; Griffith 73–74; Stam "Beyond Fidelity" 76; Sadlier 190; Cardwell 19; Hutcheon 85).

While an analysis that slips into "a game of anecdotal semblance between distinguishing features" (Eisenstein 437) should be avoided, there is a greater risk that by consciously sidestepping fidelity criticism, theorists are failing to pursue rewarding lines of inquiry. Colin MacCabe opened his recent collection, *True to the Spirit*, by arguing that if the academy chooses to ignore "the grammar of value . . . those colloquial forms that are used to discuss books and films," it is sealing itself "hermetically off from the general culture" (9). Although this collection was criticized by established scholars for not recognizing recent interventions,[21] MacCabe is one of a number of commentators trying to engage productively with fidelity. Similarly, in his article, "The Persistence of Fidelity," J. D. Connor states that the "campaign against fidelity" has failed and that scholars need to recognize "the role fidelity discourse plays in the layman's discussion," while Costas Constandinides recently argued that "various attempts to demonize fidelity criticism or value judgments contradict the field's collective call for diversity" (2).

As Connor suggests, discounting fidelity discourse is at odds with the field's wider calls for audience-centric research (Pietrzak-Franger 113). For instance, Cartmell and Whelehan, citing Corrigan, recently argued that "if we can rescue the film audience from the derisory view of them as primitive . . . we might also be better able to assess the fate of literature and film adaptations in the contemporary market-place" (*Screen Adaptation* 54), and Andrew believes that if we turn our attention to "ordinary viewers . . . we might find ourselves listening to a vernacular version of comparative media semiotics" ("Economies of Adaptation" 27).

As will be explored in Chapter Three, fidelity is a marker of quality for many audiences. In recent years, producers have been forced to recognize the concerns of the digitally bolstered consumer. Consequently, fidelity discourse has become one of the key determinants that shape film adaptations, and ignoring such discussions, as many scholars imply, would limit meaningful engagement with the audience and the marketplace. It is here that the audience research described earlier will prove most useful: by engaging with a heterogeneous cinema audience the study provides insights into how and why audiences place an emphasis on fidelity. Such "affective mapping" (Proctor *Star Wars* 207) not only meets calls for greater audience research in adaptation studies, but progresses fidelity criticism into new territory.

The reluctance of adaptation studies scholars to apply fidelity criticism is understandable given the reductive analysis of the past that catalogued variations between a source and its adaptation without probing further. However, here instances of fidelity/infidelity will not be avoided, but rather treated as crosses on a treasure map—not the end of an investigation, but rather a good place to start digging.

(C) Prioritization of the Original

A further oft-cited impediment to the development of adaptation studies is the prioritization of the "original" by the audience, critics, and filmmakers, with the adaptation considered derivative. This bias has been identified since the earliest days of adaptation studies with George Bluestone succinctly articulating the prevailing prejudices: "the novel is a norm and the film deviates at its peril" (5). Yet many of today's theorists, armed with poststructuralist concepts and terminology, challenge the supposed superiority of the "original." With his 2000 essay "Beyond Fidelity: The Dialogics of Adaptation," Robert Stam led this poststructuralist turn in adaptation studies. Citing Mikhail Bakhtin's concept of "dialogism," "intertextuality" as coined by Julia Kristeva, and the transtextual relations Gérard Genette puts forward in *Palimpsests*, Stam suggests that adaptations are "caught up in the ongoing whirl of intertextual reference and transformation, of texts generating other texts in an endless process of recycling, transformation, and transmutation, with no clear point of origin" ("Beyond Fidelity" 66). Many scholars have adopted a similar stance: Hutcheon favors "palimpsest" in her challenge to the perceived superiority of the source, stating "an adaptation is a derivation that is not derivative—a work that is second without being secondary. It is its own palimpsestic thing" (9), while Brooker describes *Batman Begins* as fitting a "promiscuous poststructuralist model" that he excitedly dubs "the Batman matrix" (*Dark Knight* 62).

Comic book fans, like the readers of most cult texts, prioritize the source. However, they are not as dogmatic about the original's primacy as some literary purists. Although readers prize "fidelity," the term most often used is "continuity." Comic book continuity refers to character consistency, interrelated books, and cumulative events. As continuity is more concerned with uniformity between the differing versions rather than adherence to a particular story, it mirrors the open intertextuality that Stam describes. The concept of continuity sees comic book fans adopting a less hierarchical view of the relationship between source and adaptation, and welcoming elements introduced by adaptations. Thus, by being attentive to the "grammar of value," the scholar might be able to borrow some useful concepts and terminology from the reader.

When asked how he felt about Hollywood adaptations of one of his books, pulp writer James M. Cain responded, "They haven't done anything to my book. It's right there on the shelf" (Leonard). Although the *Mildred Pierce* author may have been being somewhat facetious, it is true that novels and other similarly inert texts are less affected by audiovisual interpretations than episodic works. Conversely, the Sisyphean stories of mainstream comic books are susceptible to the influence of their adaptations. For instance, many elements of *Batman: The Animated Series* subsequently became canon when introduced to the comic books, such as the reworking of one-dimensional villain Mr. Freeze's origin in the episode "Heart of Ice" (Dini 1992). The new backstory, in which Freeze was depicted as a biologist determined to cure his cryogenically frozen wife's illness, was not only incorporated into the comics, but also the 1997 feature film *Batman & Robin* (Schumacher).

However, it should be noted that fans are not always amenable to such revisions especially when it contravenes perceived comic book continuity. For instance, many readers voiced their disapproval to the bright colored heroes of *X-Men* donning black leather costumes for the first feature-length adaptation. Despite these objections the costumes were subsequently introduced to the comics with *New X-Men* #114 (July 2001), and later audiovisual adaptations such as the video game *X-Men Legends*.

Yet despite some resistance, the successful introduction of characters, plots, and other elements to comic book continuity, as testified by "Heart of Ice," demonstrates that while the comic book may remain for fans the ultimate authority, these adaptations are not considered derivative by creator or consumer. As Martyn Pedler notes, "Continuity isn't bulletproof; it functions more like, say, a mutant healing factor. New details are absorbed into the official storyline, and older, outdated ideas are left to fade until they eventually barely leave a scar" ("Morrison's Muscle" 255). Thus, serialized "source" texts such as comic books can be effectively reverse-engineered to tally more neatly with their adaptations. Examples of this fidelity flux can be identified across the history of adaptation, becoming increasingly commonplace in today's franchise-minded entertainments.[22] Scholars can point to this fluidity to refute Romantic notions of an "urtext," and move discussion of adaptation out of the shadow of the source.

Bazin's Pyramid

Adaptation studies' abandonment of received views and stale orthodoxies has resulted in the opening up of a methodological space, with many scholars suggesting new paradigms to fill the void (Pietrzak-Franger 112). In particular, there is a concerted effort to align research with the exciting work being done on convergence culture and transmedia storytelling. However, many scholars fail to recognize the distinctions between adaptation and transmedia storytelling as described by the term's popularizer, Henry Jenkins—"unfolds across multiple media platforms, with each new text making a distinctive and valuable contribution to the whole" (*Convergence Culture* 97–98). For instance, Elisavet Ioannidou proposes that the narrative gaps a film adaptation viewer fills in by reading the source is tantamount to transmedia storytelling. However, Jenkins believes that the inevitable repetition of the source in traditional adaptation is not transmedia storytelling because it does not expand the story, it only re-presents it (*Convergence Culture* 98), a point he later reasserted in a dialogue with David Bordwell when the film theorist attempted to categorize the Bible, Homeric epics, and the Bhagavad Gita as examples of transmedia storytelling.[23]

Clare Parody has perhaps been most successful at marrying these two fields through a focus on transmedia *franchises* rather than *storytelling*. Citing superheroes as a clear example, Parody identifies how franchises "defuse some of the aspects of adaptation [e.g., fidelity criticism, prioritization of the original] that Stam identifies as charged" in that they "normalize an aesthetic of multiplicity," with each version "intelligible to franchise consumers as simply facets of an over-arching entertainment experience" (215–16). As Parody suggests, the continuity commonplace in comic books since the 1960s has become the transmedia goal of today's conglomerates, where texts are more often co-created across a number of platforms rather than simply adapted. For instance, president of DC Entertainment Diane Nelson describes the strategies by which her company produces audiovisual versions of their comic book characters as "looking at all the different faces of the prism" (Marshall "DC Entertainment President"). Similarly, when asked about transmedia franchises for this study, Marvel Comics senior vice president of publishing Tom Brevoort responded: "I think there is a desire to keep consistency, but not absolute conformity, which is to say that Wolverine basically needs to be Wolverine no matter what medium he is in. If you see Wolverine in the films, if you see Wolverine in the animation, if you see Wolverine in the comics, they essentially have to be the same individual—the same guy."

This type of adaptation, where chronological precedence is eschewed, and each version can be produced and received simultaneously, realizes Bazin's optimistic prediction of 1948:

> The (literary?) critic of 2050 would find not a novel out of which a play and a film had been "made," but rather a single work reflected through three art forms, an artistic pyramid with three sides, all equal in the eyes of the critic. The "work" would then be only an ideal point at the top of this figure, which itself is an ideal construct. ("Cinema as Digest" 26)

Less than forty years from Bazin's deadline, the co-creation described by Henry Jenkins (*Convergence Culture* 107) and practiced by conglomerates such as Time Warner and the Walt Disney Company has achieved this "ideal construct"—Nelson's "prism" even evokes Bazin's analogy.

Transmedia franchises are an intense and vivid example of the fluidity post-structuralists identify in all adaptation, in that each version of the franchise shapes and is reshaped by the others. Pessimistically, Cartmell and Whelehan believe that Bazin's forecast is "realistic in its prediction of the length of time it might take for such a paradigm shift across the disciplines of film and literary studies" (*Screen Adaptation* 24). However, the work of Parody and others hint that we might not have to wait quite so long for a more open approach to adaptation. Indeed, if scholars are looking for a vernacular template to articulate today's more amorphous, content-based adaptation, they would be well served by looking to the continuity long practiced by mainstream comic book publishers and embraced by its readership.

■　■　■

Given the attendant difficulties, one might question the wisdom in wading into the adaptation debate. However, the research quagmires of past studies have been identified, and while some correctives may go too far (e.g., the abandonment of fidelity studies), the application of poststructuralist approaches sensitive to media convergence seems to be moving the field onto firmer ground. Whether it is acknowledging consumers as participants, mapping the many determinants that shape an adaptation, or exploring how convergence has expedited the relay of codes and conventions between comics and cinema, this study is open to the fluidity Bazin predicted.

In the end, despite methodological uncertainty, the study of adaptation is important as it provides the critic with a unique opportunity that Andrew likened to a "laboratory condition" (*Film Theory* 98), in that the acknowledged relationship between the various texts, however obfuscated, provides a constant by which all other variables can be measured. Such fixed points will be essential as this study navigates the choppy waters of this important trend: the comic book film adaptation.

CHAPTER ONE

The Golden Age of Comic Book Filmmaking

Adaptation studies scholars have long been sensitive to the manner in which the "choices of the mode of adaptation and of prototypes suggest a great deal about the cinema's sense of its role and aspirations from decade to decade" (Andrew *Film Theory* 104). This sociological approach has proven productive as it allows one to move past the research quagmires identified in the Introduction, and interrogate the filmmaking or cultural environment that nurtured the development of a particular type of adaptation. It also allows one to consider the conditions that might have emerged when an adaptation proved popular or influential.

At the end of the calendar year, cultural commentators attempt to assess with newly discovered hindsight the major touchstones of the past 365 days. This process intensifies at the turn of the decade, and so it was on the eve of 2010 that many commentators looked back on the past ten years of cinema for trends and triumphs that could be catalogued and easily labeled for blogs and magazine sidebars. These critics did not need superhuman vision or aerial perspective to realize that 2000–2009 had been the "comic book movie decade" (Rogers). One could hardly miss the garish costumes, superhuman feats, and coordinated colors; but how did it happen? How did a largely maligned medium move to the center of mainstream Hollywood film production? This chapter will apply a contextual approach to address that question.

When interviewed for this study, *Batman* (Burton 1989) executive producer Michael E. Uslan described the post-*X-Men* boom as "The Golden Age of Comic Book Filmmaking."[1] Although a number of reasons have been proposed for its emergence, they could generally be arranged along three lines: cultural traumas and the celebration of the hero following real-life events, in particular the 9/11 terrorist attacks; technological advancements, most notably digital film techniques, which allow the source to be recreated more faithfully and efficiently on screen; and finally contemporary filmmaking paradigms that favor content with a preexisting fan base and an amenability to franchise opportunities. The industry interviews for this study brought a fourth factor to the fore, which Scott Mitchell Rosenberg described as "a changing of the guard" among those who make films and most importantly those who green-light them for production. In this chapter, the validity of these bodies of opinion will be considered. Despite the enthusiasm in the popular press for clear causality, no one culprit will be identified. Rather, by charting the context in which this trend emerged, one will gain a better understanding of the factors that fostered and shaped modern Hollywood's leading genre.

"In the Shadow of No Towers"

During the 2008 US presidential campaign, Democratic hopeful, and eventual vice president, Joe Biden described Republican rival and former New York mayor Rudy Giuliani's policies as "A Noun, a Verb, and 9/11" (B. Smith). A similar assessment could also be made of the many cultural commentators who linked any-and-all shifts in the arts post-9/11 to the World Trade Center terrorist attacks and subsequent events. For example, Jeffrey Melnick's book *9/11 Culture: America Under Construction* explores the proposition that "9/11 has become the most important question and answer shaping American cultural discussions" (3).

Unsurprisingly, as the modern comic book movie trend gained momentum when *Spider-Man* (Raimi) broke box-office records in the summer of 2002, many commentators and filmmakers were quick to link the unprecedented popularity of comic book adaptations and superhero movies with post-9/11 sentiment in the United States. For instance, when asked why *Spider-Man* struck a chord with audiences, director Sam Raimi alluded to 9/11, explaining, "These are tough and scary times, and during these times we always look to stories of heroes to show us the way and to give us hope" ("Making the Amazing"). Jon Favreau was more explicit when asked, "Why do you think this period of time is so good for superhero movies?" The *Iron Man* (2008) director replied, "I think 9/11 . . . was a game changer. I think people were looking for emotional simplicity [and] escapism" (Huver). Similarly, in a paper for *PS: Political Science & Politics*, Hagley and Harrison contend that the "post-September 11 resurrection of the superhero genre, particularly in film, is a direct response to the feelings of helplessness and terror that Americans experienced in the days and years following the attack" (120). This position is also held by psychiatrist Sharon Packer, who believes that "interest in superheroes surged after 9/11, as Americans suddenly felt imperilled" (48), while comic creator Grant Morrison succinctly wrote, "Scary times and superhero movies go together like dirt and soap" (375).

However, there are many who balk at this 9/11 analysis. David Bordwell challenged this argument on his blog (later collected in the book *Minding Movies*), opening his account by sardonically writing, "More superhero movies after 2002, you say? Obviously 9/11 so traumatized us that we feel a yearning for superheroes to protect us. Our old friend the zeitgeist furnishes an explanation" ("Superheroes for Sale"). To better understand what part, if any, post-9/11 attitudes played in the production, promotion, and ultimate success of comic book movies, this section will interrogate whether the 9/11 argument is as all-conquering as Favreau suggests, or as spurious as Bordwell believes.

Do Comic Book Movies Serve a Ritual Function?

To demonstrate the popularity of comic book adaptations, one might simply point to their box-office success, as these films achieve blockbuster status around the world. However, what often goes unrecognized is the disproportionate takings of these adaptations domestically (i.e., in North America) compared to overseas, particularly in the years immediately following 9/11. In modern Hollywood, big-budget films tend to gross a large majority of their box office overseas. Anomalously, in the period from 2002 to 2008, the most successful comic book adaptation produced each year, with the sole exception of the Spider-Man franchise, accumulated the majority of its gross from North America, with the 53.2 percent domestic gross of *The Dark Knight* (Nolan 2008) typical of the trend. This may seem like a narrow majority, but the differential becomes more revealing when it is compared to other blockbusters released during this time. In the same seven-year span, the most successful non-comic book derived film released each year grossed significantly more at the international box office with no exceptions. This period included two sequels to *The Lord of the Rings*, two sequels to *Shrek*, and new Indiana Jones and Star Wars films, with *Pirates of the Caribbean: Dead Man's Chest* (Verbinski 2006) typical of this pattern with only 39.7 percent of its $1,066,179,725 gross coming from North America—a reverse of the trend found in comic book adaptations.[2]

Furthermore, comic book film adaptations are at odds with wider tactics that de-emphasize "national, regional, or historical specificities" (Hutcheon 147) in a bid to attract international audiences. If anything, comic book adaptations have increasingly traded on their status as a US entertainment, a development at least partly expedited by 9/11 sentiment. For example, many elements of *Spider-Man* were augmented to tally with post-9/11 attitudes such as the sequence where New Yorkers come to the hero's aid on the Queensboro Bridge. Similarly, in the sequel *Spider-Man 2* (Raimi 2004), the protagonist's Forest Hills neighborhood is festooned with US flags absent in the first

FIG. 1.1 Similar shots from *Spider-Man* and *Spider-Man 2*. In the first film, largely produced before 9/11, the hero's Forest Hills neighborhood contains no flags, but the second film outfits each home with its own US flag.

film, which was largely shot before the terrorist attacks—an anecdotal example of the nationalism that permeates this particular stream of Hollywood filmmaking.

As will be more fully discussed in the next chapter, in the first eight years of the twenty-first century the comic book adaptation developed from a trend into a full-fledged genre. During this time, the films resisted two tendencies of mainstream production. They generated more box-office interest domestically than overseas and continually accentuated their national identity. These two countervailing characteristics suggest that comic book adaptations uniquely tally with US filmgoing interests. However, is this enough to propose that these films serve a ritual function for their most devoted audience?

Before investigating the ritual function of comic book adaptations, it is important to identify the audiences that most often attend these films in the

US. Although filmgoing in the US is particularly prevalent among young people (*Theatrical Market Statistics*), post-9/11 comic book adaptation audiences tended to be evenly split between the four sectors commentators use to analyze attendance (male, female, over twenty-five, and under twenty-five). This development surprised Brandon Gray of *Box Office Mojo* when he analyzed *Daredevil* (Johnson 2003) early in the trend: "Despite comic book origins that would suggest the picture would play mostly to young males, Daredevil's audience was actually split evenly between the genders and between those over and under the age of 25" ("Daredevil Hits"). *Superman Returns* (Singer 2006) continued this pattern with a relatively even split among the sectors, prompting Gray to note following the opening weekend, "57 percent of moviegoers were male and 63 percent were over 25 years old" ("Superman Returns Solid"). Such statistics suggest that the comic book adaptation has wide appeal within the confines of mainstream American cinema's youthful attendance.

While not subscribing to the ritual analysis of genre, Altman articulates the stance adopted by scholars such as John Cawelti, Leo Braudy, Will Wright, and Thomas Schatz: "By choosing the films it would patronize, the audience revealed its preferences and its beliefs, thus inducing Hollywood studios to produce films reflecting its desires. . . . Far from being limited to mere entertainment, filmgoing offers a satisfaction more akin to that associated with established religion" ("Semantic/Syntactic Approach" 682–83). Post-9/11, critics often credited comic book adaptations with serving three interrelated, ritual functions: nostalgia, escapism, and wish fulfillment.

Nostalgia

In his response to 9/11, collected in 2004 as *In the Shadow of No Towers*, Pulitzer Prize-winning graphic novelist Art Spiegelman borrowed icons from early comics such as *Bringing Up Father*, *Hogan's Alley*, and *Little Nemo in Slumberland* in which the city was portrayed as a playground rather than a graveyard. Such a nostalgic response is not what one might have expected from the alternative creator, but as the New York-based Spiegelman explains in the collection's introduction: "The only cultural artifacts that could get past my defenses to flood my eyes and brain with something other than images of burning towers were old comic strips; vital, unpretentious ephemera from the optimistic dawn of the 20th century." Many responses to 9/11 were similarly filtered through a nostalgic lens, with Melnick explaining that it "is not surprising that following the terrible attack filmmakers would express instant nostalgia for the recent past" (128).

Eclipsing Little Nemo and The Katzenjammer Kids, the mythic status comic book characters such as Superman, Batman, and Spider-Man have achieved through decades of adaptation has ensured they enjoy wide recognition.

Although the audience research for this study was carried out in Ireland, a similarly nostalgic current was evident. For instance, a 36–40-year-old non-fan at a screening of *Thor* (Branagh 2011) described how he would like to see future Marvel Studios productions because they "bring back childhood memories," while a 50-plus-year-old non-fan at the same screening described how she read *Thor* as a child. Unsurprisingly for a European audience, this nostalgia was particularly evident around *The Adventures of Tintin* (Spielberg 2011). For instance, one 21–25-year-old comic fan wrote prior to the screening that he expected, "A fun cartoon that can take me back to being a kid," while a 31–35-year-old respondent stated "I had read Tintin in my youth, and I would like to read it again for nostalgia."

Adaptation studies scholars have often pointed to the nostalgic appeal of film versions of childhood favorites, with Linda Hutcheon comparing them to nursery rhymes in that "like ritual, this kind of repetition brings comfort, a fuller understanding, and the confidence that comes with the sense of knowing what is about to happen next" (114).[3] Thus, many comic book adaptations, such as *Spider-Man*, *Fantastic Four* (Story 2005), and *Superman Returns*, could have benefited from the nostalgia Melnick detected in post-9/11 US entertainments.

However, Deborah Cartmell charts how adaptations will often go further to satisfy "a nostalgic yearning for a sanitized version of the past" (26) by removing elements from the source that might be considered "unpleasant." A number of post-9/11 comic book adaptations actively partook in this process, striving to provide audiences with a rose-tinted version of the fictional and real-world past. For instance, in modern comics Superman's nemesis, Lex Luthor, had become a more complex character, even ascending to the presidency of the United States. *Superman Returns*, produced at a time when a divisive real-world president was first elected under a cloud of doubt, opted to use the simplistic super-criminal version of the character that harked back to the Golden Age of Comics. Furthermore, the modern film heavily cited the 1978 adaptation *Superman: The Movie* (Donner) through music, casting, and production design, yet included none of Lois's pointed questioning of authority figures.[4] These amendments helped mitigate the darker elements of the source(s), catering to what Cartmell identifies as a "nostalgic yearning." Martin Flanagan describes a similar strategy at work in *Spider-Man*, which references Silver Age comics that "anchor the narrative in a register of sincerity that holds at bay more modern ironic tendencies" (147).[5]

While some comic book movies provide their audience with a comforting nostalgia attributable to the long-standing, cross-generational popularity of their characters, these films were also part of the "architectural nostalgia" Steven Jay Schneider identified in post-9/11 US filmgoing. Discussing this

FIG. 1.2 Images of the Twin Towers and other similarly evocative cityscapes in *Spider-Man* and *Batman Begins*.

phenomenon, Schneider notes that "some audiences went so far as to boo scenes of the New York City skyline absent the twin towers in *Zoolander*," while audiences cheered their appearance in *Glitter* (39).

US comic creators have always had a strong connection with city living, particularly New York. Spiegelman locates the birth of newspaper comics to "about a hundred years and two blocks away from Ground Zero" (*No Towers*). Similarly, Duncan and Smith point out that since the earliest days of the form, "virtually all of American comics were created by a couple hundred people in the New York metro area" (ix). Consequently, whether the city charter says Metropolis, Gotham, or Star City, all comics are thought to take place in New York, with Batman editor Dennis O'Neil explaining in the Bat-bible, "I've long believed that Batman's Gotham City is Manhattan below Fourteenth Street at eleven minutes past midnight on the coldest night in November." The parallels are also evident in the film adaptations where Superman is clearly seen flying over a New York skyline replete with the World Trade Center in *Superman: The Movie*. The Marvel Comics characters of the 1960s (e.g., Fantastic Four, Spider-Man, and Daredevil) eschewed ersatz landmarks and collectively inhabited America's first city. Referring to this strategy, Jason Bainbridge said, "Marvel confirmed what New Yorkers had long suspected, New York was not just the center of the world, it was the very center of the universe!" ("I am New York" 167).

However, prior to the release of *Spider-Man*, there was concern regarding the New York skyline appearing in an action-orientated film following the terrorist attacks. A warning from Diane Levin, professor of education at Boston's Wheelock College, appeared in a number of publications ahead of the release: "For all children, there's a potential to trigger anxiety and stress and more viewing of the world as a dangerous place" (Studio Briefing). Although shots of the World Trade Center were removed from publicity and reduced in the film itself, the Twin Towers were still visible, including during a celebratory montage sequence in which Spider-Man first comes to New York. *Spider-Man* director Raimi commented on the use of the World Trade Center in his adaptation, explaining, "I think it's like our memories of a loved one. . . . Probably right after the death of someone we love, it's sometimes hard to look at their pictures. Then later, there's a need to look at them" (Schneider 29). Thus, the appearance of specific landmarks in *Spider-Man*, and more generic, but no less evocative, cityscapes in other adaptations, allowed comic book movies to take part in the architectural nostalgia evident in other US entertainments post-9/11.

As Henry Jenkins suggested in his analysis of 9/11 comic books, "For some, Superhero comics hark back to simpler times and get consumed as comfort food" ("Sheds His Mighty Tears" 79).[6] This assessment could be expanded to include many of the film adaptations, with their cross-generational recognition and urban setting finding the genre ideally positioned to navigate the wider nostalgic currents dominating American popular culture following 9/11.

Escapism

Alongside nostalgic currents there was an emphasis on escapism in post-9/11 American popular culture. For instance, the ratings for the long-running New York-based sitcom *Friends* increased by 17 percent in the wake of the terrorist attacks, with the show having "gained some special advantage from the hunger among Americans for shows they loved . . . in the wake of Sept. 11" (Carter). Reviewing the year in film in December 2001, *New York Daily News* columnist Jack Mathews predicted that US audiences would, "be desperate for escape from the incomprehensible evil we've just endured," adding that the major studios had "escapist films lined up like planes approaching LaGuardia." Despite the unfortunate airport analogy, Mathew's assessment proved correct with the escapist films that the studios had in postproduction (such as *The Lord of the Rings* and *Harry Potter*) clearly resonating with audiences.

Escapism has long been considered one of the fundamental attractions of comic books, from their Depression-era beginnings to the respite they offer from more modern concerns.[7] This aspect of comic books formed the basis of the Pulitzer Prize-winning novel *The Amazing Adventures of Kavalier and*

Clay. Set during the comic book industry's Golden Age, the book follows a writer and artist as they create a Nazi-smashing sensation, appropriately titled, *The Escapist*. Late in the novel, one of the creators reflects on the seemingly simplistic nature of the form: "The usual charge leveled against comic books, that they offered *merely an easy escape from reality*, seemed to Joe actually to be a powerful argument on their behalf" (Chabon 575).

Whether it is a virtue or limitation, escapism has been widely recognized as a key part of comic books extending into adaptations. The audience research picked up on this; one 26–30-year-old female participant wrote that she hoped *The Adventures of Tintin* would be "a fun, happy, escape to an adventure," while a 26–30-year-old comic book fan at *Green Lantern* (Campbell 2011) expected "Mindless Entertainment," and a 21–25-year-old fan anticipated the film "to be a fun adaptation of a decent comic character. It won't change my life, but it will get me out of it for 2 hours." Aldo J. Regalado believes that adapters "choose to perpetuate the escapist fantasies and optimistic mythologies of American heroic individualism" (128) at the expense of the source's other virtues.[8] This was particularly prevalent post-9/11, when comic book adaptations often tallied with wider escapist tendencies.

The action sequences of comic book movies did not simply revisit the events of 9/11, but offered a window into a world in which the tragedy could have been prevented. For instance, just as superheroes were portrayed in the 1930s comics as being the only ones capable of fully negotiating big-city living, in modern adaptations the superhero continues to be depicted as the ideal inhabitant of the American city, uniquely situated to deal with its obstacles, from delivering pizzas in rush-hour traffic to stopping runaway trains (*Spider-Man 2*).[9] Increasingly those obstacles reflected and/or reimagined 9/11, from saving a falling airplane (*Superman Returns*) to stopping terrorist attacks (*Batman Begins*). As Scott Bukatman concludes in his book *Matters of Gravity*, "superheroes exist to inhabit the city. . . . They hold their shape as do the other skyscrapers and monuments of the metropolis" (222–23).

The marketing for *Superman Returns* even went so far as to make escapism a central selling point of the film. The blurb that accompanied the DVD release reads "HE'S BACK. A hero for our millennium. And not a moment too soon, because during the five years. . . Superman sought his home planet, things have changed on his adopted planet. . . . Filmmaker Bryan Singer gives the world the Superman it needs." However, this promotional copy does not describe the Metropolis of the film, which shows no signs of disarray since the hero's departure. The film's marketing suggests that it is the real-world audience that needs the hero. The blurb even dates Superman's departures from Earth (five years prior to the film's 2006 release) to coincide with the terrorist attacks. Further evoking 9/11, while the cover image for the international DVD had a

FIG. 1.3 *Superman Returns* DVD covers in the US and Europe, respectively.

generic image of the hero flying, the US version displayed Superman saving a falling airplane, thereby compelling audiences to imagine escaping to a world where the events of 9/11 could have been averted. Writing in the Bat-bible prior to 9/11, Dennis O'Neil attributes gothic avenger Batman's popularity to the assurances he provides to the terrified city-dweller, "The Batman is nothing if not urban," adding, "where is a citizen safe? Certainly not in New York, nor in New York's mirror-world counterpart, Gotham." O'Neil concludes, "We have coopted [*sic*] the grimmer archetypes, embraced them, declared them, with all their ferocity and relentlessness and inhuman competence, our allies. One of the names we call them is Batman." Post-9/11, the comic book hero as the unflappable defender of the modern US city was ideally positioned to tell stories on screen that renewed confidence in the city structure through escapist imagery and optimistic reworkings of 9/11 narratives.

Wish Fulfillment

Comic books are also noted for the wish fulfillment they provide their readers, a role their adaptations also perform. A key aspect of this wish fulfillment is the transition of comic book characters from anonymous "mild-mannered" weaklings to unassailable heroes, which allows readers to identify with the protagonist's secret identity while aspiring to his heroic persona. Comic creators often played on this identification, with Stan Lee concluding *The Amazing Spider-Man* #9 (February 1964) with the following caption: "the world's most amazing teen-ager—Spider-Man—The superhero who could be—You!" As Umberto Eco noted in his oft-cited essay, "The Myth of Superman," through Clark Kent's "fearful, timid, not overly intelligent, awkward, near-sighted, and submissive" manner, he "personifies fairly typically the average reader who is harassed by complexes and despised by his fellow man" (14–15).

This spectator identification is facilitated, in part, by the simplicity of comic book art, as Scott McCloud explains: "When you look at a photo of a realistic drawing of a face you see it as the face of another. But when you enter the world of the cartoon you see yourself" (*Understanding Comics* 36).[10] This aspect of self-identification may help account for why stars are so rarely cast in the lead roles of comic book adaptations.[11] James Naremore notes how film stars are "iconic, extra-cinematic characters" ("Acting in Cinema" 115), a quality that would detract from the wish fulfillment of these escapist fantasies. Accordingly, comic book adaptations frequently feature relative unknowns in the lead roles who do not obstruct self-identification. In fact, the first live-action actor to portray Superman, Kirk Alyn, was not even billed in the serial's credits (Gordon Bennet and Carr 1948), with only the character's name appearing. Even today, an actor's name will rarely be prominently placed in promotional material for a comic book movie. Thus, it is not Henry Cavill flying, but Superman, Clark Kent, and the spectator.

However, as Bainbridge points out, "because they are wish fulfillment, a study of superheroes is therefore also a study of the perceived deficiencies in society and what 'being heroic' necessarily entails" ("Worlds Within Worlds" 64). Thus, Superman's efforts to rescue a falling plane, Batman's desire "to conquer fear," and Tony Stark's personal guarantee that "the bad guys won't even want to come out of their caves" were symptomatic of a wider desire to reassert control in a post-9/11 world.

Do Comic Book Movies Have an Ideological Agenda?

The ritual functions (nostalgia, escapism, and wish fulfillment) that comic book adaptations serve may go some way towards explaining their increased popularity following 9/11, as US audiences craved the comfort that these films could provide, and which profit-minded studios were eager to supply. However, despite the seeming amenability of comic book adaptations to the desires of post-9/11 audiences, there was one area where these films struggled to match other entertainments: celebrating community.[12]

Comic book characters have long been noted for their individualism, whether it is the "conservative, individualist Batman spirit" (Dubose 921) of Frank Miller's *The Dark Knight Returns*, the Randian ideals Robert Genter identifies in Spider-Man (972), or the Howard Hughes-inspired eccentricity of Iron Man's alter ego, Tony Stark.[13] This individuality is frequently portrayed as threatening, as Jamie A. Hughes notes of superheroes, "their absolute power and freedom from the law make superheroes both an asset and a liability to the RSAs [Repressive State Apparatuses]" (547). Lee and Ditko's Spider-Man was one of the earliest examples of this equally cursed-and-blessed approach to comic book heroes, with the city of New York widely considering the hero a menace, including the protagonist's genial aunt: "Oh dear, I certainly hope they find that horrible Spider-Man and lock him up before he can do any harm!" (*The Amazing Spider-Man* #1: March 1963).

However, the threatening individuality of the comic book character did not tally with the celebratory spirit of post-9/11 US entertainments where the dominant mood was: heroes among us, not above.[14] In *Spider-Man*, one can discern a tension between the traditional aspects of the character and a need to chime with post-9/11 sentiment.[15] In the montage where Spider-Man is first established in New York, man-on-the-street interviews are used to demonstrate the differing opinions of locals with one disgruntled New Yorker stating: "He stinks, and I don't like him." This is typical of the character as depicted in the comic. However, in post-9/11 amendments, this aspect of the vigilante was diminished. For instance, the film's climax sees the city's citizens coming to the hero's aid on the Queensboro Bridge—an element identified by the filmmakers as being added in response to 9/11 ("Weaving the Web"). The city's residents attack the villain, the Green Goblin, yelling, "You mess with Spidey, you mess with New York!" and "You mess with one of us, you mess with all of us." Scenes such as these, where the hero's wings are clipped and he needs the help of "ordinary people," serve to emphasize a community where everyone is equal, and everyone can be a hero. Such superficial egalitarianism is challenged in *The Incredibles* (Bird 2004) where the mother of a superpowered family tells her son, "Everyone is special." The son replies, "Which is another way of saying no-one is."

The emphasis on community continued throughout the Spider-Man franchise with no sense that the city's population harbored differing opinions. The sequel included a reworking of the bridge sequence from the first film, with railway commuters defending Spider-Man from Doctor Octopus. Even the hero's once skeptical aunt becomes a champion of Spider-Man saying, "Everybody loves a hero." This sense of community reached its zenith in the trilogy-closer (Raimi 2007), with Spider-Man honored with a parade and the Key to the City, as revelers held up banners declaring "New York's Hero"—another story element at odds with the source material yet perfectly in keeping with the mood of the nation.[16] This trend of unequivocal celebration of the hero and community spirit was also evident in *Superman Returns*, with the patriotically dressed alien's first act, landing a crashing plane in the middle of a baseball stadium, prompting citywide cheers and later American-themed salutes.

However, the integration of the hero into the community was at odds with the source material and the central tenets of the superhero. Over the decade, films in which comic book heroes were perceived as threatening individuals began to dominate the genre. While these films may not have met the ritual functions of other post-9/11 entertainments, they did forward a mythology that would have greater resonance in the wake of 9/11.

In *Spider-Man*, a rooftop encounter between the hero and his archenemy, the Green Goblin, sees the villain trying to form a partnership with the selfless defender by warning him, "In spite of everything you've done for them, eventually they will hate you." When the people of New York rally to Spider-Man's side at the film's climax, the hero's faith in community is rewarded. However, outside the film's narrative, the Green Goblin's prediction was proven correct, as skepticism, even outright antagonism, to clear-cut heroics began to seep into comic book adaptations. Cosmo Landesman picked up on this trend in his review of *The Dark Knight* for the *Sunday Times*, "Heroes, in our egalitarian age, no longer embody the dream of the superior individual who is greater than humanity; nowadays, superheroes must be as flawed and screwed up as we are."

Despite efforts to temper the individualism of comic book heroes post-9/11, these characters represent the latest iteration of a mythological tradition of exceptional individuals who seek revenge for injustices wrought on themselves, their homes and society, or as Tony Stark threatens Loki, "if we can't protect the Earth, you can be damned well sure we'll avenge it." Many of these heroes are not sanctioned by the groups they seek to protect and could be categorized as vigilantes. Rosenbaum and Sederberg note in their appraisal of crime control vigilantes that "American history is replete with examples of private groups restoring 'law and order' where it has broken down or establishing it in areas into which the government's formal apparatus has not yet effectively extended" (549). A number of these real-life vigilantes and social bandits, such as Joaquin Murrieta, Jesse James, and William Bonney, had their more antisocial traits glossed over by the media of the time, entering the country's mythology as heroes. These myths inspired such fictional gunslingers as The Virginian, Hopalong Cassidy, and Zorro, thereby ensuring that the vigilante archetype and revenge narrative would become cornerstones of American folklore. As will be more fully examined in the next chapter, the comic book movie is a continuation of this archetype, but the comparisons between the westerner and the comic book hero go deeper than surface similarities to a shared ideology that underlies much of American mythology and was evoked by its leaders post-9/11.

In "The Media's Frontier Construction of President George W. Bush," Ryan Malphurs charts how 9/11 "reinvigorated President Bush's connection to cowboy mythology" (191). The commander-in-chief employed many western tropes such as his oft-cited response to the question, "Do you want bin Laden dead?" when addressing reporters less than a week after the 9/11 attack: "I want justice, and there's an old poster out West, as I recall, that said Wanted: Dead or Alive." Stacy Takacs describes how such rhetoric—successful at home if not overseas—allowed the US government to portray its actions as those of a "reluctant gunslinger forced by circumstances to resort to violence" (153). However, these folkisms did not facilitate the re-emergence of westerns on screen. Ever since the genre's revisionist turn in the 1950s, it has been difficult for westerns to slip back into the black-and-white morality that marked the genre's classical period. The few westerns that did appear during this time tended to adopt a critical stance (e.g., *There Will Be Blood*, *No Country for Old Men*, and television's *Deadwood*), prompting Dina Smith to note that "not even the western could mediate us out of this mess" (173).

As superheroes are part of the same mythological tradition as the cowboy, it is unsurprising to find responses to 9/11 also evoking comic books, such as the Tribute in Light used to mark the anniversary at Ground Zero, which calls to mind the signal used to contact the hero in Batman comics. Similarly, President Bush's use of the term "Axis of Evil" recalls stock comic book villains like the Masters of Evil. Justine Toh goes so far as to suggest that a nebulous concept like the "War on Terror" is tantamount to the Sisyphean tasks superheroes undertake and that "without super villains (like Osama bin Laden) in the 'real' world, there would be no meaningful existence for a regime that devotes itself to his capture and the supposed eradication of terror" (138).

Thus, the individualistic heroes of comic book movies were well placed within a country and presidency that valorized the lone gunslinger and adopted preemptive, almost vigilante-like, activities in its foreign policy. This became the preferred right-wing reading of *The Dark Knight*, with many conservative commentators suggesting that the superhero's use of extraordinary rendition and illegal surveillance to stop a terrorist validated the Bush administration's oft-criticized War on Terror tactics. Typical of this reading was the *Wall Street Journal* op-ed by Andrew Klavan, "What Bush and Batman Have in Common," in which the mystery novelist describes the film as "a paean of praise to the fortitude and moral courage that has been shown by George W. Bush in this time of terror and war." Klavan argues that like "W, Batman is vilified and despised for confronting terrorists in the only terms they understand. Like W, Batman sometimes has to push the boundaries of civil rights to deal with an emergency, certain that he will re-establish those boundaries when the emergency is past."

Equally right-wing currents were identified in adaptations such as *Iron Man* and *300* (Snyder 2007), although these films also invite more liberal assessments. For instance, writing in the *Sunday Times*, Cosmo Landesman argued that *The Dark Knight* "champions the antiwar coalition's claim that, in having a war on terror, you create the conditions for more terror." Such multiplicity of readings is made possible by the manner in which many of these films evoke contemporary issues without adopting a firm stance. For instance, in both The Dark Knight and Iron Man franchises, the billionaire protagonists move their companies away from military contracts and into clean energy (which is ultimately weaponized), yet maintain arms development to stock their personal arsenals. While supporting characters voice concerns regarding vigilantism (Alfred and Rhodes) and escalation (Gordon and Fury), as critic A. O. Scott pointed out, "stating them . . . is not the same as exploring them." Indeed, it is often difficult to isolate a consistent view in these films: Weapons manufacturing is amoral, but this hardware can prove useful if you want to wage a one-man war on crime ("I've successfully privatized world peace"— Tony Stark, *Iron Man 2*); terrorism is evil, unless you are the one doing the terrorizing ("I seek the means to turn fear against those who prey on the fearful"—Bruce Wayne, *Batman Begins*); and heroes should not cross certain lines, except when it is necessary ("There's a point, far out there when the structures fail you, and the rules aren't weapons anymore, they're shackles letting the bad guy get ahead"—Commissioner Gordon, *The Dark Knight Rises*).

As these franchises continued, and the vague references began to pile up, further inconsistencies emerged with the characters even contradicting themselves. For instance, in *Iron Man 2* (Favreau 2010) Tony Stark proudly states before a Senate hearing that he is America's "nuclear deterrent," yet in *The Avengers* he chastises S.H.I.E.L.D. director Nick Fury for weaponizing alien technology by sarcastically stating "a nuclear deterrent . . . that always calms everything down." Thus, these allusions, which Landesman describes as "the artistic equivalent of a fake tan," seem to be less about meaningful engagement than creating a semblance of sociopolitical relevance.

A similar strategy could also be identified in comics, with many post-9/11 books commenting on America's domestic and foreign policy. For instance, *Marvel Comics: Civil War* (Millar and McNiven 2007) followed the consequences of a 9/11-evoking disaster in the Marvel Universe with half of the characters, led by Iron Man, agreeing to a government-imposed Superhuman Registration Act, while the opposing heroes, under Captain America, deemed it an unacceptable encroachment of their civil liberties, prompting the titular conflict.[17] These sociopolitical references found the comic garnering the attention of the *New York Times* and many other mainstream media outlets, with the title subsequently becoming the bestselling comic book of 2006.[18] Creator

Mark Millar explicitly cited the political allegory when discussing *Civil War*, but reminded interviewers that "Kids are going to read it and just see a big superhero fight" (Gustines). Millar's caveat underscores the enviable position that comic books occupied in the post-9/11 American market: They gained attention and sales by alluding to larger events, but when asked to take a firm stance they could deflect scrutiny by pointing to the fantasy setting.

Similarly, adaptations such as *The Dark Knight* and *Iron Man* embraced a political hybridity, tantamount to the genre hybridity of the blockbuster, which enabled them to appeal to a wide audience while their fundamentally apolitical position avoided alienating anyone. As Bordwell suggests, this "constitutive ambiguity . . . helpfully disarms criticisms from interest groups . . . [while] it also gives the film an air of moral seriousness" ("Superheroes for Sale").[19] Just as comic books gained wider attention and acclaim through allusions to 9/11 and the War on Terror, the supposed political relevance of adaptations, which a number of commentators have noted (Schatz "Too Big to Fail" 202; Brooker *Dark Knight* 200), led to greater press attention, more favorable reviews, and industry acclaim. However, when pressed, many of these filmmakers, like comic creators, maintained the ambiguity of their films or cited their heightened reality, with Christopher Nolan responding to suggestions that Batman is a right-wing character in a *Rolling Stone* interview by saying, "Yes, if you assume Gotham is the same as a place like New York City, but that's not the case" ("Christopher Nolan").

Wheeler Winston Dixon argued in his 2004 publication, *Film and Television after 9/11*, that "the bulk of mainstream American cinema since 9/11 . . . seems centered on a desire to replicate the idea of the just war" (1). Thus, despite early, often toothless, attempts at self-reflection, comic book movie convention dictates that by the third act some undeniable evil requires the hero to (re)assume their mantle. This inevitable threat, alongside some bombastic explosions, ultimately drowns out any moral questions. It is here the secret identity of the comic book adaptation might be revealed. Despite the veneer of sociopolitical relevance, the colorful costumes and fantasy setups of these films deflect the criticism leveled at more "grounded" fare such as westerns and action movies, yet the fantasy contains the same vigilante ideology that mainstream cinema had perpetuated from John Wayne to John Rambo. These films tend to validate individualistic, even illegal efforts, to defend a community that will not defend itself. This narrative tallied with a government increasingly at odds with the international community, seeking revenge by methods that were widely considered illegal, in defense of a community (domestic and international) that increasingly cast them as "outsiders."

Faultline Texts

By building on America's national myth, these films may perpetuate its attendant ideology, but the multiplicity of readings and outward resistance of audiences to the rhetoric of films such as *300* (even while they enjoy its spectacle),
suggests that these films are not simply dull instruments shaping a passive
audience's worldview.[20] For instance, one 31–35-year-old fan displayed greater
awareness when asked if she would attend future Marvel Studios productions
following a screening of *Thor*, "I have problems with the ideologies in some of
those films." As Steve Neale argues, a stringently ideological approach is "open
to the charges of reductivism, economism, and cultural pessimism" ("Questions of Genre" 65). Similarly, even if audiences do gravitate to comics and
their adaptations for nostalgia, escapism, and wish fulfillment, this is not necessarily a regressive activity. Far from mindless drones, the audience research
found participants who sought these pleasures, while also recognizing how
fleeting or empty they may be.

Given this contestation, these films are a good example of what Alan Sinfield describes as "faultline stories . . . they address the awkward, unresolved
issues, the ones in which the conditions of plausibility are in dispute" (47).
Brooker (*Dark Knight* 209) and Alex Evans have applied Sinfield's approach to
Batman and Superman, respectively. Evans suggests that in a cultural materi-
alist paradigm "no ideological domination is total" (122), and that we should
view these heavily reinterpreted heroes as faultline texts, which are more than
simply "a tool of hegemony and imperialism but also a site of considerable
resistance and conflict" (117). Thus, these comic book movies provide a space
where cultural hegemony can meet resistant readings.

That these conflicting concerns rarely appear to chafe may be explained
by how they are codified by the genre. Rick Altman sought to organize the
ideological and ritual methods of genre studies with his article "A Semantic/
Syntactic Approach to Film Genre." As will be more fully discussed in the next
chapter, the comic book film adaptation has been channeled by methods of
production and promotion into a group of films with the shared attributes of
a single genre, the comic book movie. The semantic/syntactic method of genre
analysis goes some way towards explaining the comic book movie's recent
popularity and unprecedented sustainability. Altman explains his theory as
follows:

The structures of Hollywood cinema, like those of American popular mythology
as a whole, serve to mask the very distinction between the ritual and ideological
functions. Hollywood does not simply lend its voice to the public's desires, nor

does it simply manipulate the audience. On the contrary, most genres go through a period of accommodation during which the public's desires are fitted to Hollywood's priorities (and vice-versa). . . . Whenever a lasting fit is obtained—which it is whenever a semantic genre becomes a syntactic one—it is because a common ground has been found, a region where the audience's ritual values coincide with Hollywood's ideological ones. (688)

Applying Altman's semantic/syntactic approach, one can see how the US mythological tradition of selfless, individualistic heroes facilitating community through vigilante action has been made over with the semantic elements or "building blocks" (684) of the comic book movie: superpowered protagonists, urban settings, heightened reality, and distinctly comic book imagery. Altman goes on to note how the "Hollywood genres that have proven the most durable are precisely those that have established the most coherent syntax (the western, the musical); those that disappear the quickest depend entirely on recurring semantic elements, never developing a stable syntax" (690). In the past, consistent comic book movie production has never been maintained; however, a post-9/11 context found Hollywood fully utilizing the ideological underpinning of the comic book movie, the foundational myth that once fueled production of the western, but with semantic features that were more amenable to modern audiences, and thus, to paraphrase Altman, a lasting fit seems to have been obtained where the audience's ritual values coincide with wider ideological interests.

Clambakes and Empty Offices

> V: The building is a symbol, as is the act of destroying it. Symbols are given
> power by people. Alone, a symbol is meaningless, but with enough people,
> blowing up a building can change the world.
> —*V for Vendetta* (McTeigue 2006)

Echoing Slavoj Žižek's contention that the events of 9/11 were "much more symbolic than real" (388), this dialogue from *V for Vendetta*, which does not appear in the source material, hints at how comic book adaptations have been shaped by 9/11 and subsequent events.[21] Although some may balk at the suggestion that 9/11 was a catalyst in the modern comic book film adaptation trend, nonetheless the attack and the "War on Terror" have left an unmistakable inflection on these films, and US entertainment in general.

For instance, when asked for this study if he believed that 9/11 had contributed to the comic book movie trend, *Green Hornet* (Gondry 2011) screenwriter Evan Goldberg said, "I don't think so. I think terrorists [as villains] are standard." However, while terrorist antagonists were common in action films and thrillers, this had not been the case with early comic book movies. In the first Batman film franchise, the hero fought costumed criminals such as the Joker, but in the post-9/11 adaptation, *Batman Begins* (Nolan 2005), the hero faces the Eastern-based terrorist Ra's Al Ghul who wants to "watch Gotham tear itself apart through fear." When the Joker did re-emerge in the sequel, *The Dark Knight*, he was also ascribed political motivations, with the one-time "Clown Prince of Crime" depicted organizing bombings and sending threats via videotaped executions—actions that prompt a number of characters to dub him a "terrorist." This remaking of the supervillain as a terrorist is also apparent in the X-Men series. In the pre-9/11 franchise-starter, *X-Men* (Singer 2000), the antagonist Magneto was simply a "very powerful mutant," but by *X2* (Singer 2003) he was a "mutant terrorist," held by the government following an attack on the Statue of Liberty. In the film, the imprisoned Magneto is beaten and drugged by authorities to extract information. By the third film, *X-Men: The Last Stand* (Ratner 2006), the character's terrorist makeover is complete, as he is depicted leading a fanatical group, organizing terrorist attacks, and making video threats from his underground bunker, prompting the film's US president to respond, "On principle I can't negotiate with these people."

For their part, comic book heroes were also shaped by 9/11 and subsequent events. For instance, the many Marvel characters relaunched under the publisher's *Ultimate* imprint in 2002 gained a militaristic dimension, with heroes such as Captain America, Thor, Iron Man, and Hulk now working for the government and wearing costumes that more greatly resembled army fatigues. Creator Jim Lee noted of this development, "In some ways, the government is now our version of radiation. Radiation used to be the reason why people got superpowers. Now the government is" (DeFalco *Comic Creators on Fantastic Four* 190). This militarization carried over into Marvel Studios productions where the major thread linking the films is the presence of the military espionage and law-enforcement agency S.H.I.E.L.D., which subsequently received its own television series. This trend was also evident in *Batman Begins*, with Justine Toh writing that the hero's arsenal, cherry-picked from Wayne Enterprises' military prototypes, "encapsulates the militarization of popular culture" (128). Thus, where once comic book characters and their origins reflected anxieties such as the impact of scientific research, a post-9/11 preoccupation with militarism (bordering on fetishism) is apparent in more recent comics and their adaptations.

Perhaps the most immediate impact of 9/11 on comics was the necessary reworking of the comic book trope of "ever escalating stakes" (McCloud *Reinventing Comics* 114). One need only contrast Spider-Man's reaction to the

FIG. 1.4 The destruction of the Twin Towers in *X-Force* #3 (full page) and *Spider-Man* #16 (panels).

FIG. 1.5 The destruction of the World Trade Center in the post-9/11 comic *The Amazing Spider-Man* #36 (double-page spread).

destruction of one of the Twin Towers in a 1991 story arc "Sabotage"[22] with the commemorative 9/11 issue of *The Amazing Spider-Man* (November 2001) to see how this motif was tempered by real-world considerations. In the earlier story, on seeing the tower explode, all Spider-Man offers is a comedic, "uh-oh," while in the more recent comic, the hero is stunned into a muted ". . . God . . ." as he is dwarfed in the foreground by the enormity of the destruction, with the image given a double-page spread traditionally set aside for action sequences.

Where comic books used to rarely be concerned with collateral damage, books like *Marvel Comics: Civil War* showed the heroes acknowledging the civilian casualties of their superpowered clashes. While today comics have returned to the large-scale action sequences with which they are synonymous, these spectacles are often punctuated by moments that assure readers that there are no civilian casualties. For instance, in the last panel of the 1991 story arc "Sabotage" Spider-Man's costars, the mutant team X-Force, leave the smoldering rubble of the World Trade Center with the pithy line, "Let's blow this clambake and go home!" By contrast, the more recent *Superman Unchained* #2 (July 2013) finds moments to convey to readers that no lives are lost in the superpowered punch-ups, with the Man of Steel, on being knocked into a building by a giant robot, thinking, "Lucky You. Empty Office."

Similarly, comic book adaptations and other action cinema demonstrated greater restraint in the wake of 9/11. For instance, on the director's commentary for the 2005 DVD rerelease of *Batman Forever* (1995), Joel Schumacher noted of a sequence in which a helicopter crashes into Gotham's equivalent of the Statue of Liberty, "Pre-September 11th this was all fun and games. I'm not so sure after September 11th we would have wanted to do anything like that. It's amazing how that image takes on a whole new meaning." Many post-9/11 comic book movies display the awareness Schumacher describes. For instance, in *Superman Returns* the hero leaves the Kryptonite landmass growing off the coast of Metropolis to fly back and protect the city's residents from falling debris. Likewise, when depicting the third-act invasion of New York in *The Avengers* (Whedon 2012), there was a concerted effort to show the impact of the destruction with shots of candlelight vigils and a wall of remembrance. Furthermore, "containment" was made the heroes' priority, with the team spending as much time liaising with emergency services and saving civilians as they did tackling the invading army.

Unlike Marvel heroes, DC Comics characters are based in fictional cities. This may account for more recent DC Comics adaptations returning to traditional large-scale action sequences. In Christopher Nolan's trilogy-closer *The Dark Knight Rises* (2012), Gotham is devastated by a terrorist takeover that not only evokes 9/11, but the more recent Occupy Wall Street protests. Most controversially, the Superman reboot *Man of Steel* (Snyder 2013) culminated in the decimation of Metropolis' city center on a scale previously unseen in cinema. Unlike his comic equivalent who lands in "empty offices," this "hero" shows little regard for the destruction (and inevitable loss of life) his conflict must have wrought. *Man of Steel* was the first comic book movie to return to the careless destruction of the pre-9/11 source. However, although the devastation took place in one of DC's New York analogs, this did not stem widespread criticism of these sequences.[23]

Whatever boost the comic book movie gained in the wake of 9/11 seemed to dissipate as the genre moved into its second decade. Production regularized into predictable patterns, international grosses caught up with and then exceeded domestic box office, and national specificities were diminished— Batman retired to Florence, Tony Stark went to China for open heart surgery, and Spider-Man no longer swung through a canopy of unfurled flags. Nonetheless, the disapproval that greeted the third act of *Man of Steel* suggested that audiences were not ready for the carefree action of pre-9/11 comics, and that perhaps these films will forever be produced in the Shadow of No Towers.

Conclusions and Counterarguments

In 1938, Cleveland residents Jerry Siegel and Joe Shuster introduced Superman to the world. One year later, the city welcomed the arrival of another comic book icon, writer Harvey Pekar, whose autobiographical comics, published from 1976 as *American Splendor*, charted the file clerk's daily difficulties.[24] It is hard to imagine a comic further removed from the escapist fantasy of Superman than Pekar's independent work, a juxtaposition the 2003 adaptation of *American Splendor* (Springer Berman and Pulcini) was quick to point out. The film's opening narration, delivered by the real-life Pekar, concludes, "If you're the kind of person looking for some romance or escapism or some fantasy figure to save the day, guess what? You got the wrong movie." The presence of *American Splendor*, alongside a number of other film versions of alternative comics (e.g., *Ghost World*, *Road to Perdition*, *A History of Violence*, and *Art School Confidential*) would seem to refute the argument that an environment of uncertainty and powerlessness was responsible for the large-scale adaptation of comics in the early 2000s.

However, *American Splendor* and similar adaptations (e.g., *Ghost World*, *Mystery Men*, and *Kick-Ass*) define themselves in juxtaposition to mainstream productions. From its opening voiceover to its marketing—"At last a comic book hero that we can all relate to"—*American Splendor* is characterized by its opposition to the popular power fantasies. It is likely, given the finite readership of *American Splendor*, that without the larger comic book adaptation trend to play off, the film may not have been produced. Thus, as a number of recent adaptations of alternative comics can be linked to the wider trend, the appearance of films such as *American Splendor* does not sufficiently weaken the arguments that place 9/11 at the start of this trend.

Analyzing the year 2009 in American cinema, Dana Polan notes how the popular press was eager to draw connections between film attendance and the Global Financial Crisis (GFC) (220). Indeed, in the wake of the GFC, the recession began to replace 9/11 as the most cited cultural catalyst for the comic book movie. Echoing earlier arguments, the belief was that these high-flying characters provided spectators with an escape from their financial woes. Contributing to a report for the BBC News program *Talking Movies*, *Wall Street Journal* entertainment reporter Lauren Schuker said that "the economy has been stumbling further and further into disrepair and so films like *Iron Man* and *The Dark Knight*, where there is a very clear hero who seems to sort of rescue audiences, [are] much more appealing than some of the films which have struggled with less clear heroes and villains" (Brook). It is doubtful whether the billionaire playboy protagonists of *Iron Man* and *The Dark Knight* would have provided relief for cash-strapped audiences, but the recession may have had a more indirect effect on attendance. As discussed, many comic book characters have wide recognition. Thus, the relative reliability of a time-tested favorite, such as the adaptation of a comic book, may have seemed like a better investment than buying a ticket for an unproven property during the economic downturn.

Like the allusions to the War on Terror, some films began to reference the recession—most notably the parallels between Bane's revolution and the Occupy Wall Street movement in *The Dark Knight Rises*. Nolan again attempted to maintain the ambiguity of his film, saying, "We throw a lot of things against the wall to see if it sticks" ("The Dark Knight Rises Isn't Political"). Yet unlike Nolan's earlier Batman film, there was a general consensus among commentators that *The Dark Knight Rises* criticized populist movements and supported a conservative agenda (Shoard; Sirota; Gibbs). But it would be surprising if these films did not draw from the headlines, and while these references may have enabled the film to appear more politically engaged, the GFC did not have anywhere near the same impact on comic book movies as 9/11.

A further challenge to sociological assessments, such as the 9/11 argument, was put forward by Eileen Meehan in her study of the 1989 adaptation of *Batman*. She criticized an approach that attempts to understand the popularity of the film as a reflection of the American psyche, "such speculation requires an assumptive leap that reduces consciousness, culture, and media to reflections of each other." Meehan counters such modes of analysis by stating, "Profit, not culture, drives show business: no business means no show" (48). Like Meehan, Bordwell offers a number of counterarguments to the zeitgeist-based approaches, including how the popularity of many different types of films would suggest a "fragmented national psyche" ("Superheroes for Sale").

Heeding Meehan and Bordwell's well-founded reservations, more quantifiable factors will be considered in the sections that follow, including: technology, conglomerate practices, and generation change. However, it is difficult to ignore the central role that 9/11 played in the evolution of this genre. The first films seemed to meet many of the immediate ritualistic desires of audiences, while later adaptations propagated US mythological traditions and their underlying ideology. Undeniably, a number of comic book adaptations displayed a sociopolitical inflection, and this apparent relevance went some way towards legitimizing and sustaining this influential trend.

You'll Believe a Man Can Fly

He began not as flesh and blood, but as a simple line drawing. His comic strip has thrilled millions around the world. The magic of radio gave to his name a breathless signature and sound. Then with television came a whole new generation who idolize his exploits. Today, at last, his evolution is complete. Brought to life by the awesome technology of film. . . . Until now his incredible adventures had been beyond the power of any known medium to realize, but now the greatest creative and technical minds of the motion picture world have gathered to meet the challenge of *Superman*. He has come of age, our age. This Christmas Superman brings you the gift of flight. Superman is now the movie.
—*Superman: The Movie* original trailer

From the earliest adaptations, filmmakers have emphasized the importance of the latest technology in bringing comics to the screen. For instance, the framing device for the appropriately titled *Winsor McCay, The Famous Cartoonist of the N.Y. Herald and his Moving Comics* (Blackton and McCay 1911), saw McCay (playing himself) proposing to a roomful of doubting colleagues that he will "make four thousand pen drawings that will move." Following one month of toil, the naysayers (and audience) are stunned when McCay brings his *Little Nemo in Slumberland* characters to life by using animation techniques more sophisticated than anything previously seen. Over sixty years later, *Superman: The Movie* traded on its spectacular effects with the tagline, "You'll Believe A Man Can Fly."[25] More recently, chairman of 20th Century Fox, Tom Rothman, argued that a leaked workprint of *X-Men Origins: Wolverine* (Hood 2009), which included the full footage, was a "complete misrepresentation of the film" as "none of the effects shots were in any remotely final form" (Spines "Exclusive: Fox Chairman").

Thus, it is unsurprising that the most widely cited catalyst for the modern comic book adaptation trend is technical innovations, in particular digital technologies. For example, without exception, all of the comic creators and filmmakers interviewed for this study cited technology as one of the causal factors for the comic book adaptation trend, with *Green Hornet* screenwriter Evan Goldberg eschewing ritualistic necessity, ideological precepts, and a variety of other possibilities to confidently state, "I think it is only because of effects."[26] Many commentators echo the industry. For instance, zeitgeist skeptic Bordwell notes the "importance of special effects" in his assessment of the trend ("Superheroes for Sale"). Similarly, Bukatman comments, "It's no accident that this wave of superhero films followed the development of ever more convincing CGI [computer-generated imagery] technologies" ("Why I Hate Superhero Movies" 122). How fans used digital technologies to increase their visibility, and the visibility of their objects of devotion, will be explored in Chapter Three, and this causal factor should not be undervalued or ignored. However, taking its cue from the industry and commentators, this section will focus on the argument that digital filmmaking techniques were the catalyst for the unprecedented number of comic book film adaptations produced since 2000.

There are a number of persuasive arguments to support this technological determinist position. Firstly, many commentators believe that special effects attract audiences, with D. N. Rodowick contending that CGI allows for "market differentiation" and the chance to "bolster sagging audience numbers" (1398). The audience research for this study certainly supports this argument. For instance, fourteen of the eighty-two respondents who qualified their expectations of the surveyed films offered some variant of "special effects," with responses including: a 26–30-year-old male non-fan at *Thor* who expected a "good action movie with very good special effects (to be seen in the cinema)," a male fan (21–25) who anticipated that *Green Lantern* would be a "CGI heavy film with more action than story," and a 26–30-year-old female non-fan who hoped that *The Adventures of Tintin* would have "good 3D effects."

This argument is further supported by the unique events surrounding the leaking of the *X-Men Origins: Wolverine* workprint one month before its May 1, 2009, release. The print, which 20th Century Fox estimated was downloaded 4.5 million times, included all the footage that appeared in the theatrical version with the greatest difference being that some effects shots were unfinished. Rather than detract from the film's box office, *Entertainment Weekly* cited tracking figures that suggested the leak might have helped generate interest in the film (Spines "Tracking Data"). Despite the ready availability of the film for weeks prior to the official release, the attraction of the completed effects in a cinematic experience (i.e., surround sound, big screen, and a large audience) was enough to ensure that the film still achieved blockbuster status ($373 million worldwide). Such examples suggest that special effects are important to the comic book adaptation and its audience, which makes a compelling case for filmmaking technology to be recognized as one of the chief causal factors in this modern filmmaking trend.

Another point raised by those who subscribe to the technology argument is that comics have been waiting on film technology to reach the point where their often-heightened images could be convincingly portrayed. In discussing the green screens used in his comic book adaptation *Sin City* (2005), director Robert Rodriguez states, "Technology helps push the artform and create new ideas" ("15 Minute Flick School"). Echoing Rodriguez, Bordwell suggests that the "fantastic powers of superheroes cried out for CGI (computer-generated imagery), and it may be that convincing movies in the genre weren't really ready until the software matured" ("Superheroes for Sale"). Similarly, comic book creator Grant Morrison writes in his book *Supergods*, "Technology had caught up with the comics and believing a man could fly was as easy as believing a giant could be a midget" (322).

Such arguments are not unique to comic book adaptations. Even a cursory view of film production history provides many examples in which filmmaking technology was seen to influence what sources were adapted and how they made their way to the screen. For instance, Naremore notes how the advent of sound "produced a great appetite for literature among Hollywood moguls" ("Introduction" 4), and Michele Pierson writes that "the real history of science-fiction film is the history of its production technology" (165).

Perhaps the connection between technology and adaptation is more forcibly made with comics because the source material, particularly in its mainstream American form, has often aspired to cinematic qualities. Comic books first gained popularity by featuring the power fantasies that no other medium could effectively convey.[27] Readers would see heroes perform feats that could only be described in novels and on radio or poorly presented in cinema. Despite the potential for comics to mitigate many of cinema's limitations, American comic books still often sought cinematic qualities. For instance, it has been noted that many comic book stories and characters were inspired by cinema (Feiffer 30), yet developed in directions the film form was still unable to travel. Thus, Batman was Douglas Fairbanks released from the confines of gravity and 1930s film production technology; the impossible beasts of 1950s Marvel comics, such as Droom, The Living Lizard!, confidently stomped across cities when the best that film could offer was a rubber-suited stuntman shuffling down a scale-model Tokyo; and *Sin City* achieved a true film noir aesthetic of startling whites and impenetrable blacks that traditional cinematography was unable to create. As Stan Lee summarized, "We had to wait until the special effects were developed to the point where they could do all those things" (Burke *Superhero Movies* 151–52).

Thus, the argument seems to be that many of the most popular comic book stories were merely in a seventy-year incubation waiting for a more appropriate medium—cinema—to develop the tools necessary to depict these power fantasies.[28] While such arguments further position technology as the chief causal factor in the development of today's comic book adaptation trend, they are open to charges of reductionism. At the very least, the suggestion that comics were a placeholder for these stories diminishes the form's status as its own vital art form with a unique means of expression. Furthermore, technology is not Batman—it does not appear from nowhere, exert its influence, and then retreat into the shadows. Its relationship to the social sphere demands a more nuanced understanding.

■ ■ ■

Murphie and Potts describe a technological determinist position as "one-sided" (17), and suggest Brian Winston's linguistics approach to modeling change as a possible corrective. In his historically based analysis Winston describes how "generalised forces coalesce to function as a transforming agency" which he calls "supervening social necessities." It is these supervening social necessities that move a prototype "out of the laboratory and into the world at large" (6). Possible factors that might have compelled the development and wider diffusion of digital filmmaking technologies include: the audience's appetite for greater screen realism, the filmmaker's wish for absolute control, and the financier's need to reduce budgets. While comics often aspire to cinema, Chapter Four will demonstrate how filmmakers regularly borrow from comics. This relay back-and-forth may be partly attributable to the representational overlap that these graphic narrative mediums enjoy. The desire to narrow this semiotic gap might also be considered one of the supervening social necessities that compelled the innovation of digital filmmaking techniques and influenced their wider diffusion.

While filmmakers adapting comics might have only enjoyed certain technical standards with the advent of digital cinema, prior to such innovations they did not confine themselves to the limits of their era, but expanded their range of tools to better match the source material. For instance, many critics have discussed how the oft-cited special effects have brought about changes that are "conceptual rather than fundamental" (Sutton 388).[29] Comparing an underwater sequence from *The Spirit* (Miller 2008) with one from the much earlier adaptation *Danger: Diabolik!* (Bava 1968), one can see an example of how many modern special effects are often little more than digitally upgraded smoke and mirrors. *The Spirit* producer Deborah Del Prete boasted that the use of digital backlot technology allowed the film's cast to appear as if underwater while maintaining their hair and makeup, much as they would in a comic (*The Spirit* DVD commentary). However, a similar effect was achieved four decades earlier by simply placing a water tank between the camera and actors for *Danger: Diabolik!* Similarly, Michael Cohen, in his essay "Dick Tracy: In Pursuit of a Comic Book Aesthetic," demonstrates how the 1990 film used pre-digital technology (e.g., makeup, costumes, and mattes) to match its source as effectively as more modern films. Thus, the desire to adapt comics, and adapt them faithfully, predates the recent advent of digital technologies.

Furthermore, many filmmakers, inspired by comics, went beyond such creative solutions to push forward the technologies of the time. Winsor McCay is arguably the father of the comic book film adaptation. In order to bring his *Little Nemo in Slumberland* characters to the screen in 1911, the innovative creator advanced the techniques developed by film pioneers Emile Cohl and J. Stuart Blackton (who would co-direct McCay's film) to create the first sophisticated animated film, *Winsor McCay, The Famous Cartoonist of the N.Y. Herald and his Moving Comics*. Similarly, as this section's epigraph points out, "the greatest creative and technical minds of the motion picture world . . . gathered to meet the challenge of *Superman*." One of those challenges was the application of motion-control photography, popularized by *Star Wars* (Lucas 1977), to live-action actors rather than model spaceships. Thus, even though the special effects breakthroughs of *Star Wars* might have provided filmmakers with the confidence to adapt Superman in the late 1970s, the comic character's specificities compelled them to push the technology further. This cyclical relationship between comic book adaptations and technology continued into the digital age.

As the McCay example suggests, many filmmakers have gravitated towards animation as a way to replicate comics. Animation afforded filmmakers a mastery of mise-en-scène absent in pre-digital cinema, and through its application one can see filmmakers reaching for qualities that would later be realized in the digital age. For instance, in the first live-action *Superman* serial (1948), sequences in which the character would fly saw actor Kirk Alyn substituted with a cel animated hero.[30] While the application of this technique was dictated somewhat by budget, thirty years later animation was still being considered to make Superman fly for the blockbuster *Superman: The Movie*.[31] Today, a number of adaptations still incorporate basic animation with live-action footage to approximate the source material and demonstrate fidelity (e.g., *American Splendor*, *The Losers*, and *Scott Pilgrim*).[32]

Such examples tally with cartoonist Robert C. Harvey's celebration of the more malleable comic form in his 1996 book *The Art of the Comic Book*. Harvey begins his argument by stating that the "images in comics can be more readily tampered with and modified than the images in film, which must reproduce pretty much what the eye sees in nature," before conceding that animation allowed for some of the control comic creators enjoy and ultimately suggesting that "animated cartoons are a third medium" (175). However, in the years

FIG. 1.6 In the 1948 *Superman* serial, actor Kirk Alyn was replaced by cel animation during the flying sequences.

following Harvey's statement the wider proliferation of digital filmmaking techniques dramatically reshaped the ontology of the film image, with many suggesting that cinema had now joined the plastic arts.

Many scholars agree that the "in-your-face special effects of these films are red herrings" (Prince "Film Artifacts" 24), and that the most important consequence of digital film technologies is the degree of control it confers on the filmmaker. For instance, commenting during the early days of digital filmmaking, *Batman & Robin* (Schumacher 1997) visual effects supervisor John Dykstra said, "When the ability to create images in the digital environment a pixel at a time arrived [the visual effects supervisor role] got to be much less an engineer [role] and much more a designer [role]" ("Freeze Frame"). Citing Soviet montage theorist Lev Kuleshov, John A. Berton predicted this shift in a prescient 1990 essay, writing, "Kuleshov seems to call for exactly what digital cinema offers: complete control over every structural element in both the world space and screen space of the shot" (8).[33]

Echoing Harvey's earlier observation, new media scholar Lev Manovich believes that many of the antecedents of digital filmmaking can be found in animation, a viewpoint shared by several commentators and borne out by the history of the comic book adaptation.[34] Where once Kirk Alyn took to the skies as Superman through the use of a hand-drawn hero, today Henry Cavill allows a digitally constructed Man of Steel to carry out much of the high-altitude heroics—a more convincing, but no less constructed intermediate. Comic book adaptations are not simply at the vanguard of the transition to a more malleable film image. The desire to achieve the high aesthetic criterion set by the handcrafted comic book source was one of the supervening social necessities compelling development of these digital filmmaking techniques.

Bullet-time, the slow-motion technique in which the camera appears to move around a near-frozen object, was first popularized in the 1999 film *The Matrix*. The film's creators, the Wachowskis, have cited comics as the inspiration for the technique, with Lana (then Larry) explaining, "Comics are a graphic-type storytelling where you could freeze a moment and make an image that sustains. As a counterpart, you can't really do that in film. We tried to do that" ("Follow the White Rabbit"). Antecedents to bullet-time exist, including comic book adaptation *Blade* (Norrington 1998), but as the film's visual effects supervisor John Gaeta explained, "bullet-time is something that was conceived for *The Matrix* specifically, but I think it's the by-product of the directors observing the controls coming into place. And then they asked the right questions at the right time" ("What is Bullet-time?"). Thus, without their comic book inspiration, the Wachowskis might not have asked the "right questions," and bullet-time would not have been applied in *The Matrix* where its popularity led to the technique's wide diffusion. Thus, in much the same way that the *Little Nemo in Slumberland* comic provided the impetus to develop more sophisticated animation techniques, the desire to achieve comic-like images has propelled digital technology in directions unforeseen by its creators.

It is not only the heightened imagery of comics that has prompted this innovation, but also the creators themselves. Like McCay's foray into early animation, today's comic creators have proven to be among the artists best positioned to shape this more malleable film image. Prior to the success of *Sin City*, the only Hollywood film to use a digital backlot for the entirety of its production was *Sky Captain and the World of Tomorrow* (Conran 2004), which, despite a large budget and A-list cast, underperformed at the box office.[35] By contrast, the co-director of *Sin City*, comic book artist Frank Miller, was described as having "not only mastered the technology but . . . used it with artistry" (LaSalle 1). Furthermore, the film's graphiation,[36] attributed to Miller, was cited by many as one of the reasons for the film's success.[37] Also released in 2005 was the low-budget, digital-backlot production *MirrorMask*, directed by *Sandman* artist Dave McKean and written by his comic book collaborator Neil Gaiman. Although this film garnered less attention than *Sin City*, critics uniformly cited comic book creator McKean's effective use of digital technology as the most successful aspect of the production.[38]

Clearly, Miller's and McKean's experiences in the traditional arts advantaged them in the realm of digital film production. Berton predicted in 1990 that such skills, which not all traditional directors share, would prove beneficial:

> More so than any other cinematic medium, digital three-dimensional synthetic cinema relies on the skills of the plastic artist to create images, to shape, color and arrange every facet of every object within the screen. The process involves the skills of the painter, the sculptor and the architect. (6)

More than fifteen years later, similar statements were made by many of Miller's collaborators, who suggest that there was always a desire to bring his unique images to the screen; the technology just needed to reach the expressivity of the pencil and ink medium.[39] As Uslan explained when interviewed for this study, with studios viewing comics as "frozen movies" and "storyboards," comic creators have emerged as the "latest talent pool being drawn into the world of motion pictures and animation as directors." Thus, recent innovations did not simply create the desire to bring comic book-like images to the screen; rather, it was a confluence of new technologies and preexisting ambitions.

Adopting a cultural determinist stance, André Bazin believes that "any account of the cinema that was drawn merely from the technical inventions that made it possible would be a poor one indeed" (*What is Cinema?* 18). Instead, Bazin argues that the development of cinema is not driven by technology, but by the desire to reproduce reality, which he calls "the myth of total cinema." He expands his argument in claiming that "every new development added to the cinema must, paradoxically take it nearer and nearer to its origins. In short, cinema has not yet been invented!" (21). As Bazin suggests, just as cinema's desire to replicate reality is a Sisyphean task, so too is the impulse to faithfully replicate comics, as film can never be "better" at being a comic book than a comic book already is. Nonetheless, this goal has motivated past technological breakthroughs, and comic book adaptations continue to expand the scope of digital filmmaking techniques.

In opening his article "The Digital World Picture," Jean-Pierre Geuens notes that it should "not surprise us that digital moviemaking is . . . urging us toward certain objectives rather than others" (18). The increased aesthetic freedoms of the digital filmmaking era certainly seem to have compelled Hollywood to gravitate towards graphic narrative mediums (e.g., video games, cartoons, toys, and illustrated books); with comic books perhaps the most relied-on source.[40] Thus, one could confidently categorize digital technology as one of the chief causal factors in the current comic book adaptation trend. However, we must also recognize how the presence of comics may have served as a supervening social necessity, raising filmmaking technologies to new standards before their wider application. The aesthetic impact of these techniques will be considered in Chapter Four, where it should not be forgotten that despite the role technology played in the emergence of the comic book adaptation at the start of the twenty-first century, the cause-and-effect is not always so easily delineated.

The Conglomerate Argument

While favorites such as Austen, Dickens, and Shakespeare have provided reliable source material since the earliest days of the film industry, it is difficult to imagine a rollercoaster based on *Pride and Prejudice*; *Great Expectations* does not lend itself to an endless cycle of sequels; and no one is clamoring to guide Hamlet through a video game version of late medieval Denmark. Following the decline of the studio system in the 1950s, large companies greedily bought up the failing studios leading to the development of the media conglomerates that dominate today's entertainment industry (Comcast, 21st Century Fox, CBS Corporation, the Walt Disney Company, Viacom, Time Warner, and Sony Corporation of America).[41] These conglomerates favor reliable formulas that yield multiple opportunities to profit from a film. Thus, while the adaptation of comics to cinema might have been compelled by the possibilities of digital technologies, and found popularity by fulfilling certain ideological and ritual functions, they were also well suited, perhaps ideally suited, to today's mainstream filmmaking paradigms.

This section will map how conglomerate strategies were a key causal agent in the emergence of the comic book movie. However, much like the circularity of the technology argument, it should be noted that the comic book industry anticipated many of the wider shifts in the entertainment industry, with film studios and other subsidiaries in this conglomerate structure now adopting paradigms that the comic book industry has practiced for decades. To illustrate the points made, this section will pay particular attention to Sony Pictures Entertainment's Spider-Man films, which were typical of this era.

Built-in Audience

One of the primary economic motivations for basing a film on preexisting material has been the built-in recognition the source enjoys, with scholars describing film adaptations as "pre-sold" products (Ray 43; Hark 173), "safe bets with a ready audience" (Hutcheon 87), or, as Kerry Gough wryly summarized, "new and improved, and cheap at half the price" (63). As the cost of film production increased following the replacement of the studio system with the blockbuster paradigm, these pre-sold commodities moved to the center of Hollywood filmmaking.

Long before today's movies, many comic book characters enjoyed recognition that extended beyond their finite readership, prompting Bordwell to equate them with the stars and genres of the studio system ("Superheroes for Sale"). Consequently, adaptations of these sources offered producers the opportunity to lessen the risks associated with big-budget film production. Movie executive Jeff Katz cites the comic book's reputation as "proven material" for the sustainability of this trend, adding, "studios are going to feel even more comfortable making comic book movies" (Rogers). Similarly, Sony Pictures Entertainment's co-chairman Amy Pascal admitted, "Brands are great, because they do a lot of work for you in the marketplace. If you have a brand, a video-game or a comic book, you don't have to create a whole new business" (Braund 93–94).

In discussing *The Lord of the Rings*, the film's producer, Bob Shaye, equates the novel with comic book characters suggesting, "It was so wonderfully pre-sold. It was like *Superman* or *Batman*" (K. Thompson 31). However, while many sources have pre-sold potential, few (*The Lord of the Rings* included) can match popular comic book characters such as Batman, Superman, and Spider-Man. With decades of non-stop publication, constant and far-reaching adaptations, and incalculable amounts of merchandise, these characters have few rivals.[42] Furthermore, since the early 1990s, the core fan base of comic book adaptations has developed into a digital-connected press corps, with a dedication and influence that few sources can match. The importance of such enthusiasts to this trend and the mainstream industry will be the subject of Chapter Three.

Thus, the built-in audience for popular comic book characters is one factor that would have prompted profit-minded studios to develop comic book adaptations in the early twenty-first century.

Wide Demographic Reach

In 1954, psychiatrist Dr. Fredric Wertham published the influential book *Seduction of the Innocent: The Influence of "Horror Comics" on Today's Youth*, in which he linked a post-World War II rise in juvenile delinquency to comic books. Wertham claimed that horror comics were "apt to interfere with children's sleep" (106); he suggested Superman inspired speeding (97); and gave examples throughout the work that linked crime comics to copycat activities.[43] Following the convening of a Senate subcommittee on juvenile delinquency, the comic book industry implemented the self-censoring Comics

Code Authority. All comics fulfilling the Wertham-inspired criteria would receive the "Approved by the Comics Code Authority" stamp required to be sold through mainstream outlets (e.g., newsstands and drugstores). Consequently, the comic book industry began moving away from the then popular crime and horror comics and back to the more widely acceptable action fantasies of superheroes.[44] Among the new characters to emerge under this remit was Spider-Man, who first appeared in the appropriately titled *Amazing Fantasy* #15 (August 1962).

As mainstream Hollywood cinema entered the 1990s, the R-rated protagonists of action films such as *First Blood* (Kotcheff 1982), *Commando* (Lester 1985), and *Die Hard* (McTiernan 1988), who dispatched vaguely motivated terrorists with a violent flourish and wry remark, increasingly fell out of favor. During this time, the conglomerate-run film industry—striving for the widest demographic reach—sought content that would not incur restrictive age classifications. Like the comic book industry fifty years earlier, many filmmakers turned to the seemingly benign comic book heroes.

While it could be argued that comic book heroes are no less violent than their action movie equivalents, their fantastical setups and all-ages reputation have consistently seen them gain the lower ratings classifications that studios favor. For instance, a new "12" certificate was introduced in the UK to coincide with the release of *Batman*, which enabled younger audiences to see the occasionally violent film (Shaw). The annexation of action cinema by comic book characters was expedited post-9/11 when public sentiment shifted against violent, terrorist-bashing fare. As *New York Daily News* journalist Jack Mathews remarked of Arnold Schwarzenegger's terrorist film *Collateral Damage* (Davis 2002), "If you know someone who wants to see that film, please ask them why." Fortunately, for an industry desperately in need of a ready-made hero who would not painfully evoke 9/11 or require an R rating, one was already on the way.

Released in 2002, *Spider-Man* met the complicated demands of modern filmmaking: an all-ages action hero who could anchor a post-9/11 release without the risk of being considered exploitative or politically incorrect. At a time when existing action films needed to be shelved and/or neutered,[45] the seemingly black-and-white, fantastical conflicts of most comic book adaptations (alongside fantasy films like *Harry Potter*, *The Lord of the Rings*, and *The Chronicles of Narnia*) filled important gaps in studio schedules. For instance, some parents in the UK complained to the British Board of Film Classification (BBFC) that they could not bring their young children to see the "12" certificate *Spider-Man* (USA: PG-13). Like *Batman* before it, the BBFC responded by introducing the more inclusive 12A ratings certificate, which allowed children under the age of twelve to see the film if they were accompanied by an adult

(Chrisafis). Conversely, in 2008, the BBFC's decision to grant *The Dark Knight* (USA: PG-13) a 12A certificate was criticized by some community leaders who felt the film warranted a higher certificate. Even so, the BBFC cited the film's "superhero context" (Sparrow) to defend its decision. Such examples testify to the suitability of comic books, and their seemingly benign protagonists, to mainstream film production, with Mark Tappan concluding that these adaptations have become "thinly disguised action movies" masquerading as family entertainment.

Success, Trends, and Genres

When asked for this study why Hollywood was now so receptive to comic book film adaptations, *30 Days of Night* creator Steve Niles responded: "With Hollywood it's all going to depend on last week's box office, and that's the only reason they are going to do anything—for the money." Like comic book publishing and other entertainment industries, mainstream filmmaking follows trends, with producers hoping to increase their box-office potential by emulating popular releases. So dominant are these economic cycles that Lawrence Alloway called for film scholars to discard thematic genres inherited from art history, as "Hollywood production was typified by ephemeral cycles seeking to capitalize on recent successes" (Langford 27).

It has been suggested that after *Batman & Robin* crippled the once-thriving Batman franchise, *Spider-Man* reignited interest in adapting comic books.[46] However, while *Spider-Man* did renew confidence in these adaptations, this trend was already gaining momentum. Although *Blade*, an adaptation of the Marvel Comics *Tomb of Dracula* character released in 1998, made little reference to its source material in promotion, the film was a surprise hit, grossing $131 million on a $45 million budget, warranting two sequels and a spin-off television series. Many of the more "comic book" elements of the film (bullet-time; a trench coat-wearing protagonist who mixes martial arts with gun play) reappeared in the 1999 hit *The Matrix*. While *The Matrix* had no acknowledged source material, it was heavily influenced by comic books, with Bordwell going so far as to suggest its success "helped legitimize the cycle" ("Superheroes for Sale").

Prior to the release of *X-Men* in 2000, *Entertainment Weekly* ran a feature that examined the various reasons why comic book adaptations did not have a sustained presence in mainstream filmmaking. In the article, *Watchmen* co-creator Dave Gibbons was interviewed regarding the likelihood of his graphic novel ever being adapted to cinema. Citing the cyclical and trend-orientated nature of mainstream film production, Gibbons's response was both pessimistic and prescient, "It was most likely to happen when Batman was a big success, but then that window was lost. If this new X-Men movie is a big hit, maybe that will open up another window. But to be honest, I'm not holding my breath" (Tucker). However, the unexpected success of *X-Men*, a comic book adaptation that embraced its source, initiated a trend that would eventually see *Watchmen* adapted in 2009.

Thus, by the time *Spider-Man* broke box-office records, *Daredevil*, *X2*, *Hulk* (Lee 2003), and *The League of Extraordinary Gentlemen* (2003) from *Blade* director Stephen Norrington were already in production.[47] Consequently, one could suggest that just as mainstream film producers gravitated toward comics for their built-in appeal, so too did they favor a trend that was proving increasingly reliable. How this trend developed into a genre will be explored in the next chapter.

Rights and Ownership

Copyright and other legal considerations are an under-recognized determinant in the study of adaptation generally, and the emergence of the comic book adaptation specifically. The industry's biggest publishers, Marvel and DC Comics, are unsurprisingly also involved in the majority of Hollywood adaptations, but until recently their corporate structures were very different. By the end of the 1960s, the licensing profits of DC Comics exceeded the revenue from comics, which prompted Warner Communications, Inc., to acquire the publisher in 1971 (Meehan 52; Gordon 153). Within this conglomerate structure DC Comics characters were adapted to other media more consistently than their Marvel equivalents. Attempts were made to adapt Marvel Comics characters, but without the shelter of a parent company the rights became increasingly diluted and complicated. For instance, during the same period Superman and Batman were each the basis of four Warner Bros. feature films, various attempts were made to adapt Spider-Man to the screen. In the late eighties, rights-holders Cannon Films even went so far as to take out advertisements in trade magazines announcing "Spider-Man: The Movie, Coming from Cannon Xmas '86," yet no film was ever produced.

In 1998, Gordon observed, "In the long term Marvel's weakness, compared with DC, has been their inability to invigorate their characters through Hollywood blockbuster movies" (156).[48] However, following Marvel's bankruptcy declaration in 1996, the publisher was taken over by Toy Biz heads Avi Arad and Isaac Perlmutter, whose company already had licensing deals with Marvel. Recognizing that the financial viability of both Toy Biz and Marvel was dependent on licenses, the pair "were committed to putting their characters on the screen" (Thomas and Sanderson 182). Arad and Perlmutter managed to untangle the legal difficulties surrounding Spider-Man, enabling the 2002 adaptation, and Arad served as a producer on *Blade, X-Men, Daredevil*, and a number of other Marvel Comics adaptations.[49]

In light of the success of Marvel Comics' adaptations, in 2003 *Variety* cited an analysis of Time Warner by the investment bank Thomas Weisel Partners, which described DC Comics' characters as a "hidden asset" that is "buried" within Warner Bros. (Brodesser). Eventually, Warner Bros. began consistent production of adaptations, sustaining the comic book movie genre. However, as it was the success of Marvel Comics adaptations that initiated the trend, the hurdle that ownership presents should not be overlooked when charting the emergence of the Golden Age of Comic Book Filmmaking.

Furthermore, although Marvel may have experienced some logistical obstacles bringing its characters to the screen, the publisher, and its mainstream rival, continually avoided a second set of rights issues that beset many film adaptations: creator control. Writer Stan Lee and artist Steve Ditko created Spider-Man, yet unlike their equivalents in other fields, these creators were treated as work-for-hire artists, with Spider-Man remaining the property of the publisher.[50] Although the balance between creator and publisher has been redressed in recent years, many of the most widely recognized characters remain under publisher control. Demonstrating the lack of influence the majority of comic creators wield in the adaptations of their characters, Lee responded to the planned 2012 Spider-Man reboot, *The Amazing Spider-Man* (Webb), with the following statement: "It was not my decision, I was not consulted" (Crocker et al. 92).

There is a significant distinction between popular comics and many novels, plays, and other works that have not yet fallen into the public domain. With fewer parties to be considered, it is often easier for a comic to move into film production. This process is further expedited as many of these publishers are now part of the same conglomerates as film studios (not to mention television networks, video game developers, and theme parks) and therefore rights negotiations are simplified further. Thus, the production of a comic book adaptation is often more straightforward than the adaptation of a novel or play where the author will generally retain some ownership. This publisher-control has enabled comic book characters to move more easily in the conglomerate structure and helped facilitate the comic book adaptation trend.

Franchise

As New Hollywood was usurped by the blockbuster paradigm, the conglomerate-run film studios welcomed the development of the franchises initiated by *Jaws* (Spielberg 1976), *Star Wars*, and *Raiders of the Lost Ark* (Spielberg 1981). Comic book adaptations also took part in this process. Although *Superman* was subtitled "The Movie," it more accurately could have been described as "The Movie and a Half" since the film and its sequel were intended to be shot simultaneously. However, looming release dates resulted in *Superman II* (Lester 1980) only being partly completed, with further footage shot following the success of the first film. Nonetheless, franchises began to dominate Hollywood film production as it moved into the 1980s, a process that has only intensified in recent times and to which the comic book has again proven uniquely compatible.

As mainstream cinema becomes increasingly episodic, past sources have proven themselves ill-suited to corporate strategies, as Kristin Thompson observes, "not just any movie can generate a franchise. Musicals, biopics, and adaptations of most literary classics don't offer much potential for follow-ups" (6). While not all comic book movies are adapted from episodic texts, many are. These characters rarely change or develop in their native medium; to do so could prove detrimental to the characters and their world, not to mention the publisher's finances. Consequently, Superman and Batman find themselves in much the same position more than seventy-five years after they were first introduced, as one-time Spider-Man editor Danny Fingeroth observes: "Comic writers refer to their characters being allowed the illusion of change" (34). Thus, comic narratives, in only presenting the semblance of change, seem to be perpetually in a narrative structure comparable to the second act of a film. As described by Syd Field, in the second act the main character encounters obstacle after obstacle that prevents him from achieving his dramatic need, but the episodic comic book protagonist can never move into the third act and achieve his "dramatic need," a just and crime-free world. This inability to move forward is neatly summed up with respect to Batman by Pearson and Uricchio:

> Justice-seeking becomes an endless process, with the Batman a Gotham Sisyphus who can never reach the crime-free summit of the mountain. Just as Sisyphus may roll the rock up a different path each time but not achieve his goal, the Batman may combat different criminals with different methods but not achieve his goal. The endless repetition accounts for the non-accruing nature of most of the events. (195)

Thus, many comic narratives rest on the precipice between the second and third acts, able to look over, but never commit to the closure therein, for it would signal the end of the hero.[51]

Duncan and Smith describe the "serial aesthetic" of comic books as one of the limitations of the form (120). However, for conglomerates hoping to develop franchises, a "serial aesthetic" has become one of comics' most desirable attributes. As Peter Lunenfeld noted of today's media, "narratives are developed to be unfinished" adding, "The entire American comic book industry serves as a model of the perpetually suspended narrative" (16).

Today, comic book adaptations that are building to franchises have begun emulating the storytelling style of the source. These films have increasingly staggered the progression of their characters in order to extract further installments, leaving just enough closure to abate the hunger of the audience, while whetting their appetites for further exploits. Thus, at the climax of *Spider-Man* the hero manages to vanquish one foe, Norman Osborn, but creates another, Osborn's son, Harry, who promises, "One day Spider-Man will pay," a storyline that was gradually developed across the film's two sequels.[52]

The rooftop coda from *Batman Begins* is one of the most cited examples of a series adopting the staggered narrative of a comic. In the franchise re-starter, the hero is made aware of a new menace by the appearance of a Joker playing card, which, to anyone familiar with the Batman mythos, indicates that the hero's archenemy will appear in the next installment. That the first film in a burgeoning franchise did not play its trump card (while the earlier Batman series had not only introduced, but killed the Joker by the end of the first film) highlights how these adaptations have learned from comics' more conservative storytelling. Furthermore, when the Joker did appear in the sequel, the villain did not die in the climax, but survived, taunting Batman, "I think you and I are destined to do this forever." This suggested that, much like the comics, he would be back.

Mark Waid directly attributes this development to the influence of the source material, noting in the months ahead of the release of *The Dark Knight Rises*, "Clearly, as [Nolan] said, a lot of what happens in the third Batman spins out of the decisions he made at the end of the second movie. Again, that's very much in the comic book tradition." Indeed, much like *Spider-Man 3*, *The Dark Knight Rises* saw the child of the first film's villain, in this case Talia al Ghul, orchestrating a campaign of revenge against the hero. Thus, the episodic comic book eclipses other seemingly franchise-appropriate sources like *Harry Potter* and *The Lord of the Rings*, as boy wizards will grow up and trips to Mordor come to an end, but seventy-five years after they first appeared, comic book heroes are still engaged in the same never-ending struggles, a boon to filmmakers aspiring to franchise longevity.

Furthermore, while up until the late 1990s "it was a rare Hollywood sequel that made more than the original film" (K. Thompson 3), film series based on serialized fiction such as *The Lord of the Rings*, *Harry Potter*, and *Twilight*, alongside planned franchises such as the *Star Wars* prequels and the later *Fast & Furious* films have managed to mitigate diminishing returns. Comic book adaptations have also demonstrated the ability to reverse this trend. Much like other planned franchises, today's comic book film adaptations have displayed greater continuity between installments. For instance, in the earlier Batman franchise few elements were retained from one film to the next, as the hero gained a new love interest, faced different villains, and many secondary characters were discarded or recast.[53] By comparison, many elements are continued and expanded on in the *Batman Begins* sequel, *The Dark Knight*, such as the reappearance of love interest Rachel Dawes (albeit with a recast actor), a cameo from first film villain, the Scarecrow, and the introduction of the Joker, as hinted at in the coda of *Batman Begins*. Such strategies serve to sustain fan and wider interests by creating an ongoing narrative and prolonging the introduction of elements synonymous with the source, with *The Dark Knight* becoming the most successful Batman adaptation ever at the time of release and outgrossing its predecessor by a factor of two-and-a-half times. Similarly, *Spider-Man 3*, which resolved the Osborn/Spider-Man conflict, and finally introduced fan favorite villain Venom to the series, had the largest gross of all three films. Other sequels such as *Blade II* (del Toro 2002), *X2*, *X-Men: The Last Stand*, *Hellboy II* (del Toro 2008), *Iron Man 2*, *The Dark Knight Rises*, *Iron Man 3* (Black 2013), and *Thor: The Dark World* (Taylor 2013) also outgrossed their predecessors by adopting similar tactics—a further incentive for film studios gravitating towards comic book adaptations in recent years.

This continuity reached its zenith with the Marvel Cinematic Universe. Crossovers, where characters from different books would appear together, are a proven method for generating comic book sales.[54] While successful in themselves, these crossovers also introduce fans to characters they may not regularly read, and therefore the book has the potential to attract new readers.[55] These crossovers were only possible because of the continuity that existed between a publisher's titles. Similar team-ups between Marvel characters were previously untenable in cinema as the comics were licensed to different studios such as 20th Century Fox (*X-Men* and *Fantastic Four*), Sony Pictures Entertainment (*Spider-Man*), and Universal Pictures (*Hulk*). However, once Marvel Entertainment began producing its own adaptations, there was a concerted effort to establish continuity between the various films. The first Marvel Studios production, *Iron Man*, included a post-credit cameo from Samuel L. Jackson as Nick Fury, who announced the "Avengers Initiative." Fans familiar with the comics would know that the "Avengers" is a superteam made up of Marvel characters—among them Iron Man, The Incredible Hulk, Thor, and Captain America.[56] These were the first four planned productions from Marvel Studios, and following the success of *Iron Man*, Marvel Studios greenlit and secured release dates for the solo films starring these characters, as well as the crossover Avengers film.

The second release from Marvel Studios, *The Incredible Hulk* (Leterrier 2008), exceeded most box-office analysts' expectations (Rich). This could partly be attributed to the film's explicit continuity with the already successful *Iron Man* film, as well as the burgeoning Marvel Cinematic Universe. For example, the film's coda included a cameo from Iron Man's alter ego Tony Stark, who was again played by Robert Downey, Jr. This brief appearance was then used in TV spots to promote *The Incredible Hulk*.[57]

Reviewers and fans described these crossovers, which are common in comic books, as the most engaging aspect of the films. As *Ain't It Cool News* (*AICN*) founder Harry Knowles wrote, "For the first time in our lives as crazy geeky fanboys . . . the MARVEL UNIVERSE is moving at 24 frames a second in a theater near us" ("The Incredible Hulk"). Similarly, 81 percent of those filmgoers surveyed following screenings of *Thor* answered "yes" when asked: "Will this film compel you to see other Marvel Studios' productions (e.g., *Captain America*, *The Avengers*, and *Iron Man 3*)?" while a further 6 percent stated they would be seeing these films anyway. Typical responses from comic book fans included, "[It] will lead to an awesome collection of the Marvel Superhero Movies" (26–30-year-old male), while many non-fans also demonstrated an understanding and enthusiasm for Marvel's shared universe, with a 26–30-year-old female saying, "The Captain America trailer looks good, Iron Man has been good so far. I enjoy most films from Marvel."[58] Thus, by creating a measure of the continuity traditionally found in comics, Marvel Studios increased the box-office possibilities of all its productions.

In the past, the release of a crossover such as *Frankenstein Meets the Wolf Man* (Neill 1943), *King Kong vs. Godzilla* (Honda 1962), and *Freddy vs. Jason* (Yu 2003) suggested that a genre or franchise was struggling to retain an audience. However, *The Avengers* was not a desperation move but rather a way to consolidate Marvel's thriving franchises, cross-pollinate the audiences, and generate wider interest. Concerns that the culmination of "Phase 1" of the Marvel Cinematic Universe in *The Avengers* would diminish interest in the individual series proved to be unfounded ("10 Lessons Learned From the $1.5 Billion AVENGERS Movie"). Much like solo comic book titles gaining readership following a large crossover event, the Marvel Studios films released in the wake of the record-breaking gross of *The Avengers* have all experienced a box-office boost.[59] Thus, Marvel has successfully applied the strategies for a shared universe, refined across decades of comic book publication, to film franchises. The success of *The Avengers* has led to other studios announcing plans for similar crossovers, further demonstrating that comic book adaptations are not merely the product of conglomerate strategies, but often inspire them.[60]

A further boon that comic books offer to film franchises is their amenability to reinvention. Many different creators have interpreted comic book characters over decades of publication. Consequently they lend themselves to franchise reinvigoration more readily than comparatively inert sources like novels and plays. In comic book fandom, the refreshing of a comic or character by streamlining their fictional history is known as "retroactive continuity" or "ret-con." For example, Spider-Man's backstory was simplified in the 2007 storyline "One More Day," where complicated character developments (including the hero's marriage) were "ret-conned" out of continuity. Modern film studios have adopted a similar process, regularly announcing the "rebooting" of a franchise. While similar "reboots" may have been employed in the past (e.g., the changing of the James Bond actor), the reboots in comic book adaptations more often go back to the character's origin and offer a significant stylistic departure from the previous franchise entrant.

This trend emerged following the successful reinvigoration of the Batman franchise with the more faithful *Batman Begins* just seven years after the widely derided *Batman & Robin*. Equating the Spider-Man reboot, *The Amazing Spider-Man*, with *Batman Begins*, *Entertainment Weekly* described the film as "a reboot of the franchise, not a continuation of the series Sam Raimi created back in 2002" (Sperling). These various versions are assisted by the multiplicity of interpretations found in the comic books; where Raimi's films relied on Silver Age comics, the new franchise cited the more modern *Ultimate* line.[61] In fact, Sony Pictures Entertainment's co-chairman Amy Pascal pointed to the comic books when defending the reboot, "If you look at the comic books, Marvel was constantly refreshing Spider-Man, so I think Spider-Man fans are comfortable with new interpretations" (Braund 92). Other examples of this trend include *Punisher: War Zone* (Alexander 2008), *Dredd* (Travis 2012), and *Man of Steel.*

Thus, comic books, by virtue of their serialized narratives, fertile publication history, and openness to reinvention, are ideal franchise material, which no doubt helped propel them to the screen in recent times. However, comic book properties are not simply franchise fodder that conglomerates can enlist to start a new series. Rather, they stem from a publishing industry whose long-standing practices are now influencing Hollywood. As Bart Beaty points out, the high volume of comic publishing, "has a great deal to teach us about collaborative authorship, audience knowledge, and editorial oversight in the culture industries" (109).

Transmedia Storytelling

Exploiting Marvel Entertainment's status as a subsidiary of the Walt Disney Company, the Marvel Cinematic Universe (MCU) has been extended to television with the series *Marvel's Agents of S.H.I.E.L.D.* (Whedon 2013). This show joins DVD "one-shots," such as *Item 47* (D'Esposito 2012) and *Agent Carter* (D'Esposito 2013), as well as prequel comic books like *The Road to the Avengers* (David, Gage, and Chen 2012) in filling in the narrative gaps between film installments. Thus, the MCU could be considered a textbook example of the fluidity Bazin anticipated and Jenkins characterizes as transmedia storytelling.[62] Describing transmedia storytelling in relation to *The Matrix* franchise, Jenkins explains how it "unfolds across multiple media platforms, with each new text making a distinctive and valuable contribution to the whole," adding that "reading across the media sustains a depth of experience that motivates more consumption" (*Convergence Culture* 97–98). The financial incentives of this greater consumption have compelled conglomerates to embrace transmedia storytelling.

While embedding film franchises in transmedia stories is relatively new, like many other conglomerate strategies, comics have practiced this co-creation for decades. For instance, when Spider-Man married longtime love interest Mary Jane in 1987, it became "Marvel's most successful media event of the eighties" (Thomas and Sanderson 148). Demonstrating Jenkins's contention that in transmedia storytelling each form will play to its strengths, the wedding occurred in different, medium-specific storylines in the comic books (*The Amazing Spider-Man Annual* #21) and comic strip; Mary Jane's dress was commissioned by fashion designer Willi Smith; and a live-action version of the wedding was held at New York City's Shea Stadium on June 5, 1987, with Stan Lee presiding.

This type of "co-creation" has also led to long-running episodic comics being effectively reverse-engineered to tally with the more widely seen film adaptations. For instance, the "One More Day" storyline was considered by many as an attempt to increase the consistency between the Spider-Man comics and films (Ahmed). Derek Johnson has described how, in an era of transmedia storytelling, Marvel's licensing strategies, "first required the elimination of difference between the comic and audiovisual versions of its character properties" (66–67), a development Johnson identifies in Marvel Comics' X-Men series.[63] This is a further example of the continuity described in the Introduction, where creator and fan seek uniformity between the various versions. The amenability of episodic comic books to this fidelity flux makes them an ideal hub for transmedia storytelling.

Despite the newfound enthusiasm for co-creation, Jenkins cautions that not every text can support such transmedia storytelling. Citing Pierre Lévy's *Collective Intelligence*, he describes *The Matrix* as a good "cultural attractor" as it has "enough depth that they can justify such large-scale efforts: 'Our primary goal should be to prevent closure from occurring too quickly'" (*Convergence Culture* 97). Similarly, one would also consider most mainstream comics as good "cultural attractors." As discussed, comics often only offer the semblance of change, with these open-ended narratives perpetuated across innumerable iterations. Thus, it is unsurprising to find the transmedia practices Jenkins describes at work in the many comic book adaptations produced by media conglomerates.

Furthermore, Jenkins quotes an "experienced" screenwriter's reflections on conglomerate-run filmmaking in the era of transmedia storytelling: "When I first started, you would pitch a story because without a good story, you didn't really have a film. Later, once sequels started to take off, you pitched a character because a good character could support multiple stories. And now, you pitch a world because a world can support multiple characters and multiple stories across multiple media" (*Convergence Culture* 116). Few sources can match the scope for transmedia storytelling inherent in the ready-made worlds of comic book mythology. Thus, when Marvel Studios boasts that it is "one of the world's most prominent character-based entertainment companies, built on a library of over 5,000 characters featured in a variety of media over seventy years" ("Disney to Acquire Marvel Entertainment"), it is easy to see why a conglomerate such as the Walt Disney Company would wish to acquire not just part of the world, but the whole "Marvel Universe."

As demonstrated by the thriving Marvel Cinematic Universe, Marvel Entertainment, and its parent company, will continue to mine the transmedia potential of these characters. While cinema has replaced the comic books as the most popular entry point for these transmedia stories, comics have long practiced such narrative techniques and can serve as a template for filmmakers and scholars who wish to better understand this new paradigm. Thus, it is unsurprising that in an era of media convergence film studios have eschewed more inert texts and have chosen to plunge into the depths of a comic book universe.

Merchandise

With the realization of Bazin's pyramid in today's transmedia franchises, consumers have a number of entry points into a fictional universe. Lunenfeld suggests that conglomerate strategies have "bloated the paratext to such a point that it is impossible to distinguish between it and the text" (14). Conglomerates embrace such multiplicity, as it not only provides a number of opportunities to entice consumers, but each line has its own financial rewards. Perhaps the most lucrative is merchandise, those consumer products branded with a film title or character image. The financial incentives offered by merchandise frequently dictates what sources are adapted and which films are made.[64] For instance, when one considers that Hasbro, Inc., paid Marvel Comics a $70 million licensing fee for the rights to make the toys for *Spider-Man 3* (Duncan and Smith 91–92), the importance of merchandise is clearly not to be undervalued.

Comics have always lent themselves to merchandising opportunities. Ian Gordon notes how the American toy industry in the 1920s regularly turned to comic strip characters for "marketable images" (83), while Pasko describes Superman as "an early proponent of official merchandising" (28). This successful merchandising continued into adaptations with Brooker noting that the 1960s *Batman* television series "was the hottest product since sliced bread; and indeed, the Bond company did market Batman sliced bread in 1966" (*Batman Unmasked* 212).[65]

Although successful feature films occasionally resulted in the production of tie-in products, the mass-merchandising characteristic of modern mainstream productions is thought to have begun with *Star Wars*.[66] George Lucas retained the licensing rights for the film (evidence of how unimportant 20th Century Fox considered them to be), enabling the director to make his fortune through action figures, T-shirts, and other branded products (Emerson). However, the true merchandising potential of *Star Wars* was only realized after the film was a box-office hit. For instance, Kenner Toys was unable to produce the tie-in action figures in time to meet the film's release and instead sold "empty boxes" for $10 that promised the first four action figures would be mailed as soon as they were produced (Sansweet and Vilmur 30).

Mass production of merchandise (much of it by conglomerate affiliates) to coincide with a film's release is now standard practice, and it is often considered to have begun with 1989's *Batman* (Bordwell "Superheroes for Sale"; Pasko 177; Mendelson). In her oft-cited essay, "Holy Commodity Fetish, Batman!", Eileen Meehan describes how "WCI [Warner Communications, Inc.] created an internal market where product for one unit could be recycled to provide product for multiple units" (52). In this merchandising blitz, Warner Bros. recording artist Prince produced an album of tie-in music, DC Comics published a comic book adaptation of the film, and future Marvel partner Toy Biz received the license to produce the action figures. Describing the period, producer Mark Canton said, "People were buying the Batman ties, the T-shirts, the hats, the cuff links, the underwear, everything" ("Shadows of the Bat"). This merchandising frenzy was referred to in the media at the time as "Bat-Mania" and earned an unprecedented $750 million (D. Hughes 42).[67] The push towards merchandising has only intensified since *Batman*, with film studios and publishers striving to achieve lucrative licenses, but what are the attributes that make comics and these characters so amenable to merchandise, and consequently, so sought-after by conglomerates?

As the pop art of Andy Warhol, Roy Lichtenstein, and others suggests, comic book characters are as transcendent as Mickey Mouse and movie stars.[68] In fact, many commentators equate the recognition of comic book characters with movie stars (Gordon 45; Bordwell "Superheroes for Sale"). It could even be argued that under today's filmmaking paradigms, comic book and other franchise characters have come to supplant the role traditionally occupied by stars. For instance, of the 119 covers of the popular British film magazine *Empire* in the 1990s, fifty-three could be said to be of a movie star (i.e., an out-of-character image), with the actor's name more prominent than the film they were promoting. However, of the 120 covers produced in the 2000s, eighty-four were film characters, with the actor's name often omitted. During this decade, in which Spider-Man received five dedicated covers, only eighteen could be considered to be "movie star" covers, with Megan Fox (May 2009) and Johnny Depp (November 2004) the last actors to feature on covers that did not rely on characters they played.[69]

It is easy to understand why film producers have gravitated towards characters such as those derived from comics. Their recognition and existing fan base fulfill many of the same functions of movie stars. However, unlike a specific actor, they can be reiterated countless times across a variety of media—the transmedia strategy of most conglomerates. Describing the Spider-Man suit, actor Andrew Garfield reflected, "You very quickly realize that it's not you in the suit. It is *the* suit. . . . Whatever body is in that suit it doesn't really matter" ("Costumes"). Thus, by basing film franchises and merchandising opportunities around existing comic creations, studios are not beholden to the whims of a particular star, but rather are able to repurpose these characters at every available opportunity, such as the recasting of the lower profile (and much lower paid) Garfield as Spider-Man only five years after Tobey Maguire vacated the role.[70]

Furthermore, comic book characters, unlike their equivalents in text-based sources (e.g., Harry Potter, Frodo Baggins, and Edward Cullen), have very clearly defined and recognizable imagery. For instance, Morrison notes how artist Carmine Infantino's decision to add the yellow oval to the Bat-symbol "turned the chest emblem into a logo and a marketing tool" (105). Similarly, Bukatman describes how the "mask, costume, and logo are marks that guarantee the superhero body passage into the field of the symbolic (the logos)" (*Matters of Gravity* 54). Thus, even before these characters are adapted to cinema, they have already achieved the iconic status central to merchandising. This symbolism was evident in the promotion of *Spider-Man*, which despite being the first feature film adaptation of the character, was effectively marketed through minimalist imagery that proved instantly recognizable. For example, the central image in the first teaser trailer was of a helicopter trapped on a web between the Twin Towers of the World Trade Center. The advertisement contained only fleeting glimpses of the hero, demonstrating a confidence that the web motif would convey the message.[71]

Claire Parody notes how "franchising characteristically makes extensive use of infant media technologies" (213). Comic book brands lend themselves to conglomerate ambitions to exploit the merchandising possibilities of convergent technology. For instance, Kristin Thompson notes how mobile phone company Cingular "linked with *Spider-Man* and saw its sales spike, particularly in downloads of graphics, ringtones, and games based on the film" (106). Similarly, comic book adaptations proved amenable to the home entertainment market, which gained a digital boost in the late 1990s through the introduction of DVD. With the emergence of DVD, studios encouraged consumers to buy rather than rent films. Thompson also describes how "studios noticed that buyers favored franchise films over single features" (204). Consequently, the film franchises to which comic book characters are so amenable became integral to conglomerate strategies that hoped to optimize convergent technology such as DVD. It was not merely new technology that the studios exploited, but also its early adopters and most avid users. How a mutually beneficial relationship developed between studios and online fans will be explored in Chapter Three.

In studying the heyday of the comic strip, Gordon summarizes that by "stressing individual characters, the new comic art form lent itself to promotion and marketing because these images provided a means for embellishing commodities with personality" (7). Today, these transcendent symbols not only help to distinguish mainstream movies, but all the merchandising expected to flow from these big-budget productions; simply put, a T-shirt with a superhero emblem is more likely to sell than one without.[72] Thus, as widely recognized symbols that lend themselves to everything from bubble gum to video games, comic books and their characters are central to the merchandising strategies that conglomerates favor—attributes that have expedited their passage to film production.

Universal Communication

Bolter and Grusin consider remediation to be the "defining characteristic of the new digital media" (45). Remediation describes how new media rework older forms, and how those traditional media respond to competition from these upstarts. In the shift from command-line to graphic user interfaces, digital technologies achieved real-world immediacy through icons and displays that evoked offices, postal services, and a host of other everyday systems. With its familiar integration of text and image, the language of comics was also absorbed by new media, which may help account for the form's extended media presence today.

It has frequently been asserted that image-based communication came to the fore in the twentieth century (Varnum and Gibbons ix; Beronä 19; Wolf 411). Eisner went so far as to argue that "comics are at the center of this phenomenon" (*Graphic Storytelling* 3), a position Duncan and Smith recently reiterated (14), and which is supported by many examples. For instance, Gordon notes in his comprehensive study *Comic Strips and Consumer Culture* that the "importance of Buster Brown's marketing [a comic strip character used to sell merchandise, most famously shoes] is that it predated, and presaged, a wholesale shift from text-based to visual, image-centered advertising" (38). Gordon goes on to convincingly demonstrate how, "by the 1930s comic strips, and the techniques of communication they employed, were embedded in American daily life" (89).[73]

The integration of comic book idioms into everyday communication has intensified with media convergence. Foreshadowing the proliferation of digital technologies, Marshall McLuhan suggested in 1964 that "when electric speed further takes over from mechanical movie sequences. . . . We return to the inclusive form of the icon" (13). Writing in 1994, during the very earliest stages of what would later be called convergence culture, McCloud presciently wrote, "Ours is an increasingly symbol-orientated culture. As the twenty-first century approaches, visual iconography may finally help us realize a form of universal communication" (*Understanding Comics* 58).

As the flow of content across media increased, comics emerged at the center of this image-based communication. The amenability of comic idioms to modern media is attributable to the form's use of iconic text and symbolic images. As McCloud illustrates, "When pictures are more abstracted from 'Reality,' they require greater levels of perception, more like words. When words are bolder, more direct, they require lower levels of perception and are received faster, more like pictures. Our need for a unified language of comics sends us toward the center where words and pictures are like two sides on one coin!" (*Understanding Comics* 49). Matthew T. Jones suggests that comics' place in this continuum make them "especially suitable material for adaptation to film" (7–8). Chapter Four will examine how filmmakers engage with these representational overlaps in an effort to narrow the semiotic gap between the comics and cinema.

The central position occupied by words and images in comics allows text to be perceived as images and requires images to be deciphered. Creators Grant Morrison and Andy Kubert played on this relationship for an innovative sequence from *Batman* #656 (October 2006), in which the hero tackles terrorists during a pop art exhibition. The setting allowed the background

FIG. 1.7 The close association of text and image in comics is underscored by this self-reflexive moment from *Batman* #656, where "BLAM!" acts as both diegetic image and non-diegetic text.

paintings to serve as both diegetic images and non-diegetic text (i.e., sound effects), thereby illustrating how text and image can be used interchangeably in comics.

The use of the "unified language of comics" in advertising, instructional manuals, and diagrams has been described as more "economic" (Taylor 56) and accelerating understanding (Eisner *Graphic Storytelling* 5), with Samuel Y. Edgerton going so far as to suggest that one needs to learn "basic neo-Renaissance conventions as in the adventure comics [to] succeed at all in our diagram dependent technological world" (33). Eisner valorizes comics over other media in this capacity when he notes that "there is no pressure of time as there would be in a live action motion picture or animated film. . . . Unlike the rigidity of photographs, the broad generalization of artwork permits exaggeration which can more quickly make the point and influence the reader" (*Comics & Sequential Art* 144).[74]

Today, comic idioms enable consumers to navigate new media and convergent technology. Many comics scholars have commented on this development, with Mario Saraceni describing how the move towards user-friendly displays contributed to the adoption of comic devices: "What is more direct, easier, more familiar and friendlier than comics?" (90). Similarly, Duncan and Smith state that "the habits and skills developed by reading comics have helped make the Web both more acceptable and more comprehensible for many people" (15). Many examples could be used to support such assessments, such as the Microsoft Office assistant Clippy, who helps users navigate the software through speech balloons. Similarly, Saraceni makes the pertinent observation that computer text has gradually gained comic-like iconicity through a mix of font styles, sizes, colors, and effects (92). Beyond computers, much of today's technology, from smartphone displays to the rebus-like SMS language, rely on the type of graphic communication that comics have pioneered and practiced for decades.

Responding to the emergence of web comics, journalist Paul Gravett makes an observation that echoes the cyclical patterns that have appeared elsewhere in this section: "Just as in the late nineteenth century comics had anticipated many of the techniques and the public's acceptance of cinema so that comics then developed alongside film, so a century later a similar fin de siècle interaction has emerged with the visual and verbal language of comics informing the Internet in its design and navigation, and again with both media expanding them in tandem" (*1001 Comics* 9). If the need for a universal language pushes us toward the center of the image-word continuum (where comics reside), it should be unsurprising that comics provide much of the icons and formal systems of our symbol-orientated culture. As Ahrens and Meteling point out, "The medium 'comics' is not only reflected in the plethora of film adaptations or in the ever growing global fan culture, but also in the ubiquitous use of comic contents, icons and aesthetics in all aspects of modern life" (2). Deborah Cartmell echoes such comments in her analysis of the fidelity debate by suggesting that "adaptation is, perhaps, the result of an increasingly post-literate (not illiterate) world in which the visual image dominates" (145). Consequently, as communication becomes more visually dependent, it is unsurprising that comics should find themselves at the vanguard of post-literate adaptation. Much of new media has remediated comics; perhaps the glut of comic book film adaptations is simply an explicit example of this wider trend.

From Publisher to Licensing Company and Media Conglomerate

Marvel's transition from a publisher to a licensing company, and ultimately to a major subsidiary of the world's largest media company, is a vivid example of conglomerate strategies at work and therefore is an appropriate example to close this section. In the early 1990s, the comic book speculator boom enabled Marvel owner Ron Perelman to expand the publisher into sectors such as trading cards, themed restaurants, and comic book distribution.[75] Johnson characterizes Perelman's ultimate goal as a desire to "become a kind of mini-Disney" (70). However, the speculation market crash of the mid-1990s saw the Marvel Entertainment Group (MEG) filing for Chapter 11 bankruptcy protection in late 1996. After a two-year period in which a number of parties fought for control of Marvel, MEG was merged with Toy Biz, which ended the bankruptcy. This move led to Toy Biz heads Avi Arad and Isaac Perlmutter running Marvel and implementing a number of strategies that realized Perelman's earlier ambitions (Howe 396). As Duncan and Smith, who also equate Marvel's strategies with the Walt Disney Company, note, the company in the twenty-first century was "successful in transforming Marvel into more of a licensing company than just a comic publisher per se" (90).

The potential financial windfall from bringing Marvel's characters to the screen was the main incentive for resolving the operational confusion. Howe notes how Avi Arad fought off an ownership bid from businessman Carl Icahn with a "stirring speech" to the banks in which he claimed "that Spider-Man alone is worth a billion dollars. But now, at this crazy hour, at this juncture, you're going to take $380 million—whatever it is from Carl Icahn—for the whole thing? *One* thing is worth a billion! We have the X-Men. We have the Fantastic Four. They can all be movies" (392). When Arad's prediction proved correct in the summer of 2002, it was unsurprising that Marvel soon implemented plans to produce its own adaptations.

This process gained momentum in 2005 when the recently created Marvel Studios division of Marvel Entertainment secured $525 million from the Merrill Lynch Commercial Finance Corp. by using ten of its characters, including Captain America, The Black Panther, and Nick Fury, as collateral. However, with their most widely recognized characters licensed to other studios, such as *Spider-Man* at Sony Pictures Entertainment, the newly formed studio turned to the lesser-known Iron Man for its first production. Nonetheless, when *Iron Man* exceeded all expectations by opening with a $98 million weekend, Marvel quickly announced release dates for its other adaptations, *Thor, Captain America: The First Avenger* (Johnston 2011), and *The Avengers*.[76] These actions led to a stock increase of 9 percent, with Marvel Entertainment garnering the attention of larger conglomerates (A. K. Smith).

With many equating Marvel's licensing strategies with Disney's, it is perhaps appropriate that the Walt Disney Company acquired Marvel Entertainment for $4 billion in 2009 ("Disney to Acquire Marvel Entertainment"). That in little over a decade Marvel could go from being a bankrupt publisher to the prime acquisition of the world's most profitable media conglomerate demonstrates how amenable comic books and their characters are to conglomerate strategies.

Comics fulfill many of the goals of today's media enterprises. These properties have a built-in recognition that dates back over generations. The depth and sustainability of mainstream comic books ensures that they are well suited to film franchises and cinematic reinvention without incurring diminishing returns. These characters have achieved a transcendent symbolism that facilitates diverse and large-scale merchandising opportunities. Finally, comics have proven uniquely positioned to navigate and thrive in the universal communication of convergence culture with its many transmedia ties. It was perhaps inevitable that conglomerate practices would lead filmmakers to comic books at the start of the twenty-first century, thereby facilitating one of the most influential trends in modern Hollywood production.

Changing of the Guard

Critics and commentators regularly credit cultural traumas, technological advancements, and conglomerate practices with facilitating the emergence of the comic book movie in the early twenty-first century. Although the professionals interviewed for this study echoed these views, they also put forward a less cited factor, which *Cowboys & Aliens* (Favreau 2011) producer and Platinum Comics CEO Scott Mitchell Rosenberg articulated as a "changing of the guard"—a new generation of filmmakers and producers with a greater enthusiasm for comic books. However, filmmakers as early as Orson Welles expressed an affection for comics (McBride; Inge), so what makes this era different? Marvel Comics senior vice president of publishing Tom Brevoort, who also suggested that the catalyst for the trend might be "generational," reflected, "I don't think it's any real surprise that we had Superman and Batman in the sixties and seventies because at that point those characters had been around for twenty years and the generation that grew up with them were in a position to be able to say, 'OK, let's make a Batman TV show, let's make a Superman TV show.' We're now at a point where people who were readers or fans of Marvel are in a similar position."

However, this reasoning does not explain why adaptations of books such as *Wanted* (comic, 2003; film, 2008), *RED* (comic, 2003; film, 2010), and *Scott Pilgrim* (comic, 2004; film, 2010) were produced only a few years after their introduction, while icons such as Superman, Batman, and Spider-Man had to wait decades for a feature-length version. Writer Joe Kelly, who also cited the generational shift, provided a more nuanced explanation: "Comics have obviously been around for a very long time, but it only became integral to your teenage years in the eighties. Those kids are now moving up [in the industry] and they have a reverence for the material." *30 Days of Night* creator Steve Niles experienced this transition firsthand: "When I first started pitching, the only people who knew my work were the guys at the front desk: the assistants. Now those assistants are the ones running the office."

As Kelly points out, while comic books have been published since the 1930s, they tended to be treated as disposable kids' stuff. This reputation is not wholly undeserved; one of the earliest examples of the form, *Funnies on Parade*, produced in 1933, was a Proctor and Gamble giveaway designed to appeal to children (Harvey 17). Throughout their publication history, the comic book's status as ephemeral children's entertainment has been reinforced by paper drives, the censorship of the Comics Code Authority, marketing considerations, and a myriad of other factors. However, with the emergence of fan culture in the 1960s, comics began the slow road towards cultural credibility.

As will be charted in Chapter Three, in the 1960s disparate fans were organized into a more cohesive community through letter columns, fanzines, and conventions. This period also saw comic book collecting become more commonplace. By the time dedicated stores appeared in the mid-1970s, comic book readership may have shrunk, but those readers that remained were more committed and often continued reading into adulthood. It is these devotees, who did not exist during earlier epochs, that Kelly is pointing to when he discusses executives with enough power and enthusiasm to soften Hollywood's resistance to comic book movies.

Comics also gained credibility outside of the core fan base during this time. For instance, since the 1960s the mainstream press has regularly reported on the huge sums collectors are willing to pay for rare comics. In 1965, *Newsweek* was stunned that *Action Comics* #1 (Superman's first appearance) was "able to draw 1,000 times its original asking price!" (89) of 10 cents, while in 2011 a copy of the same comic was sold at auction for $2.16 million ("Action Comics Superman debut copy sells for $2.16m"). Such staggering numbers routinely fill column inches to the point that even if one does not value the form, they cannot ignore its dollar-and-cents worth. As Jeffrey A. Brown notes, "Many fans have learned to validate their interest and lend it a degree of status in the eyes of non-fans by citing the economic value of their hobby" ("Comic Book Fandom" 27).

A second infusion of respectability came with the introduction of the "graphic novel." Although many saw the graphic novel as a marketing ploy, with Roger Sabin believing that "the idea of the 'graphic novel' was hype—the invention of publishers' public relations departments" (165), it was nonetheless effective in bringing much-needed credibility and sales to a maligned medium. As Stephen Weiner notes, "By the late 1990s, public libraries were adding graphic novels to their popular collections, and graphic novels were being awarded prizes previously given only to prose works" (xv). Among the awards and accolades comics received were *Watchmen* appearing on *Time* magazine's list of the 100 best English language novels; *Sandman* #19, "A Midsummer Night's Dream," winning a World Fantasy Award; and *Maus* being awarded the Pulitzer Prize in 1992.

With fans becoming industry players, disposable kids' stuff earning more at auction than fine art, and graphic novels winning awards traditionally reserved for literature, it is unsurprising that in recent years Hollywood has been more receptive to comics. However, it should be noted that the adaptations also played their part in increasing the recognition of the form. This is discernible in the reviews of many film critics. For instance, *Chicago Sun-Times* reviewer Roger Ebert described *X-Men* readers in 2000 as almost delusional for believing "the medium is as deep and portentous as say, *Sophie's Choice*" and celebrated Ang Lee for "transforming" the comic books on which the *Hulk* was based. However, as the trend developed and adaptations such as *Spider-Man*, *Ghost World* (Zwigoff 2001), *Road to Perdition* (Mendes 2002), *Hellboy* (del Toro 2004), and *The Dark Knight* received awards and critical acclaim, reviewers such as Ebert tempered their earlier disdain. For instance, in 2009 the critic gave comic book adaptation *Watchmen* a glowing review that reflected positively on its source material, writing: "It's a compelling visceral film—sound, images and characters combined into a decidedly odd visual experience that evokes the feel of a graphic novel."

It is not simply a coincidence that many comic book enthusiasts emerged in key creative industry roles, especially when you consider the relatively finite readership of comics. The former president of DC Comics, Paul Levitz, who began his career on the fanzine the *Comic Reader* before moving into the industry, explained that "until the last five or six years the means of production of film or television were way beyond the average young person's reach" while comics are "fairly short" and are "often very simple in their drawing, so the apparent barriers to entry are not as high." Thus, the form engendered a degree of experimentation not possible in cinema and more resource dependent media. Furthermore, as will be explored in Chapter Three, the industry facilitated a participatory culture long before the Web made such practices commonplace. Accordingly, fan creators had more opportunities to move into professional roles. As Tom Brevoort, citing the "artists' alleys" found at many conventions, observed: "It's a fairly democratic artform."[77]

Thus, it is unsurprising that one finds many comic book enthusiasts among Hollywood filmmakers. Whether working on direct adaptations or films with no declared source, these filmmakers are a good example of the textual poachers Henry Jenkins described in his landmark publication (27), in that they borrow elements from their object of devotion (comics), and repurpose them for a new context (cinema). How these textual poachers have fostered a comic book aesthetic in modern mainstream cinema will be the focus of Chapter Four.

But this is not a one-way street; a number of successful filmmakers create and write their own comics between productions, including Joss Whedon, Kevin Smith, Guy Ritchie, Shakar Kapur, Neil Gaiman, and J. Michael Straczynski. Many of these creators are not simply indulging a childhood passion; instead, they are using comics strategically as a cost-effective step in bringing their ideas to the screen. When asked why so many comic book adaptations are produced today, *30 Days of Night* creator Steve Niles responded, "Producers don't want to read novels anymore." Niles is not simply being facetious; he described the years he spent verbally pitching the premise of *30 Days of*

Night—"vampires invade a town in Alaska"—to "blank faces" who "must have been picturing all these Bela Lugosis," but "the day I had a comic to show them that's when it sold." A number of other creators have shepherded their ideas to the screen via comics with the films announced soon after the first issue hit the shelf, including *Kick-Ass, I, Frankenstein* (Beattie 2014), and *Kingsman: The Secret Service* (Vaughn 2015). In the case of *Oblivion* (Kosinski 2013), the "graphic novel" it was supposedly adapted from was never even published. As Grant Morrison notes, "The comic book was just a pitch now, a stepping-stone to celluloid validation" (380).

Thus, the ascendency of comic book fans, and other executives weaned on visual entertainments, seems to have cultivated an atmosphere receptive to image-led pitches. When one factors in the cost of film production, in particular expensive production design and effects, it is unsurprising that comics have been positioned as the experimental wing of larger conglomerates. As Joe Kelly explained when interviewed, "[comics] are the ultimate R&D . . . we have the fewest number of steps, we have the least amount of budget, and our ideas can be fully realized."

Many high-profile fans see this as a victory for comics and its long-standing fan base. Grant Morrison opens *Supergods* by stating, "It's with amazement and a little pride that I've watched the ongoing, bloodless surrender of mainstream culture to relentless colonization from the geek hinterlands" (xvi). Actor Nicolas Cage, who reportedly once owned the issue of *Action Comics* #1 that sold for $2.16 million, told *Empire*, "People have attached words to me like 'comic book geek' . . . [but] lo and behold, it's a multi-billion dollar industry, so how big of a nerd can I be?" (Plumb). Michael E. Uslan and Mark Waid both reflect on this Golden Age of Comic Book Filmmaking in almost identical terms: "What I say to all of my fellow fanboys and comic book geeks is 'We win!'" (Uslan); "Guess what? The nerds won and now we don't have to hang our heads in shame" (Waid). I have argued elsewhere that while comics may currently enjoy an unprecedented influence on wider entertainments, the industry itself may be diminished by the need to appease its conglomerate masters ("Special Effect"). This argument will continue, and time will ultimately cast the deciding vote. For the moment, it is impossible to ignore how comics are increasingly positioned as pitch-ready material by a generation of filmmakers more enthusiastic about comics than any before—a development that undoubtedly eased their passage to the screen.

Hot Gates

The important question of why so many comic book movies have been produced since the year 2000 has unleashed an onslaught of possibilities. Taking inspiration from the Spartan use of a narrow mountain pass to corral an invading army, this section will try to organize these various arguments into a single line of analysis by focusing on one example from this trend. As this over-egged analogy suggests, this case study will be Zack Snyder's 2007 adaptation of Frank Miller's 1998 graphic novel *300*.

In the retelling of the Battle of Thermopylae, King Leonidas is portrayed as going against the orders of pacifists and bureaucrats in leading a small group, the eponymous 300 Spartan warriors, in a preemptive strike against a massing Eastern threat. In the film, Leonidas manages to form a weak coalition (with the Arcadians), but is largely a go-it-alone hero. These elements appeared in Miller's original graphic novel, and thus it could be argued that parallels with modern conflicts were coincidental, but the few amendments and additions to the largely faithful film reinforce its pro-War on Terror stance. In one sequence, which appears in both the comic and film, the Spartans express their warrior heritage by thrusting their spears into the air. In the comic this moment is a solitary, silent image, but in the film it is given a contemporary militaristic inflection as the Spartans use, what director Snyder describes as "an homage to the marine corps," with a cry reminiscent of the corps' traditional "ooh-rah" (*300* DVD commentary). Similarly, Queen Gorgo's role is expanded from one panel in the comic to an entire subplot revolving around her attempts to persuade politicians to send more troops: "We are at war, gentlemen. We must send the entire Spartan army to aid our king in the preservation of not just ourselves, but our children." The film also expands upon the graphic novel's tension between a Western conception of freedom and reason, and a perceived Eastern fixation on subservience and mysticism. In one exchange between Leonidas and Xerxes, the Persian king taunts, "Imagine what horrible fate awaits my enemies when I would gladly kill any of my own men for victory." This dialogue does not appear in the graphic novel, with its place in the film highlighting a greater use of right-wing rhetoric. Xerxes, in his reliance on superstition, and by his willingness to sacrifice the lives of his men, is comparable to a modern-day terrorist leader, who organizes suicide bombings by promising rewards in the afterlife.

Across his work, Miller has oscillated between suggesting his books are too fantastical to be taken seriously—"anyone who really believes that a story about a guy who wears a cape and punches out criminals is a presentation of a political viewpoint . . . is living in a dream world" (Sharrett 43)—to pointing to their propagandist traditions—"Superman punched out Hitler. So did Captain America. That's one of the things they're there for" (Mount). Snyder is more consistent but less committal, responding to charges of the film's conservative agenda with evasive responses that point to the film's comic book origins: "It's a graphic novel movie about a bunch of guys that are stomping the snot out of each other" (Welland). Similarly, as Lev Grossman noted of *300* in *Time* magazine, "Maybe that's the only way to make a war movie right now, or at least, the only way to make a war movie that's not an antiwar movie . . . it's to the movie's credit that it doesn't confuse what it's doing with anything real . . . *300* is a vision of war as ennobling and morally unambiguous and spectacularly good-looking." Thus, *300* might be considered another example of a comic book movie that perpetuates US mythological traditions, while using a fantastical setting to defuse criticism and appeal to a wider demographic audience.

300 was released at a time when ephemeral concepts such as "War on Terror" were being challenged, and there was a concerted effort to replace crude terms with more nuanced language (P. Reynolds). Similarly, while *300* scored the type of box office and subsequent DVD sales that indicate audiences enjoyed its escapist heroism, there was wide recognition that this was a simplistic interpretation, generating considerable criticism (Welland). Such resistant readings suggest that not all audiences were disarmed by the film's fantastical setting, and *300* might best be described as another faultline text, in that it points to the many conflicting impulses and opinions prevalent at that time.

Of course, *300* is not the first cinematic depiction of the Battle of Thermopylae. In fact, Frank Miller credits the 1962 CinemaScope film *The 300 Spartans* (Maté) with inspiring his graphic novel.[78] Thus, again one finds a comic book aspiring to cinematic qualities (Miller even used double page spreads to recreate the aspect ratio of CinemaScope), even while embracing the freedoms that did not exist in pre-digital cinema. When it was released in 2007, *300* was one of the first examples of a comic book transformation (Andrew *Film Theory* 98), in that the adaptation does not simply borrow some characters or the premise from the source, but attempted to bring the work to the screen with the fewest changes possible. The filmmakers may have been emboldened to take on such a faithful adaptation following the technical and economic success of the earlier Miller adaptation *Sin City*, where digital backlot technology was used to recreate the source. However, by positioning the adaptation as a transformation, the producers set an aesthetic criterion that the film's green screen technology was expected to meet. This went beyond recreating the comic's seas of expressionistic claret and disfigured assailants, to a concerted effort to capture the book's graphiation. Miller, who co-directed *Sin City*, said that "with this magnificent green screen process this *is* drawing, you just get to draw with Bruce Willis in the foreground" (*Sin City* DVD commentary). Although Miller's role on *300* was as a consultant and executive producer, his boldly expressive art was evident from the very first shot, of which Zack Snyder commented on the film's DVD, "That lightning is the lightning from the book . . . it is also in some other Frank Miller books like *The Dark Knight*."

 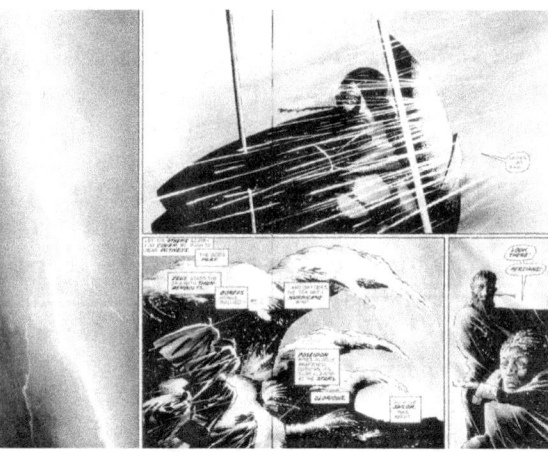

FIG. 1.8 Miller's graphiation is evident in the digital films based on his work. Here, Miller's trademark lightning bolt as it appears in *The Dark Knight Returns* and *300* is recreated for the film adaptation of *300*.

The filmmakers were able to use the more malleable digital film image to not simply capture the story, but also the style. As Deborah Del Prete, producer of *The Spirit*, noted, "In previous comic book movies you got the story, but a key part of comics is the work of artists, and that was missing . . . with Sin City and 300 you finally got the artist's work up there on the screen" (Vaz 63). While the literal translation some filmmakers aspire to is impossible, like Nemo's adventures and Superman's flight, the imperatives established by a comic book source inspire technological advancements and innovation. Thus, comic book adaptations are not merely a response to cinema's digital turn, but have been active in shaping the development of new filmmaking technology.

300 was also well placed in the conglomerate structure. The film benefited heavily from a proactive Web community, with the DVD going so far as to include a list of online fans that Snyder introduces with: "Thanks to everyone in the online community for getting the word out on 300. There'd be no 300 without you guys doing the work" ("Be 1 of 300"). Such online enthusiasm is somewhat surprising given that the five-issue series was not widely known outside the comic book community, or even within it. However, the adaptation was well positioned within the larger trend as it was aligned with

earlier successes, such as *Sin City*, in promotional material.[79] Furthermore, Warner Bros. used the highly anticipated film version of *Watchmen* to foster interest in the adaptation of the lesser-known *300*. For instance, Snyder was announced as the director of *Watchmen* prior to the *300* panel at the 2006 San Diego Comic-Con, which ensured greater attendance and fan interest in this panel. Later in the promotion, an early test image of the popular *Watchmen* character Rorschach was inserted into an extended trailer for *300*. Fans who discovered the image prided themselves on their investigative abilities and quickly began sharing the image online, with *AICN* reporting, "the web is a-buzzin" ("From 300 Trailer Comes One Helluva Rorshach [*sic*]"). This move served to not only generate interest for the in-production *Watchmen*, but also the recently released *300*.

The eventual success of *300* saw Warner Bros. eager to develop the seemingly finite story, with Miller tasked with coming up with a new graphic novel to fuel this burgeoning franchise (Schaefer). Ultimately, *300: Rise of an Empire* (Murro) was released in 2014. This film charted the battles of Artemisium and Salamis leaving the Battle of Plataea, hinted at in the original film's coda, for a future franchise installment.

In this Golden Age of Comic Book Filmmaking even limited series such as *300* have proven fertile fodder for conglomerate aspirations, with the comic adapted to the screen less than a decade after its original publication. This enthusiasm contrasts starkly with the well-publicized resistance Miller faced when he first went to Hollywood in the late 1980s (Clayton). The respect this generation of filmmakers and the industry has for Miller and the wider form is evident from their desire to replicate the creator's style, the prefixing of Miller's name to the *Sin City* title, and comments from directors like Robert Rodriguez:

> The only way to do a movie this faithful is to have Frank Miller co-directing with me. Frank is a natural story-teller, he's a visual storyteller and I thought he had a different approach to it. I didn't think someone from the comic world, like Frank, who does what Frank does should come to Hollywood and suddenly start down here and work his way up, I thought he should be right at the same level, as he's doing what I'm doing—he's graphically, and with character and with visuals, creating stories, telling stories, so I thought he should just be co-directing the movie. ("How It Went Down")

Thus, like the many other comic book movies considered in this chapter, *300* was well suited to the diverse demands of early twenty-first century Hollywood filmmaking. Behind its heightened setting the film engaged with post-9/11 sentiment. It made good use of existing digital technologies while also applying them to new considerations. The graphic novel moved fluidly in the conglomerate structure with Warner Bros. using the adaptation to cross-promote *Watchmen*, while also developing the first film into a larger franchise. Furthermore, the film's fidelity demonstrated the growing respect in Hollywood for graphic novels, which would have expedited the transition of *300* to the screen.

Commenting on his idiosyncratic take on Batman, Miller observed: "He is so simple in his design and concept that he is open to an incredible number of interpretations" (*Comic Book Confidential*). Many commentators have considered how variations in long-running comic books allow us to map the impact of the cultural context. For instance, Alex Evans describes comic book heroes as a "mythic palimpsest" (121), Andy Medhurst sees them as a "cultural thermometer" (154), and Danny Fingeroth believes the genre's "lack of self-consciousness may enable us to read cultural signposts that would be harder to discern in a cultural vein more knowingly developed" (56). Such comments echo François Truffaut's stance that adaptation is "an instructive barometer for the age" (Andrew *Film Theory* 104). Yet what do today's comic book film adaptations suggest about our time?

- Do they tap into a desire to escape to halcyon days when faced with global conflicts, or a need to validate vigilante-like activities in domestic and foreign policies?
- Are comic book adaptations an opportunity to demonstrate digital filmmaking technology, or a high aesthetic criterion that these new techniques are striving to recreate?
- Is this trend further evidence that conglomerate strategies have overtaken the entertainment industries, or are comics part of the new universal language of convergence culture?
- Does the unprecedented number of films produced suggest that comics have gained greater cultural legitimacy, or are they evidence of the infantilization of mainstream filmmaking?

No satisfying, all-conquering reason exists for why comic book adaptations are being made right now. The professionals interviewed for this study offered a variety of equally persuasive arguments, with Mark Waid articulating many of the most popularly held beliefs in a response that merits being quoted in full:

> I think the biggest catalyst for this trend was that people who had grown up reading comic books were running film studios in 2000; that was never the case before. In the sixties and seventies movie studios were run by old men who

thought comics were kids' stuff, and basically they kind of were kids' stuff. What we were lucky enough to see, starting with the *X-Men* movie in 2000 and moving on from there, is a culture of studio executives who were reading comics in 1985 and remember *Maus*, *Watchmen*, and *Dark Knight*, and remembered, "Oh my god comics can be something more than just kiddie fare," and sure enough they rose to power and positions of prominence in Hollywood, and suddenly it made the world safe for comics.

When pressed to consider why the audience was so responsive to these films, Waid added:

Certainly in America, it's a cowboy story. All of them still boil down to good versus evil, and the sheriff versus the rustlers and that basic cowboy mentality has always been a big part of what we enjoy in stories. Beyond that, it lends itself to spectacle even if you don't think that the story is particularly good, they still probably look really interesting, it still has a visual whiz-bang and a lot of pyrotechnics and stuff for the kids. It's all cyclical, eventually there will be enough bad comic book movies in a row that there will have to be a chill on it, but for the time being we're going to keep riding that wave.

As Waid articulates, a myriad of factors are responsible for the successful emergence of the comic book adaptation trend and for propelling it to previously unmatched levels of production and influence. Furthermore, given Hollywood's many priorities at the start of the twenty-first century, these goals were frequently intertwined: released in the summer of 2007, *300* married technological marvels and post-9/11 sentiment, while still maximizing its merchandising, franchise, and transmedia potential.

In summation, no single reason can cover this diverse trend. Although the multiplicity of factors may not make for good copy, this book brings all these factors together to demonstrate how these films were well suited, perhaps ideally suited, to the cultural, technological, and economic concerns that beset Hollywood production at the start of the twenty-first century. That comic book adaptations could meet and surmount such demands, and achieve unprecedented levels of popularity, testifies to their importance within modern Hollywood filmmaking. To paraphrase the oft-quoted conclusion from *The Dark Knight*: They may not be the films the audience and studios deserve, but they are the ones they need right now.

CHAPTER TWO

The Comic Book Movie Genre

From social anxieties to the novelty of digital effects, Chapter One considered a number of reasons why comic book adaptations have achieved unprecedented popularity among modern filmgoers. It also described how studios recognized and began to capitalize on a wide and enthusiastic audience for comic book adaptations following early successes such as *Blade* (Norrington 1998), *X-Men* (Singer 2000), and *Spider-Man* (Raimi 2002). Perpetuating the trend, filmmakers targeted this largely non-reader audience by trading on and emulating previously popular adaptations. Today, the comic book film adaptation has developed into a full-fledged genre: the comic book movie. By drawing on industrial discourses and the audience research described earlier, this chapter will chart how this genre emerged and its impact on Hollywood filmmaking.

Thomas Leitch persuasively argues the merits of analyzing adaptation as a genre in his 2008 article, "Adaptation, the Genre." Opening his account, Leitch states: "It may seem perverse to argue that cinematic adaptations of literary works constitute a genre when this genre has attracted so little analysis or attention" (106). As Leitch notes, it is surprising that adaptation is so rarely viewed in generic terms by the academy, especially when one considers the parallels between these systems. For instance, many scholars believe that the pleasure of adaptation comes from "the comfort of ritual combined with the piquancy of surprise" (Hutcheon 4). A similar response is elicited by the genre film, with Langford suggesting that the "combination of sameness and variety is the linchpin of the generic contract" (7). Thus, the certainty of the familiar, balanced with the possibility for innovation, entices filmgoers to adaptations and genre films alike. Furthermore, in the same way that a genre film will suggest a context to its audience through familiar conventions, adaptations will often signal their status as *adaptations*, with Leitch identifying cues such as "period setting," "period music," "obsession with authors, books and words," and "intertitles" ("Adaptation, the Genre" 111–13). This chapter will identify similar markers for the comic book movie genre.

Despite the novelty of Leitch's approach, a number of scholars had already identified adaptation-derived genres. In his list of "major genres," Geoff King includes "the literary adaptation" (119); Ken Gelder argues for the inclusion of *The Piano* (Campion 1993) to the genre he calls "literary cinema" (158); and Cartmell and Whelehan describe the "literary film" as a genre "narrowly defined as canonical literature on film" (*Screen Adaptation* 85). Similarly, Jonathan Loucks has considered comics-derived film genres in other national cinemas, such as "Japan's cinematic versions of Manga," leading him to question, "Is there such a genre as the comic-book film?" (148).

In addressing Loucks's question, this chapter will also try to identify the boundaries of this nascent genre. For instance, *The Piano* is not based on an existing work, but Gelder argues it earns its place in the "literary cinema" genre by virtue of its "special debt to Emily Brontë's *Wuthering Heights*" (158). Stam also picks up on the evocation of Brontë's book in *The Piano*, describing it as a "non-explicit intertextual relation" and categorizing the film as an "unmarked adaptation" ("Introduction" 30). Similarly, Cartmell and Whelehan describe "found" adaptations as "a text which seems to owe part of its impetus to an unacknowledged source" (*Screen Adaptation* 18). Examples of unacknowledged sources abound in the comic book movie genre. For instance, the EC Comics-inspired *Creepshow* (Romero 1982) was marketed as comedy/horror when it was first released during the comic book movie's period of articulation.[1] However, in a 2007 retrospective documentary, artist Bernie Wrightson said, "They set out to make a comic book movie, and I think it's the best comic book movie" ("Just Desserts"). Thus, while *Creepshow* may not have declared its source(s) during its initial release (EC comic books such as *Tales from the Crypt* and *Vault of Terror*), they were subsequently ascribed to the film. As will be demonstrated, such undeclared adaptations have been essential to spreading comics' influence on Hollywood cinema in recent years.

In his challenge to the strict "one-to-one case study" of past scholarship, Leitch "proposes a different model based on a different context by defining adaptation as a genre with its own rules, procedures, and textual markers that are just as powerful as any single ostensible source text in determining the shape a given adaptation takes" ("Adaptation, the Genre" 106). Building on Leitch's approach, this chapter will identify how comic book film adaptations have been channeled by methods of production, promotion, and reception into a distinct genre—the comic book movie. The many antecedents and sister genres of the comic book movie will be acknowledged, before the unique conventions and iconography are identified. This chapter will also consider what effect this fledgling, yet important, comic book-derived genre has had on Hollywood cinema, particularly through the increasing number of mainstream films that are vying to be affiliated with this trend. While these genre conventions often tally with the fan desire for fidelity, occasionally these two determinants come into conflict. Where this tension can arise, and the manner in which it is negotiated, will be addressed in the case study that concludes this chapter, which focuses on two very different adaptations from the work of Alan Moore, *Watchmen* (Snyder 2009) and *The League of Extraordinary Gentlemen* (Norrington 2003).

The Comic Book Movie in the Inter-textual Relay

It is widely suggested by film scholars that a genre's status and significance is derived from the industry and the audience (Grant 20; Altman *Film/Genre* 16). When Leitch describes adaptation as a genre, he suggests that it has "flown beneath most observers' radar" ("Adaptation, the Genre" 106). However, despite not garnering much scholarly attention, adaptation as a genre has not escaped the notice of filmmakers, publicity, distributors, reviewers, and the audience, or what Steve Neale, borrowing from Lukow and Ricci, collectively refers to as "inter-textual relay" (*Genre and Hollywood* 2). This section will trace the comic book movie's successful migration through this inter-textual relay, which makes a persuasive argument for it to be recognized as a genre.

In his 2005 book *Film Genre: Hollywood and Beyond*, Barry Langford notes how "only very recently has the focus on industrial discourses and 'relays' suggested a means of squaring this circle" (13) of genre definition. Nonetheless, the abundance of paratextual material often means it is comparatively easy to identify industrial recognition, while the audience, often considered the chief arbitrator of the inter-textual relay, remains more elusive. One approach for this study might have been to focus on online comments and discussions, and indeed there is a wealth of examples. For instance, in May 2011 *Entertainment Weekly* ran an online feature ranking the "21 Worst Comic-Book Movies" (Ward), with many readers making use of the term "comic book movie" and treating the films as a genre. For instance, one post claimed that *Ghost Rider* (Johnson 2007) is the "worst comic book film I've ever seen!!!" Taking the opposing view, another reader argues that, "Ghost Rider and the Punisher are two of the BEST comic book films ever made!", while a *Daredevil* (Johnson 2003) detractor reiterates the widely held view that "when you make a comic book movie you need to stay close to the source to appease the fans."

However, as the next chapter will explore, many of these online comments are provided by a small subset of fans and enthusiasts. Identifying this space in past studies, Neil Rae and Jonathan Gray adopted a dualistic strategy "to answer a question that is often overlooked in reception studies focusing solely on fans: how do viewers read and make sense of comic book movies differently when they have and have not read the original material being adapted?"

(86). However, as Rae and Gray's central research question was posed in relation to adaptation, it seemed destined to fall under the yoke of fidelity, with non-readers considered "intertextually poor" because they "watch the films as films, and largely as distinct texts" while "readers, predictably, looked at any adaptation as part of an episodic text" (99).

To give nuance to such findings, the audience research I carried out for this book moved beyond the source, with many non-readers proving themselves to be textually rich in the manner in which they compare these films to other entries in a newly emerging genre. Like Rae and Gray, my study sought to engage respondents on both sides of the fan divide. Accordingly, it eschewed Internet sampling and asked heterogeneous cinema audiences about their "expectations" of the film, what other films they thought it would "be like," and how they would "describe the film to a friend?" In order to achieve the most accurate responses, there was no reference to comic books in the survey until after these questions were answered, and open-ended responses were post-coded based on emerging patterns and recurrent phrases.

It was clear from the audience research that fans and non-fans alike placed *The Adventures of Tintin* (Spielberg 2011) in a very different category than *Thor* (Branagh 2011) and *Green Lantern* (Campbell 2011). When describing their expectations of *Thor* and *Green Lantern*, the key term most often used was "comics" followed closely by "action" and "special effects." However, those respondents attending *The Adventures of Tintin* adopted a different stance. Although they often alluded to the source, *The Adventures of Tintin* audience placed a greater emphasis on the filmmakers and their earlier work with one 21–25-year-old male's response typical of most comments: "I would imagine it will be good based on the quality of the Tintin series and Peter Jackson and [Steven] Spielberg's previous material." Conversely, most participants referenced previous adaptations when discussing their expectations of *Thor* and *Green Lantern* with responses including "similar to Iron Man 1 and 2" and "Superman in Green."

This trend intensified when the audience was asked to suggest other films they thought would be similar to *Thor* and *Green Lantern*. By a wide margin, comic book adaptations and superhero films such as *X-Men*, *Iron Man* (Favreau 2008), and *Spider-Man* were the most frequently referenced films by non-fans.[2] On the strength of *Green Lantern* screenings alone, *Thor* was cited five times, with the yet-to-be released *Captain America: The First Avenger* (Johnston 2011) referenced three times. Outside of comics, fantasy films such as *Clash of the Titans* (Leterrier 2010) and *Percy Jackson* (Columbus 2010) were compared to *Thor*, and two audience members expected *Green Lantern* to be similar to *Avatar* (Cameron 2009). Nonetheless, despite the mythological and sci-fi inflections in *Thor* and *Green Lantern*, these films were overwhelmingly compared to popular comic book movies. This trend was not evident in *The Adventures of Tintin*, where *Indiana Jones* was cited by eleven of the twenty-eight respondents, with no other film generating more than two mentions.

When asked about their generic expectations, respondents proved more diverse in their replies. For *The Adventures of Tintin*, "adventure" led the way, followed closely by "action," and another contentious genre, "animation."[3] The responses to *Thor* and *Green Lantern* were more consistent, with "action" being the most cited generic framework, followed by "sci-fi," "comic," "superhero," and "fantasy." These results suggest that the comic book movie and superhero are still not as widely recognized as the action genre, or perhaps filmgoers consider them subgenres of the action movie. Further clarification was provided in the answers to question nine, "How would you describe the film to a friend?" Here "comic" and "superhero" eclipsed "action" across all three films, with comments including, "Superhero Movie from Comic Book" (*Green Lantern*), as well as, "Comic book adaptation with the same directors as The Lord of the Rings" (*The Adventures of Tintin*).

However, what is more interesting is how the terms were used. Much of genre studies has focused on when a loose assemblage of films can be deemed a genre. Rick Altman suggests this shift takes place when an adjectival term, such as "*western* melodrama" or "*musical* comedy," goes through a substantiating process, "loosened from the tyranny of that noun" (*Film/Genre* 50). In answering the question, "How would you describe the film to a friend?", non-fan responses included, "A comic book fantasy"; "comic thing, like X-Men"; "action comic book"; "one of those comic book films"; and "action and CGI heavy comic book movie." From this research, one finds "comic book" used as both an adjective and noun, with the terms "comic book movie" and "comic book film" most often employed, suggesting that the *comic book movie* adaptation is going through a substantiating process and is beginning to be recognized as a genre by audiences.

Yet not every comic book adaptation is immediately placed in this fledgling genre. Comments such as, "Animated Indiana Jones," illustrate that audiences brought a number of frameworks to *The Adventures of Tintin*, including comics, animation, action-adventure, with director Steven Spielberg and his *Indiana Jones* films coloring most answers. One respondent even went so far as to suggest that *The Adventures of Tintin* "was good, but it was a copy of Indiana Jones."[4] Conversely, filmgoers consistently applied the term "comic book movie" or its variants to *Thor* and *Green Lantern*, and compared the films to other such movies (including each other). To chart how audiences have developed such expectations, it is prudent to look at another key area of the inter-textual relay, promotion.

FIG. 2.1 Comic book images and fonts are used in these posters to suggest the generic status of the films to the spectator.

Neale contends that "the indication and circulation of what the industry considers to be the generic framework—or frameworks—most appropriate to the viewing of a film is therefore one of the most important functions performed by advertising copy, and by posters, stills and trailers" (*Genre and Hollywood* 35). The comic book movie entered a more mature phase in 2000, and this cyclic shift was apparent from the changes in the promotional material that accompanied these releases. As will be explored in Chapter Three, during this period a number of comic book adaptations began highlighting their status as *comic book* adaptations. However, as Gray reminds us, "paratexts regularly address the non-fan, even when attached to fan properties" (17). Thus, this strategy not only mollified the fidelity-focused fan base, but often provided generic markers for the more mainstream audience. For example, in its promotion *Ghost World* (Zwigoff 2001) not only used the unambiguous tagline, "The underground comic book comes to life," but also included the original comic book art juxtaposed with pictures of the actors, thereby signaling its status as a "comic book movie." As the comic book movie's popularity increased, overt signifiers permeated promotional material, such as caption boxes (*Sin City*), comic book panels and fonts (*American Splendor*), comic book-style renderings of the cast (*The Losers*), and newly created images designed by comic book artists (*Iron Man*), with promotional material for some films adopting all of the above (*The Spirit*).

Thor and *Green Lantern* were also firmly positioned in the comic book movie genre by paratextual materials. For instance, the first poster for *Thor* featured a color pop (Thor's red cape) over a black-and-white image, which had become synonymous with comic book movies since the success of *Sin City* (Rodriguez 2005).[5] Publicity material also emphasized the connection to other Marvel Studios productions through the use of the company's logo and the tagline, "From the studio that brought you 'Iron Man.'" Early promotional material for *Green Lantern* also attempted to align the film with Marvel's success, with the first trailer matching *Iron Man*'s promo beat for beat. A talented but cocky sports-car-driving playboy is involved in a life-changing incident, following which he learns responsibility and develops feelings for the co-worker who recognized his true potential from the beginning. One survey respondent even expected the DC Comics adaptation "to follow the general Marvel Genre."

Given the responses from the audience research, it should be unsurprising that the publicity for *The Adventures of Tintin* did not explicitly cite its comic book source or allude to a wider comic book movie genre. Instead paratextual material emphasized the film's creative team with the trailer card: "From the two greatest storytellers of our time . . . director Steven Spielberg and producer Peter Jackson . . . This Christmas a race against evil . . . a world beyond imagination . . . an adventure beyond belief." However, the fan audience was not forgotten with promotional material often including markers that conveyed fidelity. For instance, one of the earliest publicity images, which appeared exclusively on the cover of *Empire* magazine, reworked an iconic comic book image of Tintin and his dog Snowy running in front of a spotlight—a move that would have appeased fans while also targeting the wider audience.

As the *Thor* tagline suggests, inter-genre referencing has increased since the maturation of the comic book movie. While some citations can be found in early paratexts, adaptations have increasingly referred to past successes. For example, the trailer and poster for *Elektra* (Bowman 2005) claimed that

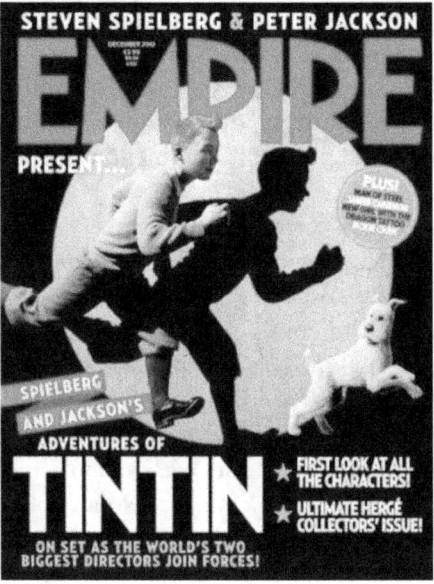

FIG. 2.2 The "first look" at *The Adventures of Tintin: Secret of the Unicorn*, as it appeared in the December 2010 issue of *Empire*. This early piece of promotion signaled the film's intended fidelity by mirroring an iconic comic book image.

it was "from the forces that brought you X-Men," even if those "forces" did not include the director, writer, or stars, but rather three of the film's nine producers. The promotion for *300* (Snyder 2007) alerted potential audiences through poster taglines that it was "from the creator of 'Sin City,'" with its success resulting in the release of *Watchmen* being heralded as "from the visionary director of '300'." More recently, the publicity for *Man of Steel* (Snyder 2013) built on these recognized comic book movies with the tagline: "From Zack Snyder director of Watchmen & 300 and producer Christopher Nolan director of The Dark Knight Trilogy." Even adaptations of alternative comics seem eager to be considered alongside this increasingly popular genre, at least in how they are promoted. For instance, *Ghost World* is firmly set in an everyday milieu, albeit with heightened flourishes. The only moment from the film that could be misconstrued as related to the comic form's most popular protagonist, the superhero, involves Enid trying on a cat mask from a sex shop. Though the mask appears in only two scenes, and is in no way integral to the plot, the image of Enid in the cat mask was reproduced in much of the film's publicity, misleadingly accentuating the film's comic book movie status.[6]

Through direct promotional strategies such as these, film marketing has attempted to prepare other participants in the inter-textual relay to view these films as comic book movies, with ample evidence suggesting they have been successful. For example, in 2008 the comic book movie genre seemed to achieve its peak of productivity. At this time, the British Film Institute (BFI) held a season of films entitled "Comic Book Movies"; that this season was not limited to superhero films but also included *Persepolis* (Satrapi and Paron-naud 2008), *A History of Violence* (Cronenberg 2005), and *Danger: Diabolik!* (Bava 1968) indicates the recognition of a more inclusive genre. The online introduction to the film season went one step further, describing these films as "a genre too often unfairly dismissed as mindless entertainment" ("Comic Book Movie Season").

Popular film magazines also adopted this term, with the cover of the November 2006 issue of *Empire* promising a "Huge Comic Book Movie Special." Rival publication *Total Film* ran a similar feature in their March 2009 edition, with the cover carrying the slogan, "The Comic-Book Movie Preview." Other film journalists also regularly employed the term, with many identifying films that elevated the genre. For instance, *Chicago Sun-Times* critic Roger Ebert described Ang Lee's *Hulk* (2003) as "a comic book movie for people who wouldn't be caught dead at a comic book movie," and *Washington Times* reviewer Sonny Bunch opens his account of *The Dark Knight* (Nolan 2008) by writing, "To say that *The Dark Knight* is the finest comic book movie of all time sounds tinny—relegating this movie to the ghetto of mediocrity inhab-ited by films like *Wanted* or *Hellboy II* is insulting. *The Dark Knight* transcends its genre."

Other examples of this generic evolution within the inter-textual relay include: the popular website *ComicBookMovie.com*, which positions itself as "a super news source for comics adaptations," but also includes all those works gravitating toward a comic book movie genre (e.g., *G.I. Joe*, *Transform-ers*, and *Riddick*); a dedicated *Comic Book Movies* edition of the *Virgin Film* series, which is normally reserved for distinct genres (e.g., *Film Noir*, *Horror Films*, and *Gangster Film*); and the Scream Awards—"The event that honors the best in comics, fantasy, sci-fi and horror"—changed the name of its "Best Comic-to-Screen Adaptation" award to "Best Comic Book Movie" in 2008 ("Scream 2009").

Today, the term "comic book movie" has become the de facto name for this genre; a phrase that has moved between the various organs of the inter-textual relay (production, promotion, press, and audience), migrating back to film-makers who have adopted it. For example, the term "comic book movie" is reg-ularly employed in a generic context by filmmakers such as Bryan Singer (*The Mutant Watch*), Zack Snyder (Frosty), with *The Amazing Spider-Man* (2012) director Marc Webb explaining on the DVD commentary, "I never thought I would do a comic book movie. It just was never part of my DNA." When interviewed for this study, Steve Niles stated, "we definitely have a subgenre now of comic book movies and I'm glad that people know there's *Batman* and *Spider-Man*, but that there's also *Road to Perdition*, *30 Days of Night*, and even *Kick-Ass*." Such is the industry recognition of the genre that in his opening to the Eighty-first Academy Awards, host Hugh Jackman sang a tribute to the overlooked *The Dark Knight*, with the lyrics, "How come comic book movies never get nominated?"

There are some who resist this categorization. Michael E. Uslan described one of the obstacles he faced in bringing Batman to the screen as trying to "convince the studios and all the powers that be that, unlike what they were thinking, comic books are not a genre . . . they are a source of stories and characters the same way as novels and plays." Uslan is right to argue that despite the dominance of power fantasies, comic books play host to a wider variety of genres. However, the resistance he has faced in Hollywood only testifies to the industry's desire to corral this potentially wide-ranging medium into a finite film genre, with evidence from the audience research and inter-textual relay suggesting that these strategies have been successful. In fact, the term has made its way back to the source material itself: comics. In the opening caption of the 2008 comic *Kick-Ass* (Millar and Romita), the amateur superhero wonders, "Why nobody did it before me. I mean, all those comic book movies and television shows, you'd think at least one eccentric loner would have stitched himself a costume."

The only group seemingly reluctant to treat the comic book movie as a genre are scholars, with Gordon et al. describing them as a "trend" (xvi). But the academy is often a step behind, for as Altman reminds us, "if it is not defined by the industry and recognized by the mass audience, then it cannot be a genre, because film genres are by definition not just scientifically derived or theoretically constructed categories, but are always industrially certified and publicly shared" (*Film/Genre* 16). The comic book movie's acceptance and propagation in the inter-textual relay strengthens the argument for it to be ratified as a genre. Thus, the time has come to not only recognize this genre, but also position it as one of the key determinants shaping the modern comic book film adaptation.

From Cowboys to Capes

Film genres do not appear fully formed, but rather evolve from traditions within cinema and beyond. As discussed in Chapter One, the comic book movie is the continuation of a US mythological tradition best exemplified by the western, a genre to which the comic book movie is greatly indebted. During the superheroes' brief sojourn from the heights of comic book popularity, the cowboy helped fill the void, with Duncan and Smith noting that by the late 1940s western comics had overtaken superheroes in popularity (37). However, when the successful reintroduction of The Flash in *Showcase* #4 (October

1956) ushered in the Silver Age of Comics, superheroes quickly annexed most mainstream titles.

Just as the western protagonist proved readily interchangeable with the superhero in comics, the comic book hero now fills a role once held by the cowboy on cinema screens. The many qualities the comic book hero shares with its natural antecedent hint at the ideological precepts that underlie American mythology. As Harvey points out, the "superhero, after all, is but the Western heroic persona elevated to near omnipotence. And in the superhero's vigilante adventuring outside the law (however ostensibly on the law's behalf), the internal conflict in the national mythology once again finds expression" (65).

Many scholars have identified this conflict between the individual and community as one of the thematic interests of the western (Schatz *Hollywood Genres*; Kitses "Authorship and Genre"; Grant *Film Genre*). However, some critics argue that this opposition can be found in other Hollywood genres, to which Jim Kitses responds, in a revised edition of *Horizons West*, that such arguments only underline "the centrality of both the genre and its frontier mythology to the American cinema" (13). Indeed, as identified in Chapter One, such oppositions are fundamental to the comic book movie. For instance, early in the genre's classical stage, the villain in *Spider-Man* proclaimed that the community would tire of the hero's individualistic accomplishments, "the one thing they love more than a hero is to see a hero fail, fall, die trying. In spite of everything you've done for them, eventually they will hate you." Like the self-aware Hollywood westerns of the 1950s (e.g., *Winchester '73*, *High Noon*, and *The Searchers*), this examination became more focused as the genre progressed.

In the closing moments of *Superman: The Movie* (Donner 1978), the Big Blue Boy Scout simply swooped down from the heavens to deliver Lex Luthor to prison, pausing before leaving to assure the bewildered prison warden, "We are all part of the same team." However, in the more recent adaptation, *Man of Steel*, the US military arrests and ultimately attempts to control Superman, with his efforts to convince them that he is on their side met with skepticism, "I grew up in Kansas . . . I'm about as American as it gets." Likewise, Spider-Man may have been honored with a parade from the city of New York in the final part of the original Spider-Man trilogy, *Spider-Man 3* (Raimi 2007), but in the franchise reboot, *The Amazing Spider-Man*, he is branded an "outlaw" by Police Captain George Stacy, who argues that Spider-Man's seemingly pro-social actions are actually the unintended consequence of his "personal vendetta"—an argument increasingly levied against comic book movie protagonists.[7] In particular, each of Christopher Nolan's Batman films articulated the tension between individuality and community. For instance, in *The Dark Knight* District Attorney Harvey Dent responds to calls from the people of Gotham for Batman to turn himself in by arguing, "The Batman is an outlaw

FIG. 2.3 Comparable moments from the codas of *Spider-Man* and *My Darling Clementine*, where the hero chooses to abandon his love interest to answer a higher call for justice.

. . . [but] we've been happy to let the Batman clean up our streets for us until now." In the film, Dent also remarks "you either die a hero or you live long enough to see yourself become the villain," a prophetic line that applies to both the western vigilante and comic book hero.

Many more western conventions are mirrored in these modern films. Where once a western hero was motivated to seek redemption upon the discovery of a burnt-out settlement or the murder of a family member (e.g., *Stagecoach*, *The Searchers*, and *Winchester '73*), today the comic book hero often resolves to seek justice when faced with the death of a parent or loved one (e.g., *Batman*, *Spider-Man*, *Daredevil*, and *The Punisher*). Similarly, where Wyatt Earp, Shane, and countless other gunslingers rode off at the film's denouement, the heroes of comic book movies jump, swing, or fly from the rooftops in search of the next threat. The selfless protectors do not need a thank you, as the hero of *Batman Begins* (Nolan 2005) reminds Lieutenant Gordon before leaping from a building (and into the sequel). Also, just as a western hero was uniquely suited to the Frontier's rugged terrain, only a superhero can fully utilize the city's concrete canyons with Bukatman describing how "the Man of Steel has the constitution, organs, and abilities equal to the rigors of the Machine Age" (*Matters of Gravity* 53).

Furthermore, as in westerns, the abilities that make the comic book hero most apt to defend the community are the same traits that prevent him from becoming part of that community. For instance, in the sequels *Superman II* (Lester 1980), *Spider-Man 2* (Raimi 2004), and *The Dark Knight*, the central characters contemplate giving up their heroic personas to be with the women they love. However, threats to the community ultimately force the protagonist to assume the mantle of the hero and sublimate his desire once more. This trope is made explicit in the comic book movie *Hancock* (Berg 2008) where the hero is weakened and ultimately loses his powers whenever he is near his soul mate. An echo of this convention across both genres can be seen in the codas of *My Darling Clementine* (Ford 1946) and *Spider-Man*, where the heroes leave their love interest waiting as they answer a higher call for justice. In many respects, Spider-Man's mantra "With Great Power Comes Great Responsibility" is a modern update of the western maxim, "A Man's Gotta Do What A Man's Gotta Do."

When the cowboy vacated his role as the cinematic avenger *du jour* in the 1960s, the comic book hero, by then an unwitting icon of the camp, did not immediately take up the mantle. Rather, the western gunslinger transitioned into the renegade cop and urban vigilante of films such as *Dirty Harry* (Siegel 1971), *Death Wish* (Winner 1974), *McQ* (Sturges 1974), and *Taxi Driver* (Scorsese 1976), who patrolled a new frontier between law and disorder on modern urban streets.

Comic book heroes have been seeking justice in an urban milieu since their inception, with Ben Highmore describing them as "a species that has adjusted to the modern city" (124). However, comic book characters took on a grittier dimension following the popularity of cinema's urban vigilantes. In the same year *Death Wish* proved to be a surprise hit, Marvel introduced their own vigilante, the "deadly" Punisher, to *The Amazing Spider-Man* #129 (February 1974). The character proved popular enough to warrant several dedicated comic books in the 1980s.[8] Like Paul Kersey in *Death Wish*, the Punisher (Frank Castle) became a no-holds-barred urban vigilante following the murder of his family. At a time when Spider-Man and other popular Marvel heroes were finding the transition to cinema difficult, the Punisher was adapted to an eponymous 1989 film.

Similarly, Mike Dubose identifies a "Dirty Harry-esque style" (920) in Miller's Batman comics of the 1980s, a trait that reappears in the brutality displayed by Tim Burton's caped crusader.[9] Furthermore, the neon-drenched paranoia of *Watchmen*'s Rorschach—"I wish all the scum of the Earth had one throat, and I had my hands around it"—is clearly indebted to another New York vigilante, Travis Bickle (*Taxi Driver*), "someday a real rain will come and wash all this scum off the streets." Today, urban crime movie conventions remain a vibrant part of comic book movies such as *Daredevil*, *The Dark Knight*, and *Dredd* (Travis 2012).

Cinema's urban vigilantes would transition in the 1980s to the action heroes of *First Blood* (Kotcheff 1982), *Commando* (Lester 1985), and *Die Hard* (McTiernan 1988).[10] Like the western gunslinger or urban vigilante, action heroes had the unique abilities necessary to meet threats to the community, but were distanced from past avengers through spectacular action set pieces, muscular heroes, and, frequently, a tongue-in-cheek style. However, as discussed in Chapter One, while the comic book movie includes many of the same attributes as the action film, it wraps them in a more inclusive fantasy. Furthermore, while action movie heroes may have been "mavericks" (Langford 234), they still tended to be sanctioned by institutions such as the police force (*Die Hard*, *Beverly Hills Cop*, *Lethal Weapon*, and *48 Hrs.*), the military (*Rambo*, *Predator*, and *Aliens*), or the government (*True Lies*, *Mission: Impossible*, and the James Bond franchise), while the independent, unsanctioned actions of comic book heroes recall the mythic vigilantism of the American West.

Unsurprisingly, the traditional action movie of the 1980s and 1990s entered a period of decline in 2000 as the comic book movie's superhuman protagonists usurped the place of the musclebound and Earth-bound action hero. As Martyn Pedler notes, "If action stars are superheroic, it only takes some quick box-office maths to see that superheroes are now action stars" ("Fastest Man Alive" 252). The traditional action films made since 2000, such as *Die Hard 4.0* (Wiseman 2007) and *Rambo* (Stallone 2008) have fallen well below previous box-office highs, with the former acknowledging its comic book competition with the tagline, "No Mask. No Cape. No Problem."[11] While the *Die Hard* sequel may have attempted to challenge the comic book adaptation, star Bruce Willis seems to have fallen back on the following axiom: "If you can't beat them, join them." Many of Willis's recent mainstream roles have been in comic book movies, including *Sin City*, *Surrogates* (Mostow 2009), and *Red* (Schwentke 2010), with the star's presence adding to the action movie conventions already present in these films.

Beyond vigilante archetypes, the comic book movie is also indebted to the science fiction and fantasy genres. Bukatman goes so far to suggest that the "superhero film is surely a variant of the science-fiction film" ("Secret Identity Politics" 115). These films do share a reliance on special effects, using the latest technology to "create an imaginatively realized world which is always removed from the world we know of" (Sobchack 87). Bukatman has cited this heightened quality in a number of publications, also linking the superhero movie and the musical: "It centers on the expressiveness of bodies and the eroticism of human movement" ("Why I Hate Superhero Movies" 119). Bukatman's arguments are persuasive, with both the musical and comic book movie focusing on protagonists whose physicality enables them to transcend the limitations of the city. However, with the notable exception of the jazz club scene from *Spider-Man 3*, comic book movies rarely embrace this parallel, an opportunity Broadway briefly exploited with the musical *Spider-Man: Turn Off the Dark* (2011–14).

Comic book creator Grant Morrison opens his book *Supergods* by suggesting that "someone, somewhere figured out that, like chimpanzees, superheroes make everything more entertaining. . . . Add superheroes and a startling and provocative new genre springs to life. Urban crime thriller? Seen it all before . . . until Batman gets involved" (xvi). However, comic book movies are not merely an inflection on existing film genres, but rather they are the product of a variety of influences (vigilante archetypes, urban crime, action sequences, and heightened reality) coming together and evolving into a genre with conventions all of its own. Identifying those conventions will be the focus of the next section.

Defining the Comic Book Movie

Any attempts to analyze the conventions of a genre face charges of reductionism, as the critic can sometimes use a sampling of films to meet a preconceived definition of the genre, while ignoring those texts that appear contradictory. Andrew Tudor suggests a solution by leaning "on the common cultural consensus as to what constitutes a [genre], and then go on to analyse it in detail" (138). As this study is responding to audience research and industrial discourses, it is hoped that it avoids any simplifications in its attempts to identify the corpus of the comic book movie and its conventions.

The most logical criteria for inclusion in this canon would seem to be if a film is actually based on a comic book. However, this would allow for the addition of adaptations that made no attempt to indicate their relationship to their source material in their promotion, nor did they adopt any of the stylistic or narrative strategies of comics in their production. For example, *Road to Perdition* (Mendes 2002) made concerted attempts to obscure its source material, including dropping the "graphic" from the "based on a graphic novel" credit in its early promotional work (D. Hughes 224). Comparable examples might include *Annie* (Huston 1982), *A History of Violence* (Cronenberg 2005), and *Tamara Drewe* (Frears 2010). Similarly, even though 70 percent of respondents knew that *The Adventures of Tintin* was based on a comic, unlike in the *Thor* and *Green Lantern* screenings, few came to the film expecting it to conform to comic book movie conventions, with the adaptation more often compared to Spielberg's earlier films.

Furthermore, to only include those films based directly on comic books would omit films that have attempted to align themselves with the genre, particularly since its rise in popularity.[12] Examples of undeclared adaptations that have benefited from inclusion in the comic book adaptation trend include *Hancock*, a superhero film that made $227 million at the US box office. The script for *Hancock* (originally titled *Tonight, He Comes*) had been in development since 1996, but was only advanced into production in the post *Spider-Man* boom. In the film, the protagonist dismisses a comic book superhero as a "homo," while his spokesperson says, "Let's move past the comics, let's get into something a little deeper." Nonetheless, by the third act, Hancock—both the costume-clad hero and the film itself—had appropriated many of the tropes of a comic book adaptation.

A number of other productions not based on comics have also vied to be affiliated with this genre, such as *Jumper* (Liman 2008), *Max Payne* (Moore 2008), and *Push* (McGuigan 2009). Among the strategies these films employed to establish their relationship to the comic book movie were: promotion at the San Diego Comic-Con; the publication of prequel comic books; and the inclusion of motion comics as DVD special features.[13] To further accentuate their status as comic book movies, each film used narrative and visual cues that played on previous genre entrants, and included markers in their paratextual material that hinted at a comic book movie to a knowing audience.[14] These undeclared adaptations have been so successful at being positioned in the comic book movie genre that they are often recognized as such by the inter-textual relay. For instance, when *Total Film* ran its "Comic-Book Movie Preview" in March 2009, it included many related films such as the toy-based *G.I. Joe: Rise of Cobra* (Sommers 2009) and *Transformers: Revenge of the Fallen* (Bay 2009).

Accordingly, a comic book movie does not need to actually be based on a comic book to be included in this genre; it simply needs to adopt elements synonymous with the comic book movie. Thus, to organize the body of films that everyone would consider comic book movies, one might include most, but not all, comic book adaptations, without omitting those "original" films vying to be affiliated with the genre.

Protagonists

To identify the key features of a genre it is perhaps best to start by examining the central protagonist and familiar narrative. Unlike the western, with its gun-toting loner out to protect the frontier, few genres have a recurrent central character. Many would identify the superhero as the main protagonist of the comic book movie genre, with Uslan explaining that there is a "perception in Hollywood that comic books and superheroes are synonymous." Indeed, in much the same way as it would be myopic to identify the recurrent, but not omnipresent detective as the film noir's only protagonist, to qualify the superhero as a required convention of the comic book movie would ignore recognized protagonists such as: Dick Tracy, The Spirit, Harvey Pekar, Marv, King Leonidas, Scott Pilgrim, Constantine, Enid, Ghost Rider, Jonah Hex, Hellboy, and Frank Moses. However, there are recurrent traits among this diverse group of characters, allowing us to isolate a generic archetype.

As will be explored in Chapter Five, comic books are built on succinct signifiers. This quality extends to many comic characters, making them ideally suited to genre filmmaking where "characters are more often recognisable types rather than psychologically complex characters" (Grant 17). Examples of such concise characters might include King Leonidas and the handsome, heroic Spartans who confront the disfigured and fey Persian army in *300*; the alternative teenagers of *Ghost World*, who set themselves apart from the social cliques through their retro clothing; and the leads of *Sin City*, each of whom is outfitted with a trench coat and a hardboiled attitude.

The characteristics and motivations of King Leondias and the *Sin City* protagonists are very similar in that they are avengers hoping to prevent or rectify perceived transgressions against themselves, their homes, or their loved ones. If anything, comic book movies accentuate this aspect of the characters. For instance, although the emergence of the franchise paradigm has seen a staggering of cinematic narratives, audiences still expect a degree of closure. One device by which these films provide resolution is by reshaping the origin of the comic book protagonist. While in the comics many of these characters garnered their desire for vengeance at the hands of random criminals, a number of the films have modified these criminal identities to that of the villain whom the hero will confront at the film's climax. Consequently, in *Batman* (Burton 1989), Bruce Wayne's parents are not killed by the lowlife Joe Chill, but rather by a young Joker whom the adult Bruce Wayne, as Batman, will later confront; Daredevil's father is no longer murdered by average mobsters, but the future kingpin of crime in his formative years; and the "lone criminal" who shot Spider-Man's uncle was revealed to have an accomplice in *Spider-Man 3*, Flint Marko, one of the film's villains. As Peter Coogan points out, "Folding together the murderer of the Waynes and the Joker gives a dramatic unity to the Batman film and helps the story loop back on itself. This concision makes for good storytelling" (10). Further examples of this type of "concision" in comic book movies can be identified in *Iron Man*, *The Spirit* (Miller

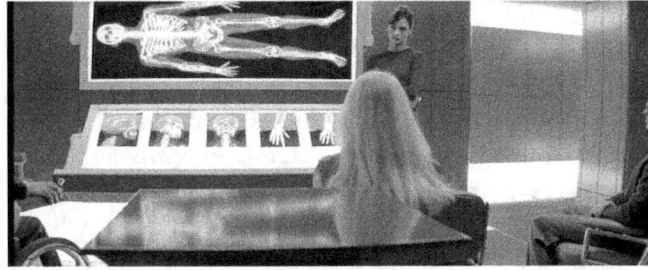

FIG. 2.4 Comic book movie *Kick-Ass* emphasizes its superpowered vigilante convention by referencing earlier comic book movie *X-Men*.

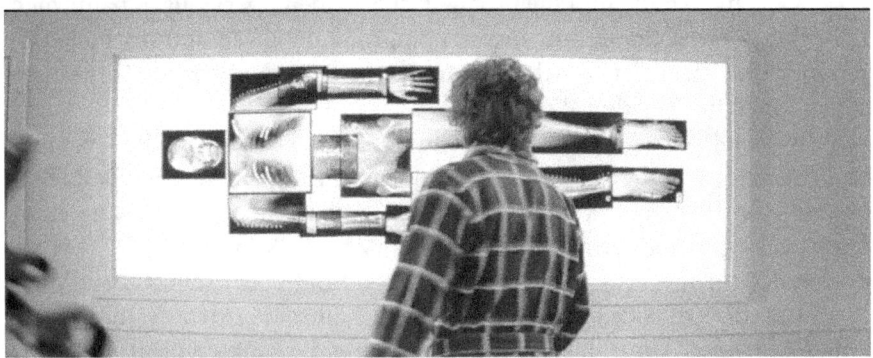

2008), and *Kick-Ass* (Vaughn 2010), with the largely faithful *300* introducing a new character, Theron, a greedy Spartan bureaucrat who conspires with the enemy, but who is ultimately killed by Leonidas's wife, Queen Gorgo. Thus, revenge can be identified as a recurrent narrative structure in comic book movies, often at the expense of fidelity.

Like their vigilante antecedents, comic book movie protagonists are often heralded as the only ones with the skills necessary to exact vengeance, with Leonidas explaining to the Arcadians that a Spartan's profession is "war," and Dwight reflecting, in *Sin City*, how Marv would be "right at home on some ancient battlefield swinging an axe into somebody's face." However, these heroes are distinguished from past vigilantes by how their abilities are articulated. From John Wayne to John Rambo, past heroes may have been quick on the draw, but Leonidas and Marv's abilities are exaggerated to a supernatural level that is supported by the genre's heightened verisimilitude. Accordingly, Leonidas seems impervious to the slings and arrows of his assailants as he relentlessly attacks Immortals, giants, and crab-limbed assailants in slow-motion flourishes, while Marv, despite operating in an urban milieu that recalls crime films, can survive a drop from a seven-story height and even a stint in the electric chair. These supernatural abilities reach their zenith in superheroes who can fly (Superman), teleport (Nightcrawler), and become invisible (Susan Storm), while possessing heightened senses (Daredevil), magic rings (Green Lantern), and an arsenal of "wonderful toys" (Batman and Iron Man) that no traditional action hero could match.

Again, this convention is more greatly emphasized in adaptations. Although Batman could swing from rooftop to rooftop in comics, he could never glide as effortlessly as "memory cloth" allows him to in *Batman Begins*; despite his supernatural pseudonym, the Spirit possessed no paranormal abilities in the comics, but in the adaptation he is made invincible through the Octopus's genetic manipulation; and while a "realistic" hero is the premise of the *Kick-Ass* comic, in the film the protagonist is made impervious to pain when, following a car accident, his nerve endings are damaged and his bones are reinforced by steel plates—which prompts the hero to observe, "This is awesome! I look like fricking Wolverine!"

As with all genres, not every film meets every convention. For instance, one character who does not neatly conform to this genre archetype is Enid (*Ghost World*). As an alternative high-school student, Enid does meet the "outsider" type. Yet the most defining trait of Enid's motivation is that she does not have one. As an apathetic teenager, Enid may use pithy putdowns as a mild form of social revenge ("I just hate all these extroverted, pseudo-bohemian losers"), but this is not of the same order as the typical genre protagonist. Similarly, while Tintin seems to enjoy supernatural luck, he does not have any heightened abilities. Furthermore, he is motivated by curiosity rather than revenge. Nonetheless, looking at the protagonists of the genre not based on comic books, one sees that Neo (*The Matrix*), David Dunn (*Unbreakable*), Mr. Incredible (*The Incredibles*), David Rice (*Jumper*), Nick Gant (*Push*), *Hancock*, and *The Green Hornet* all conform to this type, and that comic book movies generally involve an outsider, traditionally a vigilante, with heightened abilities that enable him/her to prevent and/or avenge threats to the community.[15]

Verisimilitude

A man meets a mysterious woman on a skyscraper balcony; they share a cigarette and a stolen kiss before he shoots her once in the chest. The opening scene of *Sin City* is washed in chiaroscuro lighting and accompanied by a cynical voiceover typical of many film noirs. In the first of the film's three main narratives, an equally noirish loner, Marv, is wrongly pursued by police for the murder of a prostitute. But rather than duck and double-deal his way out of trouble, the seemingly mortal Marv ploughs through a team of heavily armed officers, drops unhurt from a seven-story height, before crushing a moving police cruiser by jumping through its window. But none of this fractures the film's verisimilitude. *Sin City* may be a film-noir pastiche, but the audience

FIG. 2.5 Comic book movie signifiers (color pops, silhouettes and exaggerated perspective) from the opening scene of *Sin City*.

accepts actions and narrative moments at odds with that genre because this noir aesthetic is pierced, from the very first scene, by comic book imagery, including color pops, silhouettes, and exaggerated depth of field. These flourishes serve to inform the viewer that they are watching a comic book movie, not a film noir, and that it will therefore inhabit a different plane of reality.[16]

A comic book aesthetic is not only an important signifier to the *Sin City* audience, but is a key feature of the larger genre. How comic book codes have been adapted by cinema will be explored fully in Chapter Four, yet even a cursory glance reveals distinctly comic book imagery proliferating through the comic book movie genre, such as the onscreen sound effects of *Scott Pilgrim* (Wright 2010), *Wanted* (Bekmambetov 2008), and *Kick-Ass 2* (Wadlow 2013); the bordered aesthetic in *Ghost World* and *Hulk*; the motion lines of *Superman: The Movie*, *V for Vendetta* (McTeigue 2005), and *Green Lantern*; or the superpowered exaggerations of the many superhero films.

These tropes are recognized as comic book devices, even by those with little familiarity with the source (one need only think of their appropriation by pop art and advertising). Unsurprisingly, many of the undeclared adaptations have adopted these codes, thereby better positioning them within the comic book movie genre. For instance, the television series *Heroes* (Kring 2006) approximated a number of comic book codes such as speed lines and speech bubbles; reviewers described how *Max Payne* had a "quasi-expressionist take on comic-book grammar" (Dwyer 13); and in *Push*, which director Paul McGuigan describes as belonging to the "comic book genre" (*Push* DVD commentary), a rainbow effect is used to suggest the hero's telekinetic abilities.

The increasing application of this comic aesthetic in undeclared adaptations extends the boundaries (and influence) of the genre.

Genre films are noted for their intertextual referencing of other films within the same genre and larger generic tropes; as such a genre can be considered a hermetically sealed world orbiting at its own level of reality (Altman *Film/Genre* 25-6). Recognizing this, Langford describes how "regimes of verisimilitude are generically specific, and each bears its own relation to reality as such" (15). Yet many genre films are far from consistent in their "regimes of verisimilitude," instead oscillating about a baseline of reality with the verisimilitude of the piece becoming most exaggerated from physical laws during the moments that characterize the genre. For instance, a musical's reality is most stretched when the characters break into song and dance. Likewise, an action film pushes its verisimilitude during over-the-top action sequences, with the content of these heightened moments being key features of the genre. As the comic aesthetic suggests, comic book movies differ from this trend. While in many genre films moments of heightened reality are there to allow a generic motif, for the comic book movie heightened reality is a generic motif.

Whether it is a knowingly artificial aesthetic (e.g., *Sin City, Dick Tracy, The Spirit,* and *Scott Pilgrim*),[17] characters who could be defined as myth (most superhero films), or an ability to break the fourth wall (e.g., *American Splendor*), comic book movies are pitched at a heightened reality that is not confined to key moments such as action sequences or musical numbers. Even comic book movies based on actual events display this heightened reality, such as *300*'s inclusion of giants, crab-like warriors, and goat-headed musicians at the Battle of Thermopylae, or the surreal twists on everyday life, like the animated interludes in the autobiography *American Splendor* (Springer Berman and Pulcini 2003).

It is the continuity of this generic world that allows audiences to accept the superhuman actions of supposedly mortal characters such as Marv (*Sin City*), Leonidas (*300*), and Batman, and gives license to surreal moments unforgivable in other genres, such as the constant shift between the real-life and film version of Harvey Pekar in *American Splendor*, the lovelorn guitarist Scott Pilgrim using martial arts to compete for a girlfriend, or Kato's ability to slow time in *The Green Hornet* (Gondry 2011). Thus, heightened reality could be identified as a convention of the comic book movie.

Some films seem to challenge this convention. *Batman Begins* distanced itself from the playful Schumacher adaptations *Batman Forever* (1995) and *Batman & Robin* (1997) through a realistic tone, with Brooker arguing that *The Dark Knight* is more closely aligned with the "crime film, rather than the over-the-top styling of other comic-book movies" (*Dark Knight* 91). However, Altman suggests that "by definition all films belong to some genre(s) . . . but only certain films are self-consciously produced and consumed according to (or against) a specific generic model" ("Cinema and Genre" 277). In its opposition to the heightened reality of earlier Batman films and contemporary comic book movies, *Batman Begins* is shaped by the genre's history and conventions even while it is subverting them.

Furthermore, while commentators acknowledged that *Batman Begins* was a more realistic comic book movie, it was still, as *Empire* reviewer Kim Newman observed, "removed from reality." Likewise, former editor and writer Dennis O'Neil argued, "Batman's world is recognizably ours, but it is a tweaking of reality, it is a heightening. I think that's exactly what [*Batman Begins*] does, and that's what the best Batman stuff has always done" ("Genesis of the Bat").[18] Moreover, as discussed in Chapter One, this genre convention was used by the British Board of Film Classification (BBFC) to defend its granting of a 12A certificate to *The Dark Knight*, with the organization arguing that the "cartoon atmosphere . . . ultimately lessens the impact of the aggression" (Shaw). *Packaging Boyhood* co-author Mark Tappan is unconvinced by such arguments, describing these films as "thinly disguised action movies." Nonetheless, this disguise is an important distinction within the inter-textual relay. Just as the urban crime movie was the western relocated to the modern city, the heightened flourishes of *Batman Begins* and other comic book movies distance the films from the urban crime films and action movies to which they are indebted.

Talent and Techniques

Beyond characters, narrative features, and a general verisimilitude, many other elements can become synonymous with a genre. For instance, Altman describes how certain names "guarantee a certain style, a particular atmosphere and a well-known set of attitudes" (*Film/Genre* 25). A number of high-profile directors have fostered their careers on comic book movies, including: Sam Raimi (*Darkman* and the Spider-Man trilogy), Joe Johnston (*The Rocketeer* and *Captain America*), Mark Steven Johnston (*Daredevil* and *Ghost Rider*), Bryan Singer (*X-Men* and *Superman Returns*), Guillermo del Toro (*Blade II* and *Hellboy*), Matthew Vaughn (*Kick-Ass*, *X-Men: First Class*, and *Kingsman: The Secret Service*), and Jon Favreau (*Iron Man* and *Cowboys & Aliens*). Filmmakers returning to the comic book movie genre will often have their previous successes highlighted for the audience, suggesting they should expect "more of the same." For instance, the *Watchmen* trailer did not even name the director (Zack Snyder) presuming audiences would be content that the film was "from the visionary director of *300*."

Similarly, other roles on comic book movies are frequently filled by filmmakers experienced in the genre, such as cinematographer Bill Pope (nine films including *The Spirit* and *Scott Pilgrim*), special effects supervisor John Dykstra (six films including *Hancock* and *Spider-Man*), and composer Danny Elfman (twelve films including *Wanted* and *Hulk*). The iconography of the comic book movie also extends to stars, such as Chris Evans (*Fantastic Four, Push, The Losers, Scott Pilgrim, Captain America: The First Avenger*, and *The Avengers*), Ryan Reynolds (*Blade Trinity, X-Men Origins: Wolverine, Green Lantern*, and *R.I.P.D.*), and Ben Affleck (*Daredevil, Batman v Superman: Dawn of Justice*, and arguably *Hollywoodland*). Without even including his many turns as the Marvel Cinematic Universe's Nick Fury, Samuel L. Jackson has appeared in five comic book movies.[19] This ready association saw *Entertainment Weekly* reporting on the actor's casting in *The Secret Service* (Vaughn 2014) with the headline "Samuel L. Jackson's next Comic Book Movie" (Franich).

How these leads and supporting actors conform to the comic book convention of muscular, square-jawed heroes and wild-eyed villains will be considered in Chapter Five, where it is also noted that many filmmaking techniques have been employed in distinctive, often exaggerated ways within comic book adaptations. Furthermore, many digital innovations such as bullet-time (*The Matrix, V for Vendetta, 300*, and *Watchmen*), digital backlots (*Sin City, 300*, and *The Spirit*), and motion capture (*Watchmen* and *The Adventures of Tintin*) are regularly employed in these films. These techniques have become associated with comic book movies in much the same way that Technicolor was linked to the Hollywood musical of the late 1950s, and chiaroscuro lighting with film noir, providing yet another set of conventions for this new and influential genre.[20]

Through this analysis, the various features of the comic book movie have been identified, and a broad definition of the genre can be attempted:

> The comic book movie genre follows a vigilante or outsider character engaged in a form of revenge narrative, and is pitched at a heightened reality with a visual style marked by distinctly comic book imagery.

The following section will consider how the comic book movie tallies with genre cycles identified elsewhere and what this means for the genre's future.

Cycles and Trends

Once a genre is identified, attempts are often made to plot its progression. The revisionist films of New Hollywood are often credited with giving rise to life models to chart the development of genres. Building on the work of Henri

Focillon, who put forward a path of "the experimental age, the classic age, the age of refinement, the baroque age" (10), the models of John Cawelti and Thomas Schatz have proven popular with film scholars. Cawelti suggested in 1979 that

> one can almost make out a life cycle characteristic of genres as they move from an initial period of articulation and discovery, through a phase of conscious self-awareness on the part of both creators and audiences, to a time when the generic patterns have become so well-known that people become tired of their predictability. It is at this point that parodic and satiric treatments proliferate and new genres generally arise. (260)

Thomas Schatz offered a similar analogy for genre development, suggesting an evolutionary model of "straightforward storytelling to self-conscious formalism" (*Hollywood Genres* 38).[21]

Steve Neale and a number of other scholars have criticized models such as Schatz's on the grounds that they are "teleological," "mechanistic," and treat "genres in isolation from any generic regime" ("Questions of Genre" 58). These objections will be addressed in due course, however a further shortcoming of these models might be that they only provide a linear progression of a genre with no indication of how these phases affect levels of production. For an organic model that considers the number of films produced, one would be advised to consider the growth cycle of bacteria. Furthermore, given how genre films are often treated as a pernicious and unrelenting infestation of the cinematic form, this analogy is doubly fitting.

In vitro bacterial growth goes through four distinct phases: the lag, log, stationary, and death phase ("Bacterial Growth and Multiplication"). Applying the characteristics of bacterial growth to Schatz and Cawelti's organic models allows for a refinement of these paradigms as it accounts for production levels. During the articulation (lag) phase, "growth is slow at first, while the 'bugs' acclimate to the food and nutrients in their new habitat" ("Bacterial Growth and Multiplication"). If we consider genre films as the "bugs," and the novel genre conventions and naïve audience as their "new habitat," then one can see how the genre is first defined during this articulation phase. In the next stage, the classical (log) phase, "the metabolic machinery is running, they start multiplying exponentially" ("Bacterial Growth and Multiplication"). Now that the genre's machinery is running (i.e., conventions are established and an audience is identified), the films are produced in ever-increasing numbers. However, as with the bacterial stationary phase where "more and more bugs are competing for dwindling food and nutrients" ("Bacterial Growth and Multiplication"), competition from a large number of genre films results in

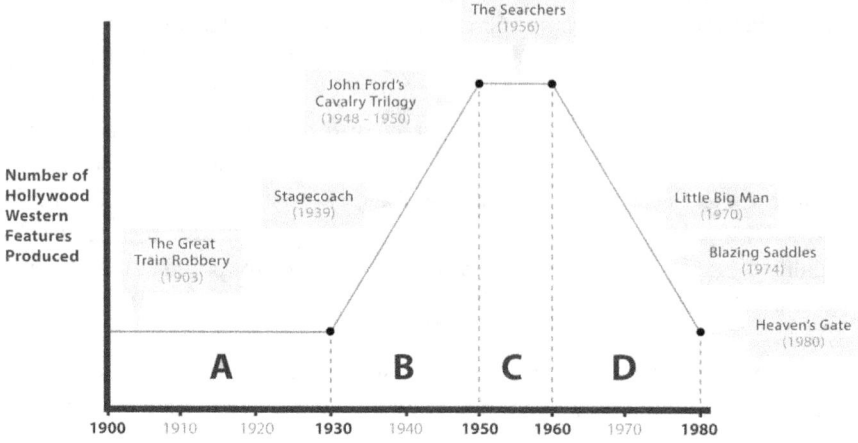

FIG. 2.6 Bacterial Growth Model for the Genre Cycle—the western.

the levels of production reaching a plateau, often with revisionist or self-aware work being produced. The final phase for the bacterial growth cycle is the death phase in which "toxic waste products build up, food is depleted and the bugs begin to die" ("Bacterial Growth and Multiplication"). The "toxic waste products" that send a genre into decline include conventions becoming tired and clichéd, thereby inviting satire and parody.

Since the western and the comic book movie share many parallels, it is fitting to illustrate the effectiveness of the bacterial growth model by first applying it to the comic book movie's natural antecedent. The graph in figure 2.6 uses the bacterial growth cycle to chart the progression of the Hollywood western from the release of proto-western *The Great Train Robbery* (Porter 1903) to the "death" of the western with the release of *Heaven's Gate* (Cimino 1980), whose failure "to recover even a proportion of its huge costs made Hollywood executives wary of further adventures out west" (Buscombe 293). During the articulation phase (A), the western conventions, though already identified in the popular culture of the time, were transferred to cinema. In this era, the release of western shorts and serials led to the establishment of much of the iconography and narratives that would make up the features. Yet the early films were inconsistent, as the realistic William S. Hart films competed with the anachronistic fantasies of Tom Mix. Soon, major western features were produced, including *The Covered Wagon* (Cruze 1923) and *The Iron Horse* (Ford 1924), as the genre's identity began to cohere. The advent of sound posed a problem for westerns as the technical requirements of early equipment did not facilitate location shooting—a staple of the genre. However, the

"1930s saw the series Western flourish once it had adjusted to the introduction of sound" (Buscombe 291), thereby enabling the genre's move into the classical phase (B).

Throughout the 1930s, the western largely remained a B-movie genre (albeit a popular one), but with the release of *Stagecoach* in 1939, the genre received an injection of credibility that propelled feature production into the heights of the 1950s. Production remained consistent throughout the decade as the genre entered its stationary or revisionist phase. Many of these post-World War II westerns were self-aware, and critically examined the role of the western hero, community, and Manifest Destiny (e.g., *Devil's Doorway* 1950; *High Noon* 1952; and *The Searchers* 1956). Yet in the 1960s Hollywood production of westerns sank from 128 features to just twenty-eight (Buscombe 292). This drop signaled the genre's progression into the decline phase (D). The "toxic waste" that produced this downturn included conventions becoming tired and clichéd and therefore ripe for satires such as *Little Big Man* (Penn 1970) or parodies like *Blazing Saddles* (Brooks 1974). This model has proven reliable when charting the development of the western. However, is it also applicable to the more recently established comic book movie? And what does this suggest about the genre's future?

Hollywood adaptation of comic books began in earnest in 1978 with the release of *Superman: The Movie*. Although earlier films had been based on comics, most were shorts or serials with the few features often mediated through a separate form, such as the feature film version of the popular television series *Batman* (Martinson 1966). Yet, even following the success of *Superman: The Movie*, the trend went through a long period of articulation. During this time a smattering of comic book movies were made with differing styles, tone, and fidelity, in a process Rick Altman calls the "Producer's Game" (*Film/Genre* 38):

1. From box-office information, identify a successful film.
2. Analyse the film in order to discover what made it successful.
3. Make another film stressing the assumed formula for success.
4. Check box-office information on the new film and reassess the success formula accordingly.
5. Use the revised formula as a basis for another film.
6. Continue the process indefinitely.

Following the success of *Batman* in the summer of 1989, producers hoping to emulate its popularity accentuated different aspects of the film. Some adaptations, such as *Dick Tracy* (Beatty 1990), *The Rocketeer* (Johnston 1991), *The Shadow* (Mulcahy 1994), and *The Phantom* (Wincer 1996), played upon the retro styling of *Batman* with adventures set during the late 1930s and 1940s. Other films emulated the blockbuster's gothic avenger, including *Darkman* (Raimi 1990), *The Crow* (Proyas 1994), and *Spawn* (Dippé 1997), with *The Crow* even going so far as to suggest it was "Darker than the Bat" in its promotional material. Nonetheless, these films failed to achieve similar success and no clear generic identity was codified.

Even two decades after *Superman: The Movie* initiated the trend, the release of *Mystery Men* (Usher 1999) and *Unbreakable* (Shyamalan 2000) indicated that any potential genre was still in its formative stage. Released in 1999, *Mystery Men* was a comic book parody that, despite high production values and a "name" cast, underperformed at the box office with a worldwide gross of $33 million against a $66 million production budget. It is unsurprising that the film did not find a receptive audience, as Barry Keith Grant points out that parody "requires viewers literate in generic protocol" (35). The comic book movie's lack of industrial recognition was also evident in the promotion of *Unbreakable*. M. Night Shyamalan's film is a superhero origin story, which, as will be discussed in Chapter Four, trades heavily on a comic book aesthetic. However, none of these elements were made obvious in the film's marketing, with Aldo J. Regalado observing that *Unbreakable* "presented unsuspecting American moviegoers with a story about comic books and superheroes" (116). *Unbreakable* is yet another example of an undeclared adaptation, with its affiliation to the comic book movie genre only acknowledged after the genre gained visibility (and credibility). For instance, in an interview on the tenth anniversary of the film, Shyamalan explained that he was told by the studio that "we can't sell this as a comic book movie," as that was a "fringe" market, and that the decision was instead made to position *Unbreakable* as "an eerie movie from the guy who made that other movie [*The Sixth Sense*]" (Rosenberg).[22]

Unbreakable might be considered the last major film in the formative stage of the comic book movie, with *X-Men*, also released in 2000, ushering in a period of archetypal expression.[23] *X-Men* continued successful generic tropes identified in the articulation stage and proved popular enough to instigate the exponential production of the classical period.[24] In the 2011 article "Why I Hate Superhero Movies," Bukatman suggests that the superhero movie trend is still in its articulation phase:

> The superhero film genre in the first decade of the twenty-first century yielded a glut of nearly identical films featuring dumbed-down versions of characters that were all appearing, to better effect, in the comics, just as the early musical films out of Hollywood dumbed down Broadway song lyrics for a non-urban and non-urbane audience. So I'm far from certain that superhero movies have discovered their real voice. (119)

FIG. 2.7 In *Hancock,* the hero's costume is said to be a "tight-ass Wolverine outfit," an inter-generic reference to the comic book movie version of Wolverine rather than the comic book.

However, while the relatively recent emergence of the comic book movie makes it difficult to gauge important shifts in production than in more established genres, the superhero movie and comic book movie genres arguably found their "real voice" in 2008, as the enthusiasm of the classical stage settled into the more self-aware films of the stationary phase.

When interviewed, Michael E. Uslan dismissed the term "comic book movie" as "an easy characterization best utilized by the press." The *Batman* producer argued that the "thematic importance" of *The Dark Knight* means that "you can't simply dismiss it and say it's a comic book movie and expect that term to define it." Uslan's resistance seemed to stem from a Romantic notion of originality that deems any art produced within an identifiable formula as hackneyed or derivative. However, Leo Braudy argues, "such absolute creativity is finally a fraud because all art must exist in some relation to the forms of the past, whether in contrast or continuation" (107). Similarly, Thomas Schatz celebrates how "each genre incorporates a sort of narrative shorthand whereby significant dramatic conflicts can intensify and then be resolved though established patterns of action and by familiar character types" (*Hollywood Genres* 24). For instance, in the final moments of *Iron Man*, Tony Stark takes great joy in dispensing with his secret identity, as he confidently announces at a press conference, "I am Iron Man." This celebratory moment would not resonate as strongly in an "original" film, as it is only after audiences have watched countless heroes wrestle with their dual identities could this convention be reworked.

The progression from the classical phase to the revisionist stationary stage is also apparent in the increase in inter-genre referencing. For example, in *Hancock*'s coda, a criminal describes the hero's costume as a "tight-ass Wolverine outfit." This is not an allusion to the brightly colored comic book character, but rather to the leather-clad version of Wolverine in the X-Men films. The way in which these films reference elements from other comic book movies, not found in the source material, demonstrates that these films have become a distinct body of work with their own history and identity.

Furthermore, many of the most effective moments from *The Dark Knight* came from subverting audience expectations. For instance, a number of comic book movies include sequences in which the villain forces the protagonist to choose between saving the woman he loves or other innocents (e.g., *Superman: The Movie, Batman Forever,* and *Spider-Man*), with the hero eventually saving both. This convention reappeared in *The Dark Knight,* with the Joker making Batman decide between rescuing District Attorney Harvey Dent and his love interest, Rachel Dawes. For an audience weaned on comic book movies, the assumption was that at the very least the hero would save Rachel. However, subverting tradition, Rachel dies in a timed explosion and Dent is badly scarred, ultimately becoming the criminal Two Face. Thus, the richness and complexity of stationary phase films such as *Iron Man, Hancock,* and *The Dark Knight* was only possible because the conventions had been established during the classical stage. All three films were met with positive critical response and box-office success when released in summer 2008—the year the comic book movie came of age.

In the excited rhetoric of participatory culture, non-fan audiences are often characterized as passive. As discussed, in their study of comic book adaptation audiences, Rae and Gray describe non-readers as intertextually poor because they "watch the films as films" (99). However, while non-fans may not be able to carry out the same "conceptual flipping back and forth" (Hutcheon 139) between source and adaptation that fans enjoy, as the stationary stage films suggest, they are active in the way that they view these films in the context of a maturing comic book movie genre.

A number of commentators picked up on the increased introspection of the genre. *New York Times* critic A. O. Scott compared the films to the revisionist westerns of the 1940s and 1950s, which were "obsessed with similar themes." Similarly, filmmakers were anticipating this shift. For instance, Evan Goldberg was interviewed for this study a few weeks before the release of *Iron Man* ushered in the revisionist stage. At the time, Goldberg was linked to an adaptation of the self-aware comic *The Boys.* Recognizing the need for a knowledgeable audience, Goldberg explained, "The trick is we need to wait for a few more superhero movies to come out, so everyone gets superheroes and then we can be critical of the superhero." While the project was never produced, Goldberg brought the same self-awareness to *The Green Hornet* (Gondry 2011) where the hero regularly acknowledged the tropes of the comic book movie—"It's in every movie, it's in every comic book, it's in everything, it's so stupid."[25]

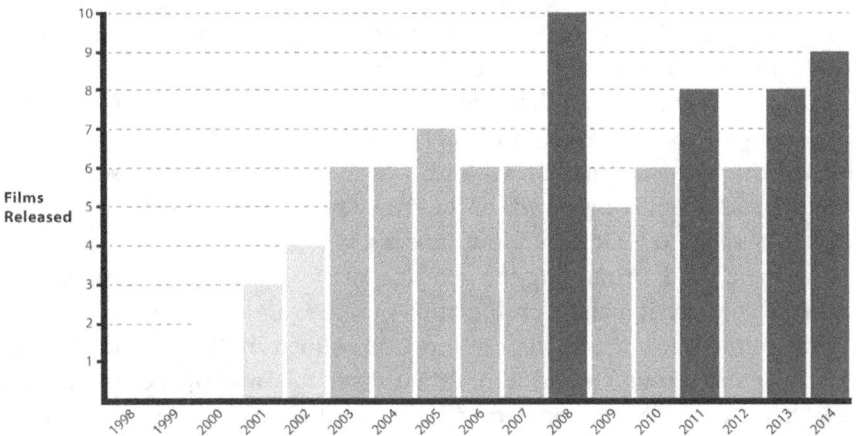

FIG. 2.8 The number of comic book movies released each year between 1998 and 2014.

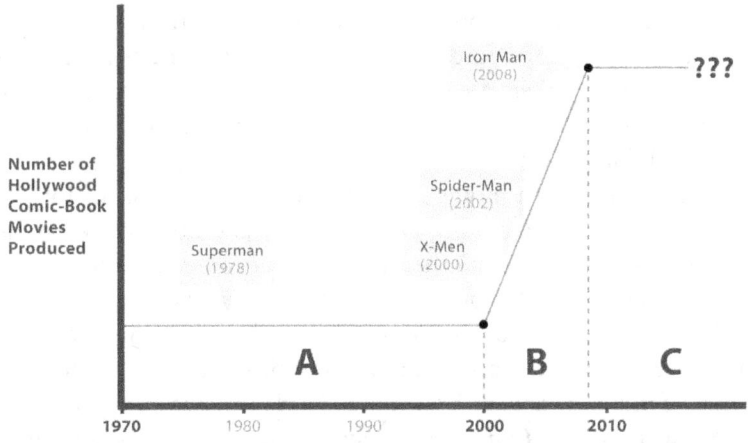

FIG. 2.9 The Bacterial Growth Model for the Genre Cycle—The Comic Book Movie.

2008 was also marked by the release of an unprecedented number of comic book movies, with ten films that could be categorized as within the comic book movie genre receiving wide distribution.[26] Given the number of films produced, and the self-conscious stance many adopted, some commentators believed the genre would soon peter out. In fact, A. O. Scott embraced such a development: "Still, I have a hunch, and perhaps a hope, that 'Iron Man,' 'Hancock' and 'Dark Knight' together represent a peak, by which I mean not only a previously unattained level of quality and interest, but also the beginning of a decline." While 2008 was a peak in productivity, the genre has not declined, but rather, like other genres entering a mature phase, reached a plateau with steady production marking this postclassical stationary stage.[27]

Furthermore, the box-office success of later parodies *Meet the Spartans* (Friedberg and Seltzer 2008) and *Superhero Movie* (Mazin 2008), alongside the satire *Kick-Ass*, signaled that audience members were now so familiar with the codes and conventions of the comic book movie that they could be effectively spoofed.[28] However, it is too early to forecast when these elements will become tired, prompting the genre to enter a decline phase marked by decreased production and a proliferation of satires and parodies.

The comic book movie fits the models outlined by Schatz and Cawelti, as it has gone through a period of articulation, followed by a classical stage of archetypal expression coupled with exponential production, and now the genre has settled into a stationary phase with the films produced displaying a degree of self-awareness. However, unlike genres such as the western or musical, comic book movies have progressed from a classical to a revisionist stage in a matter of years rather than decades. Langford suggests that a move away from the studio system with its production-line adherence to genre blueprints means that new genres "are far more likely to appear as relatively short-lived cycles" (26). Thus, with many competing studios and companies producing comic book movies, filmmakers are compelled to innovate on recent entries. This rivalry has expedited the genre's movement through the model's various phases. Accordingly, any effective genre model needs to be cyclical.

While the bacterial growth model may seem finite, it does allow for the re-emergence of a genre. If genre films are the "bugs," and novel conventions and naïve audiences their "habitat," then the habitat can be refreshed facilitating a new cycle. For example, the slasher-horror as a subgenre began with *Psycho* (Hitchcock 1960) and concluded its period of articulation with *Halloween* (Carpenter 1978). The success of *Halloween* prompted the production of an increasing number of slasher-horrors such as *Friday the 13th* (Cunningham 1980), *A Nightmare on Elm Street* (Craven 1984), and the belated *Psycho* sequels (1983 and 1986), all of which conformed to the genre's blueprint. This classical period eventually gave way to a revisionist stage with self-aware slashers like *New Nightmare* (Craven 1994) and *Scream* (Craven 1996), which came out before the inevitable emergence of parodies like *Scary Movie* (Wayans 2000). Yet the presence of these films did not spell the end for the slasher; to the contrary, the success of *Scream* saw the revival of slasher-horrors in the classical mode (*I Know What You Did Last Summer*, *Urban Legend*, and *Valentine*) and the return of previous franchises (the sequels *Halloween: H20*

Bacterial Growth Model for the Genre Cycle - Cyclicism

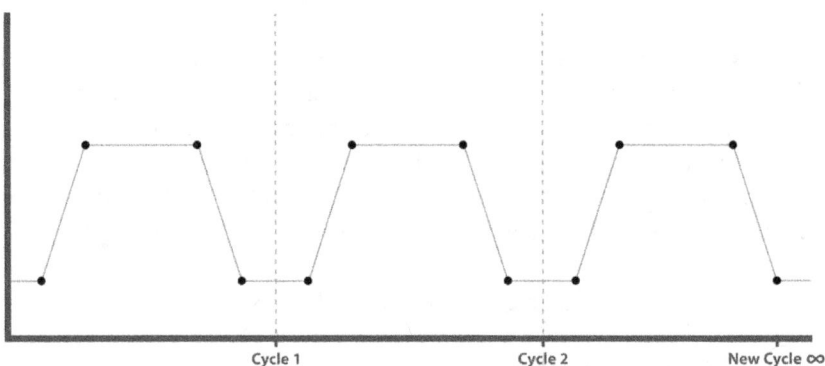

FIG. 2.10 The Bacterial Growth Model for the Genre Cycle—Cyclicism.

and *Jason X*, as well as the remakes *Psycho*, *The Texas Chainsaw Massacre*, and *The Hitcher*).

Thus, the growth model went through a further revolution finding itself back at the beginning with a new audience and refreshed conventions. Hence, a genre could potentially move through any number of bacterial growth models over the years, progressing as outlined above. When viewed in a sequence, with a number of cycles, one can see how the bacterial growth model lends itself to charting genre cyclicism in a way previous organic models did not. While the comic book movie is still in its earliest cycle, a model such as this suggests that the inevitable decline phase will not be the end of the genre, but rather an opportunity for re-articulation and for the cycle to begin anew.

The comic book movie fits with the bacterial growth model, which expands upon the work of Schatz and Cawelti to consider levels of production as well as cyclicism. Despite these refinements, organic models still draw criticism. Steve Neale suggests these models treat genres in "isolation from any generic regime" ("Questions of Genre" 58). The bacterial growth model for the genre cycle, like the *in vitro* scientific procedure on which it is based, is not expected to take place in exactly the same way *in vivo* where any number of factors (e.g., the 2007–2008 Writers Guild of America strike) can and will influence progression.[29] This study has already considered the wider industrial and cultural factors that gave rise to the genre, and mapped its recognition across the inter-textual relay. Genre models such as these are simply another tool for understanding the emergence of the comic book movie, and anticipating the next phase in the genre's development.

Fearful Symmetry: How the Comic Book Movie and Source Material Shape Adaptations

Unsurprisingly, given the importance of genre frameworks to filmmakers, publicity, and the audience, the presence of a distinct comic book movie genre has had a far-reaching impact on the comic book adaptation. This section will consider some of the deepest effects of this recently emerged genre, before concluding with a focus on adaptations from the work of Alan Moore, in which this genre collided with source fidelity.

Conventions and Expectations

Linda Hutcheon describes how adaptations "function similarly to genres: they set up audience expectations . . . through a set of norms that guide our encounter with the adapting work we are experiencing" (121). However, the comic book movie takes this one step further as the adaptations do not simply "function similarly to genres"; they are a genre. Thus, the non-reader audience has been ingrained with expectations that filmmakers often strive to fulfill even if the necessary elements cannot be found in the source. Accordingly, this comic book movie genre has narrowed comic book adaptations and related films into a discrete group with shared conventions.

One example of this process is the manner in which adaptations will often adopt a "comic aesthetic," even if it is inconsistent with the source material. For instance, *The Spirit* applies a misty grey look enlivened by instances of primary color that was previously made popular by *Sin City*. This serves to accentuate the film's status as a comic book movie, yet is at odds with the more realist aesthetic of the original comic strip. Similarly, *Ghost World* was colored in pale green hues on the comic book page. However, the adaptation has a brightly colored mise-en-scène, described by the film's cinematographer, Affonso Beato, as "enhanced and coordinated, as in comics" (Said 22). Furthermore, despite the reputation of film adaptations for refining the excesses of comics, many comic book movies have heightened the fantastical elements of the source. For instance, *300* screenwriter Kurt Johnstad was asked by the film's director to add "more weirdness" (*300* DVD commentary), which resulted in monsters and goat-headed musicians appearing at the Battle of Thermopylae. From these concessions one can see the development of a comic aesthetic, with filmmakers often making choices that are more influenced by the genre's conventions than the source material.

Throughout the development of the comic aesthetic, filmmakers have acknowledged the importance of a coherent look, with the production manager of *Dick Tracy*, Jon Landau, explaining, "It's not a building with green windows that makes a comic book. It's the same building with a Flattop character walking out of it, getting into the biggest, bluest limousine you've ever seen, and driving off on a red street into a matte painting. *That's* a comic book!" (M. Cohen 14). This increasingly unified generic style has not only emerged as a result of the desire to reference and emulate previously successful genre entrants, but it is also industrially dictated.

When Marvel Comics began producing their own film adaptations, the shared universe necessitated a shared style. Jon Favreau, the director of the first of these films, *Iron Man*, remarked on how the second entrant in the Marvel Cinematic Universe, *The Incredible Hulk* (Leterrier 2008), "was successful in keeping a tone that did not seem inconsistent with our film" (Huver). Dedicated production companies and partnerships such as these are reminiscent of the Freed Unit that produced many classical era musicals (e.g., *An American in Paris, Singin' in the Rain*, and *The Band Wagon*) and in the process created and propagated much of the genre's style and iconography (Schatz "Hollywood" 228–29). Filmmaking strategies such as these may limit the opportunities for new entrants to the comic book movie genre, but they also serve to further codify the genre and organize a distinct aesthetic.

Narratives are also often modified to tally with genre conventions. For instance, one of the few amendments in the largely faithful adaptation *Kick-Ass* was the motivation of the "hero" Big Daddy. As in other comic book movies, Big Daddy's vigilantism is instigated by a grave injustice. He was once a celebrated cop framed for a crime he did not commit by the film's antagonist. However, in the original series, Big Daddy is a deluded comic book enthusiast with no real vendetta against the villain. In changing this subversive character trait, the film is better able to meet one of the comic book movie's key conventions: a hero motivated by revenge.

The comic book movie is an expanding club with many filmmakers eager for membership. While the price of admission may be the idiosyncrasies and specificities of a source, the reward is inclusion in modern Hollywood's leading genre. As the examples from *Ghost World* demonstrate, it tends to be alternative comics, rather than the power fantasies of mainstream comics, that are most significantly modified to meet the conventions of the genre and audiences' expectations. This process will be examined in the final part of this chapter, which demonstrates how Alan Moore's Victorian literary pastiche *The League of Extraordinary Gentlemen* was adapted into a conventional comic book movie.

Move into the Mainstream

In the opening to *Fortune and Glory* (2000), Brian Michael Bendis's graphic novel account of his efforts to adapt his comic *Goldfish* for the screen, the creator describes himself as "an alternative comic book artist." He attempts to further qualify this term: "Alternative to what? I don't know. . . . Alternative to popular? I don't come up with these nonsense labels. See in the world of comics, if you don't do superheroes you're alternative." In recent years the lines between mainstream and alternative comics have started to blur with creators, including Bendis, becoming major industry players and non-superhero titles like *The Walking Dead* occasionally breaking into the top ten. Nonetheless, the dichotomy still exists with superhero titles from mainstream publishers dominating sales.[30]

In their introduction to the edited collection *Film and Comic Books*, Ian Gordon et al. pick up on this contrast, suggesting that the "sustained presence of alternative comics and graphic novels have often combined with the 'indie' film movement or modestly budgeted studio films to serve as an innovative counterbalance to the blockbuster superhero movie" (xi). Yet these parallels do not bear the scrutiny of further analysis. As Bendis suggests, in comics any book without a superhero character is quickly classed as "alternative" with sales to match. However, even though vampire comic *30 Days of Night* was not a superhero book, the adaptation (Slade 2007) was produced and marketed as a mainstream film, with a corresponding budget and eventual box-office total. When asked about the imbalance for this study, *30 Days of Night* creator Steve Niles explained, "Comics are ruled by Marvel and DC. They're ruled by the leotard boys . . . if I walked through a bookstore and all they had were cookbooks, I'd lose my mind. I love superheroes but we've got it covered; let's work on some other stuff." Scott McCloud used a similar bookstore analogy in *Reinventing Comics*, as he lamented the dominance of a "single genre" (121).[31]

Niles and McCloud's argument is supported by sales figures. For example, *The Punisher* massively outsold *30 Days of Night* both as a comic book and trade paperback.[32] However, the film adaptation of *30 Days of Night* outgrossed *The Punisher* (Hensleigh 2004) in North America (by $5,758,807) and internationally (by $20,394,982), despite both films having comparable IMDB user ratings and production budgets.[33] This trend of "alternative" comic book adaptations performing as well as, if not better, than the adaptations of "mainstream" superhero books recurs across the process. One of the examples cited by Gordon et al., *A History of Violence*, only marginally trailed "blockbuster superhero movie" *The Punisher* with a domestic box-office gross of $31,504,633 to *The Punisher*'s $33,810,189 and bettered it by $5,633,959 internationally. A dramatic example of this trend was the success of *300*. The original miniseries peaked at 49,000 preorders in May 1998. In the same month, *Uncanny X-Men* #357 and *Fantastic Four* #7 had preorders of 143,000 and 102,300, respectively. Yet the *300* film adaptation had an international box-office total of $456,068,181, almost equivalent to the box office of X-Men sequel *X-Men: The Last Stand* ($459,256,008), and vastly exceeding the international gross of *Fantastic Four: Rise of the Silver Surfer* ($289,047,763). Clearly, the production and later box-office performance of comic book movies are not always dependent on the source's popularity, sales, or generic affiliation within the comic book industry, thereby complicating any blockbuster-superhero/indie-alternative dichotomy.

Altman argues, "Even when a genre already exists in other media, the film genre of the same name cannot simply be borrowed from non-film sources, it must be recreated" (*Film/Genre* 35). Filmmakers adapting comic books have managed to mold these sources into a group of films that attract a wide audience by trading, in part, on earlier successes in the comic book movie genre. In the audience research, the dominance of the comic book movie stifled the mythological and science fiction traditions in *Thor* and *Green Lantern*. Similarly, *30 Days of Night* made no reference to horror in its promotion, but rather to "the groundbreaking graphic novel" on which it was based, while the historical action film *300* cited film noir pastiche and comic book movie *Sin City* in its promotion. The production and promotion of *30 Days of Night* and *300* demonstrate that while these adaptations often maintain elements of their comic book genre, the source only creates an inflection on the all-encompassing film genre—the comic book movie. Accordingly, one of the most strongly felt consequences of this comic book movie genre is the manner in which these filmmaking strategies have enabled comic book characters and stories, branded "alternative" in their native industry, to move into the "mainstream," with the greater visibility and economic rewards that label suggests.

The Comic Book Movie Fan

One of the most surprising findings of the audience research was that little more than half of self-described comic book fans actually still read comics. Furthermore, when asked at the screenings of *Thor* whether the film would compel them to seek out the comics only 22 percent of respondents indicated that they would. Based on this result, the survey for *Green Lantern* was amended to ask participants if they would be interested in following *Green Lantern* in any other format. While 50 percent indicated that they would, they were more interested in audiovisual interpretations than the comics. These findings are reflected in comic book sales. When *Spider-Man* was released in 2002, sales of *The Amazing Spider-Man* from North American comic book stores increased on average by only 15,000 copies from the year before (*CBG. Xtra*). Whether the increase in sales could be attributed to new readers generated by the successful film is difficult to quantify, as sales from September 2000 to September 2001 had increased from 49,300 to 90,000—a much more significant upturn, suggesting the character was enjoying a revival long before the adaptation was released. Equally, sales of *The Amazing Spider-Man* were unaffected by the release of the sequels, with any further sales boosts coming from major "events."[34] These figures indicate that comic book readership has not significantly increased as a consequence of adaptations. Rae and Gray arrive at a similar conclusion in their reception study of *X-Men*, noting that "non-comics-readers have generally not found the need to engage with the film text in its regular serialized comic book format" (100).

However, although filmgoers have not gone to the source, they have returned in ever-increasing numbers to comic book movies, with the genre developing a fan base that rivals comics in dedication, and dwarfs it in size. As will be discussed in the next chapter, fan forums such as the San Diego Comic-Con have seen huge upswings in attendance since the comic book adaptation boom. Film and non-comic book panels tend to attract the largest number of attendees—further evidence that the comic book movie is developing dedicated fans that are uninterested in the source material.[35]

This fandom could only emerge and be sustained through the consistent production of a genre. These non-reader comic book fans engage in many of the same practices as traditional fans. For example, Rae and Gray describe how the comic book reader comes to an adaptation "prepared for certain readings, looking out for others, and even hypersensitive to yet other meanings" (88). However, this experience is not confined to readers. A spectator who has seen a number of comic book movies can also display sensitivity to earlier work, viewing each new genre entrant with reference to previous films. It is this intertextuality that gave wider resonance to the genre redefining films of the stationary phase such as *The Dark Knight, Hancock,* and *Watchmen.* As a result, while comic book fans have a wider catalogue of texts that they can use to decode an adaptation, both audiences could be considered textually rich and have earned the status of "fans." Thus, one of the most significant consequences of the emergence of the comic book movie is that the genre has created new fans, though many of these enthusiasts will never read a comic book.

The comic book movie is one of the chief determinants shaping the comic book adaptation, and often wider Hollywood productions. Some of the most immediate examples of this influence might include the increasing number of films that actively conform to the genre and its audience's expectations; the movement of once obscure characters and stories into the mainstream; and the development of a non-reader fan base, which has seen a semblance of the participatory practices of comic book fandom reappear in mainstream film fandom. It is essential when studying the comic book film adaptation to recognize the role that this genre has played in shaping these films. Anticipating Chapter Three's focus on fans and fidelity, this section, and the chapter, will conclude by considering what happens when the comic book movie collides with the source text.

■   ■   ■

In the audience research, one fan's response to the importance of fidelity articulated the central conflict of comic book film adaptation production in the early twenty-first century: "It's important that the film can appeal to both fans of the comic book and a general audience." While this fan displays a greater critical distance than many other enthusiasts, his assessment is widely held by many commentators. For instance, Bordwell makes a similar point: "A comic-book movie can succeed if it doesn't stray from the fanbase's expectations and swiftly initiates the newbies" ("Superheroes for Sale"). The industry is not oblivious to this demand, and the manner in which these films try to address these imperatives has colored much of the Golden Age of Comic Book Filmmaking.

Both this chapter and Chapter Three examine the two broad audiences for comic book adaptations. As will be explored in detail in the next chapter, fans tend to view these films as *adaptations* and place a premium on the source, often using their online presence to safeguard fidelity. The non-fan audience shows less dedication to the source material and more often views these films in the context of the comic book movie genre. However, these groups are not mutually exclusive, many non-fans value fidelity and are sensitive to online discussions, while a large number of self-described fans do not read comics, and, like their non-fan equivalents, they are well-versed in comic book movie conventions. By focusing on the adaptations of one of the industry's most celebrated and idiosyncratic creators, Alan Moore, this section will illustrate the shared interests and inevitable conflicts between these groups, and how these films address them.

Of the four films that have been adapted from Alan Moore's comics—*From Hell* (Hughes 2001), *The League of Extraordinary Gentlemen* (Norrington 2003), *V for Vendetta* (McTeigue 2005), and *Watchmen* (Snyder 2009)—*The League of Extraordinary Gentlemen* and the slavishly faithful *Watchmen* most firmly inhabit the differing positions an adaptation can take. The concept for *The League of Extraordinary Gentlemen* (hereafter abbreviated to *The League*) was licensed from Alan Moore based on a four-page treatment prior to the publication of the comic book series. What attracted producer Don Murphy was the concept of a team of superheroes based on Victorian literary characters.[36] As development of the adaptation began prior to the comic's publication, it is unsurprising that the film displayed little fidelity to the source, prompting fans of the comic book to express their discontent online following the film's release (Garret). However, *The League* never strived for comic continuity; rather, it followed the conventions of the emerging comic book movie genre.

The comic centers on aging Victorian icons—Allan Quatermain, Captain Nemo, Dr. Hyde, The Invisible Man, and Mina Harker—in a story that is in keeping with their literary origins. Yet the adaptation bears little resemblance to the comic book. For instance, much like *The Spirit* and *Kick-Ass*, the characters are each given heightened powers and abilities in the film (e.g., Mina Harker is altered from a human in the comic book to "Dracula's Bride" with the ability to fly, suck blood, and command legions of bats), and younger characters such as Tom Sawyer and Dorian Gray are introduced. With these more traditional comic book movie elements, the film more closely resembled the already popular X-Men films that were produced by 20th Century Fox, the same studio adapting *The League*.

Further efforts to link *The League* to *X-Men* in the minds of the audience saw the film's title briefly changed to *LXG*, with promotional material for *The League* mirroring that of *X-Men*.[37] The adaptation also affirmed its comic book movie status by emphasizing the director's past success in the genre, with the tagline "From the director of *Blade*" included in trailers and TV spots. Thus, while the film's promotional material made no reference to the comic book, a mainstream audience, unfamiliar with the source, was positioned to expect a film similar to past comic book movies through the use of intertextual references and generic markers.[38]

Unlike *The League*, fidelity was fetishized at each turn in the production and promotion of *Watchmen*. For example, the producers hired the original artist Dave Gibbons as a consultant.[39] Gibbons produced new artwork for the film's first poster, which was distributed to fans at the 2007 San Diego

FIG. 2.12 Many tactics were employed to link *The League of Extraordinary Gentlemen* with the already popular X-Men films, including mirroring the title and theatrical trailer.

Comic-Con. Gibbons also attended panels with the filmmakers and cast at fan events including the 2008 Comic-Con. The film's screenwriter, David Hayter, even wrote an open letter to fans, in which he frequently asserted the filmmakers' status as "fans," stressing that continuity with the source was important. The film further emphasized its fidelity in its promotional material. While *The League* did not cite its source, the trailer for *Watchmen* carried the tagline, "The most celebrated graphic novel of all time." Furthermore, many of the key images from the trailers and posters directly mirrored the comics. Yet these references would have been lost on a non-fan audience unfamiliar with the source, and possibly on many who were.

Some concessions were made to the wider comic book movie audience, such as the frequent citation of Zack Snyder's status as "the visionary director of *300*." For the most part, however, the film's promotional material was considered too esoteric for non-fan audiences. For instance, the first theatrical trailer for *Watchmen*, which played before *The Dark Knight*, carried little meaning outside of the context of the source, providing no clear indication of the plot and containing only two lines of dialogue. In contrast, the many trailers for *The League* clearly conveyed the premise. Unsurprisingly, Brandon Gray of *Box Office Mojo* cited the "diffuse storyline and marketing" of *Watchmen* for limiting its appeal ("Watchmen Burns Out").

The studio, according to producer Don Murphy, mandated the more conventional elements of *The League*. For example, to entice the non-fan audience, the producers cast a star, Sean Connery, in the role of Allan Quatermain.

This strategy was at odds with the wider tactic in comic book adaptations of casting relative unknowns and relying on the popularity of the source material. However, as *The League* was not widely known outside the comic book community, or even within, this was a sound economic strategy. As Murphy explained, "What I set out to make was a summer blockbuster. In order to do this right and to do it period, I was going to need $100 million. In order to get $100 million, I was going to need a movie star" (Ambrose 120). Nonetheless, as seen with the casting of stars in previous adaptations, this decision further diluted the adaptation's fidelity, with Allan Quatermain becoming the central protagonist and the team's leader (a role filled by Mina Harker in the source).[40]

James Naremore characterizes stars as "iconic, extra-cinematic characters" ("Acting in Cinema" 115), and indeed the casting of Connery saw a move away from the opium-addicted has-been of Moore's comic to a more vibrant adventurer in the style of one of Connery's most celebrated roles, Henry Jones, Sr., from *Indiana Jones and the Last Crusade* (Spielberg 1989). This allusion was further emphasized in trailers where the "the greatest adventurer who ever lived" is introduced with images of a line traced on a globe—an overt reference to the map sequences from Indiana Jones. In contrast, *Watchmen* displayed a confidence in its source material by not casting any stars.[41] While this may serve to bolster fidelity, since *Watchmen* was not as well known as Batman or Spider-Man, this was a gamble that arguably did not pay off.

Although casting a star is atypical of comic book movies, elevating a character such as Allan Quatermain from the ensemble does frequently occur. Due to various production constraints and marketing concerns, these films favor clear central protagonists more than their source material. Examples of this trend can be seen in the *X-Men* films, where Wolverine was positioned as the protagonist, even becoming the team's leader by the trilogy-closer—a characterization at odds with the loner of the comics. Thus, even when using unknown actors, comic book movies are often tailored to meet the tastes of the wider audience. However, in a further contrast to traditional genre fare, none of the titular *Watchmen* were elevated to the role of lead protagonist, a strategy that some reviewers felt may have benefited the narrative.[42]

In discussing the graphic novel on the DVD commentary for *The League*, actor Shane West notes, "It was just a shame we couldn't do it as close to the comic book as we could; but it probably would have made $7 million if we did it that way." Whether the film would have been more successful if it had been a faithful adaptation is difficult to gauge. What is certain is that a faithful adaptation of Alan Moore's graphic novel would have resulted in an R rating for the film. When *The League* was released in 2003, of the few R-rated comic book adaptations none had generated significant box office. By 2009,

FIG. 2.13 The costumes in *Watchmen* were criticized for emulating *Batman & Robin* and not the source. However, this was a conscious decision on the part of the filmmakers to reference past comic book movies.

the success of the R-rated *Sin City* and *300* enabled the production of a more faithful adaptation of Alan Moore's most popular graphic novel, *Watchmen*.

However, despite its fidelity, it should be noted that *Watchmen* is also shaped by the comic book movie genre. In perhaps the greatest change from the source, the film's ending is amended to achieve the "concision" Coogan identified in the reworking of Batman's origin (10). In the adaptation, Ozymandias frames Dr. Manhattan for the destruction of New York, rather than concocting the extraterrestrial threat of the comic. Through this infidelity the adaptation achieved a more symmetrical narrative typical of comic book movies. Furthermore, the film is littered with allusions to past comic book movies. For instance, in defending how the costumes chosen for some characters in *Watchmen* echoed the much maligned suits of *Batman & Robin*, director Zack Snyder said, "You must acknowledge where comic book movies are right now, in the same way that *Watchmen* referenced and took apart the comic book genre . . . you have to make some references to those same decisions that were made in cinema" (Frosty). Equally, although a loose borrowing, *The League* does not completely dismiss its source. On release, the full title was reinstated, and the film included some references to the comic book's *War of the Worlds*-themed sequel.

Furthermore, the interests of the fan and mainstream audience often coincide, with an adherence to fidelity preventing conventions from descending into cliché. For instance, having read the books, fans would have known that at the climax of *Watchmen* the heroes fail to stop mass murder. But this moment would have surprised mainstream audiences who were led to expect a last-minute rescue—a comic book movie staple. Thus, in this instance, fidelity confounded genre expectations, thereby satisfying fan interests and creating a more rewarding experience for the non-reader viewer.

In the end, *The League* was a largely unfaithful comic book adaptation that made little attempt to pander to fans (of which there were few) and instead was produced and promoted within very clear genre parameters. When interviewed for this study, comic creator Joe Kelly described *The League* as "an excellent example of, for lack of a better term, exploitation. An 'exploitation film' ultimately means we know there's a bandwagon, let's jump on it and bang them out as quickly as possible." Kelly concluded his point by noting how these films "stray" from the source material in a way that isn't "organic," adding, "I think that's a danger studios are very aware of now . . . they know there's a very vocal audience that before a movie even comes out that will tell you whether or not they are going to like it." Despite negative fan attention, however, the film was moderately successful, grossing $179 million worldwide, which was the same as fellow 2003 release *Daredevil*, but below *Hulk* ($245,369,480) and *X2* ($407,711,549).

Despite some allusions to the wider genre, *Watchmen* would still be considered a "transformation" in Andrew's terms (*Film Theory* 98), with the source material the key determinant shaping the adaptation. Ultimately, the film failed to successfully cross over beyond its core fan base as demonstrated by its 67.7 percent drop at the box office from weekend one to weekend two. Steve Niles suggested that such a revisionist work arrived too early in the genre for non-fan audiences: "It took comics 75 years to reach that point. I still think that the biggest problem [with *Watchmen*] was that we asked too much of people. First, accept superheroes. Now accept that the world wouldn't be the same without them. There's a lot to swallow." The inability of *Watchmen* to break out beyond its core fan base illustrates the folly of overly relying on a built-in audience, even one as dedicated as comic book fans. As *Variety* noted, "a few hundred people on a message board or even the few hundred thousand who visit these sites each month will hardly register a blip when it comes to

FIG. 2.14 Later promotional material for *Green Lantern* emphasized comic book fidelity.

the number of people that a big-budget actioner needs to make a profit" (Fritz "Net Heads").

On a larger budget of $130 million, *Watchmen* grossed $182,735,282 worldwide, which, adjusted for inflation, would be less than *The League*'s gross (budget $78 million). However, the film did perform better in the US and sold an unprecedented number of graphic novels for DC Comics and its parent company Time Warner (Boucher). Furthermore, the film garnered more positive reviews than *The League*.[43] Ultimately, neither film achieved the critical and financial success the filmmakers would have hoped for, as both managed to alienate a sector of the audience.

Although an argument could be made that *The League* and *Watchmen* were never likely to match the profits of more widely known adaptations, the success of *Iron Man* demonstrates that even relatively obscure characters have the potential to cross over into the mainstream. As *Variety* assessed, Marvel "was especially encouraged when Iron Man, who wasn't as well known as Spider-Man, Superman or Batman, was able to cross over and launch a new franchise with a $582 million haul at the worldwide B.O." (Graser). As will be demonstrated in the next chapter, *Iron Man*, like similar adaptations, utilized fidelity-evoking publicity to generate interest among fans, and then expanded that interest through generic markers, star casting, clear promotion, and other non-fan focused strategies.

Of the films surveyed in this study's audience research, *The Adventures of Tintin* was distanced from the comic book movie genre, and even its source material, through publicity that primarily traded on the reputations of its filmmakers. *Green Lantern* tried to appeal to both groups, but at different stages, which resulted in a muddled marketing campaign. As discussed, the first trailer for *Green Lantern* targeted the wider comic book movie audience. However, it was not well received by comic book fans (Fritz "Green Lantern"), with Warner Bros. striving to appease them with publicity that concentrated on the Green Lantern Corps and evoked the covers for writer Geoff Johns's celebrated comic books.

While this strategy did serve to quiet fan discontent, it seems to have been off-putting to mainstream audiences. Furthermore, the heavy emphasis on the Green Lantern Corps in publicity led many to believe that they would be a major component of the film. When the Corps' presence amounted to little more than a second act montage and abbreviated action sequence, reviewers and fans felt the film had broken the fidelity contract. Testifying to this confused marketing, when asked whether they thought *Green Lantern* was accurately represented in publicity materials (such as posters, television ads, and trailers), one fan responded that "it looked a lot worse in trailers," while a clearly knowledgeable non-fan noted that it had "less of the Green Lantern Corps."

Conversely, *Thor* achieved box-office success through fan-appeasing fidelity and mainstream-targeting strategies. For example, 31 percent of the non-fan audience surveyed cited the film's stars and director as a reason for seeing the film, with no one citing *Green Lantern*'s cast and crew. While both films cast award-winning actors alongside upcoming movie stars, in moving from a comic book movie model to one that emphasized comic book fidelity, the actors in *Green Lantern* were pushed to the sidelines in favor of CGI creations, many of which received little screen time. Consequently, an opportunity was lost to entice mainstream audiences as testified by the audience research and ultimately the film's box office, which, like that of *Watchmen*, experienced a massive decline in week two.[44]

As the 31–35-year-old Tintin fan cited at the start of this section pragmatically suggested, fans can ignite a profitable box-office run, but the mainstream audience is necessary to sustain it. Filmmakers have come to recognize this imperative, with successful adaptations today tailored for both audiences, the fan and non-fan filmgoer. How the industry has met the demands of the comic fan will be the focus of the next chapter.

CHAPTER THREE

Fans, Fidelity, and the Grammar of Value

In a brief moment of levity before the third-act fisticuffs of *X-Men* (Singer 2000), new teammate Wolverine, sitting uncomfortably in a leather uniform, asks, "You actually go outside in these things?" Team leader Cyclops curtly responds, "Well, what would you prefer, yellow spandex?" Fellow X-Man Jean Grey conceals a smile; a self-satisfied smirk shared by the knowing members of the audience. This brief reference to the brightly colored costumes of the comics serves as both a concession and a reminder to fans, "Yes, X-Men was a comic first, but remember, this is a *movie.*" *X-Men* was released during the nascent days of the comic book movie genre, when all a comic book fan could hope for was a vague resemblance to the source, a halfway decent movie, and a smattering of such self-referential moments. Little over a decade later, *X-Men* received a prequel, *X-Men: First Class* (Vaughn 2011), which saw the heroes ending the Cuban Missile Crisis, wearing the comic book attire that seemed so ridiculous ten years prior. This chapter explores how fans in the digital age gained a measure of control over the production of comic book adaptations and the impact of this development. "What would you prefer, yellow spandex?" Yes. But now no one is laughing.

Adaptation studies today favors a poststructuralist approach that positions each adaptation at the center of a spider's web of intertextual relations, which includes—but is not limited to—the source text. Such an approach is a direct challenge to the fidelity orthodoxy that scholars feel encumbered the field in the past, with Robert Stam suggesting that critics need "to be less concerned with inchoate notions of 'fidelity' and to give more attention to dialogical responses" ("Beyond Fidelity" 76). Providing scholars with a vivid example of such intertextual relations, media conglomerates have embraced transmedia opportunities with each version of their franchises shaping and being reshaped by the others. Comic book readers, weaned on decades of interconnected mythologies, are also open to a measure of co-creation, with popular elements introduced in one version of a transmedia franchise often spreading

FIG. 3.1 The first film adaptation of the X-Men did not include the comic's colorful costumes, but the 2011 prequel *X-Men: First Class* featured designs more reminiscent of the source.

to others. André Bazin anticipated this content-centric turn in his optimistic prediction of 1948. He hoped that the critic of the future would view multiple versions of a text as a single work, a "pyramid with three sides, all equal in the eyes of the critic" ("Cinema as Digest" 26). This study is sensitive to the many relations that shape comic book adaptations. However, despite the penchant for textual fluidity among scholars, producers, and fans, this chapter will argue that recent comic book adaptations have displayed previously unseen levels of faithfulness to their source texts and the wider tenets of the medium, and that a rounded study of these films cannot ignore fidelity as a determinant.

When *Time* magazine named "You" as the Person of the Year in 2006, it articulated a growing belief in the power of new media to "simulate an ideal public sphere" (Moyo 141) in which "consumption itself is now regarded as a positive" (Creeber 19). Although, arguably insurmountable, disparities exist between producer and consumer; it seems reckless to ignore the audience in an era marked by such participation. Thus, this study of comic book adaptations allows one to reopen the fidelity debate, not as a return to the reductive research that ignored wider determinants, but rather as a means of productively addressing how fan discourses, and what Colin MacCabe calls "the grammar of value" (9), can be a vibrant part of the many relations that shape an adaptation. Accordingly, this chapter will demonstrate how comic book fans (alongside other devotees of pop culture) helped facilitate Hollywood's transition to a more participatory industry. It will argue that the increased fidelity of modern comic book adaptations can be partly attributed to comic book fans, who gained wider influence over production in the digital age. This chapter will conclude with an analysis of the unprecedented fidelity of the Golden Age of Comic Book Filmmaking, which fostered the emergence of the first comic book transformations (e.g., *Sin City*, *Watchmen*, and *Scott Pilgrim*), and how, even within the larger category of borrowings, the source has become an increasingly important determinant in films such as *Batman Begins* (Nolan 2005).

As discussed in the Introduction, many prominent adaptation scholars are concerned that any focus on fidelity will eventually descend into a box ticking exercise in which the film is compared to the source and ultimately found wanting—"the book will always be better than any adaptation because it is always *better at being itself*" (Leitch *Film Adaptation* 16). To traverse such pitfalls this chapter will employ the audience research outlined earlier. While most studies of comic book adaptation audiences were distributed via fan forums (Bacon-Smith and Yarbrough; Barker and Brooks; Brooker *Dark Knight*), this survey had the benefit of being carried out with heterogeneous cinema audiences. Accordingly, it offers a more balanced insight into who "comic book fans" are, what their priorities might be, and how they engage with these films. Some findings will tally with commonly held views, while others are more surprising. However, strengthened by evidence from industrial relays, creator interviews, and the films themselves, the results of this survey chart an era in which fans and fidelity came to shape the promotion and production of adaptations like never before.

Fanboys and Forums

As many scholars are quick to point out, adaptation offers studios an opportunity to lessen the risks associated with filmmaking by using material that has a built-in audience (Ray 43; Hark 173; Hutcheon 87; Gough 63). However, the producers of comic book adaptations traditionally ignored the expectations, rituals, and strategies of their built-in audience, or fans, with *Batman* (1989) director Tim Burton suggesting ahead of the film's release, "This is too big a budget movie to worry about what a fan of a comic would say" (Pearson and Uricchio 184), and *Batman & Robin* (1997) director Joel Schumacher describing comic book fans in 1997 as "a small cult" (Broeske).

Such dismissals are unsurprising, as, despite being regarded as the research and development branch of much of today's popular culture, comic book readership has been in decline since the 1950s. For instance, in 2000 Scott McCloud estimated that there were approximately 500,000 comic book readers in North America (*Reinventing Comics* 97). While the audience research for this study took place in Ireland, many of the demographic patterns found in the US reappeared. Of the 113 audience members surveyed in this study, only thirty-eight identified themselves as comic book fans. Tallying with most assessments of comic book fans, the fan audience leaned heavily towards adults with 92 percent aged twenty-one or older.[1] All but six of the fans were male, versus a 50-50 gender split among the non-fan group.[2] These demographic consistencies have helped give rise to the term "fanboy," a label Matthew J. Pustz examines in his book *Comic Book Culture*. Pustz argues that "more than other cultures surrounding popular texts, this [comic book] culture is truly one of consumption and commodity" (18). He goes on to contrast comic book culture with television and sports fandom, where consumption "is not a requirement" and fans "only need to watch them" (18). Thus, Pustz equates comic book fandom with the purchasing and reading of comics.

As traditional comic book reading is becoming an increasingly rarefied pursuit, the attendance of comic book film adaptations regularly dwarfs the sales of the comics. For instance, the May 2012 issue of *The Avengers* sold only 67,744 copies from US specialty stores during the same month that *The Avengers* (Whedon 2012) was the number one film at the US box office (*CBGXtra.com*). However, these sales should not suggest that *The Avengers* comic has only 67,744 readers, as enthusiasts will read comics by a number of alternative means, including borrowing, downloads, and trade paperback reprints. Furthermore, this study's audience research showed that little more than half of the self-described "comic book fans" who attended the adaptations (55 percent) actually still read comic books of any kind, with two "comic book fans" indicating that they had never read comics. Marvel Comics senior vice-president of publishing, Tom Brevoort, was asked about these findings when interviewed for this study. Brevoort suggested that this non-reader fan audience might be attributable to the cyclical nature of readership:

A great demographic of [readers] as they start to get into high school ages and even into college will tend to drop off a little bit or entirely as other things crop up. And then they go off, they enter the workforce, they get a job and have more disposable income and they tend to start coming back . . . those people still are likely to go watch The Avengers movie and the Spider-Man movie, or go and watch the new Spidey cartoon or Avengers cartoon, or to experience these characters in other ways, and those avenues will tend to lead them back into the fold again.

As Brevoort points out, these fans seem to maintain their interest in the characters through audiovisual interpretations. For instance, those filmgoers surveyed at *Green Lantern* (Campbell 2011) were asked if they would be eager to follow the character in any other format, with 90 percent of fans indicating they would. A series of formats, including "novels," "musical theatre," and "Web comics," were offered. "Comic books" only narrowly edged out an "animated TV series," with significant interest in a "live action TV series," "mobile phone app," "video game," and "novel." Such responses tally with Michael E. Uslan's observation that "there are as many, if not more, fans showing up at a Comic-Con because of [video games] *Arkham Asylum* and *Arkham City* as Batman comics." Thus, the many adaptations of recent years may have increased the visibility of these characters, but they also seem to have supplanted the role of the original comics, with fans no longer needing to return to "the fold" to get their regular fix. That so many respondents still consider themselves fans even though they no longer read comics suggests that comic book fandom can also include the armchair enthusiasts Pustz identified in some sections of sport fans. This significant non-reader sector of fandom, which Pustz would have been unable to observe in his largely comic store-based study, points to the need for a new definition of comic book fandom.

Conversely, of the participants who identified themselves as non-fans, six currently read comic books. Three younger readers (under fifteen) mentioned British humor comics *The Beano* and *The Dandy*, while the other non-fan readers identified alternative titles such as *Preacher*, *Promethea*, and *Sandman*, which suggests that some readers draw a distinction between a comic book fan and someone who reads alternative and humor titles. Pustz argues that the "boundaries" between "mainstream and alternative comic book fans" are not as strong as the divisions "between readers and non readers, between fans and those in the ordinary world" (22). This survey complicates Pustz's distinctions as some readers dismiss the "fan" label, while many fans do not currently read comics. Therefore, the term "comic book fan" cannot be equated with "reader," with Duncan and Smith's suggestion in *The Power of Comics* that "a *fan* is someone who wants to take part in the dialogue about the medium" (173) seeming more apt.

Indeed, the online habits of those fans surveyed gravitated towards films and comics, while non-fans cited a wider range of interests.[3] Fans were also more active online, with the group twice as likely to leave online comments and keep blogs than their non-fan equivalents. Such dialogue has been a fixture of comic book culture since the 1960s when comic book fandom first became organized. Much of this fandom's practices were predicated on narrowing the boundaries between creator and consumer and engendering a collaborative spirit. The publishers fostered this development, creating a cooperative medium long before the prevalence of participatory culture. A key component of this emerging community were the letters pages and columns (often abbreviated to "lettercols") that appeared in the back pages of comics.[4] Marvel Comics led the way in promoting fan discourse through lettercols, printing both praise and criticism, while adopting more inclusive terms such as "we" and "us" as opposed to DC Comics "them" (Pustz 167). Most commentators credit Stan Lee with this innovation, with Mark Waid stating, when interviewed for this study, that the Spider-Man creator "certainly did much more than anybody in making fans believe: You are a part of the process. You are a part of the comics. You are a part of the movement. You are a part of Marvel. We are all Marvel."[5]

Marvel would often go to great lengths to demonstrate how lettercols were central to the creative process. As early as the third issue of *The Fantastic Four* (March 1962), Marvel's first post-World War II superhero success, one could detect the influence of the readership, as the previously plain-clothed adventurers gained coordinated costumes—a development Lee would later attribute to fan mail (DeFalco *Comic Creators on Fantastic Four* 13). The issue's lettercol solicited further feedback, with the avuncular Lee inviting opinions on a number of topics: "So let's hear from you other readers. What type of covers do YOU prefer, and how do you feel about the name Mr. Fantastic?"

Although many entertainments were shaped by their audience's feedback, few invited responses and attributed changes to fan discourse as openly as comic books. For instance, although *Star Trek* (Roddenberry 1966) was reportedly "saved" from cancellation by a letter writing campaign, NBC did not solicit such activity and called for fans to stop writing letters once the show was renewed (Gent 95). That fans could prove influential in the production of comic books is not only attributable to the inclusionary practices of creators, but also to the serialized nature of the form. As Rae and Gray explain, episodic texts "encourage fan involvement . . . [and] promise fans a certain degree of agency" (100). Thus, comic book fans were granted a measure of interaction unavailable to the fans of more inert or less frequently produced texts such as Tolkien's *The Lord of the Rings* or *Star Wars* (Lucas 1977).

Within the fan community certain stars emerged. "Letterhacks" was the term used to describe readers whose letters were regularly printed, with many of these letterhacks using their growing visibility and close contact with the creators to move into the industry.[6] However, these pages not only fostered dialogue between fan and creator, but also fan and fan. In lettercols, a reader's contribution was generally accompanied by a postal address. This allowed disparate fans to contact like-minded readers. Aldo J. Regalado notes that during this period, "these initially unorganized relationships rapidly grew into full-blown fan communities" (127). Lettercols also enabled the wider circulation of another key component of comic book culture—the fanzine.

Fanzines are amateur publications that include discussion, fan artwork, and news stories relating to a particular aspect of fan culture. Ironically, one of comics' greatest detractors, Dr. Fredric Wertham, was an advocate of the fan publication, writing in his book, *The World of Fanzines: A Special Form of Communication*, that they "constitute a vivid and vital kind of method of interchange of thoughts and opinion" (129). Lettercols made the wider circulation of fanzines possible. For example, Jerry Bails, the founder of one of the first and most popular superhero comic book fanzines, *Alter-Ego* (1961), contacted those readers who had their letters published in *The Brave and the Bold* #35 (April–May 1961) in order to gauge interest in his fanzine and distribute it to like-minded readers (Bails).

Like letterhacks, many fanzine creators used the skills and contacts they developed on their 'zines to enter the industry.[7] For instance, former president of DC Comics, Paul Levitz, who began his career as the publisher of the fanzine *The Comic Reader*, explained when interviewed that "a lot of the skill sets that I used in my professional life, I began to develop doing my own material." Reflecting on this period of greater interaction, Jones and Jacobs note, "The signal had been sent," adding, "Fans could become pros. They could actually *shape* the comics" (67); in few other industries during the 1960s and 1970s did the gap between fan and creator seem so surmountable.[8]

Today, fanzines, like lettercols, are less frequently produced, replaced by fan sites and online message boards (Stuever 1). Like those earlier forums, the Web provides the opportunity to communicate with like-minded people, but now fandom has a wider reach and greater immediacy, a development Matt Hills terms "just-in-time fandom" (*Fan Cultures* 178).

Duncan and Smith note of traditional comic book fandom, "By no means is [it] a highly centralized community, rather it is a good example of an 'imagined' or *virtual community* [Original emphasis] where people are joined by bonds of mutual interest rather than geographic proximity to one another" (175). Such practices saw comic book fans, and other pop-culture devotees, well positioned at the start of the 1990s to take advantage of emerging online communities. As Jenkins observed, "fandom has both been reshaped by and helped to reshape cyberculture" (*Fans, Bloggers, and Gamers* 5). The producers also played their part, extending their participatory practices online, as Brooker notes: "Comics boards on the Internet have eroded more completely than any other form the boundaries between 'reader' and 'writer,' amateur and pro, fan and author" (*Batman Unmasked* 265). Many professionals regularly view boards for feedback and take part in online discussions.

Just as the fans that once contributed to lettercols moved their discussions online, the enthusiasts that might have been letterhacks or fanzine editors became the webmasters of the first fan sites. While this meant that fan favorite adaptations, such as *X-Men*, benefited from positive hype, those films that were not meeting expectations were vulnerable to negative word of mouth— or as Kristin Thompson prefers, "word of keystroke" (141). The first adaptation to rouse this digitally fortified community was *Batman & Robin*, with its development and release precipitating previously unseen levels of fan discontent and demonstrating the untapped power of comic book fandom.[9]

Like Burton before him, *Batman & Robin* director Joel Schumacher dismissed comic book fans as a "cult," with *Entertainment Weekly* reporting that Schumacher blamed negative prerelease buzz on "an unpoliced Internet" (Broeske). *Ain't It Cool News* (*AICN*) became the most referenced of the "unpoliced" Internet's film fan sites. Founded by film fan Harry Knowles in 1996, *AICN* was a hub for the type of investigative fandom that comic enthusiasts practiced and movie studios feared. *AICN* made its reputation through releasing insider information and by posting early reviews (usually based on previews or test screenings). When *Batman & Robin* was released, *Variety* reported that Joel Schumacher "referred to Knowles indirectly in publicized statements denouncing the Web for its prejudicial prerelease buzz on pics" (R. Weiner). Knowles would later acknowledge that it was *AICN*'s coverage of Schumacher's comic book adaptation that "made the site visible" (*Titanic Review*). Thus, like successful fanzines, *AICN* and other fan sites flourished by providing a forum for fan discussion nestled on the industry's fringes. The increasing power of these online forums found studios striving to meet fan demands, including one of their chief priorities: fidelity.

Fidelity

It has been argued by some commentators that fidelity is less crucial in adaptations of pop cultural texts than it is in film versions of more highbrow sources (Somigli 285; Corrigan "In the Gap" 33). Yet as the audience research demonstrates, comic book fans can be every bit as precious as readers of more highly regarded texts, and are often far more vociferous in their response. Of those fans surveyed, 89 percent considered it "moderately" (35 percent), "very" (43 percent), or "extremely" (11 percent) important that a comic book adaptation is faithful to its source. While many saw little reason for a lack of continuity—"What's the point of adapting it if you're not going to be faithful?" (21–25-year-old male fan at a *Green Lantern* screening)—others were more measured, with a 26–30-year-old female fan who had never read *Thor*, but still considered it moderately important that the film was faithful to the source, explaining, "While film and graphic novels are different media, and therefore require different story types, I think it's important to honour the characters of your source material."

The emphasis fans place on fidelity can be traced, like other practices, back to traditional comic book fandom. Paul Atkinson, citing Richard Reynolds, notes how comic "stories are judged in terms of their faithfulness to earlier issues, a process that is policed by the fans" (47). A number of reasons could be attributed to this interest in continuity. In the 1960s, "readers" also became "collectors," resulting in a greater awareness of the history of a character, and consequently a premium was placed on consistency. Moreover, as the average age of readers increased, fans continued reading for years, even decades, and therefore continuity was more greatly emphasized. The burgeoning fan forums also facilitated this interest, with readers frequently discussing the minutiae of mythology, as fans became the "guardians for continuity gaffes" (Duncan and Smith 191).[10] The development of dedicated comic book stores in the late 1970s and early 1980s also fostered this interest, as direct distribution ensured fans never missed an issue. Similarly, the reprinting of past stories in graphic novel and trade paperback formats allowed readers to contrast stories from various periods in a character's publication history.

However, while still stressing the importance of consistency, fans do allow for a certain amount of play within this continuity. For instance, 2008 saw the release of two successful adaptations of long-running comics, *The Incredible Hulk* (Leterrier) and *The Dark Knight* (Nolan). However, as *The Incredible Hulk* prepared to rampage into cinemas in his familiar shade of green, a new comic was launched featuring a red Hulk as its cover star. Similarly, in the same year *The Dark Knight* topped the US box office, DC Comics killed the Bruce Wayne character in *Batman R.I.P.* with one-time Robin, Dick Grayson, assuming Batman's cape and cowl.[11]

Despite welcoming such variations in the source, readers still place an emphasis on fidelity or continuity in the adaptations. This insistence can be traced to adaptations being viewed by many who would never read the comic book, and thus a film is an opportunity for fans to display the merits of their devotion to the wider community. Furthermore, fans realize that in comics the green Hulk will reappear and that Bruce Wayne will eventually return as Batman.[12] However, a film version of a comic book becomes the definitive version for a wide sector of society, heightening fan investment in maintaining continuity. Will Brooker identified this trend in the 1989 *Batman* film:

Tim Burton's Batman . . . was not an "Elseworld" story of what could possibly have happened. It was not one narrative among the many which appear in comics every month. It was *Batman: The Movie*, a supposedly definitive representation, and the world was watching it. Tim Burton's Batman had become, as far as the wider audience was concerned, "the" Batman, and all the movie's idiosyncrasies and infidelities to the comic text—the sex life, the stocky Joker, the skinny Bruce—were now considered gospel in the eyes of the viewing public. (*Batman Unmasked* 293)

Evidently, fans want the film adaptation to best represent the "essence" of the source, an ephemeral notion, but a desire nonetheless.[13] Thus, when the camp crusader of Joel Schumacher's *Batman & Robin* became the most widely seen version of Batman, readers were unsurprisingly irate. Although producers may have ignored fans in the past, in the digital age they have been forced to recognize how this once powerless elite now has the ability to mobilize others.

The vast majority of the fans surveyed for this study attended the earliest screening. For instance, of the seven people who were at the first showing of *Green Lantern*, which was a lunchtime presentation in 3D, five described themselves as comic book fans. By comparison, a 2D screening held just one hour later saw the percentage of fans decline to 45 percent. This drop-off continued with only 22 percent of the audience being made up of fans five days after the initial release. Such findings suggest that despite premium prices and inconvenient schedules, fans are determined to attend the earliest, if not the first, screening. As Jenkins notes (*Textual Poachers* 76), from lettercols to websites, fans are more inclined to listen to their peers rather than publicity material regarding the quality of an upcoming work. The desire to interact with the fan community partly accounts for early fan attendance, as they are eager to "demonstrate the 'timeliness' and responsiveness of their devotion" (Hills *Fan Cultures* 178). The precipitous box-office drops of adaptations such as *Jonah Hex* (Hayward 2010), *Hulk* (Lee 2003), and *Watchmen* (Snyder 2009) is attributable to front-loaded fan attendance and the failure of these films to fully engage a non-fan audience. The box office for *Green Lantern* experienced a similar decline of 66.1 percent in its second week of release.

Thus, while the early attendance of enthusiasts can lead to healthy opening weekend grosses, these first audience members are also in a position to limit a box-office run though negative word of mouth. Online fan discourse can be particularly potent. The audience research demonstrated an unsurprising correlation between mainstream filmgoers and Internet use, with 57 percent of non-fans citing the Internet as one of the sources from which they get their film information, and 25 percent identifying it as their number one source (more than any other format). Therefore, online non-fan filmgoers, who may make up the mainstream audience, are in a position to become aware of negative online opinion. Such discourses do not stop at digital boundaries, as Ben Fritz reported back in 2004: "Net-savvy marketing execs note that the mainstream media often picks up on the chatter." Fritz describes how *Gigli* (Brest 2003) became the "subject of horrific online buzz" turning it into "a national joke," while comic book adaptation *Hellboy* (del Toro 2004) exceeded expectations "thanks in part to enthusiastic online fans" ("Net Heads"). Thus, fan debate, whether positive or negative, has the potential to proliferate beyond fan forums, particularly since the advent of the Web.

Applying the Shannon-Weaver model of communication to the comic book industry, Duncan and Smith discuss "amplification" of the original source:[14]

> This amplification usually occurs among two or more people who have read the same comic book, but it is also possible for a reader to relate portions of the comic book message to someone who has not encountered it firsthand. The significance of this amplification is that the final meaning that resides with a receiver might be the product of both the reading itself and the discussion that followed, or, in the case of secondhand receivers, it could be the product solely of the discussion. (13)

It is these "secondhand receivers" that give power to fan discourse, with no familiarity with the source they will propagate fan opinion, often considered expert, thereby giving the firsthand receivers wider influence. For instance, 65 percent of non-fans surveyed considered it "moderately" (30 percent), "very" (21 percent), or "extremely important" (14 percent) that "a film is faithful (i.e., matches) the comic book." This response is somewhat surprising given that few of these respondents had, according to their surveys, ever read the comic books on which the films were based. However, comments such as, "It is disappointing to fans of books/comics to see the story they love is changed," suggest that non-fan audiences value fidelity, perhaps reflecting on a film adaptation of a text they had enjoyed.

Indeed, many of the responses tally with the "constellation of substratal prejudices" that Robert Stam believes fuel "the intuitive sense of adaptation's inferiority" ("Introduction" 4) including: seniority ("comic book was the original"), anti-corporeality ("Too many comic book heroes are portrayed differently onscreen as to what may be imagined by comic book readers"), and parasitism ("I don't believe films should be made more 'Hollywood friendly' to sell more tickets"). One non-fan response even seemed to be attempting to include as many of the "moralistic" (Stam "Introduction" 3) terms that surround adaptation criticism as possible, with "credibility, truthfulness, proper building of character, authenticity" included in a litany of complaints.

Non-fans regularly cited fans when addressing the importance of fidelity in a series of comments that mixed altruism with a growing recognition of fan power. For instance, one non-fan considered it "extremely important" that *The Adventures of Tintin* (Spielberg 2011) matched its source in order "to get those who read the comics to view the movie and trust that a sequel will be as good." Similar comments from non-fans included, "Comic book movies should be made with fans of comics in mind," "[Fidelity is] important to those who are long-term fans, so not to be disappointed [*sic*]," and "For a true fan it needs to stay true to the books."

For their part, fans have also displayed a confidence in their greater influence, with many pointing to the role of fans when discussing the importance of fidelity. For instance, a 26–30-year-old female fan who had never read *Thor* stated that fidelity was still "very important" in order "to keep the fans happy." Other fan comments that drew a connection between fidelity and the fan community included: "[*The Adventures of Tintin*] is using the same name of a brand that is associated with a specific type of story. The brand attracts the fans"; "people appreciated the comic book first"; and "to appease the fans of the comic."

Furthermore, fans have displayed a confidence in the power of online trends to shape a film, with 68 percent believing that "filmmakers follow online trends and discussions" (no—11 percent; don't know—21 percent), with half of the fans confident these online discussions influence how the film is made (no—26 percent; don't know—24 percent).[15] When asked to qualify "how," respondents on both sides of the fan divide cited *Snakes on a Plane* (Ellis)—the 2006 film was described by Kristin Thompson as a "fan-generated phenomenon" when it "became an object of obsession on many unofficial websites" (183). Building on online interest, *Snakes on a Plane* was partially reshot prior to release to incorporate online discussions, prompting respondents in this survey to describe the film as "proof of a fan driven plot line" and an "obvious example, fans wrote the dialogue." Other examples of online discussion shaping productions provided by fans include: the influence of writer/director Kevin Smith's Twitter account and the "rectified" Star Wars sequels that removed Jar Jar Binks, with one fan equating mid-shoot changes to *The Lord of the Rings* to the control that fans wield over comic book adaptations: "Some films pander to fanboys i.e. Superhero films, and Peter Jackson altered some scenes in Return of the King due to online criticism (Sauron fighting Aragon)."

Such examples fuel a genuine belief among many fans, and some mainstream filmgoers, that online discussion can shape film production, a belief that partly explains why fans are so ardent in their online criticisms of planned adaptations. Mainstream audiences also value fidelity, or at least the idea of it. Thus, when negative, fidelity-centric opinion is amplified beyond the boundaries of fandom it has the potential to sway sections of the mainstream audience—a development that has had far-reaching consequences on film production and promotion, as the following sections will demonstrate.

Participation and "Good Misinformation"

In an unassuming moment, buried on the DVD rerelease of *X-Men*, the film's producer Ralph Winter is recorded giving a preproduction set tour to members of 20th Century Fox's publicity department. Winter pauses the tour to recall an incident in which a fan snuck onto the set and read a manufacturer's label "Laser" from one of the wall coverings. The trespassing enthusiast incorrectly deduced that there would be a laser in the film, information the fan eagerly put online. Describing the incident, Winter explains, "The kid comes back after the workmen are gone, goes past the yellow tape, and looks inside of a box and he sees, 'Laser! They're putting a laser in here,'" to which the marketing representatives replied, "That's the good misinformation you want" ("X-Men: Production Scrapbook"). *X-Men* was produced when the current comic book adaptation trend and (to a lesser extent) Internet fandom were still in their infancy. Nonetheless, this interaction hinted at a wider shift that would soon take place in Hollywood filmmaking. Rather than adopting the protectionist stance prevalent at the time, the producer and publicists recognized the widespread benefits of online fandom, where even misinformation could be considered "good."[16]

In his 2000 book, *Batman Unmasked*, Will Brooker described comic books as one of the "few media forms in the late 1990s whose creators regularly choose to participate in an informal online forum, discussing their own work and treating their critics as peers; where the gap between author and fan, in short, is still so narrow" (266). At a time when Schumacher described fans as a "cult" and studios leaned toward protectionism rather than collaboration, Brooker's assessment was accurate. However, the comic book industry successfully sustained a dedicated fan base by facilitating fan discourse and loosening the boundaries between creator and fan. As the number of comic book film adaptations increased, the film industry began to employ similar tactics for adaptations and beyond.

When I interviewed Stan Lee for *Superhero Movies* in 2008, I asked the former Marvel Comics editor if cinema audiences lose out on the sense of community that comic readers enjoy, to which he replied, "Oh absolutely, but I think nobody has found a way to duplicate that sort of thing in movies yet. I don't even know if they're thinking of it." But filmmakers, some of whom rose through the ranks of fandom themselves, were often the first to understand how to accommodate their fans/peers and recreate this sense of community. For instance, *Variety* reported in 2004 that comic book adaptation directors Guillermo del Toro and Bryan Singer, as well as fan-turned-film director Kevin Smith, were the "biggest advocates" of fan sites. The article also describes how the *Hellboy* production company "took a largely hands-off approach to the management of fan site publicity, letting Del Toro converse directly with the sites and provide exclusive images and info" (Fritz "Net Heads"). Following the example of Peter Jackson, who effectively engaged with his source material's fan base during the production of *The Lord of the Rings* (2001–2003), *Superman Returns* (2006) director Bryan Singer liaised with the fan site *BlueTights.net* for his comic book adaptation (K. Thompson 164). The information provided to these key fan sites was often picked up by other websites and blogs, with interest proliferating through online communities and beyond.

Eventually, the rest of the world joined these more participatory networks, with the term "Web 2.0" coined in 2004 by journalist Tim O'Reilly to describe this transition. However, the concept of Web 2.0 has been criticized by many, including World Wide Web inventor Tim Berners-Lee, who suggests that the Web has always been "about connecting people" (Anderson). Similarly, Tom Brevoort identified antecedents for today's participatory culture in comic book fandom:

> I think comics have a long history of it, going back to the days when it was just Stan Lee writing Bullpen Bulletins, letters pages and so forth, and making that a very personal interaction between himself and the Marvel bullpen and the readers. So it's something that we're steeped in as a subculture, but as the technology has become so ubiquitous, everybody else is doing it as well.

Indeed, despite his earlier reservations, Lee has found a way to "duplicate" the sense of community that comic book fans previously only enjoyed in their native medium. In regular Twitter posts, he equates social media with his earlier practices: "Years ago, during my halcyon days at Marvel, I wrote a column 'Stan's Soapbox' in order to establish a friendly rapport with our fans. Though I long ago passed the Marvel mantle of head honcho to others, tweeting with you gives me the same warm feeling that my Soapbox did." Thus, film executives, publicity departments, and filmmakers, who had initially greeted online fandom with trepidation, acknowledged its benefits, and as *Variety* reported in 2004, they began "embracing the opportunity to master a new, and relatively cheap, tool" (Fritz "Net Heads"). Nonetheless, comic books, their adaptations, and fans were at the vanguard of this transition.

To service this more inclusionary approach to film promotion, studios annexed one of the primary forums of traditional comic book fandom: the comic convention. In an era when lettercols and fanzines have been usurped by more immediate digital equivalents, this long-standing tradition has not only resisted replacement, but has seen its influence amplified. Science fiction conventions, popular since the 1940s, had traditionally offered a subsection for comic book fans. However, with the emergence of a more organized comic book community in the 1960s, dedicated conventions began to appear, such as the fan-organized New York Comic-Con in 1964. Conventions not only provided an occasion for fans to meet in person, but, like other aspects of fan culture, they diminished the gap between creator and consumer through panel discussions, autograph sessions, and opportunities to have professional artists assess your work.[17]

The popularity of comic book conventions has increased in recent years. For instance, North America's leading convention, the San Diego Comic-Con, has seen its attendance swell. In 1970, the inaugural year, the event attracted 300 attendees. However, since then numbers have steadily increased, prompting the convention to move to the 57,200 square-meter San Diego Convention Center in 1991 (Malloy). Despite the convention center's size, Comic-Con passes have sold out every year since 2007, with many suggesting that the event should be moved to cities with larger venues, such as Las Vegas or Anaheim (L. Thompson).

Two complementary factors could be attributed to the rise in popularity of comic book conventions: the successful adaptation of comic book content to other mainstream media, and the increased exposure these events have received in the digital age. Today, comic book adaptations and other films have a considerable presence at comic conventions. The benefit to filmmakers is much the same as comic book publishers. As Peter Coogan, the organizer of the Comics Arts Conference notes, "being able to expose tens of thousands of motivated and interested people to a film—whether in the planning, production, or release stage—and flatter them with inside information, advance footage, and the opportunity to meet the film's stars and creative personnel makes Comic-Con an economical way of producing buzz among the people most likely to buy tickets and promote the film to their friends and on the Web" (6). Thus, as the major comic book publishers are reorganized as mini-Disneys, comic conventions become the equivalent of Disneyland, providing devotees with an opportunity to come together in a real-world location and express their interest, while the producers can consolidate their fan base and further extend their reach.

However, it should be noted, that the presence of film productions at comic conventions is not a recent phenomenon. When interviewed for this study, Michael E. Uslan took the credit for bringing the first major motion picture adaptation to a comic convention, when he announced *Batman* at the 1980 New York Comic-Con—an event he first attended as a seventh grader in 1964. As Uslan explains:

To be able to announce my lifelong dream project of a dark and serious Batman movie, a major motion picture, at a comic book convention to the fans, and be able to communicate to them, with Bob Kane and the president of DC Comics, that "we're doing this for you because we're doing it for me, and I'm one of you" was important. When I said, "This movie is not going to be about Batman, it's going to be about 'The' Batman," they understood the coded language and they went crazy.

However, as the 1989 release of *Batman* approached, growing fan dissatisfaction over what was perceived to be a humorous adaptation led to Warner Bros. representatives being booed at conventions (K. Hughes), with their posters torn down (Bullock). While conventions have proven to be a breeding ground for fan discontent, they can also generate positive word of mouth. A suitably dark *Batman* trailer was quickly prepared to "stop the negative rumour mill" ("Shadows of the Bat") and allay concerns. Soon after, positive hype permeated through the various fan forums including conventions, where bootleg copies of the trailer were sold for $25 ("Shadows of the Bat").

This convention-fueled word of mouth has been amplified since the advent of the Web and other digital technologies, heightening awareness and interest in these events. Many recent comic book-based film and television programs cite early attention generated by convention screenings and panels for their popularity when released. Recalling his experience, *Iron Man* (2008) director Jon Favreau explained, "With all this stuff like Twitter and everyone with their little blogs and their conversations in real time, people knew about 'Iron Man' before that panel was out at Comic-Con because people were there on their laptops. So that's incredible. That's grass roots. That's mobilizing" (Huver). In fact, videos from that panel, including the earliest footage from the film, were quickly posted on video-sharing sites such as YouTube to widespread acclaim. Thus, where once a trailer was bootlegged and traded among convention attendees, now the hype generated by early footage can extend far beyond the convention floor.[18]

With the Web amplifying the reach of fan discourse, these events have become centrally important to the marketing campaigns of not just adaptations, but many mainstream films. Today, Hollywood productions regularly organize their publicity strategies around these inclusive, collaborative events. For instance, non-comic book derived films that had a presence at the 2013 San Diego Comic-Con included: *Godzilla* (Edwards 2014), *The Hunger Games: Catching Fire* (Lawrence 2013), *Escape Plan* (Håfström 2013), *Ender's Game* (Hood 2013), and *Divergent* (Burger 2014). As Brevoort noted, "There's been much greater overlap between these events that started as solely comic book events and bigger media events . . . it's a way to tap into a really hardcore, mainstream following that [producers] can capitalize on, whatever their show or their product happens to be."[19] Thus, even though convention attendees are still only a tiny fraction of the expected audience for these films, these fan events have become drops that create digital ripples, piquing fan and mainstream interests.

As the channels and forums of comic book fandom are annexed by conglomerates hoping to exploit this newly identified resource, further strategies have been developed to meet expectations and mollify concerns. Pustz notes how in the 1960s Marvel was successful at fostering the idea that "fans—as editors in absentia—and professionals were creating the comics together" (167). Similarly, the Golden Age of Comic Book Filmmaking has seen Hollywood attempting to recreate a semblance of comic book fandom's collaborative spirit.

Returning to the Shannon-Weaver model, Duncan and Smith discuss feedforward, where messages about new comic books are "sent from the source to some of the receivers" (9), enabling the reader to influence the comic ahead of publication. This type of feedforward is now regularly practiced in the production of comic book adaptations, as filmmakers hoping to keep the online community engaged will circulate teaser images, plot outlines, and casting decisions via the Web, conventions, and other fan forums, with responses fluctuating based on the released material.

Filmmakers even began to acknowledge the impact that this feedforward had on their in-production films. Discussing the "deleted scenes" on the *Scott Pilgrim* (2010) DVD, director/co-writer Edgar Wright explains that he began writing the screenplay in 2006, before Bryan Lee O'Malley had finished the comic book series. Consequently, the adaptation's original ending, Scott reigniting his relationship with ex-girlfriend Knives Chau, differed from the eventual comic where Scott finally won Ramona, the girl he had been fighting for across six books. However, as detailed on the DVD, Wright went back and reshot the ending to match the source, explaining, "When I read . . . the ending of the book I knew it was what we should do." Wright partly attributes this change to the fans he was in contact with through test screenings, fan forums, and social networking:

> I remember once after a screening . . . looking on Twitter and seeing that people had been tweeting about it, and there was this one girl, whose name was Nicole, and she said something like, "Scott Pilgrim was unspeakably awesome, but it breaks my heart to tell Edgar Wright that he needs to do a new ending," and when we did the new ending, I messaged that girl back and said, "You got your wish," and then she came to see it at Comic-Con.

This is a vivid example of how some filmmakers are engaged with fan discourse, and that feedforward can occasionally enable these fans to shape the film—often resulting in more faithful adaptations.[20]

When asked to qualify why they believed online discussions impact upon how the film is made, a number of respondents to this study's audience research pointed to test screenings in comments such as, "In a similar way that focus groups or preview audiences affect the final edit." These remarks were echoed by many of the interviewed industry professionals, with writer Joe Kelly suggesting that "the fan base, and the vocal aspect of it, has an influence on certain studio executives and development people. I think they use it as a research tool." Similarly, ahead of the production of *The Green Hornet* (Gondry 2011), writer Evan Goldberg described how he and his co-writer/star Seth Rogen went to Comic-Con to "feel it out." Ultimately, Goldberg realized that the property was not well known and that they were free to create a looser adaptation.

Steve Niles described how the serialized nature of his comics has enabled him to respond to fan discourse, "because if a fan is bitching to me about something in a current issue, I can do something in the upcoming issues to make them even madder or fix it." As comic book adaptations become franchises, a measure of this back-and-forth can be discerned in the films, with fan discourse shaping the progression of a series and even compelling reboots. For instance, the sharp contrast between the adaptations of Marvel Comics' the Hulk, ranging from Ang Lee's more melodramatic *Hulk* to the more faithful *The Incredible Hulk*, was linked to fan activity by Gale Ann Hurd, the producer of both films. Hurd noted in an interview that the earlier film was "not the Hulk everyone expects to see from having read the comics," adding of the more recent film, "This version *is* the Hulk that people know. And I think, from reading the [message] boards I read when I can't sleep at night, that the fans are happy about that" (De Semlyen 66). Here, the film's producer demonstrates how she engages with online discussion, and how the desire to placate these long-standing fans partly motivated the move away from the more individualistic earlier effort to an in-continuity adaptation. Thus, just like the episodic texts of the comics, fans have shown the ability to influence ongoing franchises.

Fans-turned-filmmakers such as Edgar Wright seemed to come by these collaborative strategies honestly. However, a more participatory era created a wider imperative that all media become more interactive or "run the risk of losing the most active and passionate consumers to some other media interest that is more tolerant" (Jenkins *Convergence Culture* 137–38). Thus, while producers recognized the benefits of engaging with fan forums, they still sought to maintain traditional divides. For instance, Jonathan Gray describes how producers will often try to corral fan activity into "policed playgrounds" such as "fan sites that invite various forms of fan paratextual creativity and user-generated content, yet often imposing a set of rules and limitations and/ or claiming legal rights over the material" (165). Similarly, the interest generated by non-profit, fan-run events like the San Diego Comic-Con has seen some studios attempting to replicate the experience, but in a format that can be more tightly controlled. For instance, in 2009 the Walt Disney Company introduced the D23 fan club, with a biennial expo held at Anaheim. The event follows the format of other conventions with panels, early screenings, and an exhibition floor, but with a focus on Disney properties, including those that traditionally would have been prominently placed at the San Diego Comic-Con. Accordingly, there was no dedicated Marvel Studios panel at the 2011 San Diego Comic-Con, but the D23 Expo, held one month later, featured early footage from *The Avengers*.

Other policed playgrounds might include *The Amazing Spider-Man* Face of the Fan contest, which Sony Pictures Entertainment ran to promote the franchise reboot (Webb 2012). The prize-winner would become the "face of the fan" at Comic-Con, and "have the opportunity to meet the talent and filmmakers and conduct an interview with them." The competition was described as an "initiative that lets moviegoers and TV viewers get involved with Sony Pictures' projects by participating in online casting calls and contests—turning today's fans into tomorrow's stars" ("The Amazing Spider-Man—Face of the Fan"). Released the same summer as *The Amazing Spider-Man*, *The Dark Knight Rises* (Nolan 2012) also used a number of strategies to suggest that the audience was a part of the filmmaking process. For instance, the voices of "hundreds of thousands" of fans were crowdsourced by the film's composer Hans Zimmer and collected into a chant that reappeared across the film's soundtrack. Zimmer described the process in terms reminiscent of comic book lettercols: "I thought it would be something nice, if our audiences could actually be part of the making of the movie and be participants in this" (Radish). These collaborative strategies fuel a genuine feeling among fans that they are collaborators, with studios hoping to parlay that engagement into box-office success. Nowhere is this active fan base more important than in film promotion.

Whether it is the changed ending of *Scott Pilgrim* or a more "Hulk Smash" version of the Marvel Comics character, where fans have been found to shape a production it has generally resulted in greater continuity with the source. Responding to this pressure, studios have adopted a number of fan-appeasing promotional tactics that emphasize fidelity. Traditionally, comic book film adaptations had endeavored to transcend or diminish their oft-maligned source in publicity material. At a time when other big-budget films indicated

FIG. 3.2 The theatrical poster for *Scott Pilgrim vs. The World* mirrored the opening image of the graphic novel. Early promotional material for *The Walking Dead* television series signaled fidelity by contrasting the actors with their comic book counterparts.

their status as adaptations (e.g., *Jaws* was marketed as: "The terrifying motion picture from the terrifying No. 1 best seller"), *Superman: The Movie* (Donner 1978) was released with the poster taglines: "You'll Believe a Man Can Fly!" and "The movie that makes a legend come to life." However, as faithful comic book-based films championed by digitally connected fans began to exceed box-office expectations, comic book adaptations started to overtly signal their status as *comic book* adaptations.

Where once the tagline for *Superman: The Movie* promised the "legend comes to life," the promotion for *Ghost World* (Zwigoff 2001) claimed the "underground comic book comes to life." *Ghost World* was the first of these new adaptations to signal its source fidelity/continuity. Since its release, the promotional materials for many comic book adaptations have relied on their source as a marketing point. The poster for *American Splendor* (Springer Berman and Pulcini 2003) proclaimed, "At last, a comic book hero we can all relate to!"; the trailer for *The Spirit* (Miller 2008) alerted filmgoers that it was "based upon the comic book series by Will Eisner"; and the *30 Days of Night* (Slade 2007) trailer ensured potential audiences knew it was "based on the ground-breaking graphic novel"—a decision Steve Niles attributed to the studio. The prominence of the source in promoting modern adaptations is also evident in the intertextual referencing used to publicize these films, with the poster for *300* (Snyder 2007) alerting audiences that it was "from the creator of 'Sin City.'"

More recently, *The Losers* (White 2010), *Scott Pilgrim*, and television series *The Walking Dead* (Darabont 2010) are typical of this strategy of engaging fans and building a core audience with promotional material that displays comic book continuity, with *The Walking Dead* going so far as to contrast images of the show's stars with their comic book counterparts in early posters. The explicit citation of the source material in paratextual materials is tantamount to the "tacit contract" ("Film Genre" 691) that Thomas Schatz describes in genre films, in that the publicity suggests certain expectations the audience should have and that the adaptation will meet—a fidelity contract.

Publicity for better-known characters rarely uses such explicit taglines or comic book images, but still often includes signifiers that suggest a comic book adaptation for the uninitiated. For instance, in the audience research 81 percent of non-fans knew that *Thor* (Branagh 2011), *Green Lantern,* and *The Adventures of Tintin* were based on comics. When asked to qualify how they knew, the most frequent replies included "having previously collected comics"; "word-of-mouth"; and "adaptations" and "parodies" such as the television sitcom *The Big Bang Theory* (Lorre and Prady 2007) and *Adventures in Baby-sitting* (Columbus 1987). Perhaps most interestingly, many cited advertising despite none of these films' promotional material explicitly mentioning comics. Yet the publicity did include markers that suggested their source.

As discussed in the previous chapter, the first teaser poster for *Thor* included a color pop that echoed the promotion of *Sin City* (Rodriguez 2005), *The Spirit*, and other adaptations. Furthermore, it should be unsurprising that despite its mythological setting half of non-fan filmgoers expected *Thor* to be like *Iron Man* as that earlier success was cited in taglines throughout the film's promotion. The presence of the Marvel logo emerging from comic book images in trailers also reaffirmed the film's source, with one respondent even expecting *Green Lantern* "to follow the general Marvel Genre."

While the publicity for better-known characters tends to suggest the source rather than explicitly cite it, they often convey fidelity through more subtle references. For instance, much like the Tintin cover discussed in the previous chapter, one year prior to the release of *Iron Man* an exclusive cover image of the character was provided to popular British film magazine *Empire*. Although for mainstream audiences this was little more than a promotional

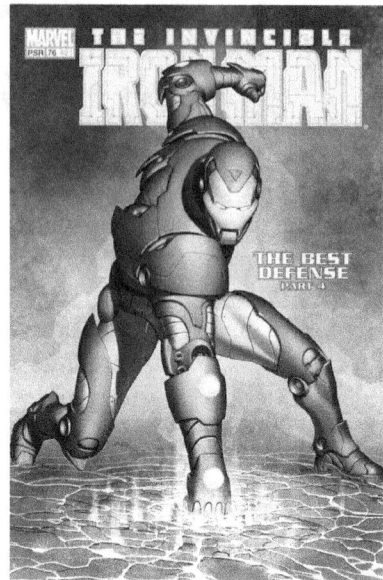

FIG. 3.3 Adi Granov's celebrated cover for *Iron Man* #76 (March 2004), which was reworked for British film magazine *Empire* (September 2007).

image, fans would have recognized it as a reworking of artist Adi Granov's celebrated cover for *Iron Man* #76 (March 2004). Thus, the image served a dual function: targeting mainstream audiences through a general interest publication, while reassuring fans of fidelity. As Jonathan Gray points out "paratexts regularly address the non-fan, even when attached to fan properties" (17).

Through this oblique reference to Granov, the *Empire* cover not only suggested fidelity to fans, but also the approval of a well-regarded creator, with Granov also accompanying the filmmakers at key events such as the 2006 San Diego Comic-Con. Such creator approval was rarely sought or signaled prior to the Golden Age of Comic Book Filmmaking. For instance, Gordon et al. suggest that "in the modern blockbuster film era, which roughly dates from *Superman* (1978) . . . motion picture creative personnel use comic book texts and comic book authorial intention in an attempt to add authenticity to comic book films" (viii). Yet there was little evidence of this "comic book authorial intention" in pre-2000 adaptations. As noted, *Superman: The Movie* barely acknowledged the comics, and it was only after a failed lawsuit and mounting pressure from high-ranking comic book professionals that Warner Bros. credited Jerry Siegel and Joe Schuster as the creators of the character on the comic book page and film adaptation.[21]

In the years since the release of *Superman: The Movie*, however, the graphic novel, along with other more individualistic work, saw a greater emphasis placed on the creators of comic books, first by fans and then by the industry.

When producing *Batman*, Warner Bros. attempted to achieve "authorial intention" by hiring creator Bob Kane as a consultant. A promotional documentary at the time of the film's release highlighted Kane's place as a beacon of fidelity, "an expert whose interpretations couldn't be disputed was hired as a consultant to the film, he is Batman creator Bob Kane" (*Batman Documentary*). Yet Kane's endorsement was more than "disputed," with an article from the *Wall Street Journal* noting, "The fans remain skeptical" (K. Hughes), as many suggested Kane was simply a corporate shill.

Under today's fan-targeting strategies, authorial intent is frequently emphasized in publicity. For instance, comic book creators regularly contribute to publicity material, with artists Tim Bradstreet, Mike Mignola, Dave Gibbons, and Jock creating posters for adaptations of their books *The Punisher* (Hensleigh 2004), *Hellboy*, *Watchmen*, and *The Losers*. Similarly, the citation of creators such as Frank Miller and Will Eisner in promotional materials, as well as Stan Lee's trademark cameo in Marvel adaptations, reinforces the importance of the creator and suggests greater fidelity. Furthermore, each film adapted from the properties of North America's largest comic book publishers, Marvel and DC Comics, open with the company's logo materializing from comic book images.[22] These comic book logos also appear before trailers and TV spots leaving little ambiguity about the source of the adaptation and further emphasizing authorial intent.

With the emergence of Web 2.0, participation became commonplace across many media forms. Comic books and their fans were uniquely suited to film production strategies that could be described as collaborative: they were a preexisting fan base with participatory experience; the presence of an urtext provided fans with a criterion to which they could compare the in-production film; and, as many of these films led to long-running series, there were numerous opportunities for fans to shape and reshape the story between installments. Although the film industry was initially resistant to fan activity, they began to recognize the benefits of an engaged fan base and started to provide them with spaces, often policed, for interactivity. Furthermore, producers sought to engender the goodwill of fans with promotional materials that emphasized fidelity. Consequently, fan-generated word of mouth began to permeate through fan channels and beyond. Although filmmakers might be characterized as kowtowing to a digitally empowered minority, the willingness of fans to act as an "unlimited press corps" has validated such actions.[23]

Power and Responsibility

When interviewed for this study, Michael E. Uslan and Mark Waid described comic book fans as "winning," because they now have their voices heard by previously protectionist industries. This period might be characterized as mutually beneficial for producers and fans with comic book devotees more heavily involved in production, while the eventual films achieve record-breaking grosses. However, behind the excited rhetoric and inclusionary terms, there are hints that this era may not be so democratic, and that its long-term ramifications could prove problematic.

Glen Creeber notes how an increasing number of critics consider participatory culture to be a "myth," with many arguing that the "participatory nature of New Media has been over-inflated to such an extent that people now refuse to see its limitations" (20). Similarly, Matt Hills identifies a recent trend in academia of challenging the leveling dream of Web 2.0 optimists and reinstating the "cultural divide between professional textual production and amateur work" ("Web 2.0" 144). Taking an example from the comic book adaptation trend, numerous news sources reported that in the hour following the announcement that one-time Daredevil Ben Affleck had been cast as Batman, 71 percent of related tweets were negative (Hayden). However, this widespread criticism had no obvious impact on the production, with Affleck remaining in the role. As Jenkins frequently points out, within convergence culture, "everyone's a participant—although participants may have different degrees of status and influence" (*Convergence Culture* 136–37). Thus, producers and rights holders can ultimately decide to ignore or even hinder fan attempts to shape a text.

Sometimes producers will go beyond disregarding fans to actively critiquing their activities. For instance, while the popular press has often depicted comic book fans as "oddly fixated and thus deservedly marginalized" (Duncan and Smith 173), such representations can also be found across texts with large fan followings. Since his season two introduction, *The Simpsons* character "Comic Book Guy" has been a way for the show's writers to parody their fan base's intense interest. This criticism became more pointed in later seasons, explicitly criticizing how fans wield their online power. For example, the twenty-first season premiere, "Homer the Whopper" (Rogen and Goldberg 2009), saw the Comic Book Guy using the Web to sabotage an unfaithful adaptation of the comic book *Everyman*, which he had created. In a similar storyline from the second season of the HBO series *Entourage* (Ellin and Farino 2005), actor Vincent Chase must first seek approval from fan site webmaster R. J. Spencer (a parody of Harry Knowles) before he can be cast as the hero in a big-budget Aquaman adaptation. Similarly, superhero movies such as *Unbreakable* (Shyamalan 2000), *The Incredibles* (Bird 2004), and *The Amazing Spider-Man 2* (Webb 2014), as well as the episodes "Beware the Gray Ghost" (Kirkland 1992) and "Action" (Dries 2007) from the popular shows *Batman: The Animated Series* and *Smallville*, respectively, feature fans whose obsessive tendencies have led them to villainous extremes. Hills, citing Derek Johnson, labels such representations "fan-tagonism," and sees them as "attempts at rein- scribing professional/amateur or producer/fan binaries" ("Web 2.0" 146).

The mercenary tactics of some fans no doubt fuel this fantagonism. Jenkins describes how the "expectation of timeliness complicates the global expansion of the fan community, with time lags in the distribution of cultural goods across national markets hampering full participation from fans that will receive the same program months or even years later" (*Fans, Bloggers, and Gamers* 141). As is evident from the audience research, fans will attend an early screening of a comic book film adaptation, if not the first, in order to engage with the fan community. This desire for "full participation" may have contrib- uted to the rise in Internet piracy, as international fans, wanting to partake in fan discourse, illegally downloaded the products not yet available in their market. Film studios have combated this problem with wide international releases. For example, comic book adaptation *X2* (Singer) had the "biggest day-and-date international release ever" (B. Gray "'X2' Unites 3,741 Theaters") when it was released in 2003, thereby catering to an audience accustomed to getting their comics in the same twenty-four-hour period as their US equiva- lents, while the producers still retained control (and profits).

Where producers fail to reassert divides, they often attempt to channel fan activity into Jonathan Gray's "policed playgrounds" (165). For example, in his book *Batman Unmasked*, Brooker identifies many examples of the "author- guessing fad" from 1960s comics, in which devoted readers would make edu- cated deductions as to which writers and artists were responsible for the new stories credited to the character's original creator, Bob Kane (255). DC Comics fostered this investigative fandom before ending the "author-guessing fad" in 1968 by including bylines for the previously anonymous artists.

Comic book fans, who rarely recognize the boundaries between media, continued their investigative fandom into the film adaptations. The producers of *Batman* regularly remarked on the difficulties of making the adaptation with fans constantly attempting to glean information from the in-production film set. However, co-producer Chris Kenny more recently suggested that the resolve to uncover early information has increased since the advent of fan sites: "You [did] have people everywhere trying to take photographs of the Batmobile for the first time. You didn't have the Internet, with all the sites now that post everything" ("Beyond Batman: Building The Batmobile").

Transplanting their investigative and deductive skills to the digital arena, fans create websites that are a bricolage of known information, educated guesses, and rumor. Initially, filmmakers were resistant to intensive fan inter- est, but ultimately they sought to harness this enthusiasm for their own interests. This shift is evident in the promotion of comic book adaptations, with studios not only allowing investigative fandom, but also facilitating it. The effective viral marketing campaign for *The Dark Knight* required fans to solve online and real-world puzzles in order to gain access to teaser images and early trailers.[24] Essentially, the publicity for the film took the practices of normal comic book fan discourse and installed them in a studio-structured campaign that encouraged fans and garnered mainstream interest. However, Margret Rossman considers this viral marketing campaign as tantamount to the "culture industry" Adorno and Horkheimer describe in that, even though the fans are active, "they are still allowing their disruptive fan behaviour to be converted to industrial, focused, fan labour in service of the marketing cause" (73). As producers began to recognize the benefits of fandom there was always a risk that this new resource might be exploited.

Comic book sales have been in a steady decline since the 1950s, prompting the industry to increasingly rely on its core readership. Accordingly, publishers have employed a variety of strategies to keep fans engaged and spending. For instance, in 1965 Marvel advertised that it would be printing the names of its fan club members, the Merry Marvel Marching Society, in its monthly comics. However, as Pustz explains, "members would not be told in which title their names would appear, so 'half the fun will be trying to find' them. And, the ad admitted, 'if this keeps you buying all our titles regularly, that won't break our avaricious little hearts either!'" (55). Such strategies have been replicated today, with the *300* DVD including a section, "Be One of 300," in which director Zack Snyder thanks the online fans before a lengthy scroll of names appears. This move may have flattered fans' sense of themselves as collaborators, but it also would have compelled them to buy a copy of the DVD (if not a few). Leitch notes how the "extended DVD edition" of *The Return of the King* also attempted to position fans as participants by including the names of the franchise's fan club members over its credits, but "the actual contribution the films ask is the purchase of something—photographs, souvenirs, commentaries on Tolkien, and, of course, later editions of the films" (*Film Adaptation* 150).

While targeting the most avid consumers is a long-standing strategy of media industries, the Web has facilitated direct engagement that encourages fans while also exploiting them. Following the disappointing opening weekend box office of *Watchmen*, screenwriter David Hayter wrote an open letter, which appeared on a number of websites (e.g., *Rotten Tomatoes*, *Ain't It Cool News*, and *IMDB*). In the letter, he asked fans—whom he presumed had all seen the film during its opening weekend—that if they were planning on seeing the film twice, to go the second weekend ("You have to understand, everyone is watching to see how the film will do in its second week") when, traditionally, the core audience is exhausted and the mainstream appeal of the film can be quantified. The letter positions the filmmakers and audience

FIG. 3.4 *Watchmen* screenwriter David Hayter accosts comic book fans for not watching the adaptation multiple times in the satirical strip "Hayter-ade," from the website *Comics Critics!*

as equals in its appeal, even attempting to embolden fans: "Demonstrate the power of the fans, because it'll help let the people who pay for these movies know what we'd like to see" (Hayter).

It is difficult to gauge what impact Hayter's letter had on the box office, but many online commentators felt the burden of responsibility should be put back on the filmmakers and the film, with one post on *Ain't It Cool News* arguing, "It isn't the die hard fans [*sic*] job to make movies like this blockbusters. It's the people MAKING the movies job to create some thing compelling enough to get fans and NON-fans alike asses in the seats. Fans who like the movie WILL see it more than once. Beyond multiple viewing and perhaps talking it up (IF they liked it) it really falls on the material and those involved who MADE the movie to deliver" (Cowtrout). Hayter's letter demonstrated a belief, which many filmmakers now shared, in the "power of fans" to create a box-office success. It is this "power" that producers have spent the past two decades trying to understand, control, and eventually harness.

In the end, despite online interest, *Watchmen* failed to maintain its opening weekend box office, dropping far below the industry average from week one to week two, which is normally a strong indicator that the film failed to cross over beyond its core fan base.[25] Such examples suggest that producers may be overinvesting in this rabid fan base, as no matter how enthusiastic fans are, they are still a small section of an adaptation's intended audience. Snickars and Vonderau comment on this aspect of the Web in their introduction to *The YouTube Reader*. Citing digital anthropologist Mike Wesch, they describe the 90-9-1 rule: "90 percent of online audiences never interact, nine percent interact only occasionally, and one percent do most interacting" (12). Correspondingly, much online discourse around comic book adaptations is provided by a narrow, heavily invested subset of the audience: the fans.

As the box-office decline of *Watchmen* demonstrates, a strong online presence does not guarantee a successful release. For instance, the oft-cited *Snakes on a Plane* proved to be something of a false dawn for a more participatory type of mainstream filmmaking, as despite online hype the film underperformed, making producers and distributors nervous about placing so much emphasis on the power of fandom and online buzz.[26] Similar examples from the comic book adaptation trend include *Kick-Ass* (Vaughn 2010), *Scott Pilgrim*, and *Dredd* (Travis 2012), all of which had successful presentations at the San Diego Comic-Con, but as Brandon Gray notes, the "Comic-Con crowd is small but vociferous, often amplifying the buzz for movies like this far beyond the reality" ("Weekend Briefing"). Ultimately, each film underperformed relative to expectations, a disparity *Variety* reporter Brian Lowry describes as the "Comic-Con false positive."

Even before the Web, comic book enthusiasts were segmented from wider society with Pustz, citing Robert Bellah, describing the fan communities as "lifestyle enclaves" (21). This separation has only been exacerbated by the narrowcast mechanisms of the Web where users will more often gravitate towards like-minded groups. Thus, blogs, boards, and social media pages can often become the echo chambers that law professor Cass Sunstein believes "exaggerate whatever consensus emerged in the group" (Jenkins *Convergence Culture* 248). Thus, the comic book community in its efforts to maintain the integrity of the source can seem unduly fixated on Bat-nipples, the ethnicity of actors, and whether or not Thor is wearing his helmet. However, where once these arcane discussions would have been confined to the corners of a subculture, the greater interaction between producers and consumers saw filmmakers, often grudgingly, acquiescing to fan concerns.

For instance, when Joe Kelly described studios using fan forums as research tools, he noted that executives look to see "what do people care about? What don't they care about? . . . Organic web-shooters versus mechanical web-shooters is a good example." Kelly is describing the fan criticism that surrounded the use of organic web-shooters in the original Spider-Man trilogy, as opposed to the mechanical web-shooters of the comics. Such was the level of criticism that the franchise reboot, *The Amazing Spider-Man*, reinstated the mechanical web-shooters, a move the filmmakers attributed to fan pressure with director Marc Webb saying on the DVD commentary, "This, of course, is the famous mechanical web shooters, which I hope the fanboys appreciate." Examples of filmmakers responding to the demands of a narrow fan base prompted Grant Morrison to colorfully comment, "Soon film studios were afraid to move without the approval of the raging Internet masses. They represented only the most minuscule fraction of a percentage of the popular audience that gave a shit, but they were very remarkably, superhumanly angry, like the great head of Oz, and so very persistent that they could easily appear in the imagination as an all-conquering army of mean-spirited, judgmental fogies" (364).

A clear example of the "mean-spirited" comments Morrison describes emerged following the casting of actress Shailene Woodley as Spider-Man love interest and sometime-model Mary Jane for *The Amazing Spider-Man* sequel (Webb 2014). Many readers on the website *SuperHeroHype* suggested that the actress was not attractive enough to play the character, with typical comments on a story by Silas Lesnick including, "She kinda looks like she has the 'girl next door' look. But if memory serves me right MJ is an aspiring actress and, according to the comic, she is suppose [*sic*] to look like a model." While some commentators challenged these statements—"the misogynist nerd crew is out in force"—similar comments followed news (S. Perry) that the character, and therefore Woodley's scenes, would not be included in the final film: "no offense to the actress portraying mj but i [*sic*] couldn't imagine her walking down the catwalk at Paris fashion week." Some journalists in the popular press linked the decision to remove Woodley's scenes to fan criticism (Moodie). It remains to be seen if Woodley will still play the role in a later franchise installment, or if fan comments had any impact on the decision to remove the scenes. Nonetheless, that fan comments such as these were widely reported points to a disquieting trend in which members of this small, largely anonymous group are given undue visibility and possibly influence.

Comic book fans regularly blame studio executives for hampering adaptations. For instance, prior to the release of *X-Men: The Last Stand* (Ratner 2006) popular fan forum *Ain't It Cool News* attested, "You want to know who the main villain of X3 is going to be? [CEO of Fox Entertainment] Tom Rothman." In an open letter to "Tom Rothman and Fox Shareholders," the site described how Rothman hated the franchise and acted vindictively to sabotage the films (Moriarty). However, as fans gain greater sway over films, they could be criticized for the same "committee thinking" as the movie "suits" they demonize on their forums.

Conglomerates may have provided the policed playgrounds, but comic book fans often play the bullies, using their newfound power to harass anyone with the temerity to play with their toys and waiver from the source material. Somewhere between complaining about organic web-shooters and criticizing a young actress for not having the catwalk-ready looks of a two-dimensional drawing, some fans seem to have forgotten that with great power comes great responsibility. Consequently, any rounded study of the comic book adaptation needs to consider this important determinant. The following section will conclude this chapter by examining the manner in which the increased fidelity of comic book adaptations has led to the emergence of the first transformations, and how, even within borrowings like *Batman Begins*, the adaptation's source(s) and its fans have become a greater determinant.

From Borrowings to Transformations

Fans and the source materials they hold dear moved to the center of comic book film production in the early twenty-first century. Although studios were initially resistant, they eventually entered into an uneasy partnership with this active group. To appreciate this transition, this conclusion will chart how looser borrowings gave way to transformations, and how, for the fans at least, Batman finally began.

In 1978, when Superman was first adapted to a feature-length film, the character was already, as promotional material for the film would frequently assert, a "legend." However, unlike his comic book adventures, Superman did not escape his original form in a "single bound," but rather through a series of interpretations. In the forty years since the character's first appearance in *Action Comics* #1 (June 1938), the Man of Steel had been adapted into every-thing from movie serials to moccasins, achieving the status of popular myth along the way.[27] In *Superman: The Movie*, this first god of a new mythology would finally realize his potential, or at least that is what the voiceover for an early trailer suggested: "He has come of age, our age. Superman brings you the gift of flight. Superman is now the movie."

Comic books were rarely acknowledged in the promotion for *Superman: The Movie*, with publicity instead suggesting that the film would be adapting the larger Superman legend. As a long-running character with many interpre-tations on the comic book page and in other media, Superman is a particularly potent example of this type of creative collage. For instance, in the twelve-part miniseries *Superman: Birthright*, writer Mark Waid updated the hero's ori-gin by drawing on a number of different versions of the character. As Waid explained when interviewed, "There's a long history with Superman of taking from other media, Jimmy Olsen and Perry White were radio characters before becoming comic characters. [The creators] realized very early on that it's a modern myth and that you can take and choose pieces." As Waid suggests, the Superman myth had been lent inflections by various forms including radio programs, film serials, and television shows. The 1978 adaptation held no ver-sion in higher regard, ignoring chronological precedence. Thus, *Superman: The Movie* would be defined by Andrew as a "borrowing," as the character was so heavily adapted it had transcended its original form and achieved the status of "myth" (*Film Theory* 98).[28] In the post-*X-Men* boom, however, loose adaptations such as *Superman: The Movie* would be tempered, as comics were positioned as the urtext and fidelity treated as a marker of quality.

The increased fidelity that characterizes recent adaptations is perhaps most evident by the emergence of comic book transformations. Andrew contends that the success of borrowings such as *Superman: The Movie* "rests on the issue of their fertility not their fidelity" (*Film Theory* 99). However, the 2005 graphic novel adaptation *Sin City* signaled the emergence of the first comic book transformations. Describing this category, Andrew writes, "Here we have a clear-cut case of film trying to measure up to a literary work, or of an audience expecting to make such a comparison" (*Film Theory* 100). As discussed, *Sin City* did not just adopt the loose premise of Frank Miller's comic book, but strived for narrative and visual fidelity at every turn, with director Robert Rodriguez stating he wanted to "make the cinematic equivalent" of the graphic novels.[29]

While comic book adaptations had made use of specific story elements in the past (e.g., *Ghost World*, *Road to Perdition*, and *American Splendor*), no film had diligently recreated the characters, plot, and dialogue of a comic book like *Sin City*. Most strikingly, Rodriguez utilized digital backlot technology, previously applied with little commercial success in *Sky Captain and the World of Tomorrow* (Conran 2004), to "translate the way [Miller] drew, right to the screen" (*Sin City* DVD commentary). A faithful comic aesthetic had been attempted by previous adaptations—for instance, Michael Cohen believes that *Dick Tracy* (Beatty 1990) was at the time of its release "the most meticulous effort to capture the aesthetic of a comic in a live-action film" (13)—but *Sin City* married narrative and visual fidelity to create Hollywood's first comic book transformation.

This fidelity was central to the film's publicity, with the trailer intercutting images from the source with clips from the film. As Brandon Gray of *Box Office Mojo* assessed, the "marketing wore the movie's dark comic origins as a badge of honor and relentlessly pursued fans, especially on the Internet" ("Living in 'Sin City'"). Furthermore, as Leitch points out, the "more strongly films wish to identify themselves as adaptations, the more likely they are to list the authors of their source texts in their titles" ("Adaptation, the Genre" 113). Thus, fidelity was further emphasized by prefixing the title with Frank Miller's name in promotional materials and the final film. Rodriguez also stated that the "only way to do the movie faithfully is to have Frank Miller co-directing with me" ("How It Went Down") and consequently Miller was credited as a director, leaving little ambiguity over the film's authorial intention, and reinforcing the intended fidelity of the project.

Sin City was soon followed by other comic book transformations, including *300*, *Watchmen*, *Scott Pilgrim*, *Kick-Ass*, *The Losers*, and *The Adventures of Tintin*. These films displayed greater narrative and visual faithfulness than the more familiar borrowings, and entered into a fidelity contract with the prospective audience through early promotional work that mirrored comic book

FIG. 3.5 Stills from the theatrical trailer for *Sin City*, which signaled the film's fidelity by intercutting images of the source with their corresponding shots from the film.

images. However, this increased fidelity is not confined to these recent trans-formations, with the formerly free borrowings increasingly cohering around comic book texts.

In discussing the various transtextual relations that shape a film, Rob-ert Stam describes architextuality as "the generic taxonomies suggested or refused by the titles or subtitles of a text" (Introduction 30). In the past, comic book adaptations simply added a Roman numeral or vague subtitle to distin-guish franchise installments (e.g., *Superman IV: The Quest for Peace*). How-ever, in today's comic book adaptation trend, marked by increased fidelity, many adaptations use this architectural relation to suggest faithfulness. For instance, *The Incredible Hulk* adopted the title of the eponymous character's longest running series after the perceived infidelities of *Hulk*; *Punisher: War Zone* (Alexander 2008) was the first of the character's adaptations (following two earlier efforts) to adopt a comic book title; and after three installments with generic titles, the X-Men series has begun to borrow from specific com-ics with *X-Men: First Class* and *X-Men: Days of Future Past* (Singer 2014). Other recent examples include: *The Amazing Spider-Man, Man of Steel* (Sny-der 2013), *Captain America: The Winter Soldier* (Russo brothers 2014), and *Avengers: Age of Ultron* (Whedon 2015). While the ultimate films may not

FIG. 3.6 Some "peak moments" from loose comic book adaptations that display a measure of fidelity.

always reflect the titles they adopt, such architextuality enables these loose borrowings to suggest fidelity to the knowing member of the audience. Moving beneath the titles, these borrowings also regularly cite specific elements from the books.

Where once comic book adaptations could rely on the long-standing, and often contradictory, publication histories of these characters to support almost any interpretation, today most adaptations strive to display a measure of fidelity while still wrestling with the character's labyrinthine past.[30] One solution is to point to key moments from the character's many titles. Discussing the first film adaptations of Shakespeare, Tom Gunning notes how early filmmakers would not adapt the whole play, but rather well-known "peak moments" ("Literary Appropriation" 44). Much like Hamlet's soliloquy or the climactic suicides of Romeo and Juliet, many modern comic book adaptations will tend to adapt "iconic" moments, which have been ratified through comic covers, pin-up images, and frequent reference. Examples of such peak moments might include: Spider-Man dumping his costume in a trash can in *Spider-Man 2* (Raimi 2004); Captain America socking Hitler on the jaw (*Captain America: The First Avenger*); and Superman lifting a car above his head in *Superman Returns*.

Focusing on the adaptations of Sherlock Holmes, Leitch describes such explicit references as "giving the appearance of fidelity by concentrating on certain kinds of details but neglecting, correcting, or improving others" (*Film Adaptation* 230). Thus, while these recent borrowings do not try to be faithful to one specific text, the emphasis now placed on fidelity, which Leitch describes as "fetishistic," is a marked change from earlier eras. Nowhere is this shift more evident than in the 2005 franchise reboot *Batman Begins*.

First introduced in *Detective Comics* #27 (May 1939), Batman was expected to augment the success of DC Comics' already soaring star, Superman. The gothic avenger would soon achieve mythic status with his first solo title, *Batman* #1 (Spring 1940), describing "The Legend of Batman."[31] Like Superman, Batman earned this position through regular adaptation. From the World War II Columbia serial to the 1960s television series, the caped crusader cast his shadow over many productions. While these versions often displayed little reverence for the original medium, they did serve to embed the character in popular culture.[32] In his 2000 monograph *Batman Unmasked*, Will Brooker concludes that "with sixty years behind him Batman has now reached the point where he could live on in the cultural imagination, as myth, if that institution [DC Comics and Warner Bros.] decided to cut him free" (11). However, despite his mythic potential, this god of popular culture has frequently found fanboys, and today filmmakers, tugging at his cape, striving to reinstate the importance of the source material.

In the late 1980s, Batman needed rescuing. Michael Keaton, a comedic actor best known as *Mr. Mom* (Dragoti 1983) and *Beetlejuice* (Burton 1988), was chosen to don the Dark Knight's cape and cowl for *Batman*, Warner Bros.' multimillion-dollar film adaptation of the DC Comics character. This casting decision provoked outcry from the longtime readership to which the film's thirty-year-old director, Tim Burton, dismissively replied, "There might be something that's sacrilege in the movie. . . . But I can't care about it. . . . This is too big a budget movie to worry about what a fan of a comic would say" (Pearson and Uricchio 184). Burton may not have worried about what a fan would say, but Warner Bros. was very concerned about what 50,000 of them might. During production, Batman fans, accustomed to the gritty avenger of Frank Miller's *The Dark Knight Returns* and *Batman: Year One*, began a letter-writing campaign to protest the humorous direction the adaptation was perceived to be taking ("Shadows of the Bat"). It was not long before the negative reader response began to rouse wider interests, including a front-page article in the *Wall Street Journal* with the headline, "Batman Fans Fear The Joke's on Them in Hollywood Epic."[33] As fan criticism began to seep into more mainstream debates, commentators started linking reader discontent to the studio's declining share price (Burton and Salisbury 72). In response, Warner Bros. hastily cut together a suitably "dark" trailer to reassure the hard-line detractors, of which Burton said, "It was a way to kind of stop the campy camp talk" ("Shadows of the Bat"). The trailer and the eventual film were a success; however, the letter-writing campaign demonstrated that while the fan base or knowledgeable viewer may be a minority of the film adaptation audience, they have the ability to sway wider interests.

In the late 1990s, the Web would heighten fan influence and embolden their resolve. When making *Batman* for Warner Bros., Burton dismissed the opinions of "a fan," but a mere eight years later Warner Bros. marketing chief Chris Pula saw one fan as a major threat: "What's disturbing . . . is that many times the legitimate press quotes the Internet without checking sources. One guy on the Internet could start enough of a stir that causes a reactionary shift in the whole marketing program" (R. Weiner). Thus, in the mid-1990s, when most media producers were battening down the hatches, comic book fans were riding the crest of the digital wave. Eventually, filmmakers adapting cult texts were forced to acknowledge these digitally empowered minorities and acquiesce to their concerns, a process that has resulted in the reshaping of many comic book adaptations.

As previously mentioned, *Batman & Robin* was perhaps the first film to fully incur the wrath of this digitally connected fan base, with Jake Rossen linking the film's financial failure to it being "deemed blasphemously stupid by fans" (250). Thomas Leitch suggests that a new version of a previously adapted source "can seek to define itself either with primary reference to the film it remakes or to the material on which both films are based" ("Twice-Told Tales" 45). In 2005, *Batman Begins* managed to distance itself from the previous franchise through a cast and star with indie credibility, a more realistic tone, and also fan-appeasing fidelity. To quantify and understand the unprecedented comic book fidelity of *Batman Begins*, and its sequels *The Dark Knight* and *The Dark Knight Rises*, it is prudent to turn to a bible: the Bat-bible.

Batman writer Dennis O'Neil was not an advocate of strict continuity in comics, describing it as a "mixed blessing . . . but something our audience demands" (Pearson and Uricchio 23). Nonetheless, when O'Neil became the editor of DC Comics' Batman titles in 1986, he introduced the Bat-bible.[34] The Bat-bible summarized the fundamental aspects of the character for comic book creators, thereby ensuring greater consistency between the many titles, with O'Neil opening the document by stating, "Herewith, in brief, everything the present editor thinks new writers and artists need to know to do basic Batman stories."[35] Among the key guidelines stated in the document are: "His determination to stop crime is exceeded only by his compassion for crime's victims"; "Wayne/Batman is not insane"; "He is celibate. . . . He appreciates women . . . but he cannot afford intimacy"; and "He never kills. Let's repeat that for the folks in the balcony: Batman never kills."[36]

The rules of the Bat-bible were flouted by the first feature-length adaptation of the comic, *Batman*. For instance, in the film's opening, Batman stands by while a family is mugged. The "hero" only confronts the criminals as they perch on a rooftop to count their spoils; not quite the "compassionate" figure O'Neil describes. Later, Bruce appears to be the model of insanity threatening the Joker, "You wanna get nuts? Come on! Let's get nuts!" In another transgression of the comic book canon, Bruce indulges in a serious, consummated relationship with Vicki Vale. Finally, in perhaps the greatest break from the comic book character, Batman kills several adversaries, including his archenemy, the Joker.

By contrast, the more recent film adaptation of Batman, *Batman Begins*, meets the Bat-bible's requirements. The character is compassionate to crime's victims, stopping at various points to give food, his coat, and even a piece of equipment to those in need. As per the Bat-bible, "obsessed the man surely is, but he is in the fullest possession of his mental and moral faculties." Furthermore, his quest for justice finds him unable to commit to a relationship with childhood sweetheart Rachel Dawes, whom he "appreciates." Perhaps, most importantly, the hero of *Batman Begins* vehemently opposes killing.[37]

While director Christopher Nolan may not have been following a DC Comics doctrine, this film clearly displays greater continuity than previous efforts. Furthermore, Nolan and his co-writer David S. Goyer referenced many fan-favorite comic books when promoting *Batman Begins*. For instance, Batman story arcs *The Long Halloween* (Loeb and Sale), *Year One* (Miller and Mazzucchelli), and the Dennis O'Neil-penned Batman comics (specifically "The Man Who Falls") were all identified by Goyer as "influential" ("Genesis of the Bat").

The miniseries *The Long Halloween* expanded on the organized crime elements that usually only serve as the backdrop for more colorful characters in Batman comics, with Goyer describing the book as a "sober, serious approach to Batman" ("Genesis of the Bat"). A central character in the storyline was mob boss Carmine Falcone, who had previously never been featured outside of the comics, but who would ultimately serve as one of the antagonists in *Batman Begins*. *Batman Begins* is also indebted to *Batman: Year One*, Frank Miller's four-part series exploring the first year of Batman's career. Goyer described how Miller developed "a great relationship" between Batman and Gordon, adding, "I think Frank was the first one to suggest that the police force in Gotham City was corrupt and that left an opening for Batman to operate in" ("Genesis of the Bat"). Goyer also cites the *Batman* comics written by Dennis O'Neil as formative, with Nolan pointing to the 1989 origin story "The Man Who Falls" as a "jumping off point" for the adaptation ("Genesis of the Bat").[38] O'Neil's story opens with a young Bruce falling down a well before retelling key moments in Batman's origin, a narrative device Nolan's film also employed.[39]

In *Hunting the Dark Knight*, Brooker charts how the filmmakers managed to suggest fidelity while still navigating the character's dense past: "So, while the production materials and documentaries suggest a broad and holistic sense of the 'source'—the entire 'history of Batman'—this vast range is narrowed down to a manageable group of texts: a small constellation of stars (O'Neil, Adams, Miller, Loeb) rather than a universe" (62). As the example of a young Bruce falling down the well suggests, these texts could be narrowed further to peak moments that signal fidelity. For instance, the closing panels of *Year One*, in which the recently promoted "Captain" Gordon waits on a rooftop to inform Batman of a new threat to Gotham who "calls himself the Joker," is reworked for the film's coda, with the recently promoted "Lieutenant" Gordon waiting on a rooftop to reveal to Batman the calling card of a criminal with a "taste for the theatrical."

Similar peak moments from the sequels might include the rooftop meeting of Batman, Gordon, and Harvey Dent from *The Long Halloween*, which then reappeared in *The Dark Knight*; and Bane crippling Batman, which was a major plot point in both the comic book story arc "Knightfall" and the trilogy-closer *The Dark Knight Rises*. Furthermore, in yet another example of the fidelity-centric architextuality identified in other recent borrowings, *The Dark Knight* eschewed the tradition of including the protagonist's name in the title in favor of a reference to one of the character's most celebrated books, *The Dark Knight Returns*.

However, while borrowings such as *Batman Begins* are showing unprecedented reverence to the source, this fidelity and its impact should not be overstated, and other influences must be acknowledged. For instance, the Christopher Nolan films may have borrowed Gotham's corrupt police force from *Year One*, but the influence of 1970s cop films like *Serpico* (Lumet 1973) and more recent police procedural television shows such as *Law and Order* (Zuckerman 1990), *NYPD Blue* (Milch and Bocho 1993), and *The Wire* (Simon 2002) could also be detected.[40] Similarly, whether it is organic web-shooters or leather costumes, filmmakers will often point to realism to diffuse charges of infidelity. As Leitch notes, if comic book adaptations were only focused on faithfulness they would be animated (*Film Adaptation* 199), or at the very least use motion capture technology, as *The Adventures of Tintin* did. But the desire for live-action credibility sees fans accepting changes from the source such as the Kevlar suits and tank-like transport of *Batman Begins*.

Equally, Nolan the auteur must not be forgotten. As Brooker, who prefers Barthes's term "scriptor," notes, "fidelity to the source is balanced with a sense of individual authorship, which lies not in original creation, but in creative selection, arranging and representation" (*Dark Knight* 40). Thus, for example, the complex plotting of *Memento* (Nolan 2000) reappears in the third act reveal of the "real" Ra's al Ghul in *Batman Begins*.[41] Furthermore, as explored in Chapter One, these films are a product of their environment, as they evoke post-9/11 discourse through the militarization of the hero. As discussed in the previous chapter, the comic book movie is also a key determinant in the production of these films, with *Batman Begins* seeking to subvert many of the genre's conventions. Finally, returning to Bazin's pyramid, it should be noted that *Batman Begins* displays the fidelity flux of other adaptations of episodic texts, with the film inspiring an armor-like redesign of Batman's costume in the comics. Thus, competing versions of these characters, other texts, and contexts do of course still influence the films. Nonetheless, from meeting the character's central tenets as identified by former editor Dennis O'Neil, through its borrowing of specific characters, scenes, and narrative devices from fan-favorite texts, *Batman Begins* is more greatly inflected by its comic book source(s) than previous adaptations of the character.

This comic book continuity clearly chimed with online fans, as long before the release of *Batman Begins* they were responding positively to the film and its perceived faithfulness, suggesting it was a significant improvement over previous adaptations.[42] As was the case with the faithful adaptations described earlier, mainstream journalists picked up on this online opinion. For example, in a prescient 2004 *Variety* article, Ben Fritz noted that "if next year's 'Batman Begins' is a hit and this summer's 'Catwoman' flops, execs at Warner Bros. can't say nobody warned them. On fan sites across the Internet, users are giving rave reviews to images of the new Batmobile and casting decisions like Christian Bale. But the initial looks at Halle Berry's Catwoman costume drew near-universal jeers" ("Net Heads"). This amplification of positive online buzz from the minority fan audience validates the studio's recognition of fans, as well as the strategies they employ to meet their fidelity-centric demands in production and promotion. Thus, given the financial imperatives, the source materials (and their fans) look set to maintain, and perhaps even deepen, their influence on comic book adaptations in the years to come.

Despite the development of strategies to facilitate audience participation, and increasing emphasis on the comic book source material in the promotion and production of adaptations, skepticism remains regarding the industrial importance of fans, as Rae and Gray point out, "although comic book readers are the most knowledgeable of audiences, they are very much in the minority within the total number of viewers for comic book movies" (86). Similarly, Brooker suggests that the paradox of adapting "cult" texts is that "the movie will be tailored for those who care least about the character, while those with the greatest emotional investment become a powerless elite" (*Batman Unmasked* 280). Richard A. Becker made a similar assessment, but added a caveat. He stated that this paradox exists because the film financers only want their "comic book adaptations to be just enough like the comic book to make a lot of money. Whatever amount of resemblance achieves the most profit is the right amount" (438–39). Hence, as demonstrated, although the fan base or knowledgeable viewer may be in the minority, they have increasingly proven their ability to sway the larger potential audience and affect the film's success. Thus, in the Golden Age of Comic Book Filmmaking, profit-minded producers regularly shape adaptations to meet the priorities of comic book fans, who are no longer dismissed as a cult.

Despite shifts within the film industry, adaptation studies scholars are reluctant to recognize fidelity as an "evaluative criterion" (McFarlane "Film and Literature" 26). In his 1957 monograph, George Bluestone observed of fidelity that, "film-makers still talk about 'faithful' and 'unfaithful' adaptations without ever realizing that they are really talking about successful and unsuccessful films. Whenever a film becomes a financial or even a critical success the question of 'faithfulness' is given hardly any thought" (114). Modern scholars such as Hutcheon have cited these earlier remarks in the hope of distancing the field from the fidelity orthodoxy of the past (7). However, as demonstrated, this assessment does not apply to many modern adaptations, particularly from the comic book adaptation trend. For instance, Warner Bros. released two film adaptations of their most popular DC Comics characters, Batman and Superman, in 2005 and 2006, respectively. With a worldwide box office of $391 million, *Superman Returns* outgrossed *Batman Begins* ($372 million), and also received more favorable reviews (a 72 percent aggregate among the "Top Critics" featured on *Rotten Tomatoes* versus 60 percent for *Batman Begins*). Nonetheless, negative fan responses following the "unfaithful" adaptation of Superman prompted Warner Bros. to "reboot" the series, while *Batman Begins* was promptly given a sequel.[43] Thus, in the fidelity-centric world of comic book film adaptations where fans hold sway, success is not only measured, as Bluestone once suggested, by box office and positive reviews, but also by the online buzz and favorable fan reactions that fidelity breeds. As William Proctor summarized of *The Dark Knight Trilogy*, "Bat-fans got what they wanted" ("Dark Knight Triumphant" 161). Thus, despite the risks associated with fidelity criticism, adaptation scholars should not lag behind the industry in recognizing that fans and fidelity are an important determinant in shaping modern comic book adaptations.

Comic book fandom has long been a participatory culture. As comic book characters made the transition to film, the fans, eschewing media boundaries, began effectively applying their collaborative traditions to cinema. This process became more intensive and far-reaching in the digital age. As Jenkins notes, "None of this is new. What has shifted is the visibility of fan culture" (*Convergence Culture* 135). Consequently, filmmakers, many of whom initially adopted a protectionist stance, have chosen to (or been forced to) recognize the merits of comic book publishing practices. In recent years, this has led to a refocusing of marketing campaigns, the development of new production practices, greater continuity between texts, as well as a number of other strategies that position fans at the center of comic book adaptation production. Nonetheless, as the previous chapter demonstrated, fans cannot be solely relied on to achieve box-office success, with studios also adopting a variety of techniques to attract the larger non-fan audience. The means by which producers continue to respond to these demands will dictate the future of the comic book adaptation.

One area where these two imperatives align is the realization of a comic aesthetic. Whether it is a convention of the comic book movie genre, or the byproduct of increased fidelity, the Golden Age of Comic Book Filmmaking has found filmmakers eager to narrow the semiotic gap between comics and cinema. The development and impact of this comic aesthetic will be the focus of the next chapter.

CHAPTER FOUR

A Comic Aesthetic

Perhaps it is the search for fidelity described in the previous chapter, or a desire to fulfill the genre conventions outlined in Chapter Two, but many modern comic book adaptations, and related films, strive to achieve a comic aesthetic. A number of commentators have identified this trend (Ndalianis "Why Comic Studies?"; Corrigan "Adaptations, Obstructions, and Refractions"), with Michael Cohen suggesting that *Dick Tracy* (Beatty 1990) was the initiator. Cohen describes the 1990 comic strip adaptation as "the most meticulous effort to capture the aesthetic of a comic in a live-action film, and [it] paved the way for the exploration of the visual correlations lying dormant between cinema and comics" (13).

As previously noted, *Sin City* (Rodriguez 2005) was the first of a new strand of transformations that mined these "visual correlations" like never before, with director Robert Rodriguez describing how he "felt the mediums were very similar. We didn't have to go make an adaptation of *Sin City*; we could just translate it the way [Frank Miller] drew it right to the screen" (*Sin City* DVD commentary). Despite the current trend of comic book film adaptations being characterized by increased levels of fidelity, many balk at the suggestion that a film can faithfully translate a story from another form given the many medium specific nuances. Unsurprisingly, comic book professionals are among the skeptics, with Robert C. Harvey arguing that the "cartoonist cannot transfer to filmmaking all the techniques of making good comics any more than the filmmaker could employ all of the devices of making motion pictures if he were to undertake producing comics" (190).

The scholarly community echoes Harvey's contention, with many commentators using linguistic analogies to challenge supposedly faithful translations. As Linda Hutcheon notes, "Just as there is no such thing as a literal translation, there can be no literal adaptation" (16). Most commentators simply point to the materials of expression being antagonistic and therefore any translation is unachievable. James Griffith, referencing structuralists William

Luhr, Béla Balázs, and George Bluestone, summarizes that this "separatist view" has become so prevalent that it is "accepted uncritically" (29).

However, comics and cinema enjoy what Timothy Corrigan describes as a "unique representational overlap" (Burke "Adaptation Studies Conference" 55). This overlap is greater than many of the media that filmmakers traditionally turned to for inspiration. As Bluestone suggested in the seminal *Novels into Film*, "it is insufficiently recognized that the end products of novel and film represent different aesthetic genera, as different from each other as ballet is from architecture" (5). However, as both comics and film are graphic narrative mediums, they at least occupy the same aesthetic genera, if not quite the same species, only being as distinct as ballet from boxing. A number of scholars point to the commonalities between the forms (Ndalianis "The Frenzy of the Visible" 239; Jones 7) with Pascal Lefèvre identifying, "a closer link between cinema and comics than between cinema and other visual arts" (2). Accordingly, this chapter will complicate the received view in adaptation studies that cinema's unique means of expression is incompatible with the media it adapts, by charting how many codes and conventions pass back and forth in the overlap that these graphic narrative mediums share.

The representational overlap between comics and cinema was largely unexploited until the Golden Age of Comic Book Filmmaking. As described in Chapter One, many in the industry and popular press suggest that the limitations of film production technology prevented traditional cinema from effectively adapting comics outside of animation, and that it was only with the advancement of digital technologies that a meaningful engagement with comics' means of expression was possible. The many proponents of the view include comic creator Marc Guggenheim (Rogers), *Sin City* director Robert Rodriguez ("15 Minute Flick School"), and *The Spirit* producer F. J. DeSanto, who stated, "We're at the really cool point—literal adaptations of comic books" (Vaz 216). Examples like Cohen's analysis of *Dick Tracy* challenge this technological determinist position, as the 1990 comic strip adaptation achieved a comic aesthetic through the use of mattes, costuming, and prosthetic makeup. Nonetheless, the possibilities of the more malleable digital image have fueled a wider interest in capturing a comic aesthetic.

The newfound freedoms of digital cinema, coupled with the representational overlap comics and cinema enjoy, has led many in the industry, and beyond, to characterize comics as idle storyboards waiting to be shot, with Michael E. Uslan noting, when interviewed for this study, that filmmakers see comics as "frozen movies." The separatist view held by many scholars finds its opposite in this storyboard analogy that a number of filmmakers seem to subscribe to. To identify one prominent example, on directing *The Adventures of Tintin* (2011) Steven Spielberg suggested that creator Hergé was "trying to squeeze out 24 frames in a single frame, and succeeding. That was, I think, the genius of Hergé. It was a movie" ("The Journey to *Tintin*"). Writing long before *The Adventures of Tintin* went into production, David Bordwell had already described Spielberg as "the live-action master of 'storyboard cinema.' And of course storyboards look like comic-book pages" ("Superheroes for Sale"). While there are many apt comparisons between comics and cinema, this storyboard analogy goes too far, as it deprives comics of their specificity. So prevalent is the storyboard analogy, that comics scholars frequently reassert the boundaries of their medium (Eisner *Comics & Sequential Art* 40; Harvey 190; Atkinson 55).

While the giddy proclamations of the storyboard analogy may overlook medium specific differences, the separatist view is also limiting as it ignores the deepening of the comic aesthetic in adaptations and related films. Accordingly, this chapter will chart a space between these opposing perspectives by arguing that some measure of translation is occurring, even if it is not literal.

Dudley Andrew contends that "if a novel's story is judged in some way comparable to its filmic adaptation, then the strictly separate but equivalent processes of implication which produced the narrative units of that story through words and audio-visual signs, respectively, must be studied" (*Film Theory* 103). This semiotic approach has been recognized as an important adaptation studies tool by a number of scholars (Stam "Beyond Fidelity" 62; Griffith 28). Cohen applied this method in his analysis of *Dick Tracy*, summarizing, "The 'comic aesthetic' in *Dick Tracy* does not transcend the ontology of cinema; it is an aesthetic translation of the characteristics and conventions from the comic medium by using the stylistic and functional equivalents in cinema" (36). Building on this observation, this chapter will seek to identify equivalences between the forms, mapping where they have been utilized by filmmakers to achieve a comic aesthetic.

These equivalents are a further example of the crosses on a treasure map described in the Introduction, with their investigation often unearthing new insights into the complicated relationship between these two media. To explore this development Brian McFarlane's concept of "adaptation proper," also discussed in the Introduction, will prove useful. In his narratological approach to literary adaptation, McFarlane distinguishes between "(i) those elements of the original novel which are transferable because [they are] not tied to one or other semiotic system—that is, essentially, *narrative*; and (ii) those which involve intricate processes of adaptation because their effects are closely tied to the semiotic system in which they are manifested—that is, *enunciation*" (*Novel to Film* 20). McFarlane describes the translation of medium specific devices to another form as "adaptation proper," examples of which will be highlighted throughout this chapter.

As noted when discussing convergent technology in Chapter One, comics enjoy a cyclical relationship with a variety of media. In particular, the overlap between comics and cinema has facilitated a steady flow of codes between the forms. So active is this relay that it is often difficult to cite the originator for shared signifiers. For example, Francis Lacassin argues that the extreme close-up was "born on a cinema screen. But only the comic strip, mirror of the imaginary, could raise it a fantasy level [sic] denied to cinema" (14). Similarly, the film adaptation of *Dream of the Rarebit Fiend* (Porter and McCutcheon 1906) is often celebrated for its pioneering use of trick photography. However, it is possible that the two earlier films, Cecil Hepworth's *The Glutton's Nightmare* (1901) and Gaston Velle's *Rêve à la lune* (1905), not only influenced the adaptation, but also McCay's original comic (Musser). In yet another example of signifiers relaying back-and-forth between the forms, Will Brooker describes how the POW! motif of the *Batman* television series, "which had been lifted straight from the comics to the TV series to give the latter a comic-book 'look', was now being used, paradoxically, to link the comic book back to the successful show" (*Batman Unmasked* 188). Of the relay between comics and cinema, Lacassin observed that "it would be rash to deduce that the latter is a tributary of the former" (14). Further examples of this relay will be identified across this chapter. In moving between comics and cinema, these codes knit the forms closer together thereby widening the overlap and increasing the opportunity for further semiotic exchange.

The many filmmakers identified in Chapter One as "textual poachers" also expedited the semiotic back-and-forth between comics and cinema. For example, Sean French describes how James Cameron "grew up writing stories and painting pictures. His interest in storytelling led him to a fusion of the two in comic books. Then he discovered the cinema and realised it was what he had been looking for" (8–9). While displaying very different styles, commentators have noted a comic book inflection in the work of directors as diverse as Orson Welles (McBride; Inge), Jean-Luc Godard (Sorlin; Morton), and George Lucas (Morrison 168).[1] When interviewed, Joe Kelly identified this comic aesthetic in comic book adaptations and wider films, linking it back to a number of fan-filmmakers:

> That aesthetic is something that's inherent to comics. So I think we're getting filmmakers who were weaned on comics, that was their initial creative outlet, or creative input depending on how you look at it . . . Edgar Wright is such a great example. He can take those graphics and they don't feel arbitrary, they feel very organic to the story and to the film as a whole. When I see that stuff happening, I couldn't be more thrilled. Guillermo del Toro is another great example. He's such

a huge comic book fan and though that aesthetic might be subtle, I think it's in those films.

Thus, as Kelly suggested, these textual poachers helped to further facilitate the development of cinema's comic aesthetic.

Furthermore, as adaptations in the form of transmedia franchises come closer to realizing Bazin's pyramid, the boundaries between the media become even more diffuse. This fluidity has seen a hastening and deepening of the semiotic exchange between comics and cinema. Claire Parody even goes so far as to suggest that this "transcoding" moves beyond translation to the "re-coding of texts and objects that may have absorbed the syntax and vocabulary of other media within their primary semiotics" (213).

Keith Cohen contends, "narrativity is the most solid median link between novel and cinema" (*Film and Fiction* 92). But, as the presence of overlaps and relays suggest, it is the visual image that combines comics and cinema. This is not to propose that comics have not influenced cinematic narratives. Chapter One described how the serialization of comics helped studios stagger their franchises, and Mark Waid attributed the world-building of television shows such as *Lost* (Abrams 2004) to comics.[2] Nonetheless, it is the contention of this study that the emergence of a comic aesthetic is the most significant impact of the Golden Age of Comic Book Filmmaking.

When Waid was asked specifically about the impact comics might have had on the aesthetics of cinema, he responded with surprise: "That's a really good question because everyone always asks the reverse question, which is how does cinema influence comics, but the other way of putting it, you know, I've never thought about it before." Indeed, the influence of cinema on comics has been an interest of scholars, and is a topic that I have tackled elsewhere (Burke "Special Effect"). However, this study seeks to address the question that Waid and others had not considered: What is the influence of comics' unique means of expression on cinema? To that end, this chapter will chart how filmmakers sought to exploit equivalents where they existed, and create them where they did not, in order to realize a comic aesthetic.

What Comics Can Do That Films Can't (And Vice Versa)

In his 1980 article, "What Novels Can Do That Films Can't (And Vice Versa)," Seymour Chatman puts forward the idea that "close study of film and novel versions of the same narrative reveals with great clarity the peculiar pow-ers of the two media. Once we grasp those peculiarities, the reasons for the differences in form, content, and impact of the two versions strikingly emerge" (123). This section will first consider the parallels and medium specific differences between the fundamental syntactic units of comics and film. It will then identify where filmmakers have exploited existing equivalents, and, in the desire to achieve a comic aesthetic, developed further, often redundant, matches.

Ever since film studies turned to Ferdinand de Saussure's theories of semiology, many scholars have subscribed to Christian Metz's view that while "the cinema is certainly not a language system (*langue*)," it may "be considered as a *language*" (71). Film academics are not alone in qualifying their art form as a language; noted comics scholars also assert their medium is a language. In *Reinventing Comics*, Scott McCloud contends that there is a comic language, adding, "its vocabulary is the full range of visual symbols" (1). Will Eisner elaborates this point to explain how "comics employ a series of repetitive images and recognizable symbols. When they are used again and again to convey similar ideas, they become a language . . . and it is this disciplined application that creates the 'grammar' of Sequential Art" (*Comics & Sequential Art* 8). Rather than argue this point, Roger Sabin definitively states "comics are a language: they combine to constitute a weave of writing and art which has its own syntax, grammar and conventions, and which can communicate ideas in a totally unique fashion" (8).[3] Thus, it is widely recognized that both forms—comics and films—are languages; but how similar are these systems and is a measure of translation between them possible?

Perhaps identifying base units is the best place to start such an analysis, before expanding further. Metz contends that in cinema one can consider the shot "the largest minimum segment . . . since at least one shot is required to make a film" (71). As detailed in the Introduction, identifying the largest minimum segment of a comic is a more difficult task, as there is little consensus as to what qualifies as a "comic." McCloud, in his landmark *Understanding Comics*, defines the form as: "Juxtaposed pictorial and other images in deliberate sequence" (9). Consequently, McCloud does not consider single panels as comics because "there's no such thing as a sequence of one" (20).[4] Applying McCloud's argument, the minimum segment of a comic would be two sequential panels. However, Harvey challenges McCloud's definition, arguing that "sequence is vital to McCloud because it creates the opportunity for closure . . . but the closure I emphasize is the closure between word and picture" (246).

Thierry Groensteen sees such an emphasis on text as the product of an outdated linguistic orthodoxy, arguing that the sequential images have narrative "without necessarily needing any verbal help" (9). Like McCloud, Groensteen suggests that the panel "never makes up the totality of the utterance but can and must be understood as a component in a larger apparatus" (5). However,

FIG. 4.1 This January 3, 1942, *The Spirit* comic strip contains a whole story segment in a single panel.

FIG. 4.2 This panel from *Captain America* #111 (March 1969) conveys a narrative sequence through the use of multiple figures within the one encapsulated image.

while McCloud asserts that single panels are "no more comics than [a] still of Humphrey Bogart is film" (*Understanding Comics* 21), Groensteen does recognize that some sequence can occur within a single encapsulated image. Citing Roger Odin, Groensteen describes how panels can be "vectorized" from left-to-right, like writing (105). For instance, in a 1942 one-panel strip, The Spirit is depicted as having trudged through snow before collapsing while a newspaper headline announces a "million" for his unmasking. Although the strip is made up of a single encapsulated image, the use of comic book vocabulary, coupled with the left-to-right vectorization provided by the footsteps, delineates a story segment without the sequence required by McCloud's definition. Groensteen suggests that such vectorization is unusual and therefore "we cannot resolve the question of the panel's internal narrativity on the basis of this particular criterion" (105). However, when comparing a panel from *Astro Boy* to Pontormo's painting *Joseph with Jacob in Egypt*, Angela Ndalianis notes how a number of phases in the same sequence can coexist in a panel with the creator guiding "the eye strategically to present a temporal unraveling of events" ("The Frenzy of the Visible" 247). For instance, in the example from *Captain America* #111 (March 1969) shown in figure 4.2, the hero goes through several discrete actions that would normally be broken into separate panels. However, in this example all the movements are contained within the one continuous image, which is discernible to the reader through the careful placement of speech balloons, as well as left-to-right vectorization. McCloud himself identifies a similar example in *Understanding Comics*, conceding that it "actually fits our definition of comics! All it needs is a few gutters thrown

FIG. 4.3 Eisner notes, "When a comic emulates film camera techniques [example 1], it can lose readability. The same event can be told more frugally [example 2]" ("Graphic Storytelling" 73).

in to clarify the sequence" (97). Although McCloud states that "not all panels are like that" (*Understanding Comics* 98), this example, and the vectorization described by Groensteen, demonstrate that a panel is capable of narrativity without the addition of a second panel, and therefore a single panel can be identified as "the largest minimum segment" of a comic. However, do these base units, the cinematic shot and comic panel, share enough similarities that the fidelity-minded filmmaker does not need to seek further equivalents?

In his analysis, Metz lists criteria by which the shot is analogous to the linguistic statement. Demonstrating the compatibility of the film and comic languages, Metz's criteria are also applicable to the comic panel. While for Metz "shots are infinite in number, contrary to words, but like statements, which can be formulated in a verbal language" (75), the potential number of panels achievable is similarly limitless. Shots, as described by Metz, "are the creations of the film-maker, unlike words (which already pre-exist in lexicons)" (75). Likewise, each panel in a comic is a novel creation designed specifically for its place within that story. Furthermore, Metz describes how a shot presents "a quantity of undefined information," is "a unit of discourse" (75–76), and contains a measure of autonomy, all attributes equally shared by the comic panel.[5]

However, the similarities between shots and panels should not presuppose equivalency. In affirming the specificity of comics, Paul Atkinson (53) and Martyn Pedler ("The Fastest Man Alive" 255) both criticize the projector analogy that was first put forward by Earle J. Coleman:

"Motion in the movies is made possible by the projector; in the comics, motion appears through our becoming, so to speak, human projectors" (97). Atkinson criticizes this comparison on the grounds that it "does not make it clear as to whether the simulated movement is in the imaginary fusion of the panels, comparable to the fusion speed of film, or in the thematic and structural difference between panels" (53). Similarly, Eisner demonstrates why the magnitude of change in comics needs to be much greater than cinema as the event must "be told more frugally" (*Graphic Storytelling* 73).

The reader participation required to stimulate movement from one panel to the next is often celebrated as comics' defining feature (McLuhan 24–25; Eisner *Graphic Storytelling* 71–72; Harvey 176; Gombrich xxvii; Bukatman *The Poetics of Slumberland* 31), with Mark Waid explaining, when interviewed, "There are many things that make comics 'comics,' but I think the one thing you can't take away from them is that in a comic you get to control the flow of information." Similarly, Italian film director Federico Fellini observed, "Comics, more than film, benefits from the collaboration of the readers: one tells them a story that they tell to themselves; with their particular rhythm and imagination" (Groensteen 11).

The panel borders and the gutter between them are the physical manifestation of the chasm in the story's action that prompts the reader to "fill in the intervening events from experience" (Eisner *Comics & Sequential Art* 38).

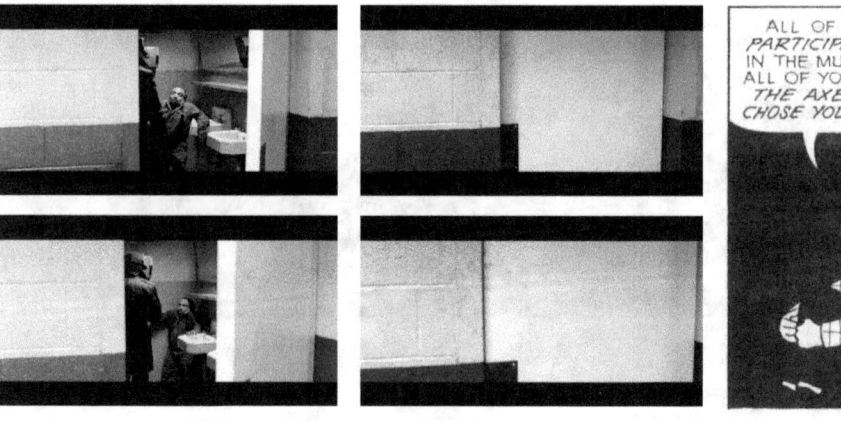

FIG. 4.5 In this sequence from *Watchmen*, the swinging door provides only brief glimpses of Rorschach approaching the criminal. Consequently, the spectator must use their imagination to fill in the rest of the sequence much as they would in a comic.

McCloud cleverly describes this defining feature of the comic form in the panels on the previous page, where he suggests that the reader is complicit in the creator's every act (*Understanding Comics* 68). Echoing the Kuleshov Experiment, McCloud goes on to argue that it is impossible for "any sequence of panels to be totally unrelated to each other . . . no matter how dissimilar one image may be to another there is a kind of alchemy at work in the space between panels which can help us find meaning and resonance in even the most jarring of combinations" (*Understanding Comics* 73). Applying Gestalt psychology, McCloud terms this process "closure," with Duncan and Smith summarizing that comics are "reductive in creation and additive in reading" (133).

On occasion filmmakers can solicit such participation. For example, in *Watchmen* (Snyder 2009) Rorschach corners a criminal behind a swinging door, which allows the spectator only momentary glimpses of the vigilante approaching the victim. In this sequence, shown in figure 4.5, the door acts as a comic book gutter would—forcing the spectator to infer what is happening in between from the isolated images. Thus, cinema has always courted some measure of participation from its spectators, with McCloud acknowledging that "filmmakers long ago realized the importance of allowing viewers to use their imaginations," while adding the caveat "film makes use of audiences' imaginations for occasional effects, [but] comics must use it far more often" (*Understanding Comics* 69). Beyond prompting the reader to make imaginative leaps, the borders and gutters have their own expressivities that modify each transition.

Notwithstanding the specificities, panel transitions fulfill much the same role in comics that cuts do in film; they both act "as a punctuator" (Eisner

Comics & Sequential Art 28).[6] As with cinematic cuts, a variety of panel transitions are available to delineate the intent of the punctuation. For instance, in the same way that a seamless cut in a film indicates that the shots are occurring consecutively, and usually within the present tense, so too in comics "rectangular panels with straight edged borders . . . [denote] that the actions contained therein are set in the present tense" (*Comics & Sequential Art* 44). Alternatively, if a dissolve is used to transition between two shots in a film, it is often meant to indicate that the following shot or scene is a flashback. Likewise, comics traditionally suggested a change in tense or shift in time by "altering the line which makes up the frame. The wavy edged or scalloped panel border is the most common past time indicator" (Eisner *Comics & Sequential Art* 44). Similarly, film can convey that a greater than normal amount of time has elapsed between successive shots through the use of a fade-to-black, while McCloud demonstrates how a wider gutter in comics can achieve the same effect (*Understanding Comics* 100–101).

Citing Benoît Peeters, Groensteen describes how most comic panels are "rhetorical" in that they "submit to the action that is described" (93). He celebrates these variable comic borders, adding that they highlight "the rigidity of the cinematographic apparatus, which is practically condemned to equip the projected image with a fixed and constant form" (40). While filmmakers rarely make use of irises and masks to modify the film frame, they will occasionally employ expressive punctuators such as wipes to create an emphasis akin to an exclamation mark at the end of a scene. However, the application of such techniques is rare, while a mainstream comic might adopt a new shape for each panel, even having a piece of art or text escape the confinement of the border.

Ultimately, film and comics are joined in a staccato rhythm of spliced-together shots and ordered panels.[7] For comics, this pace is dictated by the requirements of a medium that necessitates a number of panels to tell a story of appreciable depth. However, cinema does not have the same requirements. From the filmed-in-one-setup *actualités* of early cinema to the seamless cuts of Alfred Hitchcock's *Rope* (1948) and the shot-in-one-take *Russian Ark* (Sokurov 2002), cinema does not need to rely on montage, as Michael Anderegg points out: the "error comes from confusing what is possible for a given medium with what is essential to it" (157). Still, the cinematic language developed in such a way as to make a virtue of the assemblage of shots, rather than hide the accoutrements of the system. André Malraux said of cinema's foregrounding of editing that "it was montage that gave birth to film as an art, setting it apart from mere animated photography, in short, creating a language" (Bazin *What Is Cinema?* 24). Similarly, Groensteen believes that the comic image "finds its truth in the sequence" (114), while Lacassin suggests that montage provided both cinema and comics with their syntax (15).

FIG. 4.6 While employing their unique means of expression, these comparable scenes from the comic book *The Amazing Spider-Man* #33 and film *Spider-Man 2* have similar compositions.

Unsurprisingly, there are some grammatical correspondences between film editing and comic layouts. In comic books, the introductory panel of a story will usually be a larger panel that can take up an entire "splash" page. In this respect, the introductory panel of a comic is similar to the establishing shots often used in cinema, in that they both institute the spatial logistics for the subsequent panels or shots. Nonetheless, layout is widely considered specific to comics with Groensteen suggesting that comics scholars should "leave the editing to the cinema (and to the photo-novel) and fasten ourselves to the study of the page layout—which the cinema cannot do" (102). Indeed, in cinema each frame follows the next, while on the comic book page panels coexist. This co-presence of imagery has led McCloud to conclude that "unlike other media, in comics . . . both the past and future are real and visible and all around us" (*Understanding Comics* 104).[8] Cinema meanwhile, despite the presence of numerous past-time indicators such as dissolves, fades, and superimpositions, is inescapably fixed in the present tense.[9]

To fully appreciate "What Comics Can Do That Films Can't (And Vice Versa)," one need only look at similar sequences from *The Amazing Spider-Man* #33 (February 1964) and *Spider-Man 2* (Raimi 2004). In these two parallel moments, shown in figure 4.6, Spider-Man is pinned under tons of falling debris. The rhetorical borders of the comic allow for narrow panels to capture his anguish and pain. Although the screen size cannot change in a film, the shot scale tightens to a close-up that captures the same emotion. Furthermore, in both comic and film, the proscenium arch widens to larger panels and wider shots as Spider-Man finds the energy to lift the crippling weight; suggesting that panels and shots, though indigenous to their own forms, share some commonality.

Nonetheless, while *Spider-Man 2* may employ close-ups and wide shots in a manner similar to the comic, the spectator has neither the control nor the layout necessary to contrast the hero's efforts with his eventual triumph. Conversely, the comic's elegant layout ensures that Spider-Man's escape from the debris is more triumphant through the careful juxtaposition of the hero's struggle (conveyed in tight panels on the first page) with his inevitable emergence, which explodes into an entire splash page.[10] As Groensteen notes, in comics "the focal vision never ceases to be enriched by peripheral vision" (19).

Ultimately, comics and cinema do share some parallels—such as graphic narrative base units that have a measure of autonomy, and which are organized by punctuation-like transitions. Cinema can also achieve a measure of participation, yet the reader contribution necessitated by comics is far greater than that of film. Furthermore, while both comics and cinema rely on montage, the co-presence of images in comics (as opposed to the sequential replacement of images in cinema) can achieve results that cinema cannot match, and vice versa. Thus, while specificities make it difficult for theorists and filmmakers to draw direct comparisons, there is enough equivalency to give rise to the storyboard analogy and for filmmakers to produce faithful films that do not draw attention to the adaptation process. However, in the Golden Age of Comic Book Filmmaking there has been a concerted effort to develop further equivalences between the base elements of comics and cinema.

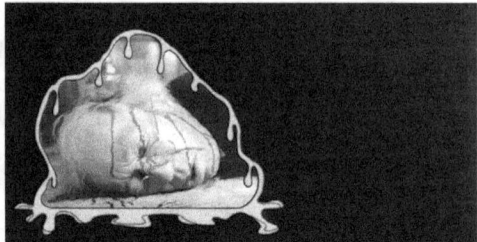

FIG. 4.7 Different techniques employed in *Creepshow* and *Popeye* to mirror comic book frames.

Many early adaptations—*Popeye* (Altman 1980), *Creepshow* (Romero 1983), and *Dick Tracy*—attempted to achieve a comic aesthetic by emulating comic book panels and transitions. For instance, Michael Cohen notes how in *Dick Tracy* "the choice to use the narrower aspect ratio of 1.85:1 was made with direct reference to the panels of the original comic strip" (32). Despite the presence of shot transitions, many self-reflexive comic book movies also employed masks and wipes to recreate the rhetorical borders of comics, including scalloped-edge borders, dripping blood irises (both *Creepshow*), and shattered frames (*Popeye*).

While these early references evoke comics, the Golden Age of Comic Book Filmmaking is marked by an even more sustained effort to emulate comics. For instance, *Hulk* (Lee 2003) and *Scott Pilgrim* (Wright 2010) eschew the availability of traditional cinematic devices (e.g., camera pans and tilts), with the film frame regularly reshaped to match the content of the shot.[11] Such "aggressive remediation" (Bolter and Grusin 48) runs the risk of rupturing the film's suture effect.[12] However, more subtle techniques have been used to suggest comic book frames.

The dimensions of the American comic book have shaped what stories appear and how they are told. While cinema's anamorphic lens may capture the breadth of Monument Valley, a comic book's portrait scale and grid-like structure is better suited to tall buildings and cityscapes. *The Dark Knight* (Nolan) may be the first film to approximate a comic book frame in cinema without fracturing the diegesis. Released in 2008, the adaptation contained six sequences shot using IMAX cameras, with the studio promotion emphasizing it as the "first time ever that a major feature film has been even partially shot

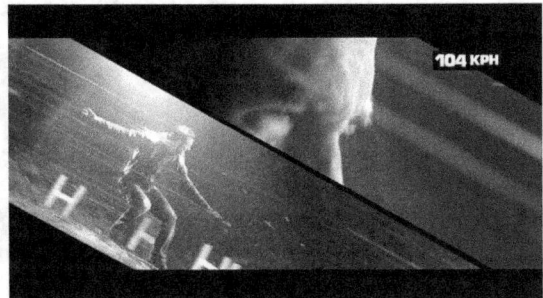

FIG. 4.8 Examples of scenes in *Hulk* and *Scott Pilgrim* in which the cinematic proscenium is modified to a more comic book-like frame.

Standard 35mm
Widescreen

FIG. 4.9 Scenes from *The Dark Knight* as presented in traditional theatres and IMAX.

FIG. 4.10 References to comic book panels and transitions in *The Warriors* and *Creepshow*. A more sustained attempt to recreate comic book panels and transitions can be found in *Hulk*.

using IMAX cameras" ("Warner Bros. Press notes").[13] As a result, in IMAX theatres, these key sequences would change from a 2.35:1 aspect ratio to 1.78:1. This had the effect of providing a more vertical frame than other mainstream films, including the standard theatrical version of *The Dark Knight*. Although the filmmakers did not state they were attempting to mirror a comic book frame, the sequences chosen to receive this vertically expanded treatment in *The Dark Knight* and its sequel, *The Dark Knight Rises* (Nolan 2012), are revealing. Each sequence was either set atop skyscrapers or within the cityscape, the very sort of moments comics traditionally presented so well within a vertical frame. Through the use of IMAX, *The Dark Knight* is arguably the first adaptation to approximate a comic's frame—an innovative example of "adaptation proper."

Moving from panels to transitions, one again finds a desire to emulate borders and gutters in comic book adaptations and related films. As early as *The Warriors* (Hill 1979), *Popeye*, and *Creepshow*, filmmakers have referenced panel transitions in their cuts. One of the most committed attempts at capturing a comic book aesthetic was Ang Lee's *Hulk*. In the film, shots would appear within shots, side by side, and in a variety of other patterns modeled on the transitions and layouts found in comic books.

However, while comic book-style transitions may be appropriate for fleeting moments in self-reflexive adaptations, the aggressive remediation in *Hulk* drew criticism from reviewers, as the overt transitions moved the film away from continuity editing, thereby reminding the spectator of the artifice of cinema.[14] As cinematic equivalents of comic book panels and transitions are already in place, such unnecessary translations failed to utilize cinema's means

FIG. 4.11 The opening of *American Splendor* approximates a comic book's paneled aesthetic.

of expression or effectively recreate the experience of a comic book. Few other adaptations attempted to continue this approach with the next Hulk director, Louis Leterrier commenting, "it was very much like a comic book, and somewhat alienating to the audience, because . . . you were never watching a real movie" (*The Incredible Hulk* DVD commentary).

Examples such as this seem to refute the comparisons of the storyboard analogy. Nonetheless, those who subscribe to a separatist view should recognize that other attempts at adaptation proper have been more successful. For instance, in the opening sequence of *American Splendor* (Berman and Pulcini 2003), the protagonist, Harvey Pekar (Paul Giamatti), is seen walking the streets of Cleveland, which is framed in panel-like borders. To further emphasize the film's comic book origins, these shots are interspersed with comic book art, and the "tracking mimics a reader following the layout of a comic book" (Hight 194). While *American Splendor* may seem to disregard cinema's unique means of expression, the film falls within the category of adaptation that Andrew calls "intersecting" in that it "presents the otherness and distinctiveness of the original text, initiating a dialectical interplay between the aesthetic forms" (*Film Theory* 100). By preserving the specificity of both mediums, their contrast is highlighted—a choice that tallies with the film's pointed examination of representation.[15] Thus, by not attempting to achieve comic book transitions in cinema, but rather maintaining both forms, the adaptation does not rupture the suture effect as *Hulk* does.

Less self-reflexive strategies for emulating comic book panels within cinema's mise-en-scène can be found throughout the 1968 Italian adaptation *Danger: Diabolik!* (Bava). In the film, many sequences are composed within diegetic frames creating a grid-like structure comparable in look, if not in function, to a comic book page. Similarly, in *Dick Tracy* the diopter lens was an in-camera means of achieving a "paneled" effect. As Michael Cohen explains,

FIG. 4.12 In *Danger: Diabolik!*, diegetic borders reference the source medium's grid-like structure. In *Dick Tracy*, a diopter lens is used to create panel-like compositions.

the rarely used diopter lens allows "the foreground and background characters and objects to be displayed in sharp focus," however it leaves "a distinct blurred line down the center of the image, which divides the two focal planes" (34).

A number of adaptations have imaginatively emulated the discontinuous images of comics. For instance, Matthew T. Jones identifies how the 1906 live-action adaptation of Winsor McCay's *Dream of a Rarebit Fiend* borrows "directly from the strip" through the use of jump cuts to replicate the "action-to-action transitions" of the comics (12). Over a hundred years later, jump cuts were still being employed to suggest the moment-to-moment actions of comics. For instance, in *Kick-Ass* (Vaughn 2010), Big Daddy's raid on a criminal's warehouse is conveyed through jump cuts that leave only the key beats of this extended action sequence.

Another inventive approximation of comics' discontinuous images is the use of intermittent lighting effects. For instance, while *Hulk* is notable for applying more comic book idioms than most adaptations, there is one sequence with no contrivances that ironically comes closest to approximating comic book transitions. At the film's climax, Hulk is carried along in a lightning bolt by his father (who has now assumed electrical form). The characters are only visible for split seconds when the lightning breaks. Each time they are seen they are in a new pose and position. Thus, the sequence is made up of a series of static images much like its source. A similar effect is achieved through the use of machine gunfire in *The Dark Knight Rises*, and through strobe lighting in *Blade* (Norrington 1998) and *Kick-Ass*, as well as in the *Smallville* episode "Checkmate" (Chisholm 2010). In these

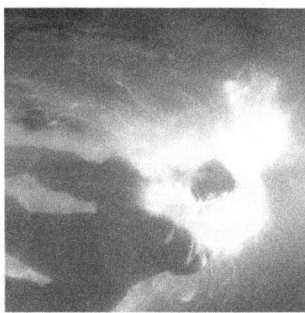

FIG. 4.13 The use of intermittent lighting in *Hulk*, *Smallville*, and *Kick-Ass* allows for comic book-inspired static images within cinema's motion pictures.

sequences, shown in figure 4.13, the intermittent lighting allows the characters to appear in discrete (often exaggerated) positions, much like they would in a comic book.

Thus, while the ready-made equivalents make it unnecessary, even cumbersome, for an adaptation to try to recreate panels and their transitions, a number of attempts have been made to bring these elements to the screen. Some examples have been self-referential (*American Splendor*), others imaginatively subtle (*The Dark Knight*), while a few transgress the specificity of both forms (*Hulk*). Nonetheless, these efforts represent a desire among many modern filmmakers to infuse film adaptations with a comic aesthetic.

While panels and gutters find easy equivalents in cinema, given the degree of control and participation conferred on the reader by a comic's layout, filmmakers have unsurprisingly found it difficult to adapt this syntactic element for the screen. For instance, Ang Lee's *Hulk* made elaborate use of split screen to try and create the contradictory experience of "watching" a comic book. Furthermore, the adaptation frequently placed shots within one larger shot in a montage comparable to a comic book's layout. However, these comic-inspired setups had to be negotiated within the relentless motion of cinema. Editor Tim Squyres explains, "If you try to lay out your movie that way and tell the story sequentially, in panels, you'll wind up wasting all your screen" ("The Unique Style of Editing the Hulk"). The solution was to have

FIG. 4.14 In *Hulk*, split screen was regularly used to evoke comic book layouts. Often, comic book-like insets were created with shots appearing within shots.

the panels coexist spatially, while also moving them forward in time, as seen in figure 4.14.

Given the simultaneity of the shots, they are closer to "insets" as identified by Groensteen than traditional panels. Describing the use of small panels ("insets") within one larger panel ("inclusive panel"), Groensteen notes how the "cartoonist introduces a frame within the frame in order to highlight a detail of his 'picture,' similar to the effect of a cinematic zoom, bringing the reader closer to the pertinent element" (87–88). The application of this technique challenges André Bazin's contention that in cinema montage "rules out ambiguity of expression" (*What Is Cinema?* 36). Each screen is a different shot (most often a different camera angle on the same action) with the spectator presented with multiple locus points on the now spatialized screen. Within the many competing images the spectator's focus will likely shift to the shot that is the most appropriate (i.e., information rich). Accordingly, the spectator is called on to demonstrate a level of decoding and participation rarely needed in cinema, but essential in comics.

A number of other comic book adaptations have adopted further devices to replicate the participation of the source. For instance, in his analysis of *300* (Snyder 2007), Jochen Ecke suggests that the filmmakers attempted to "imitate the way the human eye roams the space of the comic book page" (17) by using digital zooms and multiple cameras of varying focal lengths. Similarly, Martyn Pedler notes that the use of extreme slow and fast motion in Snyder's *Watchmen* serves to "mimic the unpredictable progress of a comic reader's time and attention across still images" ("The Fastest Man Alive" 259).

FIG. 4.15 In *Ghost World*, an innovative use of diegetic borders and juxtaposed imagery recreates the paneled aesthetic of the comic book.

However, noting the specificity of the forms, Ecke ultimately concludes that, "what Snyder offers us is the *simulation* of the spatio-topian freedom of the reader" [original emphasis] (17). Similarly, the shot compositions in *Hulk* were deemed a failure, with Pascal Lefèvre arguing that even though the "multiple-frame imagery is closer to comics, it breaks the usual cinematographic illusion" (6). Perhaps the ready-made equivalents of shots and cuts made the montage of *Hulk* redundant. Or maybe these codes were unmediated transfers rather than "adaptation proper" and therefore never likely to proliferate in the cinematic lexicon.

While efforts to replicate comics' base units in cinema could, in some instances, be characterized as ineffectual, misguided, and even unnecessary, there have been interesting examples that suggest the endeavor has been worthwhile. Combining the tracking shot as seen in *American Splendor*, with the diegetic gutters of *Danger: Diabolik!*, and the grid-like structure attempted in *Hulk*, *Ghost World* (Zwigoff 2001) achieves perhaps the clearest equivalent of a comic book's panels and layout without transgressing the film form. In the film's opening scene, the camera tracks along the side of an apartment block, peering through window frames at somber neighbors engaged in mundane tasks. These shots are juxtaposed with clips of a vibrant musical number from the Bollywood film *Gumnaam* (Nawathe 1965). In this sequence, shown in figure 4.15, the left-to-right tracking mirrors the vectorization of comics, while window frames evoke panel borders by encapsulating each shot. The use of such framing, coupled with the juxtaposition of imagery, allows the sequence to emulate a comic while still retaining its verisimilitude.

Examples such as this recall another of Bazin's optimistic observations: "The problem of cinematic adaptation is not absolutely insolvable. . . . All it takes is for the filmmakers to have enough visual imagination to create the cinematic equivalent of the style of the original, and for the critic to have the eyes to see it" ("Cinema as Digest" 20). The next section will explore one of the most successful examples of adaptation proper from the Golden Age of Comic Book Filmmaking: bullet-time.

From Discourse-time to Bullet-time

Cinema, as described by Lev Manovich, is "the art of motion, the art that finally succeeded in creating a convincing illusion of dynamic reality" (296). There are no illusions in comics; fixed images are unmistakably a fundamental feature of the medium. This section recognizes the central role that these frozen moments play in comic storytelling and charts the comic book movie's engagement with this medium specific device.

Given the possibilities of "motion" pictures, it is unsurprising that filmmakers have primarily been concerned with making comic book characters move, rather than freezing film performers. This was the main attraction of early adaptations, including the appropriately titled *Winsor McCay, the Famous Cartoonist of the N.Y. Herald and His Moving Comics* (Blackton and McCay 1911). In the film, cartoonist and animation pioneer Winsor McCay (playing himself) proposes to "make four thousand pen drawings that will move." Despite his colleagues' skepticism, McCay produces the drawings, the first of which features McCay's character from *Little Nemo in Slumberland*, Flip, inviting audiences to "watch me move," before the film segues into sophisticated animation.

McCay believed that animation would render all static forms of art obsolete, going so far as to claim that "there will be a time when people will gaze at [a painting] and ask why the objects remain rigid and stiff. They will demand action. And to meet this demand the artists of that time will look to the motion picture people for help" (Canemaker 163). Despite McCay's enthusiasm for motion picture technology, one need only look at the densely packed panels from the creator's original *Little Nemo in Slumberland* to recognize the unique possibilities of comics' seemingly stagnant imagery. Thus, before exploring cinema's adaptation of comics' frozen images, one needs to consider how this device is utilized in its native form.

A variant on the storyboard analogy that filmmakers adapting comics often assert is the snapshot fallacy. For instance, director Robert Rodriguez suggested that a film version of *Sin City* was possible because "the mediums are really very similar, these are just snapshots of movement" ("How It Went Down"). However, comic panels do not depict an indiscriminate instant, but

FIG. 4.16 Stills from the appropriately titled *Winsor McCay, the Famous Cartoonist of the N.Y. Herald and His Moving Comics* (Blackton and McCay 1911).

FIG. 4.17 Many actions take place in this panel, which is more than just a "snapshot of movement."

rather the image is carefully selected and constructed to carry the maximum amount of narrative weight. Thus, the encapsulated images of comics are very rarely a "snapshot," but more often contain a sequence lasting a longer duration. For instance, a panel will often include a speech balloon that would take minutes for the characters to speak. Or the image might convey a series of movements in one economical image, as seen in figure 4.17 (*Daredevil* #168, January 1981). In the carefully constructed panel, Daredevil is seen backflipping into the street while taunting a criminal; the criminal responds defiantly as he sets his dog (already seen jumping in midair) on the hero. Meanwhile, a homeless man resting beneath a newspaper surveys the scene—all conveyed in one panel, covering an event much longer than the oft-cited "snapshot."

These frozen images confer a measure of control not afforded to the film spectator. Not only is there great elasticity in how much time is covered by a particular comic panel, but there is also freedom in how much time the reader can devote to it. Seymour Chatman observes that, in literary descriptions, "events are stopped, though our reading- or discourse-time continues, and we look at the characters and the setting elements as at a *tableau vivant*" (123).

FIG. 4.18 The limitless discourse-time of the comic book *300* allows one panel to convey an elaborate group battle, an effect the limited discourse-time of cinema could not recreate.

Chatman goes on to demonstrate how cinema cannot achieve this "discourse-time." Eclipsing literature, comics enjoy a limitless discourse-time, as a panel can be read for as long as one pleases. While Atkinson argues that the "drive of the visual succession usually overcomes contemplation" (54), most comics scholars agree that the narrative can be arrested by a panel that invites readers to luxuriate in its encapsulated image.

As Michael Cohen asserted, a comic book panel "can be scrutinized and savoured in a way cinematic images cannot" (28), while cartoonist Harvey believes that in comics,

FIG. 4.19 The "fastest man alive" escapes the limitations of cinema's "motion" pictures to burst into comics on the cover of *Showcase* #4 (October 1956).

we are not rushed by the necessity of keeping up with images in constant motion. We can linger, taking as long as necessary to drink in all the visual information from each panel. . . . The story could be told in film. But it is impossible for film to do it effectively in precisely the same way. (188)

Thus, while the fixed image of a panel may be covering a moment of a particular duration, its frozen nature allows for unfettered attention, a virtue few other visual narrative forms, including cinema, enjoy.

As Cohen and Harvey suggest, there are a number of storytelling devices and conventions that creators regularly employ to take advantage of the form's static imagery. For example, the limitless discourse-time of comics allows for the framing of complex images with multiple points of interest. These panels cannot easily be recreated in cinema, as motion pictures would move far too fast for the composition to be fully perceived. This cinematic limitation is evident during the first encounter between the Spartans and Xerxes' personal guard in the film adaptation of *300*. In the comic, a single panel conveys the full dynamism and clamber of the battle sequence while also emphasizing how the Spartans operate as a fighting unit. This effect is lost in the film as the limited discourse-time necessitates cutting between dozens of shots.

The ability of comics' fixed images to create moments unobtainable in cinema is celebrated on the cover of the landmark comic book *Showcase #4* (October 1956), where the "fastest man alive," the Flash, bursts from the boundaries of the film frame onto the only form capable of capturing his "whirlwind adventures": comic books.[16] The Scarlet Speedster's emergence from the celluloid is a giddy riposte to those who fail to recognize comics' possibilities and extol "motion" pictures. Nonetheless, even the most ardent comic fan would have to recognize the virtues of cinema's convincing illusion of movement.

Discussing *Sin City*, Thomas Leitch observes that "Rodriguez's streaming video is constantly showing movement Miller's discontinuous tableaux can only imply" (*Film Adaptation* 201). One of the many examples of cinema easily capturing what comics struggle to convey can be found in the film's segment "That Yellow Bastard." The graphic novel contains the caption, "She tosses me a wink that'd make a corpse breathe hard." This caption is unaccompanied by an image, as it would take the comic successive panels to render this narration and still not capture the motion as aptly as the narrative description—as Flaubert argued, "The most beautiful literary description is eaten up by the most wretched drawing" (Giddings et al. 19). However, the same moment in the otherwise faithful film adaptation contains no voiceover narration, only a shot of the reviving wink, which can now be effectively rendered by cinema's motion pictures, if perhaps not to Flaubert's exacting standards.

Comic book film adaptations continue to trade on their ability to make comic characters "move," with publicity for *Ghost World* announcing, "The underground comic book comes to life." However, wider attempts to achieve a comic aesthetic have seen a number of filmmakers engaging in the seemingly counterintuitive practice of freezing *motion* pictures.

Italian film director Federico Fellini, who visited the Marvel Comics office in the 1960s, believed that "the world of comics may, in its generosity, lend scripts, characters, and stories to the movies, but not its inexpressible secret power of suggestion that resides in that fixity, that immobility of a butterfly on a pin" (Gravett *Graphic Novels* 2).[17] While the comics may not have lent cinema its "secret power," this has not stopped filmmakers from trying to discover it for themselves. Freeze-frame seems to be the most commonsensical filmic equivalent of comics' static images, and indeed it has been applied in several adaptations. For instance, in the *American Splendor* montage where Harvey Pekar finds inspiration for his autobiographical stories, everyday moments are held in freeze-frame before being rendered as comic book art.

However, there are many features of the comic book image that freeze-frame cannot replicate. As discussed above, comic book images are not split-second

FIG. 4.20 A storyboard from comic book artist Steve Skroce with its corresponding image in *The Matrix*.

moments, but cover a longer duration that freeze-frame is unable to communicate. Furthermore, Chatman challenges the use of this technique as an approximation of discourse-time noting, "Once that illusory story-time is established in a film, even dead moments, moments when nothing moves, will be felt to be part of the temporal whole, just as the taxi meter continues to run as we sit fidgeting in a traffic jam" (130). Finally, freeze-frame does not have the same suture effect of other filmic codes prompting Michael Cohen to describe it as "narratively awkward as it has the potential to disrupt spectator engagement" (30).

As noted in the last section, a number of films have used intermittent lighting effects, which evoke the discontinuous images of comics. While the 1998 adaptation *Blade* also used strobe effects, the film introduced a precursor to a more productive cinematic equivalent, which would be perfected one year later in *The Matrix* (the Wachowskis 1999): bullet-time.

Although *The Matrix* is not a comic book adaptation, it is recognized as one of the initiators of the current trend (Bordwell "Superheroes for Sale"). The creators of *The Matrix*, Andy and Lana (then Larry) Wachowski, initially conceived the concept for a comic book. To develop the idea for cinema, the majority of the film was storyboarded by comic book artist Steve Skroce, who had previously worked with the Wachowskis on the comic book *Ectokid* (*The Matrix Revisited*).[18] Thus, much like *Creepshow*, *The Matrix* could be described as an undeclared adaptation, and retrospectively be considered a comic book movie.[19]

One of the most innovative aspects of *The Matrix* was its use of digitally accentuated slow motion, which the creators termed "bullet-time." Bullet-time was achieved by filming the performer in a multi-camera rig against a green screen background, with the actor then composited back into the shot. This created the effect of the camera moving around the performer. Although antecedents exist (notably *Blade*), visual effects supervisor John Gaeta explained, "Bullet-time is something that was conceived for *The Matrix* specifically" ("What is Bullet-time?").

Although bullet-time is indebted to a number of influences, most notably slow-motion photography and wirework action sequences, the creators of *The Matrix* explicitly cited comics as a key component of the technique.[20] Perpetuating the snapshot fallacy, Gaeta explained that the "immediate result of [the Wachowskis'] comic background is their storyboards were far more dramatic, and the moments they select to actually draw, the snapshot in time, is often right on the head, the most maddening, the most emotionally evocative" (*The Matrix Revisited*). Specifically acknowledging comic books in the lineage of this technique, Lana Wachowski, recognizing the different specificities of the forms, stated that "comics are graphic-type storytelling where you could freeze a moment and make an image that sustains. As a counterpart, you can't really do that in film. We tried to do that" ("Follow the White Rabbit"). As a fan-filmmaker, Lana Wachowski does not subscribe to the storyboard analogy. She recognizes that bullet-time cannot completely recreate the limitless discourse-time of comics, but that it does allow for prolonged contemplation of interesting or complex images without the disengagement that freeze-frame creates.[21] Thus, this textual poacher positions comics as a goal to which digital cinema might aspire, which further challenges the technological determinist view of the comic book adaptation trend described in Chapter One.

Tom Gunning described the early years of filmmaking as the "cinema of attractions"; films were directly soliciting "spectator attention, inciting visual curiosity, and supplying pleasure through an exciting spectacle" ("Cinema of Attractions" 58). Many commentators have suggested that digital cinema has seen a return to the "cinema of attractions," with Andrew Darley describing these spectacles as the "antithesis of narrative" (104), and Brooks Landon calling them a type of "counter narrative" (69). However, throughout the late 1990s and into the 2000s, digital techniques moved from show-stopping novelty to one more production technique that is subservient to the narrative.[22] Comic book movies were among the films facilitating this development, with Aylish Wood suggesting that rather than being "the death of narrative . . . digital effects are able to introduce new dimensions" (386).

To support her argument, Wood cites the comic book-influenced *The Matrix* and its innovative use of slow motion. Bullet-time does not de-narrativize the film as some digital effects might, but allows the spectator to explore the narrative spatially (much as they would in a comic), viewing several areas of interest with a degree of participation rarely afforded by cinema's relentless images. Expanding on this point, Wood even goes so far as to compare bullet-time to comics, writing that there "is a need to rethink conventions of narrative in spectacular cinema, a cinema which exists in a continuum with other media that have multiple points of focus—computer games, comic book cartoons and multimedia installations" (386). This is evident from the image in figure 4.21 from a near-frozen moment in *The Matrix Reloaded* (the

FIG. 4.21 In this bullet-time moment from *The Matrix Reloaded*, the spatialized screen requires greater participation from the reader.

Wachowskis 2003), in which the spectator can choose to concentrate on five competing locus points.[23]

Although Warner Bros. trademarked the term "bullet-time," it is still applied to the many instances of digitally augmented slow motion that have permeated mainstream entertainments since the success of *The Matrix* (Wakeman). Unsurprisingly, as bullet-time proved to be an appropriate equivalent of comics' static imagery, comic book movies regularly contrived opportunities to include digitally accentuated near-frozen moments. For instance, upon taking the drug Valkyr, the hero of *Max Payne* (Moore 2008) is able to exact revenge in slow-motion flourishes. "Slo-Mo" is the drug of choice in *Dredd* (Travis 2012), with the denizens of Mega-City One using the narcotic to perceive time at 1 percent its normal speed. Commenting on the film's many "Slo-Mo" sequences, comic creator and *Dredd* concept artist Jock observed, "You almost get the effect of a comic panel" ("Slo-Mo"). Wesley Gibson (*Wanted*) and Kato (*The Green Hornet*) do not need any performance-enhancing drugs; their accelerated heart rates allow them to perceive time more slowly, thereby enabling the anti-heroes to take on multiple assailants. Following an early display from Kato, the Green Hornet excitedly explains, "You can beat the crap out of a million dudes at once because you can like freeze time or something once your heart starts pumping."

While comic book movies may have introduced and popularized bullet-time, these frozen moments are not confined to adaptations. McCloud notes that "whenever an artist invents a new way to represent the invisible, there is always a chance that it will be picked up by other artists. If enough artists begin using the symbol, it will enter the language for good" (*Understanding Comics* 129). As an increasing number of films, television shows, and other entertainments strive to be affiliated with an emerging comic book movie genre, the stylistic features of adaptations, including comic book-influenced slow motion, have been widely adopted. Whether it is the appropriately named Hiro, from *Heroes* (Kring 2006), who zips around exaggerated frozen moments, or the gladiator of *Spartacus: Blood and Sand* (DeKnight 2010), who attacks his rivals in slow-motion movements that recall the Spartans of *300*, this technique has gone beyond the boundaries of films based directly on comics. Such is bullet-time's ubiquity that it can be identified far from comic book movies. The technique has been used on television—to dissect crime scenes in *CSI* (Shankar 2009) and to suspend contestants mid-action in the game show *The Cube* (Adler 2009). For the 2009 MTV Movie Awards, a rig using forty-eight cameras captured the attendees in bullet-time ("Fashion 360"). It has also become a staple of video games such as *Max Payne* (Järvilehto 2001) and, fittingly, *Enter The Matrix* (Perry 2003).

In looking at adaptation from a sociological standpoint, Dudley Andrew writes that "the stylistic strategies developed to achieve the proportional equivalences necessary to construct matching stories not only are symptomatic of a period's style but may crucially alter that style" (*Film Theory* 104). Although bullet-time may have entered the cinematic lexicon through a desire to recreate the dynamic *tableaux vivants* of comics, the device has proliferated far beyond coloring a stylistic epoch. Since *Blade*, and more significantly since the success of *The Matrix* films, bullet-time has become commonplace in mainstream media, providing a new means by which to crystallize and accentuate movement, and finally achieve Fellini's "butterfly on a pin."

Visualizing Sound

Comics exist in a vacuum that requires the reader to see sound. The most commonsensical equivalent of this visual soundtrack in cinema is actual audio. Nonetheless, some "adaptation proper" is required. As Lefèvre points out, "in comics the visible appearance of the character and other ideograms can suggest the sound of a voice, but it remains largely an interpretation by the reader" (11), and Catherine Khordoc notes that "children are often surprised by the voices of their favourite comic book heroes adapted for film because their voices are not the ones they imagined" (159). However, this phenomenon is not confined to children, with many criticizing the vocal performances in adaptations such as *The Dark Knight* for not matching the "sound" of the comics.[24] Thus, it is not simply a case of finding a cinematic equivalent, but the *right* cinematic equivalent (if such a quality exists). Although most film adaptations simply bring resonance to a comic's symbols, the drive to create a comic aesthetic has seen a number of filmmakers attempting to remediate the many innovative ways comics visualize sound.

FIG. 4.22 The original hand-lettered example from *Watchmen* has a more organic feel than the uniform typed font.

The most frequently used device to visualize sound in comics is the speech balloon.[25] While antecedents have been identified in early forms of sequential art (Sabin 11), Ian Gordon believes that the consistent employment of balloons (which he credits to *Happy Hooligan* cartoonist Frederick Burr Opper) was one of the milestones in the development of the comic language (24). However, despite the speech balloon's central importance, Eisner describes it as, "a desperation device" as it "attempts to capture and make visible an ethereal element: sound" (*Comics & Sequential Art* 26). A number of strategies are employed to give the speech balloon greater versatility and make a virtue of this "desperation device."

As one of the graphic arts, the iconic lettering of comics achieves an auditory resonance unmatched by most printed material. Comic book dialogue traditionally was hand-lettered to ensure it had a more organic feel than the print in magazines and books. For instance, if one were to replace the comic text with rigid typeface, as in the example from *Watchmen* in figure 4.22, it is clear how the original lettering better captures the human voice than the more inert typeface of the altered example. As Mario Saraceni observes in *The Language of Comics*, the "irregular shapes of the letters resemble the irregular patterns in the way people speak, with varying tones and loudness of voice" (21). Even though many modern comics are lettered digitally, these fonts are designed to emulate handwriting, with many creators using software based on their own script.[26]

Further devices that allow comic book balloons to better echo a voice include emphasizing parts of the text. In the example in figure 4.22, the single word "dead" may solicit the reader's increased attention; however, without the use of a thicker line, "the" would not. Such variations in the text are rare in

FIG. 4.23 In these examples from *Watchmen*, *Ghost World*, and *The Dark Knight Returns*, the tone of each character's voice is inferred from the qualities of the speech balloons.

most traditional printed material and are used in comics to better approximate the sounds unavailable in the medium.

Similarly, greater characterization can be achieved through the alteration of the lines that make up the speech balloon. For example, the reader can infer from the first image in figure 4.23 that the *Watchmen* character Rorschach has a coarse voice while Dan's is smooth and regular; the broken line of the balloon in the *Ghost World* panel suggests the character is whispering; and in the third image the jagged lines, coupled with the absence of a tail, indicate that this is an off-panel character speaking through an electronic device. Describing the many types of speech balloons that a creator may use, Groensteen observes that "all these resources are intended to guarantee the intelligibility of the enunciative situation, that is to allow the reader to know who expresses what and by which method" (74).

Khordoc contends that the "ability to create the illusion of sound through visual devices is unique to comics" (173). However, during the first three decades of the medium, cinema was as silent as comics.[27] In this period dialogue would often be represented through the use of intertitles. Over time the graphics of these cards became more elaborate, as cinematographer John Bailey notes of *Sunrise* (Murnau 1927): "By this time in the silent era the intertitles started to take on a life of their own and they were used sometimes with an effect" (*Sunrise* DVD commentary). The effects used by later intertitles are comparable to those employed by comics' iconic sounds and one can see in figure 4.24 how in the early days of the form cinema did indeed "create the illusion of sound through visual devices."

Jeffrey Kirchoff makes this connection between intertitles and comic text (27), arguing that comics remediated cinema. However, Kirchoff's study is

 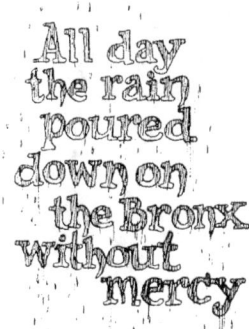

FIG. 4.24 As this intertitle from *Sunrise* (left) demonstrates, cinema has been visualizing sound since the earliest days of the form. Right (Eisner *Comics & Sequential Art* 11).

FIG. 4.25 In *Heroes*, translated dialogue follows the conventions of comic book speech balloons. *Kick-Ass 2* goes one step further by adding speech balloons around the on-screen translations.

limited to comic *books*, and therefore he does not consider the more complicated movement between the forms. Depending on your definition, comics predate film, and newspaper strips were well placed to influence all aspects of early cinema. Thus, intertitles would have gone back-and-forth between the forms in an example of the relay described earlier. While it is difficult to identify the relay's originator, as the onscreen dialogue of *Winsor McCay* suggests, animated films certainly borrowed from comics. For instance, *Soda Jerks* (1925), featuring the comic strip characters Mutt and Jeff, used speech balloons where an intertitle would disrupt the comedy.

In recent years, a further cinematic device has been tailored to match speech balloons. Subtitles, as the term suggests, typically appear at the bottom of the screen. However, in the comic book-inspired television series *Heroes*, characters who required translation had their dialogue appear in blocky paragraphs near their mouths in a close-up, or next to their body in a wide shot. In this way, the translation emulates a speech balloon as figure 4.25 demonstrates. Beyond referencing comics, these translations are an elegant solution to some of the problems associated with subtitles. Firstly, it is possible to tell who exactly is speaking, even in a crowded scene. Secondly, the visualized

FIG. 4.26 Unmediated sound effects from *Batman*, *Scott Pilgrim vs. The World* (top), and *Super* (bottom).

sounds are better integrated with the images allowing for a more cohesive mise-en-scène. This link is made explicit in *Kick-Ass 2* (Wadlow 2013), where subtitles are encased in speech balloons.

Another relied-on convention for visualizing sound in comics is the sound effect, indexical onomatopoeic signs that convey noise. Sound effects are often more expressionistic than speech balloons achieving iconicity comparable to the art. Groensteen prefers to describe comic book text as "*verbal* functions as opposed to *written* functions" because it is closer to speech in cinema rather than literature by the way in which it is integrated into the action (128). Despite the close proximity of sound effects to cinema, they are not widely remediated. Of the few films that have included sound effects, most could be considered commentaries, as they self-referentially employ a comic book code. For instance, the 1960s-era *Batman* television series and spin-off feature film (Martinson 1966) remain the most noted examples of sound effects on screen. In the series, sound effects were used even more liberally than they were in the source material to achieve a camp tone. Andy Medhurst, in describing this strategy, notes, "Camp often makes its point by transposing the codes of one cultural form into the inappropriate codes of another. It thrives on mischievous incongruity" (158). However, despite any subversive intentions, the sound effects continue to function much as they would in comics; expressionistically embellishing the actions to which they are applied. More modern examples of this self-reflexive use of sound effects can be found in *Scott Pilgrim* and *Super* (Gunn 2010).

Comic book creators have developed a number of ways to convey sound in comics and in many cases have made a virtue of this supposed limitation. However, there are areas in which comics' visualized sound trumps cinema's soundtrack. For instance, as Harvey notes, "word and picture can be coupled to reveal the hero's cheery bravado even in the very midst of thundering action, collapsing buildings, or stampeding elephants" (40). In the earlier example from *Daredevil*, the hero's repartee is clearly conveyed though speech balloons, even as he leaps from a great height into a busy city street. Cinema would struggle to recreate these moments, as any dialogue would be muted by ambient noise. Consequently heroes and villains in adaptations rarely engage in the mid-action banter of the source. Thus, it is ironic that despite the availability of sound in cinema, film adaptations often render comics' most loquacious characters mute.

Almost from its inception, cinema visualized sound. Even today, when such devices appear redundant, a few comic book adaptations and related films have sought to graphically convey dialogue and other sound effects. Although this device is not as prevalent as other efforts to cinematically recreate comic book conventions, these attempts testify to the desire among filmmakers to achieve a comic aesthetic. Furthermore, while the more direct ideograms of comic book sounds may not have been roundly embraced by cinema, as Chapter One discussed, they have been embedded in the language of new media.

Graphiation

Terms such as "voice," "signature," and "soul" are excitedly applied to novels, plays, and films in which the artist is deemed to have transcended the form and produced a work that channels their personality or worldview. Jan Baetens adopts Philippe Marion's term "graphiation" (147) to describe "the graphic and narrative enunciation" of comics. Many comics scholars argue that the medium is better able to convey the philosophy of an artist than more recognized authored mediums. For instance, citing Art Spiegelman's *Maus*, McCloud contends that "those lines speak in the distinctive voice of the artist far more than any camera or news article could" (*Reinventing Comics* 40).

Picking up McCloud's argument, Craig Hight notes how "underlying many of these works is the explicit assumption that these artists' drawing styles are much more analogous to handwriting than might be the case for the writing style of prose writers" (182). To demonstrate his point, Hight cites the work of Robert Crumb, which he describes as "unmediated" and "therefore all the more valuable as artistic expression" (182). In *Understanding Comics*, McCloud (also referencing Crumb) notes how comic book art is inescapably expressionistic (126).[28]

However, despite the more eager claims of some comics scholars, the film form's capacity for expression should not be underestimated. Indeed, the auteur theory is predicated on the belief that a film artist can "express his personality through the visual treatment of material" (Sarris "Auteur Theory" 562). Furthermore, as discussed in Chapter One, digital filmmaking techniques have afforded filmmakers greater control of the film artifact, and the form could now be considered, like comics, as one of the plastic arts. These developments prompted Robert Stam to conclude: "filmmakers no longer need a pro-filmic model in the world; like novelists, they can give artistic form to abstract dreams" ("Introduction" 12). However, is the control conferred on filmmakers by digital technologies tantamount to that of comic creators? Furthermore, has this control enabled a measure of comic book graphiation to emerge in those films striving to achieve a comic aesthetic?

As one would expect in a medium that conveys time through space, in comics space is a rapidly diminishing commodity. Indeed, Groensteen identifies "synecdochic simplification" as one of the five "principle characteristics of narrative drawing" (161). Accordingly, comic creators are often very selective in their storytelling, and rarely fill their panels with extraneous textual or visual information. McCloud celebrates this precision, writing, "The combination of simpler, more selective imagery and comics' many frozen moments lends a less fleeting, less transitory feeling to each moment, imbuing even incidental images with a potentially symbolic charge" (*Reinventing Comics* 33). As Chapter Five will explore, the necessary economy of comics' storytelling greatly influences the content of panels (e.g., the regular use of stereotypes), and how they are framed (e.g., exaggerated depth of field is often employed to convey the maximum amount of information).

Thus, a comic is similar to prose in that the "description of a scene . . . appears to be fully occupied by what it describes and never appears to lack

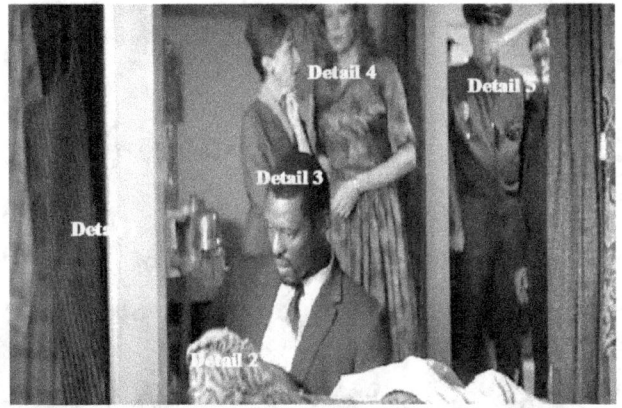

FIG. 4.28 The economic and selective imagery of comics is emulated in the opening scene of *Unbreakable*.

what it fails to mention" (Giddings et al. 18). Conversely, in a film adaptation "each frame would find itself inescapably loaded with unnecessary detail" (Giddings et al. 18). Thus, cinema's omniscience can often prove hostile to the source's selective aesthetic. Nonetheless, many filmmakers have sought to recreate comics' economic storytelling. For instance, a number of scenes in *Barbarella* (Vadim 1968), *Dick Tracy*, and *Unbreakable* (Shyamalan 2000) emulate comic books through minimal cuts and little to no camera movement.[29] For instance, in *Unbreakable* many scenes only contain a single shot, including the film's opening, which uses a carefully arranged mise-en-scène to convey pertinent information. In most traditional films, the scene's key details would be conveyed through individual shots, but, as *Unbreakable* emulates a comic aesthetic, the screen is spatialized with five different locus points.[30] The *tableau vivant*-like image in figure 4.28 allows the spectator to concentrate on different aspects of this tightly controlled shot, inviting a greater degree of participation than traditional film spectatorship.

Many filmmakers have sought to extend this economy to a selective use of imagery, including props. For instance, in *Winsor McCay* the various elements of the comic creator's studio were labelled in thick black lettering. Later adaptations, such as *Danger: Diabolik!*, employed symbols for clearer delineation of the plot (e.g., "$" bags in the opening scene). Of the 1990 adaptation *Dick Tracy*, production designer Richard Sylbert noted, "If you're going to do *Dick Tracy* there's only one way to do it, and that's with icons, where a car is just a car and a building is just a building" (M. Cohen 16). Cohen goes on to describe how the "abstraction of props extends to the use of generic labels" (26), a device that can also be found in other adaptations such as *Popeye* and *Batman*. However, like many of the techniques discussed in this chapter, the

FIG. 4.29 The use of symbolic props in *Winsor McCay*, *Danger: Diabolik!*, and *Popeye*.

FIG. 4.30 A scene from *Scott Pilgrim* that matches the source's selective use of imagery.

FIG. 4.31 Two digitally constructed images of the same street corner from *The Spirit*. The second image illustrates how comics' selective imagery can be used to highlight the pertinent details.

comic book adaptation's approximation of its source material's economic storytelling became more consistent and pervasive in the digitally bolstered, fidelity favoring Golden Age of Comic Book Filmmaking.

Art director Stuart Craig believes that the "best sets are the simplest, most 'decent' ones. . . . Reality is usually too complicated" (Bordwell and Thompson *Film Art* 117). From the expressionistic settings of film noir to the abstract backdrops of musicals, minimalist mise-en-scène can be identified throughout film history. Craig's approach to production design tallies with what McCloud sees as the goal of comic art: "By stripping down an image to its

FIG. 4.32 The mise-en-scène of *The 300 Spartans* is much more densely packed than the comic book adaptation *300*, which also depicts the Battle of Thermopylae.

essential 'meaning,' an artist can amplify that meaning in a way that realistic art can't" (*Understanding Comics* 30).

This minimalism is central to the comic aesthetic of many comic book movies. For instance, in *Scott Pilgrim* complicated or superfluous details are regularly dropped from the mise-en-scène, so that only the most pertinent features remain—much as they would in the source. Stu Maschwitz, the visual effects supervisor on *The Spirit* (Miller 2008), describes how he discovered from Will Eisner's comics that he "could express what this whole city is about with one small detail" ("Green World"). Maschwitz uses two images (shown in figure 4.31) to illustrate his point: the first is a fully detailed street corner, while the second is the same image, with all but the most pertinent details obscured by darkness. As Groensteen notes of comic creators, "The illustrator includes in his images only that which must be there" (119).

This more restrained mise-en-scène also extends to the use of props. The graphic novel *300* is loosely based on the 1962 CinemaScope film *The 300 Spartans* (Maté 1962). Comparing the film adaptation of *300* with *The 300 Spartans*, the comic book-inspired minimalism becomes evident. For instance, in the 1962 film, the Spartans' spears are one part of a costume and an even smaller part of the wider mise-en-scène. Accordingly, these weapons are no more privileged than the Spartans' headgear or Persian battlements, and are frequently left out of the frame by the medium shots the film readily employs. By contrast, the mise-en-scène in *300*, mirroring the comic, is much less densely populated with the few props each given greater prominence. Thus, in *300* the spears take on a symbolic quality and are an inextricable part of the mise-en-scène with wide shots regularly used to show their full-length as they are pointed upwards for maximum dramatic effect.

The minimalist aesthetic of comic books has extended beyond transformations to the undeclared adaptations of the comic book movie. For instance, the selective imagery of *Max Payne, Clash of the Titans* (Leterrier 2010), and the television series *Spartacus: Blood and Sand* owes much to comic book adaptations such as *Sin City* and *300*.[31] Thus, this comic book convention is moving beyond direct adaptations to those mainstream films that make up the comic book movie genre.

Jan Baetens suggests it would be worthwhile "to examine the extent to which some elements of film-making such as choice of props or casting could be compared on a structural level to graphiation in comics" (150). As detailed in Chapter One, "the graphic and narrative enunciation of the comics" has become more achievable within the malleable mise-en-scène of the digital age. As these screen spaces are more often constructed than filmed, a measure of the economy employed by comic book creators has emerged in comic book film adaptations. Thus, where once cinema's omniscient view was in danger of revealing more than is essential and obscuring what is essentially important, in these more tightly controlled mises-en-scène, comics' selective use of imagery can be better approximated.

Baetens contends that the "graphiateur is not the person in the flesh who signs the work, but an authority constructed by the reader" (151). The conception of a graphiateur with no fixed identity is a productive way of considering the creator of a comic book, as the industrial process generally finds more than one person producing a book. Two of the most overlooked roles in comic book production, which are fundamental to graphiation, are inking and coloring.[32]

With few exceptions, an inker outlines the art in a comic book. While in some cases the artist inks their own work, it is more often a separate role. The inker follows the lines of the artist to supply definition, add contrast, texture, and shading, as Lefèvre notes: "Although such outlines in drawn pictures may be less analogous to the external world, they are not necessarily inferior in their capacity for grasping the essential aspects of a scene" (7). In cinema, the delineation of props and actors is largely the responsibility of the cinematographer and is achieved through lighting; emulation of comic inking in cinema, then, is arguably unnecessary.

Nonetheless, as with other techniques in the comic aesthetic, the presence of equivalents has not deterred some filmmakers from attempting to recreate this aesthetic in the adaptation's mise-en-scène. Michael Cohen points to one early example in *Dick Tracy* where cinematic lighting achieves the same effect as comic book outlines: "Tracy walks toward the camera firing his Tommy gun. The strong backlighting from a single source forms a halo of light around the character" (29). While this sequence successfully achieves an outline, Beatty's Tracy needs to be shot in isolation against a bare black background. If props, other characters, or a detailed background had been used, the effect would have been impossible to realize with traditional cinematic lighting. However, since the digital revolution some filmmakers have successfully achieved comic book-style outlines.

Unsurprisingly, Ang Lee's *Hulk* also sought to remediate comic book inking. In one sequence, the antagonist Major Talbot is outlined in white prior to being engulfed by an explosion. This serves to prolong the character's screen presence and transition into the next shot, while also emulating the outlines of comic book graphiation. However, despite utilizing modern techniques, Talbot (like Tracy) is the sole element in the mise-en-scène. Possibly the first sustained application of comic book-style inking in an adaptation can be found in *Sin City*.

In order to maintain fidelity to Miller's graphiation, director Robert Rodriguez described how he used digital technologies to outline each figure: "The only way we'd be able to isolate actors from the backgrounds . . . was to shoot on green screen because then we could put lights anywhere" ("15 Minute Flick School"). Consequently, within the largely black-and-white aesthetic of *Sin City*, key characters and props are given their own outlines, much as they would in a comic. This technique was applied in later adaptations with digital colorists on *The Spirit* adopting the term "inked out" and applying the skills of comic book inking to all elements of the mise-en-scène ("Green World").[33] Although this "inking" is less evident in borrowings, it does enhance the comic aesthetic of these transformations while suggesting graphiation-like control of the film image.

Like inking, coloring is another key feature of comic book graphiation that is often overlooked. Comic books are known for a limited palette of bright primary colors. However, when cinema was just flickering into black-and-white life, newspaper magnate William Randolph Hearst published a comic supplement on October 18, 1896, that was "eight pages of polychromatic effulgence that make the rainbow look like a lead pipe" (Gordon 32). Ultimately, as McCloud notes, while color "hit the newspaper industry like an atomic bomb," the high cost necessitated a streamlining of the system and the "standard four color process took over" (*Understanding Comics* 187), with McCloud adding that "to counteract the dulling effects of newsprint and to stand out from the competition, costumed heroes were clad in bright, primary colors and fought in a bright primary colored world" (*Understanding Comics* 188). Thus, once the three-strip Technicolor process was introduced to cinema in 1935, film overtook comics' limited color palette.

Comics' reputation for primary colored fantasies saw many "alternative" comic creators adopting a dulled palette to signal their high-minded intentions, including *Maus* (Spiegelman 1986), *Our Cancer Year* (Brabner, Pekar, and Stack 1994), and *Ghost World* (Clowes 1997). Even when DC Comics colored *V for Vendetta* (Moore and Lloyd 1990) for American distribution, a muted scheme was maintained, and *Watchmen* (Moore and Gibbons 1987) distinguished itself from other mainstream fare through the use of secondary colors (including browns and purples).

Commenting on the comic book adaptation in his 2007 book *Film Adaptation and its Discontents*, Thomas Leitch suggested that "comics and movies deploy color very differently, since comics are normally limited to six colors" (194). However, the restricted palette Leitch describes was rendered obsolete by digital coloring. As Dennis O'Neil explained in a 1991 interview, the introduction of digital color allowed the creator to go from "sixty-four colors" to a "sixteen million color palette" (Pearson and Uricchio 26). Accordingly, subtler coloring became prevalent, even in mainstream comics.

Nonetheless, the primary colored reputation of comics pervades with many of the films that aspire to a comic aesthetic adopting this restricted range.[34] David Hughes notes that "early in the development of *Dick Tracy*, Beatty decided to make the film using a palette limited to just seven colors—primarily red, green, blue and yellow—to evoke the film's comic book origins" (54). Similarly, despite the pale green hues of the comic, the adaptation of *Ghost World* adopted the coordinated colors of other adaptations, with Linda Hutcheon summarizing that "fans felt [the adaptation] lost in the process what was considered the perfect, if sickly, analogue for the two punky girls' hyper-self-conscious and cynically ironic lives: the drained-out blue-green tint of the comics' pages" (43). Thus, the convention of distinctly comic book imagery trumped fidelity, a trend one can identify across adaptations and related films where an outdated four-color graphiation is still prevalent.

An extreme example of enhanced comic book coloring is the color pop. Even within the tightly controlled panels of comics, some information is more pertinent than others. In these instances, the artist will often highlight part of the image through distinct, often garish, color to grab the reader's eye.[35] This technique has long been employed in comic book adaptations. For example, the art director of *Batman*, Nigel Phelps, described how "it is the monochrome aspect of it that's just a really good way of keeping everything cohesive and things would pop when you need it" ("Visualising Gotham").

Coordinated palettes and color pops are obviously not confined to comic books and their adaptations. Many films, particularly those with a heightened verisimilitude (e.g., those in the musical and science fiction genres), have adopted similar approaches. However, these techniques became an integral part of the comic aesthetic moving into the modern trend. For instance, in the World War II-era opening of *X-Men*, the ethnicity of the people being herded into a concentration camp is highlighted through the use of a color pop on the Star of David.

Filmmakers using such color pops regularly acknowledged their influences, with *Thor* (Branagh 2011) costume designer Alexandra Byrne describing the techniques she employed to allow the Norse god to stand out: "I started with the comics. I would say the biggest input for Asgard was the original artwork of Jack Kirby. The world he created is amazing. . . . For the population of Asgard I wanted to keep the idea of the comic book graphics where [Kirby] ombrés out the crowd, and keeps it very monochrome. That seemed a very good way to keep the population of Asgard present but not distracting" ("From Asgard to Earth").

The increased use of color pops in comic book movies could partly be attributed to the availability of new postproduction technology. In the digital age, manipulating color to emphasize certain features and to create effects has become much simpler and more commonplace. The digital intermediate (DI) process in which a film is digitized to allow for ease of postproduction has become synonymous with digital color grading.[36] While most digital color grading is subtle (it was used in *O Brother, Where Art Thou?* to give the film a sepia tone), the technique has been used to fully realize the comic book color pop.

Sin City is home to many extreme examples of comic book color pops. The comic deals in a largely black-and-white palette, only breaking the monotone aesthetic for an eye-catching splash of (primary) color. However, rather than confine themselves to the judicious flourishes of the source, the filmmakers accentuated the comic aesthetic in *Sin City*. In the comic book only one color pop was used, the eponymous Yellow Bastard of the third story. Yet in the film a variety of color pops were employed for everything from bloodstains to

Cadillac cars. John Belton describes such images as "color for color's sake. It is an exercise in graphic stylization that experiments with various digital tools, from Photoshop to Paintbox, to see what the new medium can do" (63). This experimentation is not confined to *Sin City*; other transformations (e.g., *Scott Pilgrim*), borrowings (e.g., *Hellboy*), undeclared adaptations (e.g., *Unbreakable*), and paratextual materials (e.g., *Thor*) all emulated this approach. Thus, it is ironic that filmmakers used the same digital technologies that had freed comic creators from a limited color palette a decade earlier to achieve a comic aesthetic that no longer appeared on the page.[37]

Citing Hans-Christian Christiansen, Lefèvre describes how, in comics, "every drawing is by its style a visual interpretation of the world, in that it foregrounds the presence of an enunciator" (8). Despite comics' specificity, a number of comic book movies have taken cinema's capacity for expression, recently enriched by digital technologies, to attempt "adaptation proper" of comics' handcrafted images. While these equivalents certainly enhance the prescribed comic aesthetic of these films, is it possible to detect the presence of a graphiateur?

With his minimalist, high-contrast art, Frank Miller has one of the most idiosyncratic styles in mainstream comics. This aesthetic is perfectly in keeping with the creator's preferred character types—hard-boiled heroes who skulk around dimly lit cities. Since the start of the Golden Age of Comic Book Filmmaking, two films (*Sin City* and *300*) have been directly adapted from Miller's comics, while the creator himself stepped behind the camera for the Will Eisner adaptation, *The Spirit*.[38] In these films, many moments meticulously mirror the source, with the control filmmakers are afforded enabling them to achieve unprecedented levels of visual fidelity. One might even go so far as to argue that a measure of Miller's graphiation has seeped into the film's mise-en-scène.[39]

For instance, although Miller's solo directorial debut *The Spirit* was not based on his own work, the comic creator's style was evident in every shot. Such hallmarks included high contrast lighting, color pops, and a minimalist mise-en-scène. These techniques would have been difficult to achieve using traditional technology, but in the digital age a film can brim with Miller's graphiation. Walter Benjamin suggested that the "traces of the storyteller cling to the story the way the handprints of the potter cling to the clay vessel" (*Illuminations* 92). Similarly, whether directly involved in the adaptation or only serving as the source text creator, the presence of Miller molds these digitally augmented films.[40] Other creators-turned-filmmakers who have also shaped the more malleable digital film in their particular styles include Dave McKean (*MirrorMask*) and Kaare Andrews (*Altitude*).

Like many of the other techniques discussed in this chapter, while comic book-style graphiation is most evident in transformations, it can also be

FIG. 4.33 Frank Miller's comic book style of high contrast, minimal detail, and color pops (*Sin City*, left) can also be discerned in his digitally bolstered directorial debut *The Spirit* (right).

FIG. 4.34 The suit for *Iron Man* was based on Adi Granov's more recent comic books rather than the character's traditional look, thereby allowing a measure of the comic creator's graphiation to seep into the digitally augmented film.

discerned in borrowings and comic book movies. When developing *Iron Man* (2008), director Jon Favreau explicitly cited the more "mechanical" and "tech-based" suit designed by comic creator Adi Granov rather than the traditional design, which looked like a suit somebody "slipped on that was skintight and happened to be metallic" ("I am Iron Man"). Thus, by basing the design on specific comics, the prosthetic and digital versions of Iron Man carried a measure of Granov's graphiation over to the film.

The possibilities of digital technologies have been widely embraced by Hollywood. Nonetheless, as detailed in Chapter One, graphic narrative mediums such as video games, illustrated books, anime, and in particular comics have pushed filmmakers to embrace the plasticity and expressivity of these new techniques. While the images in a collaborative medium like cinema may never achieve the enunciation of hand-drawn lines, the small measure of graphiation that has emerged has served to deepen and enrich Hollywood's comic aesthetic.

Symbolic and Specialized Codes

In *The System of Comics,* Thierry Groensteen questions whether there are any codes specific to comics (6). However, Groensteen's analysis stops at the panel border. If one moves inside the panel some candidates emerge, including motion lines, speech balloons, plewds, thought balloons, and krackle. Such codes are so tethered to the comic form that they often defy "adaptation proper." Nonetheless, the pursuit of a comic aesthetic has seen a number of filmmakers attempting to replicate these codes with varying degrees of success.

When analyzing cinema's "signifying organization," Metz identifies two main types of code: "cultural" and "specialized." For Metz, cultural codes are "so ubiquitous and well 'assimilated' that the viewers generally consider them to be 'natural'. . . . The handling of these codes requires no *special* training" (74). Conversely, specialized codes appear "more explicitly as codes, and they require a special training" (74). This dichotomy can also be found in comics with the codes that seem to succeed in cinema more often being cultural codes, while the specialized codes usually remain lost in translation.

Many of these comic-specific codes at first seem arbitrary. For instance, Stephen Prince notes how "some pictures employ purely representational codes with no overlap in real-life experience." To illustrate this point, Prince cites the "streaky lines used to represent speed in comics" ("Discourse of Pictures" 23). However, like many seemingly arbitrary comic codes, motion lines do have an overlap in real-life experience, as recounted in David Kunzle's *History of the Comic Strip*:

> Artists ever since the Renaissance, knew that drapery carried by the wind or trailed by a running figure created lines independently suggestive of movement, and speed lines external to the object occur when the movement is through or from water or snow [and also] dust or air displaced by a striding figure. (351)

Similarly, in the 1970s, comic book creators developed variations on motion lines by abstracting from photography. For instance, Daredevil artist Gene Colan found that "if the camera moves with the moving object, that object will remain focused while the background will now be streaked," a technological quirk he then applied in comics to suggest speed (McCloud *Understanding Comics* 113).

Thus, motion lines are a symbolic exaggeration of an actual experience. McCloud identifies this process—symbolically abstracting real-life moments—as the origin of many comic book codes. He illustrates how a number of these seemingly arbitrary symbols began "as simple pictures of actual reactions [which] then drift into the more abstract territory of pure symbols" (*Making Comics* 96). One of the examples cited by McCloud is the droplets that emanate from a character's head when they are surprised or anxious, which he believes was abstracted from sweat beads. In *The Lexicon of Comicana*, Mort Walker humorously named these flying sweat droplets "plewds," a term that has been adopted by many creators who have regularly used this largely abstract symbol to suggest physical or mental stress.[41]

Another distinctive comic book signifier that could be categorized as "arbitrary," but may also have a relationship with real-life experience is the speech balloon. As explored earlier, the text in a balloon is used to visualize sound and therefore its relationship to its referent could be considered arbitrary. However, the balloon itself may have an overlap with real-life experience, with Eisner making a connection in the above image between speech balloons and the "steam from warm air expelled during conversation" (*Comics & Sequential Art* 26). The overlap of this signifier with real-world experience is further evident in the Italian term for comics, "fumetti," which translates to "little smokes," a reference to the visualization of speech balloons (Sabin 217). Thus, speech balloons can be seen as another example of a seemingly arbitrary sign that in fact has a familiar origin.

That so many of these distinctly comic book codes have their basis in real-life experience goes some way towards explaining why readers universally understand them. Nevertheless, more specialist codes can be found with McCloud identifying how some symbols "are strictly metaphorical and require you and your audience to both 'know the code' before the message can get through" (*Making Comics* 96). Providing examples, McCloud describes how certain symbols from manga are migrating to North American comics (e.g., the bulging vein-on-forehead), while "other manga symbols still seem pretty strange to western readers," such as blood shooting out of the nose to signify sexual arousal and a mucus bubble to indicate sleep (*Making Comics* 97).

As McCloud suggests, many comic codes require the reader to go through a period of training to infer their meaning. One clear example of this can

FIG. 4.36 The code to signify the hero's Spider-sense would be difficult to comprehend without further explanation.

be found in the Spider-Man comics. In the comic books, one of the hero's abilities is a paranormal "Spider-sense" that alerts him to danger. This Spider-sense is most often depicted with jagged lines that emanate from the hero's head. These lines have no real overlap in human experience, and it would be almost impossible for a reader to infer its meaning without some "training." In fact, Pierre Comtois notes how readers often misunderstood artist Steve Ditko's application of this technique (56). With repeated textual reference, however, the uninitiated reader gained the training to infer the code's meaning, thereby allowing it to be used liberally throughout the rest of the story.[42] Thus, within unique comic book codes there is a division between cultural codes (e.g., motion lines and speech balloons) that can be followed, and specialized codes (e.g., Spider-sense), which require at least some training. This is a pertinent distinction as one considers how cinema negotiates these comic specific codes.

One distinctly comic book code employed by modern comic book adaptations is the motion line. As motion lines convey movement within comics' seemingly static images, this device might seem redundant in *motion* pictures. The code was liberally applied in early animated shorts such as *Winsor McCay*, and went on to become a regular part of cartoon grammar. Among live-action features, the device was used for the climax of *Superman: The Movie* (Donner 1978) to suggest the hero's supersonic speed as he flew around the Earth. However, despite this memorable example, the use of motion lines in live-action films has been rare, but in recent years the motion line has become a more relied-on convention.

As discussed earlier, the comic book-influenced bullet-time has become a popular cinematic technique. However, due to the relative absence of movement within these near-frozen moments, it is often necessary to convey to

Comics   Cinema

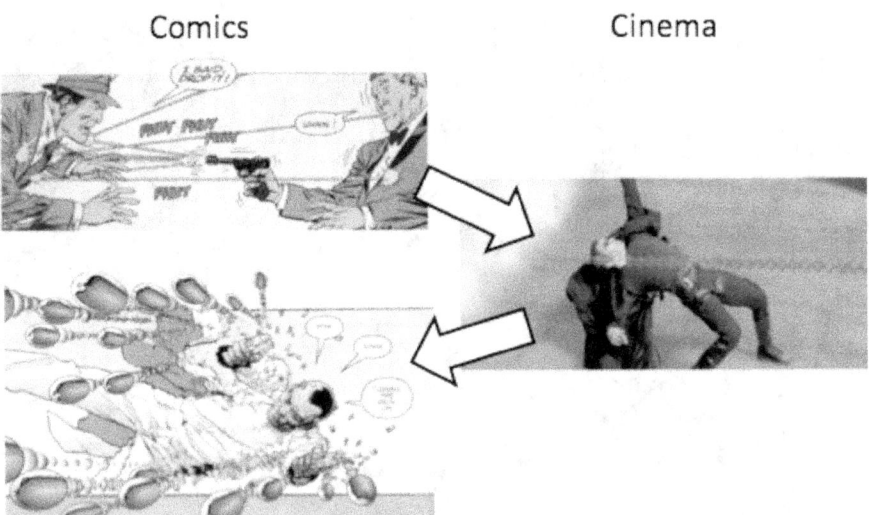

FIG. 4.37 Bullet-time, replete with motion lines, was returned to comics in *Planetary* #9 (April 2000), albeit with a cinematic inflection.

the spectator what actions are taking place, and resultantly motion lines are employed much as they would be in comics. For example, in the rooftop sequence from *The Matrix*, it is possible to infer, even within the near-frozen moment, the speed and direction of bullets from the motion lines they leave in their wake.

To achieve photorealism, digitally created motion blur had been applied to computer-generated images such as the dinosaurs of *Jurassic Park* (Spielberg 1993) (Prince "True Lies" 30). However, while the motion lines of *The Matrix* do adopt some camera mimesis, it is not the subtle motion blurring of a CGI dinosaur, but rather the exaggerated, abstracted device of comic books. The device found a similar application in the comic book adaptation *V for Vendetta* (McTeigue 2005), where the direction, speed, and even the rotation of throwing knives were all conveyed with motion lines, and in *Heroes*, where a superfast character is shown in slow motion leaving an extended trail that recalls not only motion blur, but the lines that follow comic book characters such as the Flash. Thus, in adapting one comic book technique, static motion, cinema was motivated to learn another, the motion line. In an example of the relay of codes between comic books and cinema described earlier, following the success of *The Matrix*, bullet-time was even adapted (or rather returned) to comics in *Planetary* #9 (April 2000), replete with motion lines that evoked camera mimesis.

Innovative methods for remediating the speech balloon into a film's mise-en-scène were identified earlier. In a speech balloon, the text is a specialized code

FIG. 4.38 Remediated thought balloons in *American Splendor*, *Scott Pilgrim*, and *Wanted* strengthen their comic aesthetic.

because it requires reading competence to be understood, while the balloon itself, given its overlap with real-life experience, is a cultural code. Consequently, spectators can easily comprehend the untranslated use of speech balloons in an adaptation such as *Kick-Ass 2*. Comparable to speech balloons, but signifying inaudible mental processes, is the comic book thought balloon. Catherine Khordoc praises this device over literary and cinematic equivalents due to its directness (170), but as McCloud notes, this signifier has in recent years been eclipsed by the use of captions in comics (*Making Comics* 155). McCloud, like Groensteen (128), compares comic captions to film voiceovers, and so it should be unsurprising to find that nearly all comic book film adaptations use voiceover rather than try to approximate the thought balloon. Nonetheless, like sound effects, thought balloons often appear in more knowing comic book movies such as *American Splendor*, *Scott Pilgrim*, and *Super*. Some borrowings have even managed to provide a visible manifestation of a character's thoughts. In *Wanted* (Bekmambetov 2008), the protagonist's unspoken feelings for a coworker who has been sleeping with his girlfriend are articulated in the letters and teeth that fly into the air after he hits him with his computer keyboard. Like the translated dialogue of *Heroes*, it is easy for a spectator to imagine this image encased in a balloon. The appearance of this comic book code pushes *Wanted* further towards a comic aesthetic.

Reader and spectator alike understand these signifiers. Perhaps it is their status as cultural codes, abstractions, and exaggerations of real-life experiences that allow them to be read without any training. Nonetheless, there are some

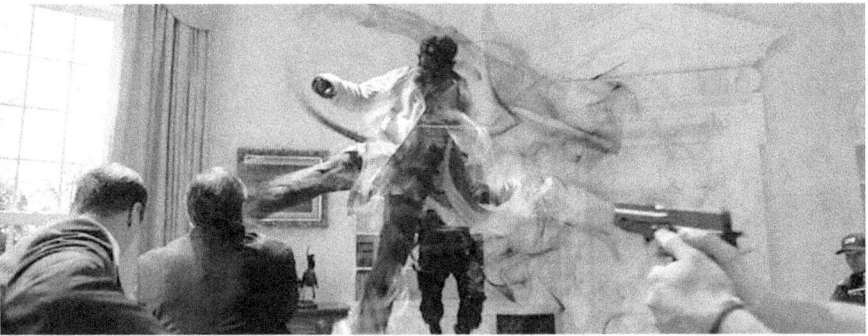

FIG. 4.39 Superpowers can be achieved in cinema without the need to remediate the abstract colored shapes of comics, yet many comic book adaptations and related works such as *Fantastic Four*, *X2*, and *Heroes* have begun to apply this signifier.

comic devices that have yet to make the transition to cinema; unsurprisingly these doggedly untranslatable signifiers are among comics' specialized codes.

As explored above, the Spider-sense device is a specialized code that requires a reader to be educated for it to be understood. This training is easily instilled in the comic reader through repeated textual referencing. However, to articulate the ability in the 2002 adaptation, *Spider-Man*, a combination of slow motion and point-of-view shots were used. In this instance, remediation of the comics' visual signifier, as had been achieved with cultural codes, would have resulted in confusion for the uninitiated audience.

However, one set of specialized codes that have recently made their way to the screen are the abstract colored shapes that convey a superpowered character's abilities, which are sometimes termed "krackle" (Mendryk). For example, the X-Men villain Magneto's ability to manipulate metal is indicated in the comics by blue shapes, but in the first adaptation no device was necessary, as the mutant moves cars, trains, and bullets about the screen. However, as audiences became more familiar with comic book movies and their superpowered protagonists, these abilities were increasingly signified via the abstract colored

FIG. 4.40 *Watchmen* not only recreates but also exaggerates the abstract colored shapes of comics, while undeclared adaptation *Push* also conforms to this genre convention.

shapes typical of comics (e.g., *X2* (Singer 2003), *Fantastic Four* (Story 2005), and *Heroes*).[43] If anything, this code has been exaggerated to meet the comic book movie convention of heightened abilities described in Chapter Two. For instance, Dr. Manhattan's powers are often displayed subtly in the *Watchmen* comic, but in the adaptation they are conveyed through large blue shapes. Similarly, the undeclared adaptation *Push* (McGuigan 2009) saw rainbow effects used to convey telekinetic abilities, a convention displayed in past films without the requirement of an overt signifier. These aesthetic decisions are in keeping with the comic aesthetic of modern adaptations and related films, and are discernible to an audience "tutored" in the cinematic translations of these once specialized codes.

Examples such as the migration of krackle from page to screen suggest that while specialized codes may not be immediately amenable to cinema, the desire to signal fidelity and bolster the heightened reality of comic book movies has seen some filmmakers ignoring preexisting equivalents in favor of aggressive remediation. Although it could be argued that such efforts are unnecessary and cumbersome, these codes, which were previously specific to comics, have become an increasingly prominent part of cinema's comic aesthetic.

Peculiarities of the Medium

McCloud optimistically suggests that media convergence "is a two-way street. As the technological distinctions between media fall away, their conceptual distinctions will become more important than ever" (*Reinventing Comics* 205). However, as convergence relies on content that can move across any number of platforms, producers are increasingly diluting specificity, with many commentators noting that the boundaries between forms have become more diffuse (Friedberg 214; Jenkins *Convergence Culture* 254; K. Thompson 249). For instance, when asked for this study whether comics had lost their specificity in the digital age, comic creator Mark Waid responded, "I've been very adamant about the fact that no matter what you do with digital comics, it's still got to look like a comic. You don't need it to have bells and whistles, you don't need it to have sound effects, voices, and limited animation because then it is another medium."[44] I have argued elsewhere that conglomerate efforts to exploit transmedia potential have deepened the influence of cinema on comics ("Special Effect"). But as the relay between these forms suggests, this process is cyclical, and so we should be unsurprised to find comics have also shaped cinema.

The Golden Age of Comic Book Filmmaking saw filmmakers eagerly engaging with the language of comics, seeking out cinematic equivalents, or developing them where they could not be found. Accordingly, adaptations sought to emulate, even replicate, panel borders, transitions, and layouts; they attempted to freeze motion pictures, visualize sound, and interpolate a host of codes that had previously been considered unique to comics. Furthermore, some filmmakers have used the malleability of digital tools to bring a measure of comic book graphiation to cinema.

The resulting comic aesthetic is most evident in the transformations that prize fidelity. Nonetheless, many borrowings have adapted aspects of these techniques. Furthermore, the comic aesthetic does not stop at the boundaries of the adaptation process. As discussed in Chapter Two, following the post-*X-Men* boom in comic book adaptations, a number of Hollywood films (e.g., *Jumper*, *Push*, and *Max Payne*) strived to be affiliated with the emerging comic book movie genre. As this chapter demonstrated, many of these films even emulated the look of popular adaptations. Thus, by proliferating through undeclared adaptations, this comic aesthetic has colored modern Hollywood cinema.

Film theorist Rudolph Arnheim argued that "in order that the film artist may create a work of art it is important that he consciously stress the peculiarities of his medium" (35). One might argue that those filmmakers aspiring to a comic aesthetic have ignored cinema's full possibilities. But could we go so far as to suggest, as Waid does when discussing digital comics, that these films have become "another medium"?

To more fully emulate a comic, filmmakers frequently place restrictions on a production. For instance, in *Dick Tracy* the action is kept within stationary frames to "encapsulate" each narrative unit. However, as Bazin asserts, the "idea of a *locus dramaticus* is not only alien to, it is essentially a contradiction of the concept of the screen" (*What is Cinema?* 105). Thus, in mirroring the panels of comics, the film limited its full expressivity. Mark Bould, citing Bolter and Grusin, notes a similar loss of specificity in *Sin City*, a film that "uses digital tools to give its viewer the immediacy of the comic book image" (112), and which at certain moments strives "to erase the new medium 'so that the viewer stands in the same relationship to the content as she would if she were confronting the original medium'" (114). However, has the adaptation "erased" the film form to the point that it could be argued that in *Sin City* the semiotic gap has narrowed beyond recognition?

Clearly, despite the eager exchange of content and conventions, medium specific distinctions remain between comics and cinema. For instance, *Dick Tracy* may aspire to Chester Gould's vignettes, but the film still employs many distinctly cinematic edits—even within the confines of its comic aesthetic. *Sin City*, despite its high fidelity to its source, finds many spaces to include moments that are unique to cinema's means of expression, such as the previously cited wink from Jessica Alba's Nancy that only *motion* pictures can effectively depict. Comic books may have had a deep and lasting influence on the aesthetics of modern Hollywood cinema, but as a "rich, sensorially composite language" (Stam "Beyond Fidelity" 61) film is capable of integrating many influences. Thus, although these films may, as Michael Cohen suggests, demonstrate a "choice to move away from the language of 'cinema' towards the language of 'comics,'" (34), they retain their medium specificity, albeit heavily inflected.

To identify this inflection and cinema's application of the comic aesthetic, this chapter will conclude by analyzing four films from the Golden Age of Comic Book Filmmaking: *Unbreakable*, *Watchmen*, *Scott Pilgrim*, and *Green Lantern* (Campbell 2011). Released just as the genre's period of articulation was ending, *Unbreakable* was marketed as a mystery, nonetheless its adherence to a comic aesthetic prompted Grant Morrison to describe the film as "faithful to the form in a way we'd never seen before on-screen or in comics" (323). As demonstrated in Chapter Two, although *Watchmen* is shaped by a variety of cinematic and extra-cinematic influences, the film's fetishization of the source text extends to its means of expression. Similarly, *Scott Pilgrim* displays many influences (especially video games and anime), but two of the greatest determinants are the source material and comic book movie genre. While writer Geoff Johns's comics were regularly cited in the production and promotion of *Green Lantern*, the film, like most adaptations of long-running characters, is a looser borrowing.

In his book, *Adaptations as Imitations*, James Griffith describes the difficulties that beset even the most fidelity-minded adapter. "Finding an equivalent for every trope would prove to be more of a problem," he wrote. "Filmmakers, therefore, may pick up and develop only selected motifs" (43). Similarly, none of these adaptations utilize all the techniques discussed in this chapter, but between them they testify to the sustained interest in translation that has marked the Golden Age of Comic Book Filmmaking.

Confirming the relative compatibility of panels and gutters with shots and transitions, many shots in these films animate the source in medium specific ways. For instance, the content of the panels in *Scott Pilgrim's Precious Little*

FIG. 4.41 The opening panels of *Scott Pilgrim's Precious Little Life* are replicated in the film using techniques appropriate to that aesthetic form.

Life (O'Malley 2004) are replicated in the first act of the film, albeit with the added tracks of motion and sound. Examples such as these challenge the stringently separatist view of some adaptation scholars that translation between cinema and the forms it adapts is impossible. Furthermore, while not quite as sustained as the multi-screen imagery of *Hulk*, *Scott Pilgrim* does contain a number of instances of split-screen that evoke the source and further its comic aesthetic. Also like *Hulk*, the film features a variable frame, with non-diegetic borders introduced in sequences that are inspired by the comic book. Similarly, while *Unbreakable* does not try to remediate panels, it does allude to the economy of comics with many scenes containing few cuts and minimal camera movement.

However, efforts to explicitly evoke comic panels are relatively finite. For instance, *Green Lantern*, like many borrowings, focuses its fidelity around

FIG. 4.42 Many of the digitally augmented slow-motion moments in *Watchmen* mirror the source material.

peak moments such as the discovery of Abin Sur's crashed ship. In an example of adaptation proper, this peak moment is depicted much the same in the film as it is in the comic without the need for elaborate framing devices. Such examples suggest that the ready-made equivalents of comics and cinema's fundamental units necessitate no further matches, even within transformations.

The parallels between panels and shots, however, should not give credence to storyboard analogies; arguably insurmountable differences between the mediums remain. As demonstrated in the example from *The Amazing Spider-Man* #33, the co-presence of images in comics can create moments unobtainable in cinema. For instance, in *Watchmen*, much of the tension in Rorschach's session with a psychoanalyst stems from the co-presence of comic panels, as the layout allows the reader to juxtapose the inkblots, Rorschach's anemic responses, and his violent memories. This effect is diminished in the film where one image replaces another. Thus, despite some compatibility, there remain important distinctions between the forms, which imbue them with their strengths and weaknesses.

While all the adaptations make some use of slow motion, *Watchmen* is the greatest proponent of the bullet-time technique that has proven so effective in capturing comics' static images. The film frequently uses bullet-time to sustain key images with many of these instances crystallizing the graphic novel's peak moments.

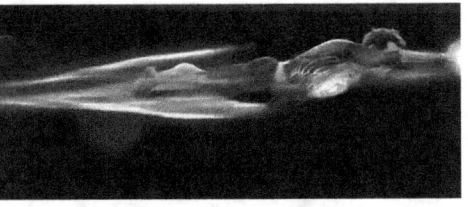

FIG. 4.43 Both *Scott Pilgrim* and *Green Lantern* contain codes once considered specific to comics such as speech balloon-like subtitles, motion lines, and abstract colors to signify heightened abilities.

All four films employ the visual economy of comic books. In *Watchmen*, for instance, key narrative clues are highlighted through color pops. One example is the Comedian's smiley badge, which despite the darkness of the opening scene is always bright yellow (an effect that could only be achieved through postproduction color correction). In *Unbreakable* and *Green Lantern*, characters peer into the minds of others where the pertinent details are separated from a black-and-white aesthetic through color pops. While *Scott Pilgrim* also includes color pops, the film takes this selective imagery a step further with many scenes set against a minimalist mise-en-scène that has all but the most pertinent details removed.

Of the films, only the more self-aware *Scott Pilgrim* attempts to remediate sound effects and speech balloon-like subtitles. However, *Unbreakable* is the only film not to include codes that were once considered specific to comics, with motion lines and abstract superpowers appearing in *Watchmen*, *Scott Pilgrim*, and *Green Lantern*.

With the exception of *Green Lantern*, each film makes a concerted effort to solicit increased spectator participation. For instance, the opening credits of *Watchmen* are made up of a series of history-redefining *tableaux vivants*. These shots contain several locus points, which are presented through deep focus. As in the example from *Unbreakable* described earlier, these story elements would traditionally be conveyed in separate shots, but in this comic

FIG. 4.44 In the opening montage of *Watchmen*, several *tableaux vivants*, with multiple locus points, are presented though slow motion and deep focus.

book-influenced film they are presented as single, densely packed shots, with the spectator afforded greater discourse-time through slow motion.[45]

A meditative take on a supernatural story that culminates in a twist ending, *Unbreakable* bears all the hallmarks of its writer/director M. Night Shyamalan. However, apart from some color correction, the film does not appear to have made the same use of digital technologies as later comic book movies. Nonetheless, the audience is provided with a glimpse of how the film might have appeared if it were a more heightened comic book movie. Following David Dunn's first foray as a vigilante, a newspaper reports on his rescue of a family. The story is accompanied by an artist's rendition of Dunn as a square-jawed hero. This clever allusion to comic book exaggerations demonstrates an artist's ability to craft an image. A semblance of this control is evident in more recent, digitally tailored comic book movies.

In terms that evoke Lev Manovich and Robert C. Harvey, *Green Lantern* actor Mark Strong picks up on how the use of digital techniques in these films allows for a control similar to comic graphiation: "The CGI suit is going to give me the physique of the comic and I can see why they have done that. If you're faithfully recreating [the comic] then the best way to do it is part animation. I like the idea that some of you will be drawn, because it is obviously a direct link back to the comics" ("Green Lantern's Light"). Similarly, *Scott Pilgrim* uses green screen technology to recreate the seemingly simplistic, video game and manga-influenced images of Bryan Lee O'Malley's original comic. Although the mise-en-scène of *Watchmen* is not as constructed as *Scott Pilgrim*, a measure of graphiation can also be discerned. For instance, the superpowered character Dr. Manhattan was digitally created in postproduction following motion capture of actor Billy Crudup's performance. As the finished film negotiates Crudup's features within the comic's art, the adaptation is infused with a measure of the source's graphiation.

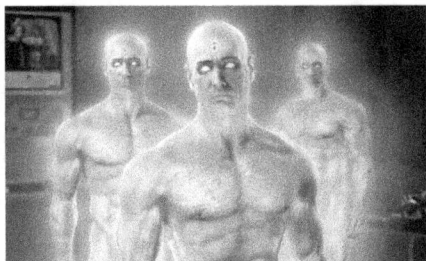

FIG. 4.45 The application of digital techniques in *Watchmen* and *Green Lantern* enabled the filmmakers to shape the films much like a comic creator.

The Golden Age of Comic Book Filmmaking saw filmmakers actively engaging with comics' previously unique means of expression. Medium-specific equivalents were applied on a number of occasions. In other examples, new strategies were developed, often by employing the freedoms offered by digital technologies. Although some of these innovations did not spread beyond their initial application, many found use in a number of adaptations and those undeclared adaptations that make up the comic book movie genre. The proliferation of such techniques should not suggest that the gap between comics and cinema has narrowed to the point that storyboard analogies have been realized, but separatists must recognize that these forms are now more closely aligned. These cinematic efforts to grasp the language of comics have not only codified a comic aesthetic within the genre, but, with many films vying to be affiliated with the comic book movie, twenty-first century Hollywood filmmaking has developed an unmistakable comic book inflection. The following chapter will consider how conventions of framing and mise-en-scène, shared by comics and cinema, have been exaggerated in adaptations, thereby deepening this comic aesthetic.

CHAPTER FIVE

How to Adapt Comics the Marvel Way

> Elijah: The thing to notice about this piece. The thing that makes it very,
> very special is its realistic depiction of its figures. When the characters
> reached the magazine they were exaggerated, as always happens.
> —*Unbreakable* (Shyamalan 2000)

Elijah, the unlikely antagonist of comic book movie *Unbreakable*, is first introduced at his art gallery showing a piece of original comic art—"a classic depiction of good versus evil"—to a prospective buyer. In his pitch, rich with subtext, Elijah articulates how mainstream comics subscribe to an approach in which no framing device is too heightened, no composition too dynamic, and no character too extreme, or as Elijah would later put it, "jazzed up, made titillating." As in Chapter Four, this final chapter will consider how the twin imperatives of fidelity and comic book movie convention, along with the presence of fan-filmmakers, has led comic book adaptations and related films to aspire to a comic aesthetic. However, where the previous chapter focused on means of expression, this chapter will look at larger flourishes that once might have been dismissed as "comic-booky," but are today among Hollywood's most relied-on conventions.

Mainstream comic book publishers are unashamed by embellishment. In fact, many hold exaggeration up as the high criterion to which artists should aspire. Published in 1978, the instructional art book *How to Draw Comics the Marvel Way* was described by its co-author, Spider-Man co-creator Stan Lee, as the first instructional book on drawing comic book superheroes. In the book, Lee (working with popular Marvel Comics artist John Buscema) explained many of the formal aspects of comic book art and how to tailor them to the "mildly magnificent Marvel style" (8).

Lee and Buscema's guide, which is still in print, has proven hugely influential on generations of comic book artists. For instance, when organizing a cover for this book, I was fortunate to commission Marvel Comics artist Will Sliney

(*Spider-Man 2099*). I offered only general guidelines—"comic book movie heroes line up outside a movie theatre"—and yet my dull suggestions were transformed into a dynamic cover populated by expressively posed figures. I asked Sliney if he had ever read *How to Draw Comics the Marvel Way*, to which he enthusiastically responded, "Yes, absolutely. It still holds up today." He later elaborated, "The best of the 'How to' books break everything down into simple steps, which are important for an artist long before their own style develops." While this book's cover is distinctly Sliney's work, the conventions identified by Lee and Buscema inform this image, as they do many contemporary artists.

While Lee jokingly concludes the preface of *How to Draw Comics the Marvel Way* by writing, "Don't tell our competition what you've learned," other mainstream publishers place a similar emphasis on dynamic storytelling conventions and adopt comparable techniques. For instance, DC Comics editor Dennis O'Neil noted in the Bat-bible that "stories should above all, move. Batman should never do something sitting that he can do running or leaping or jumping off a rooftop. Exposition and explanation should always be integrated with action." Although he does not use Lee and O'Neil's excited terms, Thierry Groensteen identifies five "principle characteristics of narrative drawing" in *The System of Comics* that tally with the instructions found in popular guides: anthropocentrism, synecdochic simplification, typification, expressivity, and rhetorical convergence (161–62).

Such strategies extend far beyond superhero titles, with Scott McCloud noting,

> After 60 years of mutations, the superhero genre currently incorporates hundreds of embedded stylistic "rules" governing story structure, page composition and drawing style and when the creative community trained in that field ventures into other genres, it tends to take many of those rules along for the ride. Such Trojan horses aren't always the creators' doing, though. From a publisher's standpoint, it may be commercial suicide to do it any other way. (*Reinventing Comics* 114–15)

McCloud explicitly cites *How to Draw Comics the Marvel Way* for perpetuating this exaggerated style, noting how "many of its basic rules still are followed—consciously or not—in today's superhero comics" (*Reinventing Comics* 123). Thus, while some comics do not employ such dynamic techniques, most mainstream comics do, including many that have been adapted to cinema. Accordingly, *How to Draw Comics the Marvel Way* provides an insight into the strategies behind Marvel Comics' production practices, as well as many of its competitors and imitators.

Commentators and critics frequently characterize films as having comic book qualities.[1] Although such descriptions are often a barely veiled criticism, the use of this term does suggest that comic book nuances can be discerned in cinematic storytelling. As this chapter will attest, such nuances have blossomed in recent years into a full-fledged style. While variants on these conventions might also be identified in other traditions (e.g., theatre, painting, and prose); as described in the previous chapter, comics and cinema share a semiotic overlap.[2] While this unique overlap might facilitate a comparatively easy back-and-forth between the forms, it also makes it difficult (arguably impossible) to identify influences that are distinctly comic or cinematic. To negotiate the active relay between the forms, Lee and Buscema's seminal guide will be used in this chapter to chart how filmmakers learned to adapt comics the Marvel Way.

Framing and Composition

As discussed in the previous chapter, comic creators can enliven a panel by modifying its border. The dynamism of these panels and layouts is often matched by the composition of the encapsulated image. Groensteen describes this principle of narrative drawing as "rhetorical convergence" explaining that the "narrative drawing obeys an imperative of optimal legibility. Consequently, it uses different parameters of the image (framing, composition dynamics, color placement, etc.) in a manner that mutually and concurrently reinforces them to the production of a unique effect" (162).

Of course, comic books do not hold a monopoly on dynamic compositions with painting, theatre, photography, and many other art forms all capable of employing medium specific devices to create energetic framing. Furthermore, a number of framing techniques have been relaying between comics and cinema for decades, such as the canted or "Dutch" angle, where a composition's horizon is set at an oblique angle to the frame. The Dutch angle is often credited to comic books, but it has many antecedents in cinema. As early as *The Cabinet of Dr. Caligari* (Wiene 1920), filmmakers were employing this disorientating effect, with the technique becoming a relied on convention of the expressionist film movements of the 1920s and 1930s. During this time, elaborate framing devices were not common in comic strips. Only when the medium moved from newspapers to its own format did more ambitious techniques such as Dutching become commonplace. The self-reflexive (over)use of the Dutch angle in the 1960s *Batman* television series brought the technique wider attention and solidified its relationship with comic books in the minds of many, including *Batman & Robin* (1997) director Joel Schumacher.[3] When Batman and other comic books made the transition to modern films many long-standing tropes (including the Dutch angle) were adapted (or returned) to cinema.

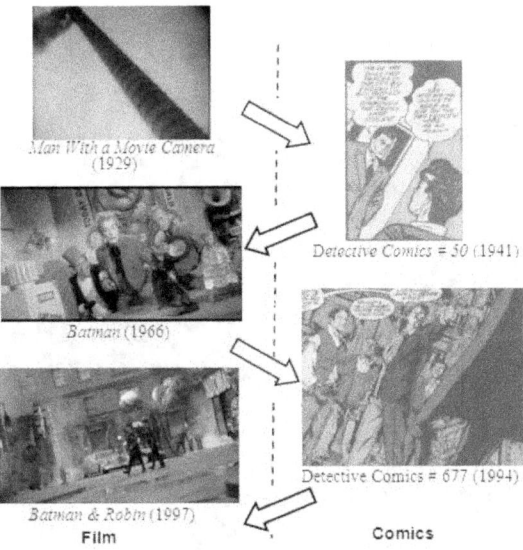

Film   Comics

FIG. 5.1 Many techniques have relayed between comics and cinema including the Dutch angle.

The shared history of comics and cinema is littered with examples of such back-and-forth, which can be attributed, in part, to the propensity of film-makers for textual poaching.[4] For instance, when Orson Welles was developing *Citizen Kane* (1941) comics was a true mass medium.[5] Welles himself was frequently associated with broad entertainments, even lending his voice to the radio adaptation of pulp hero and Batman antecedent, The Shadow. Thus, it is unsurprising to identify a comic inflection in Welles's films. Joseph McBride, who characterizes Welles as a comic book fan, describes "the influence of *Batman* in the boldly angled expressionist style of *Citizen Kane*" (276), with Thomas Inge making a similar connection (xx). Such influences might include Welles's famous use of extreme low angles, a device regularly employed by comics of the time. Furthermore, in their use of exaggerated depth of field, comic books share many qualities with Welles's lauded deep-focus photography.[6] Thus, it is easy to imagine conventions going from Bob Kane to *Citizen Kane* and back again during this fertile period of cross-pollination.[7]

In later years, filmmakers were actively advised to seek inspiration from comic compositions by university text books such as *Exploring the Film*, which urged students to study Marvel Comics' *The Amazing Spider-Man* as "one of the best sources of dynamic pictorial angles" (Edgerton 32). Accordingly, while not every filmmaker could be considered a "textual poacher," comics have been found to influence some of the more wildly expressive framing of cinema, just as comic book conventions are no doubt indebted to film. Such examples demonstrate the active relay that comics and cinema have enjoyed

FIG. 5.2 In *How to Draw Comics the Marvel Way*, various techniques are demonstrated to create a "feeling of more movement and better design" (Lee and Buscema 121).

for more than a century, and what Michael Cohen describes as "visual correlations" (13).

The emphasis that has traditionally been placed on dynamic compositions by the comic book industry is to be expected given their popularity with readers. Such conventions were overtly championed in *How to Draw Comics the Marvel Way*, in which Lee identifies the devices by which a "feeling of more movement and better design" (121) can be achieved. The example in figure 5.2 is typical of the Marvel Way in how it uses an exposition sequence to demonstrate the techniques that an artist can employ to achieve a more energetic composition. Lee writes that the first set of drawings is "the way any comic-book company might do it," while the second set is done in the "mighty Marvel style" (118).

An asymmetrical composition is one of the techniques used to enliven the second version. As Duncan and Smith note,

> symmetrical composition tends to give every character and object in the panel
> equal importance and can be visually boring. The conventional wisdom for main-
> stream comic books, with their emphasis on action and adventure genres, is that
> figures in a panel must be arranged asymmetrically to make both the characters
> and their actions more dynamic. (141)

A second technique is the mixing of angles, with Lee suggesting that in comic books some "angles are more dramatic, more interesting than others" (116). Examples throughout the book demonstrate how changing the angle can give a scene a greater "sense of urgency," make it "more compelling," or simply less "blah" (116–17). A further strategy employed by comic book artists to give compositions more energy is depth of field, which is emphasized by a constant shifting of figure size with characters and objects placed at different (sometimes over-extended) planes of perspective. Lee writes that a panel "is much more impressive when the figures are drawn different sizes. It gets dull for a reader to see characters who are pretty much the same size throughout the page" (121).

Yet comics are often criticized for the overuse of such techniques with McCloud describing "exaggerated depths of field" as "genre prerequisites" of superhero comics (*Reinventing Comics* 114). Similarly, in *Comics & Sequential Art*, Will Eisner uses one of his own science fiction stories "The Visitor" to illustrate the virtue of restraint. Eisner argues that "the temptation to go 'hog-wild' with perspective shots and panel shapes is hard to resist" (91), but that such an approach can remove "the reader from direct intimate involvement" (99). Eisner contrasts the story as it originally appeared in eyeline level framing with a version employing a variety of perspectives to demonstrate how, given the fantastical nature of the story, a dynamic composition is redundant and can lead to spectator disengagement.

Thus, while it could be argued that Lee's second layout is more interesting than its prosaic alternate, there is a risk of overusing these techniques, with even the most mundane story element deemed worthy of an elaborate depth of field, bizarre angles, and disjointed composition. Despite such creative pitfalls, and perhaps owing to the correlations with cinema, many film adaptations have framed scenes the Marvel Way.

In keeping with the heightened reality of comic book movies identified in Chapter Two, adaptations frequently rely on the same strategies suggested by Lee in what might otherwise be considered a mundane exposition sequence. An example from the 2003 comic book adaptation *X2* (Bryan Singer) can be seen in figure 5.3; the scene is set in the White House Oval Office and involves the president of the United States, a senator, and a military scientist. This is the second scene of the film to be set in the Oval Office. The earlier sequence featured the president being attacked by the teleporting demon-like mutant, Nightcrawler, and was described by reviewers at the time of its release as "startling" (McCarthy). There are no such theatrics in this scene, which is little more than an extended conversation. Following the previous Oval Office scene and other equally dramatic moments, there is a discernible desire on the part of the filmmakers to infuse this long, but necessary, exposition sequence with comparable energy.

FIG. 5.3 In this exposition scene from *X2*, a dynamic comic book-like frame is created using techniques identified in *How to Draw Comics the Marvel Way*.

Firstly, asymmetrical compositions are used throughout, with few shots equally balanced. While asymmetrical compositions are a convention of comics, as Bordwell and Thompson point out, "since the film frame is a horizontal rectangle, the director usually tries to balance the right and left halves" (*Film Art* 143). Secondly, the shots are composed so that the three characters are frequently in different planes of perspective, thereby changing their shape relative to each other and from shot to shot. The changing of figure size is used in comics to keep the panels interesting, and one can see how *X2* mirrors this in the second image (the handshake in the foreground with the third character in the background), which is very similar to the final panel in Lee's example.[8] Such extended depth of field can be found in many other films, but in this comic book adaptation it is used repeatedly from shot to shot, becoming as exaggerated as it is in the source.[9] Most noticeably, of the scene's thirty-eight shots, twenty-one are from either a high or low angle, with eyeline shots in the minority. The contrast and range of angles in this scene are even more dramatic than Lee's comic book example and serve the same function: giving the scene a greater sense of urgency.

To demonstrate how unconventional the framing in this sequence is, one need only compare it with a similar Oval Office scene from *Independence Day* (Emmerich 1996). In this sequence, the president meets with his staff and

FIG. 5.4 This brief exposition scene from DC Comics adaptation *Catwoman* conforms to a number of the exaggerated framing conventions identified in other adaptations.

advisors as the first images of an alien invasion emerge. The framing for this sequence would be considered by Lee as "average," as all of its thirty-two shots are evenly balanced; there are only five shots that are not from eyeline level, and the shallow focus photography is far from the exaggerated depth of field found in *X2*. If the exposition scene from *X2* had been shot at eyeline level like *Independence Day*, using the traditional two-shot and with characters in the same plane of perspective, it still would have conveyed the same information. However, in doing so, the scene would have more closely resembled Lee's first, more pedestrian, example. Thus, the use of dynamic framing in the comic book adaptation enables it to match the dynamic quality found in other scenes within the film and the source material.

While many of the techniques in *How to Draw Comics the Marvel Way* are evident in adaptations, this should not suggest that the filmmakers are purposely adopting this style, but rather it testifies to the, perhaps unconscious, desire to achieve a comic aesthetic. Nonetheless, a number of filmmakers have explicitly cited Marvel Comics as having informed their choice of framing, including Louis Leterrier (*The Incredible Hulk* DVD commentary) and Kenneth Branagh (*Thor* DVD commentary). Similarly, *The Amazing Spider-Man* (Webb 2012) animation supervisor David Schaub positioned comic book-style foreshortening, which Lee describes as "vitally important" (77), as an aesthetic criterion for his work, saying that "the lens is often animated throughout the shot to achieve dramatically foreshortened compositions that have become one of the signatures of the Spider-Man artwork" ("Rite of Passage").

These techniques are not confined to Marvel Comics adaptations. Films based on rival DC Comics titles also share these conventions. For instance,

FIG. 5.5 Bordwell contrasts a panel from *Watchmen* with a scene from *The Matrix* in order to demonstrate how modern mainstream films employ "graphically dynamic compositions" typical of comic books.

in a brief exposition sequence in *Catwoman* (Pitof 2004), shown in figure 5.4, a staff member confirms the villain's suspicion that her husband is cheating on her. Despite its expository nature, the sequence brims with the techniques identified in comic books and many of their adaptations: thirteen of the sixteen shots are from either a high or low angle, depth of field is accentuated throughout, and many compositions are asymmetrical with a number of shots employing Dutch angles. Thus, whether identified or not, a variety of comic book adaptations frame their shots the Marvel Way.

These devices are not confined to direct adaptation, but have been identified in the wider category of comic book movies and beyond. Citing the foregrounded bullets in *Wanted* (a comic book adaptation), the cascading bullet shells in *The Matrix* (a comic book movie), and the airborne playing cards in *21* (a non-comic book film), David Bordwell suggests that these images remind the audience of comic book panels, "those graphically dynamic compositions that keep us turning the pages" ("Superheroes for Sale"). Contrasting the cascading shells in *The Matrix* (the Wachowskis 1999) with a panel from *Watchmen* (Moore and Gibbons 1987), Bordwell's point is well made; many comic book movies adopt the convention of contrasting figure size through the use of exaggerated depth of field. Examples such as these demonstrate how framing conventions, common to both comics and film, are often given a comic book inflection in films that wish to signal their status as comic book adaptations. These stylistic flourishes are not only evident in recent adaptations, but also in related films that strive to achieve a comic aesthetic.

Performance

Comic book framing conventions may infuse even the most prosaic film adaptation sequence with energy, but these techniques are not solely relied on to achieve the dynamism of the source. One aspect of the mise-en-scène that is noted for adopting comic book conventions is performance. In his 2007 book *Film Adaptation and Its Discontents*, Thomas Leitch proposes "performance is not central to novels or illustrations or comic books as it is to the cinema" (198). However, many comic professionals and scholars challenge Leitch's view. *The Spirit* creator Will Eisner considered "the human form and the language of its bodily movements" as "essential ingredients of comic strip art" (*Comics & Sequential Art* 100), arguing that "if the skill with which an actor emulates an emotion is, in large part, the criterion for evaluating his or her ability, certainly the artist's performance at delineating the same on paper must be measured with the same yardstick" (104). Thierry Groensteen places a similar emphasis on the central figure, by including anthropocentrism and expressivity among his five principle characteristics of narrative drawing. Groensteen defines anthropocentrism as the prioritization of the character as "the agent of the action," while expressivity describes how the "characters should be as expressive as possible" (161–62).

Leitch also contends that in comic book adaptations "performative styles depend less on any medium-specific comic-book look than on the individual style of their particular source and the relation they seek to establish to that source" (199). However, looking across the modern genre, one can detect a consistent performance style. This style was identified by James Naremore when he described how the "digital era," coupled with the rise of "comic-strip films of various kinds, seems to involve a qualified return to a style that pre-dates Stanislavsky," with performances that are more expressionistic ("Acting in Cinema" 118).

Of course, larger-than-life performances are not confined to comic book movies. However, as Naremore points out, "most movies contain a heterogenous mix of performing styles and skills," adding that "Hollywood in the studio period usually required that supporting players, ethnic minorities and women act in more vividly expressive fashion than white male leads" ("Acting in Cinema" 115). Thus, perhaps the greatest distinction between comic book movies and many other genres is that it tends to be the lead's performance that is pitched at a higher register.

As Naremore suggests, the peculiar requirements of the comic book movie have given rise to less realist performances, with many of these choices stemming from conventions on the page. For instance, the demonstrative depictions of mainstream comics is partly attributable to the difficulties of conveying emotion in a medium without a soundtrack and populated by characters whose faces are often covered. As Grant Morrison colorfully observed, "Expecting these masklike, often masked faces to convey understatement was like expecting stained glass to act" (76). Similarly, Scott Bukatman suggests that the superhero, "denied the expressivity of the face, must rely on the boldness of bodily presentation" ("Secret Identity Politics" 115)—an expressivity many adaptations maintain.

In addition to masks and costumes, actors often have to contend with the exactitudes of computer-generated imagery (CGI). Strengthening Naremore's contention that digital technologies have produced a return to pantomimic traditions, Steven Spielberg described how the use of motion capture on *The Adventures of Tintin* (2011) required, "a little more projection of one's feelings. I think performance has to be, not forced, but extended a little stronger than normal . . . I went for actors who were naturally expressive and who didn't hold back" ("The Journey to *Tintin*").

Furthermore, unlike the stoic leads of westerns, crime films, and action movies, a comic book movie protagonist often creates two different personas, or alter egos, with the distinction between them enforced through pantomime-style acting. Emulating the source material, these two performances are often modeled along stereotypical gender lines. As Catherine Williamson notes, comic book heroes use "gender performance as tools to fight crime" (3). Similarly, Jules Feiffer describes how in Superman comics, "Clark Kent was the put-on. That fellow with the eyeglasses and the acne and the walk girls laughed at wasn't real, didn't exist, was a sacrificial disguise, an act of discreet martyrdom" (12); while in the Bat-bible, Dennis O'Neil describes Batman's alter ego Bruce Wayne as "not exactly effeminate, but nobody would mistake him for John Wayne—or Batman."

Naremore cites comic book movie *RoboCop* (Verhoeven 1987), in which Peter Weller plays a police officer transformed into a machine-man hybrid, as an example of this duality in cinema. However, twin performances, reinforced by expressionistic acting, can be seen in a variety of comic book adaptation roles. For instance, to accentuate the hero's two sides, Christian Bale adopted a gravelly delivery and many pronounced poses as Batman, which distinguished the crime-fighter from the foppish Bruce Wayne. Similarly, Brandon Routh, evoking Christopher Reeve, flitted between Superman as the confident hero, the indestructible "Man of Steel" and Clark Kent, the clumsy, bookish coward. Such performances prompted David Bordwell to summarize that "comic-book movies offer ripe opportunities for this sort of masquerade," concluding that performers "get no strokes for making [acting] look easy, but if you work really hard you might get an Oscar" ("Superheroes for Sale").[10]

Yet not every performance in these comic book movies is pitched at a heightened reality. In a reversal of the "heterogenous mix of performing

FIG. 5.6 Lee and Buscema explain how to create "Marvel-style drawings" (66).

styles" ("Acting in Cinema" 115) that Naremore identified in the studio era, the heightened reality of comic book movies often finds the leads behaving more expressionistically than their supporting players. Accordingly, characters that would be described in Proppian terms as "helpers" and "donors" tend to be played more understatedly. Examples would include Patrick Stewart's Professor Xavier in *X-Men*, James Rhodes as played by Terence Howard (and later Don Cheadle) in the *Iron Man* series, and Gary Oldman's Jim Gordon in *The Dark Knight Trilogy*, who Bordwell suggests seems to have "stumbled in from an ordinary crime film" ("Superheroes for Sale").

To isolate the features of "comic book-style" acting that make these leads so expressive, it is productive to return to the instructional art book *How to Draw Comics the Marvel Way*, seen in figure 5.6.

In the book, Stan Lee compares two similar ways of conveying the same pose. He suggests that the "variations may not seem to be major, and yet as simple a device as thrusting the head farther forward, or spreading the legs farther apart, can make all the difference in the world. Basically, the smaller figures are perfectly adequate drawings; but the larger ones are Marvel-style drawings!" (66). Many of Lee's tactics for suggesting power are also practiced by bodybuilders. Quoting ex-bodybuilder Samuel Fussell, Bukatman

FIG. 5.7 The expressionistic techniques used to convey power in comic books like *The Dark Knight Returns* are also employed by bodybuilders (e.g., the "Archer" pose Arnold Schwarzenegger popularized as a bodybuilder).

describes the "walk" competitors use "to emphasize their supersolidity. . . . They burrowed their heads slightly into their shoulders to make their necks appear larger. They looked bowlegged, absurdly stiff, and infinitely menacing" (*Matters of Gravity* 59–60). These flourishes are evident in the staging of many mainstream comics, where impressionism gives way to performances that express power.

Many comic book adaptations employ this dramatic posturing with each pose often maximized to the point of exaggeration. The influence of these comic book techniques becomes apparent if one contrasts the comic book film adaptation *300* (Snyder 2007), with its source material and the 1962 Cine-Scope film *The 300 Spartans* (Maté) that inspired the graphic novel. As seen in figure 5.8, the actors in the earlier film, while employing some of the theatricality expected of a period film, are far more restrained and naturalistic than the comic book-inspired dynamism of their 2007 counterparts.

Looking at comparable scenes from the 1962 film, the comic, and comic book adaptation, the influence of the comic on the performances and the staging of actors becomes clear. In the 1962 film, scenes tend to be framed in a medium shot with the performers staged, but not adopting any pronounced poses. In contrast, scenes for the 2007 adaptation were frequently filmed in long shot, which allows the full figures to be displayed. Like Spartan bodybuilders, the actors adopted dynamic poses with their heads thrust up, legs spread, and chests extended. These expressionistic performances are further accentuated by the minimalist mise-en-scène and selective use of imagery identified in Chapter Four as being typical of comic book adaptations. Isolating comparable moments such as these, one can identify many of the strategies from the Marvel Way and discern the source's influence on the performances in this adaptation.

FIG. 5.8 The influence of comic books on today's more expressionistic performances becomes apparent when one contrasts *The 300 Spartans* with the *300* graphic novel and film adaptation.

Many of the strategies suggested by Lee were echoed by *X-Men* actor Hugh Jackman when he described his approach to Wolverine: "One thing that mesmerized me about wolves, they always had their nose to the ground . . . that is why they seem to appear like they are always looking through their eyebrows, and I wanted to get that for Wolverine" (Lipton). Accordingly, during his performance, Jackman continually pushes his head forward, adopts a wide stance, and extends his chest.

A comic aesthetic calls for a performance that will not get lost in the dynamic framing, minimalist mise-en-scène, and many other heightened conventions of the genre. Responding to that challenge, today's comic book movie stars regularly deliver performances that are pitched at a heightened reality, combining the implied power of a bodybuilder with the physical virtuosity of a tap dancer. Like many of the conventions that will be discussed in this chapter, when it comes to comic book movie performances, there seems to be little room for restraint.

The Chosen Moment

Boltie: You don't see them bored in comic books.
The Crimson Bolt: That's what happens in between the panels.
—*Super* (Gunn 2010)

Part of the emphasis on the body in comics is attributable to the medium's discontinuous means of expression, which, as the epigraph from *Super* suggests, focuses on sustained moments that leave the "boring" parts out. Duncan and Smith describe each panel as a paradigmatic choice, in that the depicted image is juxtaposed by all the images that could have been chosen (133). As many commentators point out, the chosen moment needs to best summarize the sequence or action (Eisner *Comics & Sequential Art* 103; Groensteen 162; Atkinson 56). However, for mainstream comics, such as Marvel superheroes, the chosen moment must not only communicate meaning, but also be dynamic. This point is underlined in *How to Draw Comics the Marvel Way*, where it is suggested that aspiring artists "draw a series of stick figures . . . depicting as many different stages of that action as possible," before picking the pose that has the greatest impact (Lee and Buscema 60). Lee and Buscema's stick figures, each one conveying an incrementally different stage in an action, resemble the various phases of an animated figure. Hence, it is appropriate that Jack Kirby, one of the artists regularly cited for bringing a sense of movement to comics, began his career in animation (Harvey 29). Working on *Popeye* for Fleischer Studios, Kirby would draw in-between animated cels. As

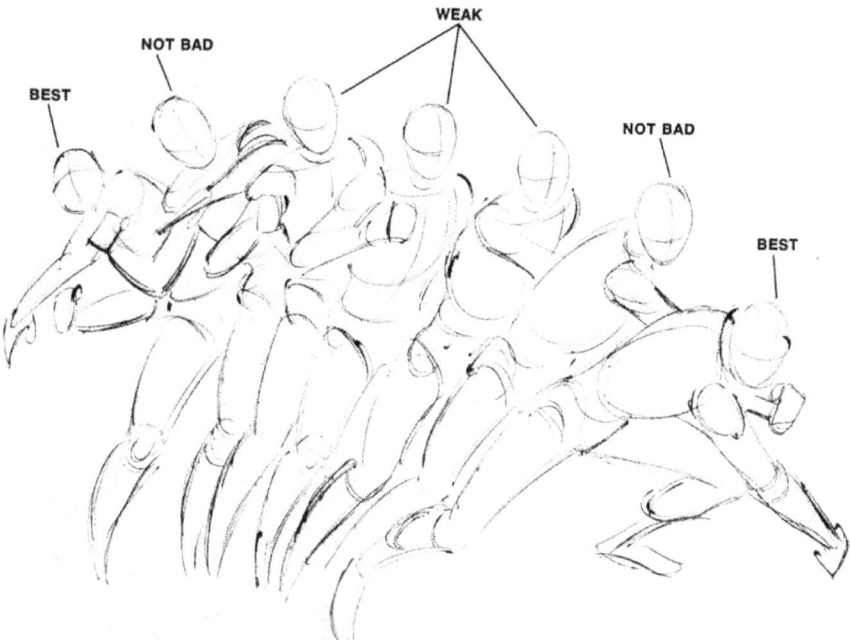

FIG. 5.9 Lee and Buscema suggest drawing a series of intermediary poses and selecting the one that has the most impact.

FIG. 5.10 Artist Jack Kirby's experience in animation would have equipped him with the skills needed to bring a greater sense of movement to comic books.

FIG. 5.11 The comic book conventions identified in *How to Draw Comics the Marvel Way* are evident in Jim Steranko's concept art for *Raiders of the Lost Ark*.

an in-betweener, Kirby would draw the moments that completed an action, which no doubt influenced his comics, as comic book artists tend to draw characters between two states—such as a punch just landing—rather than a clenched fist or the blow after (e.g., Kirby's iconic *Captain America* #1 cover).

Thus, the comic artist's primary goal is to choose the moment that will best enable the reader to fill in the narrative gaps, with a secondary concern to design the most dynamic composition. While each shot in cinema may also represent a paradigmatic choice, a different set of considerations is in play. The filmmaker does not concentrate on a single image (i.e., a frame), as the "equivalent instant for the filmmaker is usually accompanied by several minutes of a longer sequence in which that instant occurs" (Harvey 178). Furthermore, the filmmaker was traditionally not afforded much control in how the shot would proceed; as once they called "action" all they could do was act as a bystander hoping that the scene would meet their expectations.

Despite the differences, the dynamic actions sustained by comics' limitless discourse-time, what Federico Fellini called comics' "inexpressible secret power" (Gravett *Graphic Novels* 2), have inspired cinema for decades. Warren Buckland believes that one "can detect the influence of comic books, particularly in the storyboarded action sequences" (169) of *Raiders of the Lost Ark* (Spielberg 1981). Such influences are unsurprising given that celebrated Marvel artist Jim Steranko (*X-Men* and *Nick Fury: Agent of S.H.I.E.L.D.*) provided the film's concept art. Looking at the first example in figure 5.11, one can see how the expressionistic comic book posturing more recently practiced by superheroes and Spartans was previously a template for this 1980s hero. In the second set of images, the sharply curved lines of comic book characters are evident as the hero delivers a knockout blow.

Bordwell, who described Spielberg as the "live-action master of storyboard cinema," makes the point that if "you're planning shot by shot, why not create very fancy compositions in previsualization?" ("Superheroes for Sale"). Spielberg's eventual film was unable to fully recreate all of Steranko's comic book-inspired concepts. However, as the storyboard analogy described in the previous chapter suggests, today's filmmakers, emboldened by digital technologies, are eager to faithfully recreate preproduction materials, whether they are storyboards, animatics, or increasingly, comic book panels. For instance, the development of bullet-time and similar digitally augmented slow motion techniques has provided filmmakers with many creative opportunities. Most notably, these devices have allowed cinema to approximate the discourse-time of comics' static images. Consequently, filmmakers are confronted with a paradigmatic choice, one that comic artists have to make with every single panel: Which moment to freeze?

Visual effects supervisor John Gaeta described the options that confront filmmakers employing bullet-time: "I can choose at will any elapsed real-world time to photograph" ("Follow the White Rabbit"). Yet, while the decisions made by comic book artists and filmmakers are similar, they are not the same. As outlined, a comic book artist's primary concern should be to convey the maximum amount of information possible to enable the reader to fill in the intervening moments, with aesthetic values a secondary concern. However, for filmmakers, the static comic book-like images do not carry this narrative weight, as the frozen action is not a discrete image, but rather a staggered moment that follows the same tenets of any cinematic shot. Accordingly, the secondary concern of a comic book artist—aesthetics—is often the filmmaker's priority.

These instances of bullet-time evoke the pre-cinematic experiments of Eadweard Muybridge, who took successive shots of a galloping horse in order

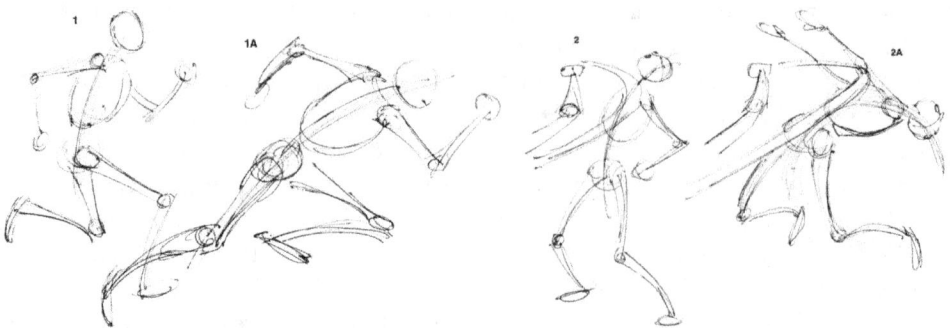

FIG. 5.12 Lee and Buscema demonstrate techniques for maximizing a dramatic moment.

FIG. 5.13 In this oft-cited use of bullet-time from *The Matrix*, the frozen performer has the "sharply curved center line" that Lee suggests brings "vitality" to comic book images.

to isolate one image that best exemplified the gait of the animal. Today, film-makers that emulate comic book techniques arrest the motion of a scene so that the spectator can more fully study and appreciate its anatomy. To understand the strategies utilized by a filmmaker in deciding which of cinema's normally relentless images to sustain, one again finds insights in *How to Draw Comics the Marvel Way*.

Harvey believes that when an artist makes the choice to draw a particular piece of action it is "already stressed . . . dramatically" (178). For those artists who subscribe to the Marvel Way, and similar mainstream comic conventions, however, this is not enough; the action needs to be maximized for dramatic effect. In Stan Lee's instructional art book, he compares two similar ways of conveying the same actions; while the first is a "perfectly clear, understandable sketch, it simply isn't done in the Marvel style. It doesn't have the vitality, the movement, the sharply curved center line of [the second]" (65).

This level of dynamism is also sought in comic book adaptations, where stuntmen, wirework, and CGI contort characters into the most dramatic

FIG. 5.14 The closing coda of *The Amazing Spider-Man* includes many near-frozen moments chosen to match the dynamism of the comic's iconic poses.

poses. One of the first and certainly most widely cited examples of bullet-time was the rooftop sequence in *The Matrix*. The filmmakers could have chosen to freeze any moment, but like comic creators who draw the Marvel Way, they waited for the moment that had "the vitality, the movement, the sharply curved center line," with the hero bent backwards, arms stretched out, as he tries to dodge an onslaught of bullets.

These frozen moments frequently occur at the midpoint of an action, much as they would in the source material. This serves to sustain the dramatic qualities of the performer such as comparable moments from *300* and *The Spirit* (Miller 2008). In these near-frozen moments, the hero is in mid-leap, arms and legs stretched out with the tails of his cape/trench coat fluttering flamboyantly in the wind, as the viewer is left to contemplate the dynamic image and whether the hero will make the next cliff-face/rooftop.

In transformations, where fidelity is at a premium, slow motion will often crystallize the peak moments of the source, thereby conveying faithfulness to the source including its dynamic chosen moments. For instance, the opening of *Watchmen* (Snyder 2009) uses slow motion to accentuate the moment in which the Comedian is thrown through a high-rise window, a moment that the comic creators also chose to depict.

Rather than being limited to a single moment, filmmakers will often choose to accentuate a number of dynamic actions within a larger sequence.

For instance, the action-filled coda for *The Amazing Spider-Man* (Webb 2012) saw the pace grind to a standstill at key moments so that the hero could be fully appreciated in iconic poses. Rearticulating the snapshot fallacy, the film's animation supervisor, David Schaub, explains, "Not only are we hitting those familiar poses from the comic books, but we are choreographing the movement in and out of the poses so that the action flows gracefully like an aerial ballet, and the comic book panels become snapshots connecting our work to the source material" ("Rite of Passage").

Thus, in the digital age, filmmakers are better equipped to tap into the once "inexpressible secret power" of comics' fixed images. This new expressivity has seen filmmakers facing a difficult decision: Which moment to freeze? Positioning panels as storyboards, many filmmakers have looked to comics to maximize the contemplative potential of these techniques. Accordingly, the comic book movie's chosen moments tend to be populated by characters who broadcast power, emotion, and vitality, thereby deepening Hollywood's comic aesthetic.

Stereotypes

It is rare to find an artist in any medium who will openly acknowledge their reliance on stereotypes, with Richard Dyer noting how the term's negative connotations stem from the "wholly justified objections of various groups . . . to the ways in which they find themselves stereotyped in the mass media" (11). While acknowledging the dangers of such simplifications, Everette E. Dennis points to how visual communicators rely on devices that "communicate dramatically and without much subtlety or nuance" (ix). Similarly, Eisner believes that stereotypes in comics are an "accursed necessity" (*Graphic Storytelling* 17), a view held by many commentators (Groensteen 162; McCloud *Making Comics* 73; Duncan and Smith 135). This necessity is borne out of comics' limited space, be it the corner of a newspaper designated for a strip, or the predetermined number of pages a comic book is set to contain. Consequently, comics rely on readily identifiable signs that leave little room for ambiguity. Thus, in the same way a clock must look like a clock, character types in comics tend to be explicit.

Antecedents to modern "typification" (Groensteen 162) include the shaved heads and facial hair used to distinguish the Normans and Anglo-Saxons on the Bayeux Tapestry; the "acrobatic dentist" and "Herculean assistant" of cartoons in the late nineteenth century (Kunzle 372); and the first recurring comic character, The Yellow Kid, who was based on a "type" by creator Richard F. Outcault, with the readers of *The World* providing the slum resident's name

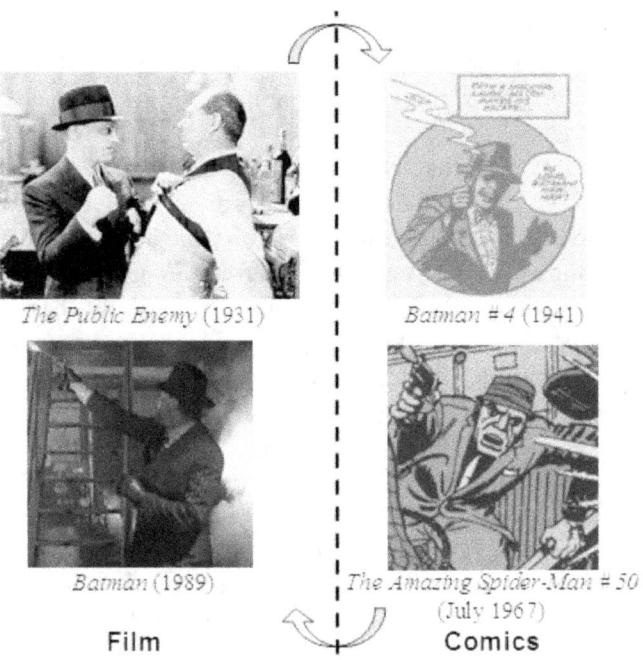

FIG. 5.15 The relay of stereotypes between comics and cinema.

(Gordon 29–32). Many of the stereotypes of early comics made the transition to cinema, such as the homeless Irish imbecile Happy Hooligan, who appeared in eleven films between 1900 and 1903. Similarly, a number of the first comic-derived animation stars, like *Krazy Kat*, are today recognized as deracinated variants of African-American types (Gordon 73; Bukatman *Poetics of Slumberland* 21).

In yet another example of the active relay described earlier, cinema returned comic's favor with many of the types that appeared in strips and books borrowed from films. As Eisner summarized: "American films, with their broad international distribution, helped establish global visual and story clichés. Comics benefited and rode on their acceptance" (*Graphic Storytelling* 74). For instance, it is appropriate that Warner Bros. and DC Comics are now subsidiaries of the same conglomerate, as so many of the publisher's character types sprung from the studio's films. Jules Feiffer noted how Batman creator Bob Kane actively strove for the "Warner Brothers fog-infested look" (30) with Will Brooker adding that he even went as far as to "include a [James] Cagney lookalike in 'Public Enemy #1,' a story from *Batman #4*" (*Batman Unmasked* 49). This gangster type continued in comics long after it had become anachronistic, with 1960s Spider-Man artist John Romita, Sr., noting that organized criminals "were all lean, mean-looking, moustached with a felt hat and a striped suit" ("Making of Daredevil"). When Batman and other comics were made into modern films, these long-standing tropes were adapted, or rather returned, to cinema.

When creating new characters, many comic book artists exploited the relay between comics and cinema. For instance, in developing *The Spirit* Will Eisner designed a crime-fighter who was "very much like Cary Grant, a nice American looking hero" ("Comics and Superheroes"). Similarly, the wild hair and immovable grin of iconic Batman villain the Joker was based on Conrad Veidt's character in *The Man Who Laughs* (Leni 1928). In discussing visual stereotypes, E. H. Gombrich describes an anonymous sixteenth century German woodcutter's attempts to portray a flood in Rome:

> He knew the Castel Sant'Angelo to be a castle, and so he selected from the drawer of his mental stereotypes the appropriate cliché for a castle—a German *Burg* with its timber structure and high-pitched roof. But he did not simply repeat the stereotype—he adapted it to its particular function by embodying certain distinctive features which he knew belonged to that particular building in Rome. (70–71)

Cinema is frequently the "drawer" comic creators poach their character types from. Like the artist who placed a German Burg in Rome, on selecting these filmic models the comic book creator does "not simply repeat the stereotype," but adapts it to its new context and function. Accordingly, movie star Cary Grant is given a mask and gloves to breathe life into The Spirit, and German character actor Conrad Veidt is reimagined with green hair and ruby lips in the creation of Gotham City tormentor the Joker.

However, as these examples suggest, the handcrafted nature of comic books has seen many of these types exaggerated further. For instance, like most World War II US entertainments, the 1943 *Batman* Columbia serial took part in the vilification of Japanese soldiers, with Pasko describing the serial's antagonist, Dr. Daka, as a "Japanese spy stereotype" (51). However, the film did not/could not fully recreate the extreme caricaturing of the comic books and other visual materials of the time, with Brooker concluding that it was "a more realist variation on the grotesque stereotypes of the poster-art" ("Batman" 188). Although film production technology in the 1940s may have prohibited the Batman serial from achieving the level of visual exaggeration practiced by comics, posters, and other propaganda material, today advanced production techniques, coupled with the expressionistic performances of the comic aesthetic, have led to more exaggerated stereotyping seeping into adaptations and related films.

For instance, in the original *Watchmen* graphic novel Richard Nixon displays the exaggerated jowls, furrowed brow, and bulbous nose typical of the

FIG. 5.16 The cover of *Batman* #18 (August 1943) contained a Japanese caricature typical of propaganda material produced during this time. The Columbia serial of the same year offered a more "realist" variation on this type.

FIG. 5.17 Nixon in the *Watchmen* graphic novel and film adaptation, alongside Frank Langella in *Frost/Nixon*.

many parodies of the much-maligned president. These features allow the reader to easily identify the figure even when presented in a one-quarter profile. This caricature is maintained for the adaptation, with heavy makeup ensuring the film's Nixon has the same exaggerated visual traits. Although this level of "synecdochic simplification" (Groensteen 162) may have been necessary in the comic book, where the world leader needed to be identified as concisely as possible, the more luxurious space of cinema coupled with the possibility of additional auditory signifiers made this level of stereotyping unnecessary. The excessiveness of this caricature becomes more evident when the president of *Watchmen* is contrasted with the Nixon played by Frank Langella in *Frost/Nixon* (Howard 2008), released one year earlier. Langella, adopting the mannerisms and speech patterns of the regularly lampooned figure, did not rely on any pronounced visual signifiers. But the restraint of *Frost/Nixon* would have been at odds with the intended comic aesthetic of *Watchmen*.

FIG. 5.18 A "classic depiction of good versus evil," from *Unbreakable*.

Frank Miller suggests that "in cartooning you make someone's physicality a metaphor for their interior reality" ("300 Spartans—Fact or Fiction?"). In Miller's own *300*, the heroic Spartans are portrayed as handsome and physically toned, while the Persians they combat are often disfigured, even inhuman. As discussed in Chapter One, the film adaptation of *300* was seen by many as perpetuating pro-War on Terror sentiment. The film was criticized for its depictions of its Eastern threat, which was interpolated from the source using a variety of old and new techniques including: makeup, digital backdrops, and color grading. Thus, like Nixon in *Watchmen*, the visual exaggerations typical of the source material continued into the adaptation. Yet these direct signifiers seem subtle when compared with some of the other techniques used to suggest heroes and villains.

Returning to *Unbreakable*, the film's self-aware dialogue frequently points to comic book conventions that make the twist ending inevitable in hindsight. In particular, the "classic depiction of good versus evil" discussed earlier prompts Elijah to comment, "Notice the square jaw of Slayer, common in most comic heroes. And the slightly disproportionate size of Jaguaro's head to his body. This again is common, but only in villains." His mother later adds, "See the villain's eyes, they're larger than the other characters', they insinuate a slightly slewed perspective on how they see the world, just off normal." *Unbreakable* replicates this "classic depiction of good versus evil," for later, when Elijah is revealed to be the film's villain, it becomes clear how he adheres to his own assessment of a comic book villain, with a "disproportionate" head on a spindly frame. Similarly, the film's hero, David Dunn, also conforms to the comic stereotype; being played by that most square-jawed of action stars Bruce Willis.[11] However, it is not only self-referential films that adhere to this "classic depiction of good versus evil." Of all the comic book types that have been adapted by cinema, the conventional representation of hero and villain is perhaps the most pervasive.

How to Draw Comics the Marvel Way places an emphasis on the imposing physicality of heroes. Comparing Captain America to an "average guy," Lee notes how the "superhero is larger with broader shoulders, more muscular arms and legs, a heavier chest, and even a more impressive stance" (46). McCloud objects to this genre prerequisite of "musclebound anatomy" (*Reinventing Comics* 114), a criticism that could also be leveled at adaptations. However, unlike action films, where muscularity is a marker of strength, many comic book movie stars meet this convention through costuming and postproduction techniques. For example, Michael Keaton, Val Kilmer, and George Clooney may have lacked the muscularity of action stars, but their molded rubber suits ensured Batman still had "musclebound anatomy." Similarly, while former bodybuilder and action movie icon Arnold Schwarzenegger was considered for the role of *Watchmen* superbeing Dr. Manhattan in the mid-1990s, when the film was eventually produced, in 2009, motion capture technology enabled indie actor Billy Crudup to have the exaggerated physique of a comic book hero. The importance of muscularity can also be seen in the fully displayed physicality of the Spartan warriors in *300*, which was accentuated through high contrast photography. This convention has become so heavily associated with the comic book movie that it was satirized in *Watchmen*, with the self-aggrandizing villain Ozymandias wearing a costume that directly referenced the sculpted rubber of the Batman suits. The *300* parody, *Meet the Spartans* (Friedberg and Aaron Seltzer 2008), went one step further in its critique of this convention by having six-pack abs painted onto the body of one of its unlikely heroes.

Increasingly actors are not simply relying on CGI or costuming, but are putting in the gym hours necessary to achieve the expected muscularity. For instance, fitness magazines and the popular press paid particular attention to Henry Cavill's transition from a bullied boarding school teenager, reportedly nicknamed "Fat Cavill," to the "superhero-shredded" physique of the *Man of Steel* (Tuthill). Since the comic book advertisements for Charles Atlas's "Dynamic Tension" exercises, the fitness industry has often enacted the wish fulfillment of superhero transformation discussed in Chapter One.[12] Continuing this productive relationship, today's comic book movie stars are ideal fodder for the fitness industry. In his study of bodybuilding, Alan Klein describes how bodybuilding poses are designed to display power: "One doesn't so much admire bodybuilders for what they can do as far as what they *look* like they can do. The look of power, virility, prowess, counts for more than function, and has more in common with the world of modelling, beauty contests, or

FIG. 5.19 Comic book movie heroes, like bodybuilders, must convey power even when they are standing still. Thus, it is unsurprising to find actors adopting recognized bodybuilder poses, such as Most Muscular (crab), in films and related promotional material.

cinema idols than that of sports heroes" (215). Thus, it is unsurprising to find comic book movie performers adopting bodybuilder-like poses (as seen in figure 5.19) in order to convey the power of their two dimensional equivalents in films and promotional material (including fitness magazines).

As the villain's monologue in *Unbreakable* suggests, a square jaw is often a more important heroic signifier in comic books and their adaptations than musclebound anatomy. Unsurprisingly, this convention is emphasized in *How to Draw Comics the Marvel Way* with one of Lee's "rules to follow" that the artist "make the chin strong and firm" (90). This feature is regularly emphasized by the hero's costume, with the lower part of their face often the only feature visible. Not only do classic heroes such as Batman and Daredevil display a square jawline beneath their masks, but characters such as the X-Men and Judge Dredd, the supposed "freaks" and "antiheroes" of the genre, also conform to this convention. This heroic type has remerged not only in film adaptations, but also in those undeclared adaptations that complete the corpus of the genre. For instance, the protagonist in *Unbreakable* finally accepts the mantle of a "hero" in the third act, with this transition signaled by David

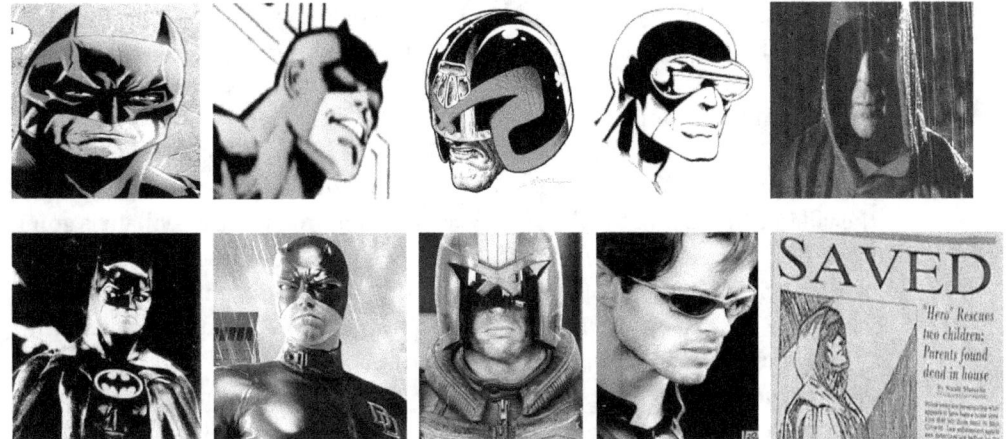

FIG. 5.20 Comic book heroes and their film counterparts conform to the square jaw convention.

Dunn donning a raincoat that leaves only this indexical symbol on display. This feature is further highlighted in the film's coda, when a newspaper artist's rendition of the anonymous hero exaggerates this signifier, making the chin "strong and firm" as Lee suggests.

In *The Amazing Spider-Man*, the hero stops to taunt a criminal: "In the future, if you're going to steal cars don't dress like a car thief." Yet this unlucky criminal did not have a chance; convention dictates that comic books and their adaptations are inhabited by characters who are distinguishable from a distance. Remarking on the recurrence of these criminal types, Pearson and Uricchio observe "nameless thugs seem driven to crime by anatomy. To paraphrase Jessica Rabbit, these criminals aren't really bad, they're just drawn bad. This 'badness' extends to their apparel, which classifies them as outside respectable society" (204). This typification becomes even more pronounced when one moves from rank-and-file criminals to evil masterminds. As Dennis O'Neil outlines in the Bat-bible, "Villains should be larger than life, and preferably grotesque. The Joker and Two-Face are perfect examples of Batman bad guys; they wear their villainy on their faces."

These villainous facades continue into the comic book film adaptations, with the reveal of these exaggerated features often denoting evil intent. For instance, right before he kills a man with a series of well-placed paperclips, *Daredevil* (Steven Johnson 2003) villain Bullseye removes his beanie hat to reveal a branded forehead. Similar examples might include the increasingly elaborate hair of *Batman Forever* (Schumacher 1995) villain the Riddler, Magneto adopting his helmet in the third act of *X-Men: First Class* (Vaughn 2011), and Hector Hammond's ever-expanding head in *Green Lantern* (Campbell 2011). As Michael Cohen observed of *Dick Tracy* (Beatty 1990), "There is no exploration of the psychology or background of each villain because the prosthetic design creates the phrenology of a criminal" (26). Thus, these conventions are an efficient way to reaffirm or signpost a character's villainy, while accentuating the film's comic aesthetic.

In *Unbreakable*, Elijah believes that he and David are "on the same curve just on opposite ends" and chastizes him at the climax for not realizing he was the villain: "In a comic you know how you can tell who the arch-villain is going to be? He's the exact opposite of the hero." Such dichotomies litter comic book movies, with characters regularly articulating this relationship—"I made you, you made me first" (*Batman*); "I've got to stop him . . . because I created him" (*The Amazing Spider-Man*); and "Why can't you be like me?" (*Green Lantern*). As Dyer notes, stereotypes function to "maintain sharp boundary definitions, to define clearly where the pale ends and thus who is clearly within and who clearly [is] beyond it" (16). Thus, the heightened visual cues of heroes and villains not only establish their individual characteristics, but also the distance between them.

The conventional depictions of good and evil, as well as other stereotypes, have passed readily from comics into cinema where they have proliferated widely. Such amenability is no doubt attributable to film being the initiator of many of these conventions, which are now being returned to cinema with a comic book flourish. This typification, coupled with the conventions described earlier, demonstrates a sustained interest among filmmakers in achieving a comic aesthetic. How these devices have been codified into a coherent style will be explored in the next section, which considers whether Marvel Entertainment's films live up to the ideals of its publishing arm.

Marvel, the Marvel Way

As discussed earlier, despite careful branding, the "Marvel Way" techniques are not confined to Marvel comics, but can be found in most mainstream books and many other titles that might be considered "alternative." Furthermore, while this chapter charted how these conventions have migrated to cinema, this is not to suggest that filmmakers are assiduously studying Lee and Buscema's 1977 guide or any other specific comic books. Rather, compelled by the twin imperatives of fidelity and genre expectations, comic conventions have ridden the semiotic relay into cinema where they have gained wider use. In concluding this chapter, there is perhaps no better way to view the consistent application of this approach than in the films that proudly display their comic book beginnings, the Marvel Cinematic Universe.

In his brief post-credit cameo in *Iron Man* (Favreau 2008), Samuel L. Jackson's Nick Fury heralded the arrival of the Marvel Cinematic Universe

FIG. 5.21 *The Incredible Hulk* filmmakers created a "Marvel Hulk Scene" using techniques similar to those identified in *How to Draw Comics the Marvel Way.*

(MCU)—"Mr. Stark, you've become part of a bigger universe. You just don't know it yet." This expanding group of films has turned comic book-like continuity into bustling box office. Each entry opens with the now familiar Marvel Studios logo emerging from comic book pages. Yet is this simply a throwaway reference to the film's origins or do these adaptations adhere to the tenets of their source material, adapting comics the Marvel Way?

This chapter has identified a number of examples of comic book framing in adaptations and related films. Nonetheless, it is rare to find filmmakers openly acknowledging the debt that these compositions owe to their paper and ink antecedents. The Marvel Studios directors, however, have proven eager to cite their comic book inspiration. For instance, director Louis Leterrier and his actor Tim Roth identified on the DVD commentary how they elevated a potentially "boring" exposition sequence in *The Incredible Hulk* (2008) through Marvel-style framing.

> We spent a good part of a day on this and we made very much a comic book—a Marvel Hulk scene (Tim Roth). That's what it is. I mean there are two ways of shooting expositional scenes, either together around the table drinking coffee and talking about it, which is fun but kind of boring, or you put them in a funky environment and tell them, "Okay, you guys run free and just take your own blocking and walk around and I'll chase you with my camera." (Louis Leterrier)

In figure 5.21, one finds the recurrence of techniques identified by Lee for achieving a dynamic composition: shots are asymmetrical, a variety of angles are used, and characters and objects frequently appear in different planes of perspective within a shot.

FIG. 5.22 The exaggerated depth of field in the comic book adaptations *Batman*, *Hulk*, and *Thor* is reinforced by architectural lines and performer staging.

The director of *Thor* (2011), Kenneth Branagh, also described how comics informed his film's propensity for heightened framing: "For me tilted angles, Dutched angles, is the way I remember comic book frames . . . that's how I perceived the dynamism of the compositions in the frames—wide-angle lenses with lots of depth—and it's why I chose it as a style for this film." As previously discussed, canted or "Dutch" angles, while not specific to comics, have become synonymous with the medium and they are used in *Thor* to achieve the desired aesthetic. However, these devices are more often used in the film's Earth-based character scenes, while the elaborate mise-en-scène of Asgard is treated to a more balanced composition. Thus, as with the example from *X2*, when confronted with a scene that does not seem to meet the genre's heightened realism, there is a discernible desire on the part of the filmmaker to enliven such moments through dynamic framing techniques.

Even when the shot has the requisite spectacle, the "more-is-more" approach of comic book movies often compels further exaggeration. For instance, in many comic book movies it is not simply enough to employ depth of field; this convention should be heightened through aspects of the mise-en-scène. Thus, in adaptations such as *Batman* (Burton 1989) and *Hulk* (Lee 2003), architecture and performers reinforce the depth of field by providing lines of perspective typically found in comics. Similar orthogonal-like staging can also be seen in Marvel Studios' *Thor*.

As in the example from *The Incredible Hulk*, there are many moments in *Thor* that combine these various techniques. For instance, the scene in which

FIG. 5.23 Many scenes from *Thor* are framed the Marvel Way.

the Earth-bound Thor is interrogated by S.H.I.E.L.D., as seen in figure 5.23, is filmed with a variety of extreme high and low angles, and every one of the thirty-one shots is canted. These devices are not only found in those adaptations in which the filmmakers explicitly cite comics. For instance, the first three shots of Nick Fury in *The Avengers* (Whedon 2012) are all from a low angle, chosen, it seems, to enliven the exposition being doled out in the opening scene.

As with the other adaptations discussed in this chapter, the Marvel Way techniques are not confined to framing, but extend to the elements of the composition. Lee and Buscema would no doubt approve of how comic book movie performers channel the "vitality" of the comics. For instance, Steve Roger's transition from a frail, but well-meaning recruit to a full-fledged hero in *Captain America: The First Avenger* (Johnston 2011) is conveyed through variations in his movement. The pre-transformation Rogers is uncoordinated while the Super Soldier stands firm, expressing the power one has come to expect from comic book heroes. Similarly, Mark Ruffalo portrays the introvert scientist Bruce Banner in *The Avengers* with his head down and shoulders hunched, which heightens the moment he unleashes the Hulk—a rampaging wall of muscle whose movements express power even before he plunges into an alien armada.

These moments of display often tally with peak moments from the comics that adapters are eager to accentuate. For instance, Ryan Meinerding, visual development supervisor for *Captain America: The First Avenger*, describes searching through the source material to "find in the comic key moments that make him who he really is" ("Outfitting a Hero"), while Marvel Studios president of production Kevin Feige noted of *Thor*, "We are going right to those

FIG. 5.24 In this sequence from *Thor,* actor Chris Hemsworth adopts a bodybuilder-like Side Chest pose that is accentuated through slow motion photography.

comic covers. In every sequence we want to hit at least two or three classic Thor images" ("From Asgard to Earth"). Similarly, when describing how one action sequence for *Iron Man* was digitally embellished, animation director Hal Hickel notes, "The jump is a lot bigger now with a more heroic moment in the middle of it. We tried to get what we've been calling a Marvel moment" ("Wired: The Visual Effects of Iron Man"). In capturing iconic comic images, the filmmakers are infusing their chosen moments with the dynamic qualities of the source, while also emphasizing fidelity.

These heightened moments are often accentuated through slow motion, such as Thor's attempts to reclaim his hammer, Mojlnir, from a S.H.I.E.L.D investigation site. This sequence also allows for another comic book movie convention to be displayed—musclebound anatomy. Thor's efforts to remove the hammer see actor Chris Hemsworth replicating a Side Chest bodybuilder pose, which enables him to convey power even though his efforts ultimately prove futile. The survey carried out for this study identified an enthusiastic audience for this convention, with some of the expectations from female respondents aged between twenty-one and thirty at the first *Thor* screening including: "He will be dreamy"; "A Hot Man"; and "I want to see sexy man meat." One participant matter-of-factly answered the fidelity question this way: "I just came for the hottie."

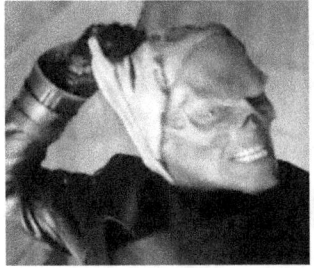

FIG. 5.25 As in other comic book movies, the antagonists of the Marvel Cinematic Universe (Red Skull, Loki, and Abomination) only reveal their stereotypically exaggerated features once they have fully embraced their roles as the villain.

Kevin Feige described how *Thor* had "the Marvel aesthetic of wish fulfilment" ("From Asgard to Earth"). While all the studio's films play on this convention, *Captain America: The First Avenger* makes it a plot device. Skinny Steve Rogers is transformed into Captain America by a Super Soldier serum. The serum's creator, Dr. Erskine, explains how it "amplifies everything that is inside, so good becomes great." This description tallies with Lee and Buscema's suggestion that when drawing Captain America, as opposed to an "average" guy, "you should always slightly exaggerate the heroic qualities of your hero and attempt to ignore or omit any negative, undramatic qualities" (46). This transition is emphasized in *Captain America: The First Avenger* through postproduction techniques that transplant actor Chris Evans's face onto a frail frame, thereby accentuating the reveal of his musclebound anatomy. This is a reverse of the tactics found in other films, where actors, through a mixture of costumes and digital techniques, would be given the conventional physicality of a hero. Nevertheless, it demonstrates the desire to fulfill the hero stereotype. Unsurprisingly, fitness magazines picked up on the transformations of Hemsworth and Evans. However, they were not the only MCU heroes to receive this attention with an *Avengers*-themed issue of *Muscle & Fitness* magazine featuring a CGI Hulk as its cover star. Even though it is unlikely that readers would ever "get huge like the Hulk," this cover is yet another example of how embedded musclebound anatomy has become in the genre.

Conforming to type, the villainy of the MCU antagonists is also made explicit through oversized heads and grotesque features. These traits are accentuated as the antagonist's malevolence deepens. For instance, the Red Skull's famous visage is only revealed following his first confrontation with Captain America; in *Thor* Loki finally adopts his horned helmet when he ascends to the throne; and Emil Blonsky becomes a true "Abomination" in the third act of *The Incredible Hulk*. A later MCU entrant, *Iron Man 3* (Black 2013), played with this convention. All publicity material for the film suggested that Ben

Kingsley would play the oriental-themed comic book villain, the Mandarin, while his accomplice would be the classically handsome Aldrich Killian (Guy Pearce). However, in a second-act reveal the hero (and audience) discovers that the Mandarin is a proxy created by Killian from stereotypical conventions, and that Killian is the real villain. The success of this reversal demonstrates how engrained the hero/villain stereotypes have become in the Marvel Cinematic Universe and wider comic book movie genre.

As the previous chapter established, in the Golden Age of Comic Book Filmmaking filmmakers engaged more fully with the language of comics than at any other time in film history. Perhaps motivated by fidelity or the perceived expectations of the comic book movie audience, some filmmakers, utilizing this new expressivity, have tailored film conventions to better emulate the source. Thus, while many of the conventions, even in their exaggerated forms, can be found in other genres, like wayward Avengers they are assembled in comic book movies striving to achieve a comic aesthetic. Consequently, in adaptations, the film frame is more dynamic—employing asymmetrical compositions, a variety of angles, and exaggerated depth of field. Equally, the stars of these films are often called upon to behave more expressionistically than in comparable genres such as the action movie or crime film. Comics have also lent cinema their "inexpressible secret power" of frozen moments, with those filmmakers adapting comics now regularly choosing static over motion pictures. Despite the comparatively luxurious running time of cinema, many adaptations have also employed the exaggerated stereotypes typical of comics' economic storytelling. Stan Lee termed these conventions "the Marvel Way," but they are now common to comics, their adaptations, and the increasing number of films vying to be affiliated with the comic book movie genre.

CONCLUSION

The Future of the Comic Book Movie

Salvador Dali believed that "comics will be the culture of the year 3794" (Gravett *Graphic Novels* 2), while former Spider-Man editor Danny Fingeroth describes them as "the pastime of a rarefied audience" (170) whose steadily declining sales will soon see them absent from our shelves. Whatever the outcome—forgotten art form or all conquering culture of the next millennium—today comics are inextricably linked to another medium: cinema. Since the success of *X-Men* (Singer) in 2000, comic books have moved from the fringes of pop culture to inspire Hollywood's leading genre, the comic book movie. With release dates planned years in advance, the comic book movie has already eclipsed the longevity of classical genres such as film noir; it has more entries than the Universal horror cycle; and in recent years these films have been better attended than adaptations of stage plays, Broadway musicals, and many other sources that regularly receive intense academic scrutiny. Despite some important early interventions, however, this topic has yet to provoke consistent scholarly debate—an imbalance this book sought to redress. To that end, this study looked to the field of adaptation studies, which was recently enlivened by an interest in convergence culture and transmedia opportunities. This methodology was not only applied to the films and comics, but also to industrial relays, audience research, and creator interviews. What emerged was a rounded account of why the mainstream American film industry was drawn to comics in the early twenty-first century, and the impact of this unprecedented level of production.

From an analysis of wider discourses, as well as direct engagement with industry professionals, the first chapter identified the most commonly held views as to why, after a century of indifference, filmmakers fixed their gaze on the comic book. Those hoping for a silver bullet would be greatly disappointed, as it was the confluence of a number of factors that prompted a refocusing of production around this previously maligned source. Heroes on the comic book page were never more popular than when they were turning over

Axis tanks or socking Hitler on the jaw. This four-color rebuttal to a real-world threat found many in the popular press linking the more recent success of cinema's heroes to the escape they offered American audiences rocked by 9/11. However, the first chapter found that while post-9/11 films such as *Spider-Man* (Raimi 2002) may have gained a boost from the wish fulfillment they offered audiences, these individualistic comic book heroes more neatly tallied with the vigilante mythology enacted by America's leaders during the subsequent War on Terror.

After digital dinosaurs and cow-tossing twisters, Hollywood was eager to find further opportunities to display its digital toolkit. While the prospect of realizing previously unachievable images through computer-generated effects may have propelled comics to the screen, Chapter One also considered how comics served as a high criterion, with filmmakers realizing that the sky is not the limit, it is only the beginning.

The 2009 acquisition of Marvel Entertainment by the Walt Disney Company provided yet another example of the annexation of mainstream media by conglomerates. These organizations favor content with name recognition, wide demographic reach, and amenability to any number of transmedia opportunities. With decades of non-stop publication under their utility belts, comic book characters were well suited to the content-based strategies of conglomerates, which hastened their movement to cinema, and to the many other media that fall under these mammoth corporate structures.

When interviewed for this study, Michael E. Uslan described this period as the "Golden Age of Comic Book Filmmaking." The executive producer of every Batman adaptation since Tim Burton's blockbuster in 1989, Uslan was among the first of a generation of fan-filmmakers who did not dismiss comics as kids' stuff, but recognized their potential as the basis for blockbuster movies. When all these factors intersected at the dawn of the twenty-first century, the previously arduous path from comics to cinema soon became a well-trod thoroughfare.

The alignment of these causal factors saw the comic book adaptation enjoy unprecedented success, and the trend quickly developed into a full-fledged genre. Chapter Two charted this development across inter-textual relays including this study's audience research. Building on these discourses, this chapter probed the boundaries of the genre, and found that it includes some, but not all, comic book adaptations, as well as a number of undeclared adaptations eager to be affiliated with the genre. Identifying the conventions of these films, a definition of the genre was offered:

> The comic book movie genre follows a vigilante or outsider character engaged in a form of revenge narrative, and is pitched at a heightened reality with a visual style marked by distinctly comic book imagery.

Refining earlier genre models with a bacterial growth analogy, the development of this genre was plotted and attempts were made to predict its next phase. In conclusion, this chapter looked at various attempts to balance the requirements of the fan and non-fan audience, ultimately suggesting that Marvel Studios' *Iron Man* (Favreau 2008) was a textbook example of how to negotiate this divide. The success of *Iron Man* is no mean feat, as Chapter Three explores, fans have gained new power and renewed purpose in the digital age.

Archie Comics' *Josie and the Pussycats* was one of the many titles adapted for the screen in the early days of this Golden Age. In the film (Elfont and Kaplan 2001), Alexandra Cabot, the enemy of the eponymous rock band, inexplicably joins the trio on their American tour. When finally asked why she would be a groupie for her rivals, the villain curtly responds, "I'm here because I was in the comic book." This brief, self-referential moment in an otherwise forgotten film could be taken as the maxim for the modern comic book film adaptation. Unlike earlier efforts, which more often displayed a loose fidelity to the source, these adaptations demonstrated previously unseen levels of faithfulness. This shift could be attributed to the increased power fans gained in the digital age, with previously protectionist filmmakers eager to engender goodwill (and online buzz) through fan-appeasing strategies. Although both sides of the fan/producer divide exploited this uneasy relationship, film adaptations created a semblance of the community readers previously only enjoyed within the confines of comic book fandom—a transition that presaged wider shifts to a more participatory culture. Central to this fidelity was the emergence of a comic aesthetic in adaptations and related films; Chapters Four and Five analyzed this development in detail.

Sacha Baron Cohen's Brüno leaps forward in a leopard-print leotard, Paris Hilton plants a kiss on a minor league baseball star, and *Jackass* star Steve-O attempts a one-handed flip. These were some of the red carpet "highlights" captured using bullet-time at the 2009 MTV Movie Awards. The technique, popularized ten years earlier in *The Matrix* (the Wachowskis 1999), allows digitally augmented moments to appear more slowly or frozen, thereby prolonging spectator contemplation. Since the success of *The Matrix*, bullet-time has become commonplace in popular entertainments including films, television programs, and video games, reaching such ubiquity that it is used to capture star-jumping teen idols attending award ceremonies. While this innovation is a continuation of cinema's experimentation with slow motion, Chapter Four argued that it was also one of the most successful attempts to narrow the semiotic gap between comics and cinema.

The Golden Age of Comic Book Filmmaking saw filmmakers engaging with the language of comics with unprecedented enthusiasm, often by utilizing the control offered by digital technologies. Bullet-time, which was innovated for *The Matrix* as a means to approximate the limitless discourse-time of comics, probably proliferated most widely. However, there were many further efforts to adapt the language of comics to cinema. For instance, film-makers often went beyond ready-made equivalents in their desire to create comic book-like panels and transitions, visualize sound, and bring previously specific codes to the screen. The enthusiasm for the comic language, coupled with the plasticity of the digital film image, even led to a measure of comic book graphiation seeping into cinema. Although many of these techniques did not enjoy the success of bullet-time, collectively they testify to a concerted effort to achieve a comic aesthetic, which has served to enrich the expressivity of mainstream cinema.

Moving beyond the language of comics to wider conventions, Chapter Five considered the approaches adopted by filmmakers to achieve the heightened realism of comics. Among the strategies employed to meet this genre expectation were dynamic framing and composition, expressionistic performances, exaggerated frozen moments, and concise, often stereotypical, character types. These conventions are so heavily influenced by comic books that they could have come from a comic publisher's "how-to" guide.

With each chapter elucidating a different aspect of the modern comic book film adaptation, a more complete picture of filmmaking in the twenty-first century emerged. Faced with cultural traumas, conglomerate imperatives, and technological possibilities, Hollywood sought to exploit comics and their built-in audience. However, the industry was seemingly caught off guard when this built-in audience had built-in practices. Nonetheless, anticipating wider shifts, filmmakers soon discovered ways to utilize this intense fan base, while simultaneously codifying the trend into a more reliable genre that appealed to a wider audience. Central to this genre was a comic aesthetic—an expectation that saw filmmakers exploit the new expressivity of digital cinema to engage with the language and conventions of comics like never before.

This book opened with an analogy of crosses on a map marking hidden treasure, and while each chapter unearthed some insights, the comic book film adaptation still holds many areas that warrant further discovery. Perhaps the most urgent continuation of this study is research that focuses on the adaptation of comic books to other media, and with television series such as *The Walking Dead* (Darabont 2010) breaking ratings records and video games like *Batman: Arkham City* (Hill 2011) generating more revenue than most feature films, it is only a matter of time before such work emerges. Similarly, the opportunities provided by digital technologies have seen filmmakers turning to a host of other visual media for inspiration, including cartoons (e.g., *Alvin and the Chipmunks*, *Scooby-Doo*, and *The Smurfs*), illustrated books (*The Grinch*, *The Polar Express*, and *The Cat in the Hat*), and video games (*Resident*

Evil, Prince of Persia, and *Need for Speed*). Although these films have not enjoyed the sustained success of comic book film adaptations, this shift from text-based to visual sources is another development deserving of analysis.

In recent years, adaptation studies has moved beyond the traditional novel-to-film debate to not only recognize a wider range of sources, but also the transmedia paradigms practiced by modern entertainment industries. This study suggested that scholars would be well advised to look to the continuity utilized by comic publishers and embraced by their readers for models to understand and articulate this content-based turn. Similarly, it will be interesting to see if adaptation studies continues its move towards audience-centric studies, with research that considers the larger audience rather than just the readily available fans.

As the conflicting estimates that opened this conclusion indicate, the future of comics is often called into question. Similarly, great uncertainty surrounds the long-term prospects for the comic book movie. As the genre path outlined in Chapter Two suggested, the comic book movie reached its peak of productivity in 2008, with the genre entering a stationary phase marked by more self-aware films. Perhaps fearing audiences would tire of comic book movie conventions, filmmakers have recently enlivened the genre with amoral protagonists, sociopolitical allusions, and greater continuity. In particular, the record-breaking gross of *The Avengers* (Whedon 2012) has resulted in studios paying the price tag necessary to produce films on a grander scale (e.g., *X-Men: Days of Future Past* and *Batman v Superman: Dawn of Justice*). However, is it only a matter of time before the comic book movie arrives at its own *Heaven's Gate* (Cimino 1980)—a film that fails to earn back its massive budget thereby sending the genre into a steep decline? Or perhaps there will be an industry revolt tantamount to New Hollywood, with a new generation of filmmakers eager to challenge a genre that has become part of the establishment? Maybe, as the bacterial growth cycle suggests, any decline in production will only be a momentary pause as the comic book movie rearticulates itself for a whole new era. While the future of the genre is uncertain, one point is clear: this Golden Age of Comic Book Filmmaking will stand as a unique moment in which cinema was stimulated, challenged, and enriched by an oft-dismissed form, and for longer than anyone would ever have expected, the comic book movie became Hollywood's leading genre.

APPENDIX

North American Box-Office Totals for Comic Book Film Adaptations

TITLE	GROSS[1]	RELEASE DATE
X-Men: Days of Future Past	$231,331,687	5/23/14
The Amazing Spider-Man 2	$202,408,526	5/2/14
Captain America: The Winter Soldier	$258,848,387	4/4/14
300: Rise of An Empire	$106,580,051	3/7/14
I, Frankenstein	$19,075,290	1/24/14
Thor: The Dark World	$206,362,140	11/8/13
Billy and Buddy	$894	11/8/13
Kick-Ass 2	$28,795,985	8/16/13
2 Guns	$75,612,460	8/2/13
The Wolverine	$132,556,852	7/26/13
Red 2	$53,262,560	7/19/13
R.I.P.D.	$33,618,855	7/19/13
Man of Steel	$291,045,518	6/14/13
Iron Man 3	$409,013,994	5/3/13
Oblivion	$89,107,235	4/19/13
Bullet to the Head	$9,489,829	2/1/13
Dredd	$13,414,714	9/21/12
The Dark Knight Rises	$448,139,099	7/20/12
The Amazing Spider-Man	$262,030,663	7/3/12
MIB 3	$179,020,854	5/25/12
Marvel's The Avengers	$623,357,910	5/4/12
Ghost Rider: Spirit of Vengeance	$51,774,002	2/17/12
The Adventures of Tintin	$77,591,831	12/21/11
Cowboys & Aliens	$100,240,551	7/29/11
Captain America: The First Avenger	$176,654,505	7/22/11
Green Lantern	$116,601,172	6/17/11
X-Men: First Class	$146,408,305	6/3/11
Priest	$29,136,626	5/13/11
Thor	$181,030,624	5/6/11
Dylan Dog: Dead of Night	$1,186,538	4/29/11
The Green Hornet	$98,780,042	1/14/11
Red	$90,380,162	10/15/10

TITLE	GROSS[1]	RELEASE DATE
Scott Pilgrim vs. the World	$31,524,275	8/13/10
Jonah Hex	$10,547,117	6/18/10
Iron Man 2	$312,433,331	5/7/10
The Losers	$23,591,432	4/23/10
Kick-Ass	$48,071,303	4/16/10
Surrogates	$38,577,772	9/25/09
X-Men Origins: Wolverine	$179,883,157	5/1/09
Watchmen	$107,509,799	3/6/09
The Spirit	$19,806,188	12/25/08
Punisher: War Zone	$8,050,977	12/5/08
The Dark Knight	$534,858,444	7/18/08
Hellboy II: The Golden Army	$75,986,503	7/11/08
Wanted	$134,508,551	6/27/08
The Incredible Hulk	$134,806,913	6/13/08
Iron Man	$318,412,101	5/2/08
30 Days of Night	$39,568,996	10/19/07
Fantastic Four: Rise of the Silver Surfer	$131,921,738	6/15/07
Spider-Man 3	$336,530,303	5/4/07
TMNT	$54,149,098	3/23/07
300	$210,614,939	3/9/07
Ghost Rider	$115,802,596	2/16/07
Superman Returns	$200,081,192	6/28/06
X-Men: The Last Stand	$234,362,462	5/26/06
V for Vendetta	$70,511,035	3/17/06
A History of Violence	$31,504,633	9/23/05
Fantastic Four	$154,696,080	7/8/05
Batman Begins	$206,852,432	6/15/05
Sin City	$74,103,820	4/1/05
Constantine	$75,976,178	2/18/05
Elektra	$24,409,722	1/14/05
Blade: Trinity	$52,411,906	12/8/04
Catwoman	$40,202,379	7/23/04
Spider-Man 2	$373,585,825	6/30/04
The Punisher	$33,810,189	4/16/04
Hellboy	$59,623,958	4/2/04
American Splendor	$6,010,990	8/15/03
The League of Extraordinary Gentlemen	$66,465,204	7/11/03
Hulk	$132,177,234	6/20/03
X2: X-Men United	$214,949,694	5/2/03
Bulletproof Monk	$23,358,708	4/16/03
Daredevil	$102,543,518	2/14/03
Road to Perdition	$104,454,762	7/12/02
Men in Black II	$190,418,803	7/3/02
Spider-Man	$403,706,375	5/3/02
Blade II	$82,348,319	3/22/02
From Hell	$31,602,566	10/19/01

TITLE	GROSS[1]	RELEASE DATE
Ghost World	$6,217,849	7/20/01
Josie and the Pussycats	$14,271,015	4/11/01
X-Men	$157,299,717	7/14/00
Mystery Men	$29,762,011	8/6/99
Virus	$14,036,005	1/15/99
Blade	$70,087,718	8/21/98
Steel	$1,710,972	8/15/97
Spawn	$54,870,175	8/1/97
Men in Black	$250,690,539	7/2/97
Batman and Robin	$107,325,195	6/20/97
The Crow: City of Angels	$17,917,287	8/30/96
The Phantom	$17,323,326	6/7/96
Barb Wire	$3,793,614	5/3/96
Judge Dredd	$34,693,481	6/30/95
Batman Forever	$184,031,112	6/16/95
Casper	$100,328,194	5/26/95
Tank Girl	$4,064,495	3/31/95
Richie Rich	$38,087,756	12/21/94
Timecop	$44,853,581	9/16/94
The Mask	$119,938,730	7/29/94
The Shadow	$32,063,435	7/1/94
The Crow	$50,693,129	5/13/94
Batman: Mask of the Phantasm	$5,617,391	12/25/93
Dennis the Menace	$51,270,765	6/25/93
Teenage Mutant Ninja Turtles III	$42,273,609	3/19/93
Little Nemo: Adventures in Slumberland	$1,368,000	8/21/92
Batman Returns	$162,831,698	6/19/92
Brenda Starr	$67,878	4/17/92
The Rocketeer	$46,704,056	6/21/91
Teenage Mutant Ninja Turtles II	$78,656,813	3/22/91
Dick Tracy	$103,738,726	6/15/90
Teenage Mutant Ninja Turtles	$135,265,915	3/30/90
Batman	$251,188,924	6/23/89
The Return of the Swamp Thing	$192,816	5/12/89
Superman IV: The Quest for Peace	$15,681,020	7/24/87
Howard the Duck	$16,295,774	8/1/86
Supergirl	$14,296,438	11/21/84
Sheena	$5,778,353	8/17/84
Superman III	$59,950,623	6/17/83
Annie	$57,059,003	5/21/82
Swamp Thing	n/a	Mar 1982
Superman II	$108,185,706	6/19/81
Popeye	$49,823,037	12/12/80
Flash Gordon	$27,107,960	12/5/80
Buck Rogers in the 25th Century	$21,671,241	3/30/79
Superman: The Movie	$134,218,018	12/15/78

NOTES

Introduction

1. Desmond and Hawkes, who also acknowledge the importance of *L'Arroseur Arrosé* in the development of narrative cinema, described how Louis Lumière "adapted a well-known newspaper cartoon" (11).

2. The many pre-cinematic examples of the *L'Arroseur Arrosé* premise that Rickman identifies include: "Fait divers" by A. Sorel published in *La Caricature* (12 March 1887), "An Urchin's Caper" by Hans Schließmann in *Fliegende Blätter* (15 August 1886), "A Public Waterer" by Christophe in *Le Petit Français Illustré* (3 August 1889), and "Public Watering" by Uzès in *Le Chat Noir* (4 July 1885).

3. Later, in the silent-film era, the popular American newspaper comic strip *Mutt and Jeff* was adapted first into a series of David Horsley-produced live-action comedies, including *Mutt and Jeff and the Country Judge* and *Mutt and Jeff and the Dog Catcher* (1911), and later as an animated series of shorts. One of the most innovative adaptations produced during this period was *Winsor McCay, the Famous Cartoonist of the N.Y. Herald and His Moving Comics* (J. Stuart Blackton 1911), which combined live action and animation to bring McCay's *Little Nemo in Slumberland* strip to cinema.

4. One notable exception to the relatively little scholarship made available in the English language prior to the post-2000 boom in comic book adaptation production is Francis Lacassin's 1972 article, "The Comic Strip and Film Language."

5. Recent publications such as *A Comics Studies Reader* and *The Power of Comics* contain no dedicated chapters on the audiovisual adaptation of comics.

6. Unadjusted box-office information for the adaptations discussed in this study can be found in the appendix.

7. Although many antecedents exist, Superman is considered the first comic book superhero. The character first appeared in *Action Comics* #1 (June 1938) in a story by writer Jerome "Jerry" Siegel and artist Joe Shuster.

8. In an updated edition of his book *The 101 Best Graphic Novels*, librarian Stephen Weiner chose to include many comic book anthologies. Weiner justified their place by arguing that "although these stories may be considered soap operas and don't end, many of these works are important contributions to the comics field, and some of these books chronicle a point of discovery within the life of an ongoing character" (ix).

9. William Proctor identifies some of the limitations of carrying out audience research via a fan site, which was necessary due to the "time-sensitive nature" of his study (*Star Wars* 205), "as with all small-scale research projects, it is difficult to ascertain if the results are representative of the large community. The people who responded to my call for volunteers may represent a

small percentage of 'full-on fan commitment' and it is important to note that some fans may not vocalise their thoughts and opinions on online forums such as TheForce.net and others, but may still consider themselves as fully-fledged *Star Wars* fans" (*Star Wars* 205–206).

10. It should be noted that Galway is a college town and that the Eye Cinema had gained the reputation for attracting more serious filmgoers, and therefore it was more likely to draw young fan enthusiasts than other cinemas.

11. In total nine screenings were surveyed, three for each film. These were the first screening and later screenings of the film in 2D and 3D. *Thor* was released in Ireland on a public holiday, Easter Monday (April 25, 2011), for one day of previews ahead of its regular release on Friday (April 29). As these screenings were open to the public, the first preview was surveyed on Easter Monday—a 2D presentation at which twenty-four surveys were completed. Five days later, two screenings were surveyed on Saturday (April 30): a 3D presentation at 7:20 p.m. and a 2D presentation at 7:40 p.m., with eleven and fourteen surveys, respectively, completed. The first screening of *Green Lantern* was a 3D lunchtime presentation on Friday, June 17, which only yielded seven completed surveys. The next screening (approximately one hour later) was in 2D and resulted in eleven usable surveys. The final surveyed screening of *Green Lantern* was five days after its initial release, a 9:20 p.m. screening in 3D on Wednesday, June 22, which resulted in eighteen completed surveys. The first day of screenings of *The Adventures of Tintin* on Monday, October 24, were "previews" that, like *Thor*, were open to the public. The first screening surveyed was a 3D presentation at 4:40 p.m. with a 2D presentation taking place at 5:25 p.m. These screenings yielded ten and seven surveys respectively. The final screening surveyed was one week later on Monday, October 31 (a public holiday). This 3D presentation was held at 7:50 p.m. and yielded eleven surveys.

12. The 113 individuals who took part in this survey identified their ages as follows: under 10 (3 participants), 11–15 (5), 16–20 (4), 21–25 (17), 26–30 (36), 31–35 (23), 36–40 (9), 41–45 (4), 46–50 (3), and over 50 (9).

13. Most adaptations of Sherlock Holmes, James Bond, and Dracula take the literary character and general premise, but create a new story, and would therefore be categorized as "analogies" by Wagner. In contrast, a number of adaptations of Dickens, Shakespeare, and Austen prefix their titles with the author's name and go to great lengths to stress their textual fidelity, and therefore could best be described as "transpositions." Perhaps most interestingly, self-referential films such as *Adaptation* (Jonze 2002), *A Cock and Bull Story* (Winterbottom 2005), and *Nightwatching* (Greenaway 2007) leave part of the source unmediated, setting up a reflexive interplay between source and film, and therefore could be considered "commentaries."

14. Although less cited than Wagner and Andrew, Klein and Parker in their 1981 book, *The English Novel and the Movies*, also propose a model that corresponds to Wagner's original concept: "the source is merely seen as raw material, as simply the occasion for an original work," "retains the core of the structure of the narrative while significantly reinterpreting or, in some cases, deconstructing the source text," and "fidelity to the main thrust of the narrative" (10). Similarly, Desmond and Hawkes suggest the categorizations close, loose, and intermediate (3), while Cahir proposes "literal, traditional, or radical" (10). Elliot expands to six categories: psychic, ventriloquist, genetic, de(re)composing, incarnational, and trumping (133–83), while Leitch, citing Elliot, proposes ten groups in a "grammar of hypertextual relations as they shade off to the intertextual" (*Film Adaptation* 95).

15. Many of the elements synonymous with Batman were not introduced until a year or more after the hero's first appearance in *Detective Comics* #27 (May 1939). For instance, Batman's loyal butler, Alfred, first appeared in *Batman* #16 (April 1943), while his base of operations, the Batcave, was first introduced in the Columbia serial before migrating to the daily comic strip (29 October 1943). Similarly, Batman villains the Joker and Catwoman did not appear until *Batman* #1 (Spring 1940).

16. Addressing the various interpretations of comic book characters, Luca Somigli concludes "a comic book character is always already a remake" (286).

17. Wagner describes the sphere of adaptation Andrew terms "intersection" as "commentary" because the film comments on the two forms and the process between them. Similarly, Keith Cohen calls these films "subversive adaptations . . . [as they carry] a hidden criticism of its model, or at least renders implicit certain key contradictions implanted or glossed over in the original" ("Eisenstein's Subversive Adaptation" 245).

18. "Nuff said" would be familiar to fans of Stan Lee's comics as one of the writer's traditional sign-offs.

19. Among the organizations challenging the past orthodoxies of adaptation studies is the Association of Adaptation Studies, an international group of scholars including Dudley Andrew, Jan Baetens, Deborah Cartmell, Timothy Corrigan, Brian McFarlane, Robert Stam, and Imelda Whelehan. The association has organized an annual conference since 2006 that seeks to "challenge assumptions concerning the boundaries of literature on screen" ("Association of Adaptation Studies"). The organization was responsible for the introduction of the Oxford University Press journal *Adaptation* in 2008, with the editors describing past criticism as "woefully predictable" (Cartmell et al. 1) in their inaugural issue.

20. In their review of the 2012 Association of Adaptation Studies conference, Blackwell and Han noted that the conference "revealed that contemporary adaptation scholars have considerably broadened the field's early fixation on novels on screen" (137).

21. In a customer review on the online retail website *Amazon.com*, Dr. Laurence Raw criticizes *True to the Spirit: Film Adaptation and the Question of Fidelity*, writing: "Sadly it does not take into account new theoretical interventions in adaptation studies." Further criticism of MacCabe's collection came from Thomas Leitch as Blackwell and Han note in their review of the 2012 Association of Adaptation Studies conference "referencing Fredric Jameson's 'Afterword' in the essay collection *True to the Spirit: Film Adaptation and the Question of Fidelity* . . . Leitch maintained that the theorist misconstrued an emerging discipline" (133).

22. Leitch identified an earlier example of an adaptation influencing the source material in the stories of Sherlock Holmes. Arthur Conan Doyle borrowed the name "Billy" from the William Gillette stage adaptations for Sherlock Holmes's previously unnamed pageboy (*Film Adaptation* 209). Similarly, author Louis L'Amour was asked by his publisher to tailor the *Hopalong Cassidy* novels to match the successful William Boyd-starring movies (L'Amour).

23. In a blog entry, Jenkins challenged Bordwell's application of "transmedia storytelling" to the Bible, Homeric epics, and the Bhagavad Gita, noting that these examples "are simply adaptations of works produced in one medium for performance in another platform. And for many of us, a simple adaptation may be 'transmedia' but it is not 'transmedia storytelling' because it is simply re-presenting an existing story rather than expanding and annotating the fictional world" (Jenkins and Bordwell *Part One*).

Chapter 1

1. The American comic book industry is loosely broken down by commentators into four distinct eras: the Golden Age (mid-1930s–early 1950s); the Silver Age (1956–70); the Bronze Age (1970–mid-1980s); and the Modern Age (sometimes referred to as the Dark Age), the last of which commentators suggest began with the publication of *Watchmen* and continues today. However, as I have argued elsewhere ("Special Effect"), the dominance of comic book adaptations, and other transmedia ties, has led to limits being imposed on the comic book industry as well as a loss of specificity. Thus, while Uslan may characterize this period as the Golden Age of Comic Book Filmmaking, it might also be described as the Celluloid Age of Comics.

2. Even when adaptations have a non-US setting, they still tend to gross more in North America. For example, the London-set *V for Vendetta* (McTeigue 2005), based on celebrated British author Alan Moore's graphic novel and produced with a largely UK cast, failed to enjoy the same success internationally as in the US with a 53.6 percent domestic gross.

3. Scholars have linked trends in film adaptation to the nostalgic respites they offer during times of unease, such as the Depression-era prevalence of the Dickensian adaptation, which "gave many Americans a sense of childhood nostalgia for the reading of 'classics,'" (DeBona 109) and heritage films (e.g., *A Room with a View*), which provided British audiences in the 1980s with a break from the perceived threat of multiculturalism as "comfortable images of a literary past often represent a therapeutic nostalgia for 'traditional' national values" (Corrigan "In the Gap" 36).

4. The nostalgia of *Superman: The Movie* was positioned as a response to the political mistrust of 1970s America by star Christopher Reeve: "We wanted to know if an innocent man from the '30s could survive in the post-Watergate '70s. Well, thanks to all of you, he's doing just fine" (*The Making of Superman: The Movie*). This aspiration is made explicit in Superman's response to Lois's question as to why he was on Earth, "I'm here to fight for Truth, Justice, and the American Way," to which the hard-nosed reporter replies, "You'll end up fighting every elected official in this country." Lois's response is to be expected from an American journalist in the wake of the Watergate scandal. Equally, Superman's comforting, George Washington-invoking reply—"Lois, I never lie"—attempted to assuage Lois's concerns, as well as those of the audience. In striving for its own measure of nostalgia, *Superman Returns* heavily cites the bucolic wistfulness of the 1978 film, but retains none of Lois's questioning of authority.

5. In his analysis of the use of Silver Age comics in the first Spider-Man film adaptation, Flanagan notes how the film's climax (the bridge-top saving of Peter Parker's love interest, Mary Jane) is a conscious reworking of the story arc "The Night Gwen Stacy Died" from *The Amazing Spider-Man* #121–22 (June-July 1973). This storyline, in which the Green Goblin killed the hero's longtime girlfriend, is often considered the end of the Silver Age of Comics. The film reworks this sequence in a scene in which the hero triumphs, thereby maintaining the film's Silver Age nostalgia.

6. As early as the 1940s, comic book characters were associated with nostalgia, with Ian Gordon, in *Comic Strips and Consumer Culture*, attributing homefront nostalgia to the popularity of comic books among World War II servicemen.

7. Martin Pasko bombastically writes of the escapism provided by the earliest comic books: "You're a kid in the '30s and you're hungry for heroes. And who isn't? The country's in the grip

of its greatest economic depression. Bread lines. Soup kitchens. Beggars on every street corner. Who did this? Who pulled the rug out from under America? And who's gonna help you get back on your feet? Who's gonna make the ones who did this pay? The heroes, of course. The heroes born of necessity, out of your despair and fear. The heroes both real and make-believe whose struggle for The Brighter Tomorrow—itself both real and make-believe—lights the way" (7).

8. Escapism was cited by Chinese officials in 1978 as the reason for removing *Superman: The Movie* from cinemas only one day after its release, with the *Beijing Evening News* describing the character as a "narcotic the capitalist class gives itself to cast off its serious crises" (Pasko 157).

9. Since their inception comic book superheroes have been portrayed as the only ones who can thrive and fully utilize the city's concrete canyons, with Superman's ability to "hurdle a twenty-story building" celebrated in his first appearance (*Action Comics* #1 June 1938). Fittingly, Ben Highmore describes superheroes as "a species that has adjusted to the modern city and overcome its obstacles" (124), and Bainbridge adds, "they are 'super' in that they can transcend those limitations (of gridlock, crime, and other urban constraint) that the city places on the rest of us" ("I am New York" 168).

10. *Hulk* (2003) director Ang Lee also notes how the comic art allows for reader self-identification: "I think in the comics nobody cares about Bruce Banner. He's a wimp, a loser. But by simplified drawings you can project your own melancholy onto him" (*Hulk* DVD commentary).

11. Film adaptations of iconic comic book characters tend to cast actors in the lead roles who were unknown (Christopher Reeve, Brandon Routh, Hugh Jackman, and Henry Cavill) or associated with low-budget and independent productions (Michael Keaton, Tobey Maguire, Eric Bana, and Christian Bale). As a consequence of these films' popularity, many actors have found mainstream success, while others became typecast in their iconic roles. An exception to this trend has been the casting of stars as less well-known characters, presumably to augment the property's relative obscurity, e.g., Keanu Reeves (*Constantine*), Nicolas Cage (*Ghost Rider*), and Robert Downey, Jr. (*Iron Man*).

12. In the wake of 9/11, much of US popular culture celebrated community. For instance, Nigel Morris notes of *World Trade Center* (Stone 2006) that "in contrast to rugged individualism—nevertheless effective within the narrative's bounds—the film honors community" (154–55). Other examples might include the songs "My City in Ruins" and "Hero," first performed at the *America: A Tribute to Heroes* (Gallen 2001) telethon by Bruce Springsteen and Enrique Iglesias, respectively; the emergency service television programs *Third Watch* (Boole Williams and Allen Bernero 2002) and *Rescue Me* (Leary and Tolan 2004); the films *Black Hawk Down* (Scott 2001) and *Behind Enemy Lines* (Moore 2001); and Anne Nelson's play *The Guys*, subsequently adapted into a film.

13. The comparisons between Tony Stark and Howard Hughes are emphasized in *Iron Man 2* (Favreau 2010) when the billionaire inventor is subpoenaed to appear in front of a Senate hearing in which he is asked to turn over the Iron Man "weapon." Stark's cavalier attitude recalls the climax of *The Aviator* (Scorsese 2004), which dramatized Hughes's testimony at the Senate War Investigating Committee in 1947.

14. Reviewing *Hulk*, Andrew Sarris suggested that the sequences in which the monster destroys US army tanks and planes were "considerably out of sync with what is perceived in

many quarters as the public's triumphant pride in the feats of our armed forces" ("The Not-So-Jolly Green Giant").

15. The conflict between traditional aspects of comic book heroes and the desire to tally with community spirit is perhaps most evident in *Spider-Man* as the adaptation was in postproduction at the time of the 9/11 terrorist attacks, prompting changes to the film and its promotion. However, these additions were often at odds with the more faithful aspects of the film.

16. In a shrewd piece of cross-promotion, just as the fictional residents of New York were celebrating the hero, the real-world city experienced "Spider-Man Week," organized by the marketing teams of Sony Pictures Entertainment and New York's tourism organization, NYC & Company, to coincide with the release of *Spider-Man 3*. Events included an appearance by the cast, a comic book artwork exhibition at the New York Public Library, displays of rare arachnids, and giveaways, with banners "The Hero Comes Home" hanging throughout the city ("Look Out! Here Comes Spider-Man Week!").

17. The allegory of *Civil War* extended to images of the heroes sifting through rubble looking for survivors, embedded reporters (*Civil War: Front Line*), a Guantánamo Bay-like prison (named "42" in the story), and Patriot Act-evoking legislation (Superhuman Registration Act).

18. Comic books were not alone in receiving increased media attention by reflecting contemporary events. In 2004, the long-running newspaper comic strip *Doonesbury* garnered massive media interest, including the cover of *Rolling Stone* magazine (#954), when one of the strip's lead characters, BD, enlisted in the US army and was subsequently injured.

19. This trend of sociopolitical relevance was not confined to comic book adaptations, with many credibility-striving blockbusters produced at this time citing 9/11 and the War on Terror, while ultimately adopting conservative or apolitical positions, e.g., *War of the Worlds* (Spielberg 2005), *Cloverfield* (Reeves 2008), and *Prince of Persia* (Newell 2010).

20. When reviewing *300* for *Newsday*, Gene Seymour concluded that "the movie's just too darned silly to withstand any ideological theorizing. And 'silly' is invoked here, more or less, with affection."

21. *V for Vendetta* writer Alan Moore described the film adaptation as "a Bush-era parable by people too timid to set a political satire in their own country" (Vineyard "Alan Moore").

22. "Sabotage" was a three-part team-up between Spider-Man and the mutant team X-Force, which took place across *X-Force* #3, *Spider-Man* #16, and *X-Force* #4.

23. *Variety* reporter Justin Chang described the "inconsequential" third act of *Man of Steel* as a "basic failure of imagination" in the article "Does 'Man of Steel' Exploit Disasters Like 9/11?"; *BuzzFeed* cited disaster expert Charles Watson in a report that compares the action sequence to the "Nagasaki Nuke" (Zakarian).

24. Regular Harvey Pekar collaborator and successful alternative comic book creator Robert Crumb said of Pekar's motivations in the preface to their collection *American Splendor Presents Bob & Harv's Comics*: "He reports the truth of life in Cleveland as he sees it, hears it, *feels* it in his manic-depressive nervous system. There's nobody else to do it. Who would want to? There's no money in it. There's no money in telling the truth. People want *escape*. They want *myths*."

25. Warner Bros. president of marketing at the time of the production of *Superman: The Movie*, Andrew Fogelson, remarked that the tagline, "You'll Believe A Man Can Fly," was "the

single most important part of the whole marketing campaign. It was our way of saying to the ticket-buying world: 'We've learned how to do things in movies you've never seen before' and what better way to do it than to give you this spectacular version of Superman" ("Taking Flight: The Development of Superman").

26. Among the interview responses to the question of why so many comic book adaptations have been produced in the past two decades were: "The most obvious reason is the technology finally advanced to the point where you can do a movie about a superhero whether it's a Silver Surfer, Green Lantern, Thor or whoever" (*Batman* executive producer Michael E. Uslan); and "one [catalyst] is simply the technology has gotten to the point where you can legitimately realize some of these characters on film in a way that you might not have been able to do twenty years previously" (Marvel Comics senior vice-president of publishing Tom Brevoort).

27. Writing in 1996, cartoonist and critic Robert C. Harvey noted, "Comic books were the ideal medium for portraying the exploits of super beings. They were nearly the only medium at the time . . . only in comics could such antics be imbued with a sufficient illusion of reality to make the stories convincing" (35).

28. A number of commentators believe that cinema's recent annexation of the mainstream comic book industry's power fantasies will benefit the form (McCloud *Reinventing Comics* 212–13), with comics scholar Brad Brooks suggesting "that since now movies can use CGI, there is no need for comics to have superheroes in them" (Regalado 118).

29. Stephen Prince notes how Georges Méliès "used papier-mâché and stop-motion tricks where filmmakers today use computers" ("Filmic Artifacts" 26). Bukatman, also citing early cinema, points out that special effects are "only a more recent manifestation of optical, spectacular technologies" (*Matters of Gravity* 91), while Aylish Wood sees little distinction between the matte paintings of *Ben-Hur* and the digitally created Colosseum of *Gladiator* (378).

30. Other serials produced by Columbia at this time also employed cel animation to create "special effects," including *Captain Video: Master of the Stratosphere* (Gordon Bennet and Grissell 1951), in which "Captain Video and the Ranger left their hidden Earth headquarters and blasted off, via a crudely animated cartoon spacecraft" (Harmon and Glut 50). Other serials to employ this technique were the comic strip adaptations *Bruce Gentry* (Gordon Bennet and Carr 1949) and *Blackhawk* (Gordon Bennet and Sears 1952).

31. Supervisor for optical effects Roy Field describes how animation was tested during the development of *Superman: The Movie*, "but alas, it wasn't photo-real enough" ("The Magic Behind the Cape").

32. Comic book adaptations were obviously not the only films to integrate live-action footage with animation during these pre-digital eras. As Paul Wells notes of Ray Harryhausen's work in fantasy and adventure films, "Animation itself, however, is also often perceived as an 'effect' within live-action film-making, for example in the work of Ray Harryhausen in feature films from *The Beast from 20,000 Fathoms* (1953) to *Clash of the Titans* (1981) in which his stop-motion animated creatures and figures were the central aspect of the narrative and spectacle" (28).

33. As one of the innovators and early practitioners of digital technologies, George Lucas, remarked in a 1995 interview, "We've changed the medium in a way that is profound. It is no longer a photographic medium. It's now a painterly medium" (*A Personal Journey*). A number of scholars have echoed Lucas's assessment that cinema is now closer to the plastic arts. John

Belton notes of the increased malleability of the film image: "In the old days, filmmakers used to say they would 'fix it in post [-production].' Now with DI, they tend to say they'll 'make it in post'" (59). Similarly, Stam believes "filmmakers no longer need a pro-filmic model in the world; like novelists, they can give artistic form to abstract dreams" ("Introduction" 12).

34. In a 2007 report on the Irish film and television industry, it was noted that "many of the skills and techniques of animation are fundamental to feature film and television drama postproduction. Indeed, as special effects continue to build importance in feature film the crossover between animation and feature film has grown significantly" (*Creating a Sustainable Irish Film* 14). Similarly, Wells believes that animation techniques are fundamental to modern filmmaking: "Arguably, virtually all contemporary cinema is reliant on animation as the key source of its story-telling devices and effects" (28). These more recent assessments tally with Lev Manovich's contention that "digital cinema is a particular case of animation that uses live action footage as one of its many elements" (302).

35. *Sky Captain and the World of Tomorrow* had a production budget of $70 million, but only grossed $38 million at the North American box office. By contrast, *Sin City* had a production budget of $40 million, yet went on to gross $74 million at the North American box office.

36. Philippe Marion in *Traces en cases* terms "the graphic and narrative enunciation of the comics" as "graphiation" (Baetens 147). It will be more fully explored in Chapter Four.

37. Mick LaSalle of the *San Francisco Chronicle* cited Miller's influence on the film in his review of *Sin City*: "The film uses a combination of live action, performed by real actors, and computer graphics to transform Frank Miller's graphic novels into moving pictures" (1).

38. On its release, film reviewers identified the inventive use of digital technologies as one of the strongest elements of *MirrorMask*, with Roger Ebert writing in his largely negative review that "the movie is a triumph of visual invention," with Lisa Schwarzbaum summarizing, "CG effects and digital animation employed with avant-garde panache in a live-action adventure . . . an unusual collaboration between lord-of-the-cult multimedia artist Dave McKean and king-of-the-comics Neil Gaiman."

39. Robert Rodriguez, Miller's co-director on *Sin City*, said of the artist: "If you read his books you see he was already a director; he was just working with paper instead of a camera, and I really wanted to emulate that in the movie and make the cinematic equivalent of his book" ("15 Minute Flick School"). Similarly, Stu Maschwitz, the visual effects supervisor on Miller's solo-directorial debut, *The Spirit*, said "everyone always suspected that Frank Miller's artwork was cinematic even though they didn't really understand how to bring it to the screen until *Sin City*" ("Green World").

40. The graphic narrative mediums cinema has gravitated to since the emergence of digital filmmaking techniques include "live-action" versions of video games (*Resident Evil*, *Max Payne*, and *Prince of Persia*), cartoons (*Scooby Doo*, *Alvin and the Chipmunks*, and *The Smurfs*), toys (*Transformers* and *G.I. Joe*), and illustrated books (*The Grinch*, *The Cat in the Hat*, and *The Polar Express*).

41. In 1966, Paramount Pictures was purchased by Gulf & Western Industries heralding the start of a shift towards studio ownership by diversified, multinational conglomerates.

42. Spider-Man first appeared in *Amazing Fantasy* #15 (August 1962) before quickly receiving his own title with *The Amazing Spider-Man*, which celebrated its 700th issue in December 2012. Soon after the character's introduction, Spider-Man began appearing in other media,

including the Saturday morning cartoon *Spider-Man* that aired on the US ABC network from 1967 to 1970; 1977 saw the emergence of a short-lived live-action television series on CBS (1977–78) and a syndicated comic strip (by Stan Lee and John Romita), while pinball machines could be found in arcades during the 1980s.

43. Fredric Wertham's work has been criticized since the publication of *Seduction of the Innocent*. In 2010, the sources for Wertham's study were made widely available, with Carol Tilley identifying in her paper "Seducing the Innocent" how Wertham manipulated evidence.

44. Although superhero comics did not prompt the same level of scorn from Wertham as horror and crime comics, concessions still needed to be made. For instance, following Wertham's suggestion that Batman and Robin's relationship was "like the wish dream of two homosexuals living together" (190), female characters such as Bat-woman (1956), Batgirl (1961), and Aunt Harriet (1964) were introduced.

45. Production of the fourth *Die Hard* film, eventually titled *Live Free or Die Hard*, was delayed following 9/11 (Brodesser and Fleming). When finally released in 2007, *Live Free or Die Hard* became the first film in the franchise to target and receive the lower PG-13 rating.

46. Popular comic book writer Jeph Loeb summarized the success of *Spider-Man* as follows: "There was no reason why *Spider-Man* should have worked. I'm sure that Sony was terrified. The Batman franchise had flamed out. The Superman franchise had flamed out before that" ("Making the Amazing"). Loeb, in trying to create an underdog story, fails to note the success of *X-Men* (and to a lesser extent *Blade*), which must have given the filmmakers some confidence.

47. At the beginning of the modern comic book adaptation trend, fan-turned-filmmaker Kevin Smith lampooned Hollywood's habit of attempting to recreate any financial success. In Smith's 2001 comedy *Jay and Silent Bob Strike Back*, the eponymous duo discover that a comic book series in which they star is about to be adapted into a blockbuster film. This development is brought to the protagonists' attention by a comic book store owner who explains, "After *X-Men* hit at the box office, the movie companies started buying out every comic property they could get their dirty little hands on."

48. Like Gordon, Derek Johnson also believes that Marvel's position outside the conglomerate structure prevented it from enjoying the same mass-media opportunities as its competitor. Johnson suggests that because "DC was part of the Time Warner media conglomerate, its comic book characters boasted a potential for synergy and profit-making that Marvel's could not match. With a single character or property, Time Warner could release a comic book through DC, a film through Warner Brothers, a novelization through Warner Books, or a television program through the WB network" (70).

49. The head of talent at the William Morris Agency, John Fogelman, described Avi Arad's involvement in Marvel Comics adaptations as "beyond fiduciary concern; it's parental" (Brodesser).

50. The publisher—not the creators—own most of the comic characters that have been the subject of film adaptations. In 2002, Stan Lee successfully sued Marvel Comics after failing to receive a share of the profits of *Spider-Man*; Marvel Comics emphasized Lee's status as an employee ahead of the case, saying, "Marvel believes it is in full compliance with, and current on all payments due under, the terms of Mr. Lee's employment agreement and will continue to be so in the future" ("Lawsuit Filed by Spider-Man Creator").

51. Writing in 1972, Umberto Eco also remarked on the non-accruing nature of comics. He suggests that the stories are told in an "oneiric climate" and efforts are made to not let the character progress, as Superman "would have taken a step toward death" (17).

52. A similar example of comics' "serial aesthetic" in cinema can be seen at the end of *X-Men*, when Magneto promises, "The war is still coming." The villain finally makes good on his threat in the third film of the series, *X-Men: The Last Stand*.

53. The earlier Batman franchise showed little regard for continuity. For instance, Billy Dee Williams played Harvey Dent in the first film, only to be replaced with Tommy Lee Jones in *Batman Forever*.

54. Pierre Comtois notes how during the 1960s, the X-Men book was not well integrated with the rest of the Marvel Comics continuity, which resulted in it losing, "opportunities to make the book more reader-friendly" (190). This lack of continuity was thought to have contributed to the book's cancellation in the late 1960s.

55. Early examples of comic book crossovers include *Marvel Mystery Comics* #8 (1940), in which the popular comic book characters Sub-Mariner and the Human Torch had the first of their many encounters. DC Comics icons Superman and Batman would regularly team up in *World's Finest Comics* starting with #71 (1954). The first issue of *The Amazing Spider-Man* (March 1963) had an appearance from the already popular Fantastic Four to spur interest in the new book.

56. An extension of comic book crossovers is the superhero team (e.g., *Justice League of America* and *The Avengers*). These are comic books in which popular characters team up on a regular basis. The Avengers first appeared in *The Avengers* #1 (September 1963) with its roster including Iron Man, The Incredible Hulk, Thor, Ant-Man, and Wasp; Captain America was added to the series in #4.

57. Not only did *The Incredible Hulk* demonstrate its continuity with *Iron Man*, but the film also established the backstory for future adaptation, *The First Avenger: Captain America*, with the villain, Abomination, using the same Super Soldier serum that transformed Captain America.

58. It is important to note that a trailer for *Captain America: The First Avenger* preceded each of the surveyed showings of *Thor*, thereby increasing awareness of the upcoming film.

59. Released after *The Avengers*, *Iron Man 3* became the franchise's highest grossing film earning $1.2 billion internationally, almost twice as much as the previous franchise high *Iron Man 2* ($623 million). Sequels, *Thor: The Dark World* and *Captain America: The Winter Soldier*, also achieved franchise highs of $644 million and $713 million, respectively.

60. Following on from the success of *The Avengers*, the 2013 San Diego Comic-Con included panels for 20th Century Fox's *X-Men: Days of Future Past*, which features both generations of characters from the X-Men films, and Warner Bros. *Man of Steel* follow-up which will include Batman.

61. Ang Lee's poorly received interpretation of *Hulk* was "rebooted" just five years after its release with the more action-orientated *The Incredible Hulk*. Kevin Feige, Marvel's president of production, equated the differing films with competing interpretations published in comics, describing Lee's version as a "one-shot" while "what we're doing now is *really* starting the Marvel Hulk franchise" (De Semlyen 66).

62. Early examples of transmedia storytelling centered on comic book film adaptations can be found in the X-Men films and its paratextual materials. For instance, the backstory between

successive *X-Men* films, *X2* and *X-Men: The Last Stand*, was filled in by the video game *X-Men: The Official Game*, which used the likenesses and voices of the film's cast and was written by comic book writer Chris Claremont and screenwriter Zak Penn. Claremont also wrote the novelizations of the two films, while the films themselves were the subject of comic book adaptations, which not only reiterated the film's narrative, but elaborated character backgrounds.

63. Johnson's primary example is the manner in which Wolverine, previously a short and brutish looking character, was consistently modified in the comics to resemble the taller and more classically handsome Wolverine of the films, as portrayed by actor Hugh Jackman. Other examples that corroborate Johnson's thesis include the heroes wearing black uniforms, Rogue reverting to a more traditional look and characterization, and the introduction of a larger student body, all elements innovated by the first X-Men film, but quickly adopted by the comics and other versions of the characters, such as the animated series *X-Men: Evolution* and the video game *X-Men Legends*.

64. Merchandising opportunities frequently influence what films are produced. For instance, the Pixar film *Cars*, despite being one of the studio's most poorly received and lowest grossing films, was only the second Pixar film to receive a sequel. The decision to produce a sequel to *Cars* and not the studio's higher grossing and better received films, *Finding Nemo*, *Wall-E*, *The Incredibles*, and *Up*, was dictated by merchandising considerations, as *Cars* generated ten times more merchandising revenue than *Finding Nemo* (Von Riedemann). Strategies such as these are typical of mainstream film production today.

65. Today, many online and independent comics make the majority (if not all) of their revenue from advertising, donations, and merchandise (McCloud *Making Comics* 247). This tactic was dramatized in the biopic *American Splendor* with Harvey Pekar trying to sell a "Harvey doll" that his wife hastily put together when interviewed on *Late Night with David Letterman*.

66. Early examples of tie-in products include a perfume to coincide with the release of the 1925 *Ben Hur* adaptation (Buchanan) and the toys and fan cards that featured Charlie Chaplin's Tramp character (Aberdeen).

67. Testifying to how important merchandising became in mainstream film production following *Batman*, director Tim Burton describes how the merchandisers were unhappy with his darker sequel, *Batman Returns* (1992) and consequently he was dissuaded by Warner Bros. from making the third film (*Batman Returns* DVD commentary). Burton's replacement, Joel Schumacher, also remarked on the push towards merchandise: "For *Batman & Robin* there was a real desire at the studio to keep it more family-friendly, more kid-friendly, and a word I had never heard before: 'toyetic,' which means that what you create makes toys that can sell" ("Shadows of the Bat").

68. Many pop artists produced work based on established comic book iconography. Jess Collins created her "Tricky Cad" collages from Dick Tracy strips during the late 1950s. Andy Warhol enlarged images of *Dick Tracy* (1960) and *Superman* (1961) on canvases and created an exhibition piece (without the approval of DC Comics), titled *Batman Dracula* in 1964. Working out of Sacramento, Mel Ramos also used comic book heroes and villains as subjects for works such as *Joker* (1962). Richard Merkin used a variety of comic book icons, including Superman, Batman, Dick Tracy, and Little Orphan Annie, for his 1965 collage, *Little Orphan Annie is Forty*.

69. In the first decade of the new millennium, franchise characters firmly eclipsed movie stars, with comic book characters dominating the covers of *Empire* magazine. Over the ten

years, there were seven Batman covers, six X-Men covers, five Spider-Man covers, three Iron Man and Superman covers, two Hulk, and one cover each for Hellboy, Fantastic Four, and Watchmen. Further indicating the dominance of comic book and other franchise characters during this period, rather than acknowledging stars, the magazine identified ten "Icons of the Decade" for the December 2009 issue, with comic book characters Wolverine and the Joker taking two coveted spots.

70. The *Sunday Times* reported that actor Tobey Maguire had signed a deal worth $50 million for the planned fourth and fifth installments of the Spider-Man series (Harlow). Ultimately, the films were scrapped with the part recast with the relatively unknown Andrew Garfield, who reportedly received the comparatively miserly fee of $500,000 for his contribution (Fleming).

71. The minimalist marketing utilized for *Spider-Man* was first innovated by *Batman*, where the teaser poster simply contained the hero's logo and the release date with no supplementary information or images.

72. The ability of comic book icons to confer market differentiation was embraced by the UK-based clothing store French Connection. The clothes retailer has produced fashion lines to coincide with the release of comic book adaptations such as *The Dark Knight*, *The Incredible Hulk*, *X-Men Origins: Wolverine*, and *Kick-Ass* (Vaughn 2010).

73. Brooker also notes the use of advertising, "clearly in the mould of contemporary comics" during World War II (*Batman Unmasked* 69).

74. Comics' "universal accessibility" (McCloud *Reinventing Comics* 85) has been recognized since the earliest days of the industry, with both Stan Lee and Will Eisner tasked with creating "teaching materials" (Comtois 68) and "instructional comics" (Vaz 29) for soldiers during World War II. Eisner even went on to form the American Visuals Corporation in the 1950s, producing instructional material for the military, government, and businesses.

75. Comic book collecting reached its saturation point in the early 1990s, when a speculation market emerged. Exploiting this trend, comic book publishers began to produce comics that catered to collectors and speculators, such as a new *Spider-Man* title launched in August 1990, and epic storylines like "Maximum Carnage" that required readers to buy fourteen issues from five Spider-Man titles to complete the story. However, with so many comics produced, these "investments" rarely maintained their cover price and certainly never reached the value speculators were hoping for. Consequently, the speculation market crashed and comic publishers' fortunes experienced a significant downturn, with Marvel forced to declare bankruptcy in 1996.

76. Following the successful opening weekend of *Iron Man*, Marvel announced release dates for future adaptations *Thor* (July 4, 2010), and *Captain America: The First Avenger* (May 6, 2011), with the crossover film *The Avengers* to be released in July 2011 (Davis 2008). These release dates were later changed to May 6, 2011, July 22, 2011, and May 4, 2012, respectively.

77. Artists' Alley is a space at many conventions for amateurs to showcase their work to professionals, receive feedback, and make industry contacts.

78. Frank Miller explains his inspiration for *300* in the letters page of the third issue: "The movie, called *The 300 Spartans*, was released in 1962. I saw it when I was five—and have been entranced with the Hot Gates ever since. While it's kind of a clunky old show, it's surprisingly accurate—and it sure inspired *this* kid" ("Glory").

79. Promotion for *300* included the tagline "From the creator of Sin City," thereby positioning this adaptation of a little-known source within the wider comic book movie trend.

Chapter 2

1. Original poster taglines for *Creepshow* include "The Most Fun You'll Ever Have . . . BEING SCARED!" and "Jolting Tales of Horror!"

2. Of the forty-nine non-fans across both *Thor* and *Green Lantern* who answered the question, "What other films do you expect this film to be like?", twenty-two cited *X-Men* (or one of its sequels); *Iron Man* received twenty mentions; and *Spider-Man* received fifteen. With two mentions at screenings of *Green Lantern*, *Avatar* was the most frequently cited film outside of the comic book movie genre.

3. Speaking on *The Incredibles* (2004) DVD commentary, director Brad Bird said of animation: "It's not a genre. A Western is a genre. Animation is an art form, and it can do any genre. You know, it can do a detective film, a cowboy film, a horror film, an R-rated film or a kids' fairytale. But it doesn't do one thing. And, next time I hear, 'What's it like working in the animation genre?' I'm going to punch that person." However, despite the variety of genres that Bird suggests can be depicted through animation, mainstream production is overwhelmingly dominated by family entertainment, prompting the audience and industry to treat animation as a genre, with the American Film Institute including it alongside the western, science fiction, and gangster in its "10 Classic Genres" ("America's 10 Greatest Films in 10 Classic Genres").

4. Suggestions that *The Adventures of Tintin* is derivative of *Indiana Jones* are ironic—Spielberg said he faced the reverse comparison when promoting *Raiders of the Lost Ark* through Europe in 1981 ("The Journey to *Tintin*").

5. Identifying the generic affiliation in the promotion of *Thor*, *Empire* reporter James White described how the *Thor* teaser poster brings "to mind the Sin City posters with its splash of red on a monochrome image" ("Thor Teaser Poster Released").

6. In his analysis of *Ghost World*, Martin Flanagan describes the cat mask scene as "the most explicit reference to superhero culture in Zwigoff's film" (144).

7. The motives of the western vigilante and comic book movie hero are often questioned because they tend to be fueled by revenge, with Peter Parker, Bruce Wayne, and Matt Murdoch joining Wyatt Earp, Ringo Kid, and Ethan Edwards in adopting vigilante-like tactics in response to the murder of family members. The legitimacy of their actions is questioned, such as Rachel reminding Bruce in *Batman Begins* (Nolan 2005) "Justice is about harmony, revenge is about you making yourself feel better," and Alfred impressing on Batman that "it can't be personal, or you're just a vigilante."

8. *The Punisher* was one of the most popular comic book characters of the 1980s, at one stage he even appeared in three titles simultaneously: *The Punisher War Journal*, *The Punisher War Zone*, and *The Punisher Armory*.

9. Creator Frank Miller offers a sly allusion to the influence of urban crime films on his Batman in *All Star Batman & Robin The Wonder Boy* #2 (October 2005), with the hero's sidekick describing Batman's voice as an "Eastwood imitation."

10. Gregory A. Waller notes how following the success of *Rambo: First Blood Part II*, "*Newsweek* affirmed that 'Sylvester Stallone has brought the hero back to the forefront of American mythology,' and it went on to link Rambo, the 'warrior' hero, with both John Wayne and the 'noble savage'" (119).

11. Both *Die Hard 4.0* and *Rambo* had the lowest box-office returns of any entry in their series at $134,529,403 and $42,754,105, respectively. These films fell well below the franchise

highs of *Die Hard 2: Die Harder* ($184,268,515 adjusted) and *Rambo: First Blood Part II* ($286,246,977 adjusted).

12. Speaking in 2010, studio executive Jeff Katz recognized comic book movies as a distinct, valuable genre, stating, "I would say, even though they technically fall into a lot of different genres, they're actually like a genre unto themselves. And it's one of the most desirable genres in Hollywood" (Rogers).

13. *Jumper*, *Max Payne*, and *Push* were the subjects of panels at the San Diego Comic-Con on the following dates: July 26, 2007, July 24, 2008, and July 27, 2008. *Jumper* included an "Animated Graphic Novel" prequel as part of its DVD features. Similarly, supplementary feature "Michelle Payne—Graphic Novel" fills in the backstory of *Max Payne*, while DC Comics imprint Wildstorm published *Push* prequel comic books.

14. Director Doug Liman stated on several occasions during the DVD commentary of *Jumper* that he was seeking to subvert superhero conventions and the "staples of the genre" that audiences familiar with Spider-Man and Superman would expect. Furthermore, there are many direct nods to comic books and their adaptations in *Jumper*, with the character Griffin referring to David Rice as "Spidey" and the hero suggesting they try a "Marvel team-up." *Max Payne* employs the minimalist, monotone aesthetic made popular by *Sin City*. *Push* was marketed with the critical notice "X-Men meets Trainspotting," and stars future Captain America Chris Evans who had already enjoyed success playing the Human Torch in *Fantastic Four* (Story 2005).

15. As a writer of an alternative comic, even Harvey Pekar is a vigilante within his medium, seeking revenge for what he sees as daily slights through his autobiographical book. Similarly, in four of the five stories that make up the horror comic book movie *Creepshow*, the protagonist is motivated by a desire for retribution, while the anthology's wraparound story sees a young boy get revenge on his father, via a voodoo doll.

16. Craig Hight notes how the use of comic book imagery (typeface, diegetic text, and panels) in the opening of *American Splendor* cues the audience to accept the many heightened moments that will permeate the biography (194).

17. In discussing the knowingly artificial world of *Dick Tracy* (Beatty 1990), Michael Cohen suggests "the artificial set refuses to let the spectator forget this film is based on a comic" (20). Similarly, on the Blu-ray commentary for *Thor*, director Kenneth Branagh describes how even in the Earth-bound sequences he wanted to create a "heightened version of a kind of Americana that I had enjoyed seeing in the comics," and *The Spirit* producer Deborah Del Prete noted of her film's verisimilitude, "We always look for heightened-reality in this kind of film" ("Green World").

18. Batman editor Dennis O'Neil includes "heightened realism" as one of the guidelines for writers and artists in the Bat-bible.

19. Samuel L. Jackson's roles in comic book movies include *Unbreakable*, *The Incredibles*, *Jumper*, *The Spirit*, and *Kingsman: The Secret Service*, as well as his numerous appearances as Nick Fury in the Marvel Cinematic Universe.

20. Noting the use of bullet-time in comic book movies, Jake Rossen recalls how William Wisher, a screenwriter for a tentative Superman adaptation, was "instructed to '*Matrix* up' Superman . . . for an audience armed with fresh expectations" (241). Such "*Matrixing* up" occurred in *X-Men*, *300*, and countless other comic book movies that employ this genre convention.

21. Comic book creator Mark Millar discusses genre cycles in relation to his self-aware comic book *Kick-Ass*: "I think it's a natural progression for superheroes. There's the first stage, which is the perfect hero, like Superman or Batman. Then you get Stan Lee, one of my idols, introducing the flawed hero who lives in a real city, in the 1960s . . . I think *Kick-Ass* is the next stage; there's a through line, in nerd terms, from Clark Kent to Peter Parker to Dave Lizewski" (Armstrong 11).

22. The promotional material for *Unbreakable* contained little to suggest that the film would be a comic book movie. For instance, the film's poster taglines were: "Are You Ready For The Truth?"; "Are You Unbreakable?"; and "Some things are only revealed by accident." Similarly, the only card carried by the trailer was, "From M. Night Shyamalan the writer and director of *The Sixth Sense*," with the trailer displaying none of the overt comic book signifiers of the film. In contrast, the film itself opens with intertitles describing the minutiae of comic book collecting and includes many narrative moments and explicit references that could have been used in promotional materials to suggest this generic framework to prospective audiences.

23. The classical genre entrant *X-Men* was released a couple of months before *Unbreakable*, which could best be categorized as within the period of articulation. Such overlaps have been cited by scholars as weakening past organic models (Grant 35). However, the bacterial growth model allows for such overlaps. For instance, while the overall number of bacteria may be increasing during the log phase, this does not preclude the possibility that individual bacteria could be dying. Applying this model to cinema, genre entrants that are characteristic of other phases will coexist throughout the cycle, but it is the dominant genre entrant that defines the phase.

24. The producers of *X-Men* openly acknowledged their debt to earlier films, with director Bryan Singer remarking, "*Batman* and *Superman* are the only two analogous films, and *Batman* is far more retro. If I had to compare it to anything, I'd compare it to the first act of *Superman*, which I'm very inspired by and love" (D. Hughes 188).

25. Like Goldberg, comic creator Mark Millar also discussed the need for levels of comic book movie production to reach a critical mass before subversive comic book movies could be produced. Millar noted of his self-conscious comic *Kick-Ass* and its film adaptation, "I think that's the future for comics, now that everyone is superhero-literate. You couldn't have written Kick-Ass five years ago: it took the Spider-Man and Batman movies to make everyone know the conventions of the comic universe. So it's time to have the heroes living in the real world and turning all those conventions on their head" (Armstrong 11).

26. The ten comic book movies released in North America in 2008 were *Jumper*, *Iron Man*, *The Incredible Hulk*, *Hancock*, *Hellboy II: The Golden Army*, *The Dark Knight*, *Punisher: War Zone*, *Superhero Movie*, *Wanted*, and *The Spirit*.

27. The levels of production reached a six-year low in 2009, with Hollywood only producing five comic book movies. This drop could partly be attributed to the 2007–2008 Writers Guild of America (WGA) strike, which resulted in the number of tentpole releases during 2009 being curtailed (Mumpower). However, the numbers have rebounded with Hollywood releasing an average of 7.8 comic book movies each year between 2010 and 2014, which suggests that the genre has not yet entered its decline phase.

28. Early parodies *Mystery Men* and *My Super Ex-Girlfriend* (Reitman 2006) grossed $33,699,000 and $60,984,606, respectively. Despite being produced on smaller budgets

and with few "stars," later parodies and satires grossed more, including *Superhero Movie* ($71,237,351), *Meet the Spartans* ($84,646,831), and *Kick-Ass* ($96,130,432). The increasing success of comic book movie parodies suggests that the audience is becoming familiar with, perhaps even tired of, the genre's conventions.

29. Neale suggests that organic genre models are mechanistic ("Questions of Genre" 58), a criticism that seems redundant given that it is industrial regimes that develop and propagate genre filmmaking.

30. In July 2012, the milestone 100th issue of *The Walking Dead* topped the US sales chart with 335,082 orders. Nonetheless, the rest of the top ten was still dominated by superhero titles, including *Avengers vs. X-Men #7* (179,208) and *Batman #11* (127,210) (*CBGXtra.com*).

31. As comics scholar Scott McCloud uses the medium of comics in his analysis, any excerpt from his work will be treated in this study as a quote rather than an image. Accordingly, these images will have an in-text citation rather than a caption.

32. The *Comics Buyer's Guide* reported that preorders of the *30 Days of Night* comic peaked at 6,900 copies in June 2002 while *Punisher #13* preorders reached 49,100 in the same month. The trade paperback (TPB) of *30 Days of Night* had final orders of 900 in August 2004 (the first month it appeared on the list), falling well below the final orders for *Punisher Max Vol. 1* (4,200).

33. *30 Days of Night* had an IMDB user rating of 6.6 and a budget of $30 million compared to *The Punisher* user rating of 6.3 and $33 million budget.

34. Sales highs for *The Amazing Spider-Man* in the 2000s have included #583 (352,847 copies), which featured just-elected US president Barack Obama on the cover; #544 (146,170), the first part of the retroactive continuity storyline *One More Day*, and #535 (117,000), part of the crossover event *Civil War* (*CBG.Xtra*).

35. The importance of comic book movies and television shows at comic conventions was evident by the size of the venues used for a series of panels, "The Visionaries," organized by *Entertainment Weekly* at the 2008 San Diego Comic-Con. The first panel was with "Comic Creators" and included popular creators Jim Lee, Mike Mignola, and Grant Morrison. The second panel, "Showrunners," included the creators of *Heroes* and was held in a space four times the size of "Comic Creators." The final panel, "Filmmakers," was held in the largest venue, the 6,500-seat capacity Hall H with a panel consisting of Kevin Smith, Frank Miller, and Zack Snyder.

36. Producer Don Murphy enthused that in "the League comic, the brilliant concept is that all these brilliant characters actually happened. They live in the same world—it's like Spider-Man meeting Daredevil" (Ambrose 120).

37. The theatrical trailer for *X-Men* included the captions, "When all that we are afraid of . . . will be all that can save us" before a series of cards introduced the adaptation's heroes and villains. The promotional material for *The League* emulated this approach with the first trailer using the voiceover: "This Summer The Bad Will Fight For The Good." Furthermore, many of the theatrical trailers and TV spots introduced the characters through caption cards. It is noteworthy that while the caption, "When all that we are afraid of . . . will be all that can save us," accurately summarizes the plot of *X-Men*, the one for *The League* misleadingly conveys the film's story. However, the tagline does manage to associate *The League* with the previously successful genre entrant.

38. Attempts to align *The League of Extraordinary Gentlemen* with the more obviously comic book-based and already popular *X-Men* series did not escape the notice of reviewers, with Kirk Honeycutt of *The Hollywood Reporter* observing, "*League* might attract the under-25 crowd . . . But these MDCCCXCIX-Men are no X-Men."

39. Following the disappointment of *The League of Extraordinary Gentlemen*, Alan Moore had his credit removed from future adaptations of his work and his royalties given to the artists. As a result, he was not involved with, or credited on, adaptations of *V for Vendetta* and *Watchmen*.

40. In the past, several comic book adaptations relied on star actors to not only attract a mainstream audience, but also to validate the project (e.g., Marlon Brando and Gene Hackman in *Superman: The Movie*). This was the stated motivation for casting Jack Nicholson in *Batman*, with the film's producer Peter Gruber explaining, "It changed the nature of the 'comic' framework into a 'film' with the inclusion of Jack Nicholson" ("Shadows of the Bat"). Yet the addition of such star attractions would often unbalance productions, with the casting of Nicholson prompting the introduction of more Joker-centric scenes in *Batman* and a shifting of emphasis away from the protagonist.

41. Peter Aperlo notes that *Watchmen* director "Snyder wanted to avoid movie stars in putting together his ensemble cast, feeling that their well-known personas might distract the audience from full immersion in the film's weighty narrative" (24).

42. *Empire* reviewer Ian Nathan noted the lack of a clear, central protagonist in *Watchmen*: "Jackie Earle Haley finds the leery, psychopathic heartbeat of the faceless Bogart, and you half-wish Snyder might have stuck with Rorschach as protagonist rather than spreading the net so wide. No doubt the purists would have wailed."

43. *Metacritic*, which calculates an aggregate of a film's reviews, finds *The League* receiving an average of 30 percent, while *Watchmen* scored 56 percent.

44. Many comic book adaptations appear on *Box Office Mojo*'s list, "Biggest Second Weekend Drops at the Box Office," including *Jonah Hex* (69.7 percent), *Hulk* (69.7 percent), *Elektra* (69 percent), *X-Men Origins: Wolverine* (69 percent), *Watchmen* (67.7 percent), and *Green Lantern* (66.1 percent).

Chapter 3

1. Estimates of the age of comic book readers vary greatly, but all lean toward adults. The website *Comic Collector Live* offers a wide demographic "The average age of a comic book reader is between 18 and 34" ("Advertise"), while *Comic Book Secrets* is more finite "The average age of todays [*sic*] comic book reader is around 28 years old" ("New Comics").

2. As terms such as "comic book guy" and "fanboy" suggest, comic book fandom is a largely male pursuit with Jeffrey A. Brown noting in a 1997 paper that 90 percent of comic book fans are male ("Comic Book Fandom" 16). However, adaptations often enjoy a more even split, with Bacon-Smith and Yarbrough observing that while only 7 percent of visitors to fan forums such as comic stores and conventions were female, screenings of *Batman* attracted a 37 percent female audience (94).

3. The audience survey's second question asked participants to "list (1–3) the news and/or general information websites that you most regularly visit (i.e., not a search engine, email,

or social networking site)." Upon categorization of the websites it was found that fans cited a much narrower range of topics, with many fans just including film sites. Other topics that garnered strong interest included news, sports, comics, and video games. Non-fans demonstrated a much wider range of interest, with the variety of sites too numerous to list.

4. Although some earlier examples of comic book lettercols exist, they became a permanent fixture in the 1960s, with DC Comics titles *Superman* and *Justice Society of America* among the first to regularly include them (Jones and Jacobs 63).

5. Marvel Comics editor Stan Lee later explained of his participatory practices: "I tried to write as if the readers were friends of mine and I was talking specifically to them" (Duncan and Smith 182). Commentators note that Lee's and Marvel Comics' practices during the 1960s created a "participatory world" (Pustz 56), a "personality culture" (D. Thompson 129), a "chummy camaraderie" (Morrison 95), and a "rapport with readers" that prompted "intense loyalty" (Comtois 97), with Bukatman colorfully describing Lee as "the babbling disk jockey whose alliterative patter bound the whole *megillah* together and cajoled the willing reader into a sense of participation" ("Secret Identity Politics" 111).

6. Noted letterhacks include "the father of comic book fandom," Jerry Bails, and future comic book writers Kurt Busiek and Ralph Macchio.

7. Many comic book professionals started their careers by founding, running, or contributing to fanzines, including former Marvel Comics editor-in-chief Roy Thomas (editor of *Alter-Ego*) and comic book writer Mike Gruenwald (publisher of *Omniverse*).

8. Pierre Comtois terms the early 1970s era of Marvel Comics, where fans began moving into the industry, the "twilight years" (154). While the creators of many popular entertainments may have started out as fans, the comic book industry better nurtured the move from fan to professional. Such leaps were made possible by the opening up of the process in publications for fans like *Marvelmania Magazine* (1970–71). As noted in the *Marvel Vault*, "Marvelmania . . . gave members of the new fan group a look at behind-the-scenes doings. For the first time, readers were able to see how an artist's penciled work appeared before it was inked, or the finished product before it was colored, or what a script looked like" (Thomas and Sanderson 107).

9. *Batman & Robin*'s final US box-office gross of $107,325,195 significantly trailed the adjusted gross of the previous installment *Batman Forever* ($192,774,430) and franchise-high *Batman* ($322,413,092). Furthermore, *Batman & Robin* received the worst reviews of any film in the series, as testified by their Rotten Tomatoes aggregates: *Batman* (69 percent), *Batman Returns* (77 percent), *Batman Forever* (44 percent), and *Batman & Robin* (12 percent). Comic creator Grant Morrison colorfully describes how the film is "widely regarded as the worst Batman film ever made and indeed reviled by some commentators as the most indefensible artifact ever created by so-called civilization" (338).

10. Readers who pointed out continuity gaffes in Marvel Comics were awarded a "No-Prize" by the title's editor if their letter was published.

11. While continuity is "the preoccupation of fandom" (Duncan and Smith 190), fans are also open to "What If" scenarios and "Imaginary Stories," such as the popular storylines *Kingdom Come*, *The Dark Knight Returns*, and *Spider-Man: Reign*, which imagined future versions of the characters. However, these stories are set outside the regular continuity (the publishers have demarcated the timelines Earth 31, Earth 22, and Earth-70237), and thus do not contravene any preexisting canon.

12. Reporting on the inevitable *Return of Bruce Wayne*, blogger Sam Otterbourg wrote, "Death [in comics] doesn't really mean anything anymore. It doesn't matter to readers, and it barely means anything in-universe. People shrug off death like it's nothing because they know they are going to come back."

13. Commenting on fidelity in comic book adaptations for this study, former president of DC Comics Paul Levitz reflected, "I think fans insist on fidelity to the *essence* of the character because, while it is a very hard thing to put into words, it is something that is peculiarly easy to get a consistent opinion on."

14. Duncan and Smith describe their use of the Shannon-Weaver model of communication in *The Power of Comics* as follows: "The basic model for a communication act was first developed by a pair of mathematicians named Claude Shannon and Warren Weaver, whose *The Mathematical Theory of Communication* gave rise to the field of information theory. Their model, with its familiar components of source-message-channel-receiver, is often taught as a foundational concept in communications studies. We begin our model of comic book communication building on the foundation of what Shannon and Weaver first proposed" (7).

15. Half the non-fan respondents believed that online trends and discussions were followed by filmmakers (No—16 percent; Don't Know—34 percent), while only 27 percent thought that they impacted upon how a film is made (No—28 percent; Don't Know—45 percent).

16. At the same time the producers of *X-Men* were embracing fan activity, many other filmmakers were resisting intensive fan interest, with Jenkins describing *Star Wars* production company Lucasfilm's efforts to control and block online fan activities as "acting like a '500-pound Wookiee,' throwing its weight around and making threatening noises" (*Convergence Culture* 156).

17. Artists who got their start in the industry by showing their work at comic conventions include Jim Lee, Steve McNiven, and Mike Wieringo (DeFalco *Comic Creators on Fantastic Four*).

18. Speaking during postproduction, *Iron Man* director Jon Favreau noted the impact that the 2007 San Diego Comic-Con was having on the film's release: "After Comic-Con, we showed the footage, people got on board and got excited about it. . . . It built from like a small, little grassroots thing into something where people are anticipating it. So, I know the awareness is there" ("I am Iron Man").

19. Of the 2009 Comic-Con, attending director James Cameron noted, "It's been co-opted by Hollywood. . . . But that's OK; it's mutual exploitation. [Fans] get the first looks and get to lord over all their friends what they saw before anyone else" (Bowles).

20. *X-Men* director Bryan Singer was one of the first filmmakers to acknowledge the impact of online fandom, with the director commenting ahead of the film's release, "Until now I've not admitted to it, but if I really think about it, somebody will say something that'll strike a chord with you and you'll sit down with everyone and discuss it. Then you'll do it" (Salisbury 52). Although this concession lacked the all-inclusive terms of a comic book publisher, it did situate the fan as part of the creative process.

21. In 1973, when *Superman: The Movie* was first being developed, the character's co-creator Jerry Siegel, who had lost the rights to Superman in 1947, took the opportunity to sue for royalties owed to him and artist Joe Schuster. Siegel lost, but mounting pressure on DC Comics from high-ranking professionals saw Siegel and Schuster credited as the creators of Superman (MacDonald).

22. The comic book-based logos for Marvel and DC Comics adaptations were first used in the theatrical releases of *Spider-Man* (Raimi 2002) and *Catwoman* (Pitof 2004) respectively.

23. When returning to the San Diego Comic-Con to promote the sequel *Iron Man 2*, Jon Favreau remarked, "You can't underestimate how powerful this group is. . . . It's an unlimited press corps, all of them knowing how to communicate in a digital age. The geeks have inherited the Earth, and that's good news for us" (Bowles).

24. Two of the many websites used to build interest in *The Dark Knight* were *ibelievein-harveydent.com*, which emulated District Attorney Harvey Dent's election campaign, and a Joker-style vandalized version *ibelieveinharveydenttoo.com*. Emails sent to this website unveiled the first image of the Joker a pixel at a time.

25. Remarking on the steep drop in *Watchmen*'s box office, Brandon Gray of *Box Office Mojo* noted, "Watchmen disintegrated 68 percent to $17.8 million for $85.8 million in ten days, trailing all previous superhero movies that debuted in the $50 million range through the same point. . . . The weekend further cemented Watchmen's status as a movie with much more limited appeal than other superhero pictures, rooted in its non-mainstream source material and its diffuse storyline and marketing" ("Watchmen Burns Out").

26. *Box Office Mojo* writer Brandon Gray noted how following the "media creation" of *Snakes on a Plane*, *Borat* (Charles 2006) was released on a more modest 1,100 screens ("'Borat' Bombards the Top Spot").

27. The first Superman movie serial was produced by Columbia and was simply titled *Superman* (Gordon Bennet and Carr 1948). An advertisement from *Superman* #8 (January–February 1941) shows licensed products including bubble gum, toy guns, undershorts, and moccasins (Pasko 29).

28. An eagerness to transcend the original form was not only apparent in the promotional material for *Superman: The Movie*, but was also emphasized in the adaptation's opening. *Superman: The Movie* begins with a shot of a theatre curtain opening partway to reveal a small cinema screen. We see a black-and-white clip with the title "June 1938" and the image of a child reading "Action Comics." A dissolve transforms the images from the comic book page to a movie serial clip replete with a black-and-white aesthetic and dated model work. Finally, the curtains draw back fully, as a color credit appears, and then escapes from the expansive proscenium. The manner in which the film's pre-credit sequence moves from a comic book to a black-and-white movie serial (one of the earliest forms to adapt Superman) and finally to a "modern" film not only acknowledges the character's history, but suggests this adaptation's transcendence of all previous forms.

29. The three *Sin City* graphic novels adapted to Rodriguez's 2005 film were "That Yellow Bastard," "The Hard Goodbye," and "The Big Fat Kill."

30. In a 1995 promotional documentary for the loose Batman adaptation, *Batman Forever*, presenter Chris O'Donnell was still able to point to aspects from the character's lengthy publication history to justify the largely free interpretation, such as describing the film's Batmoblie as a "stylized, automotive version of a bat. And this single fin here goes back to the Batmobile's first appearance in a 1941 comic book" (*Riddle Me This*).

31. Prior to being deemed a "legend" in *Batman* #1, Batman was described in the introduction to *Detective Comics* #37 (March 1940) as "an almost legendary figure."

32. The 1943 Batman serial omitted many elements of the Batman mythos established by the time of production, such as replacing Commissioner Gordon with the opportunistic Captain Arnold; Batman allowing several criminals to fall to their deaths; and instead of a comic book villain, the film introduces Dr. Daka, a "shifty eyed Jap." Although comic books were cited in the 1960s *Batman* series, these references frequently undermined the source in service of the show's camp tone and aesthetic.

33. "Batman Fans Fear The Joke's on Them in Hollywood Epic," by Kathleen A. Hughes, quoted fan criticism of Tim Burton's yet to be released Batman adaptation, and reported that "fans have circulated petitions demanding a different cast, and they booed Warner representatives who had the audacity to show up at a comics-fan convention with a photograph of Mr. Keaton."

34. Dennis O'Neil explained the Bat-bible's background in email correspondence: "I did the first version of the bible a month or two or three after taking over the batbooks [1986]." The number of titles considered part of the Batman family changes regularly. In 1989, the year *Batman* was released, the core titles under O'Neil's editorial control included the monthly comics *Batman*, *Detective Comics*, and *Batman: Legends of the Dark Knight*. Furthermore, Batman would regularly appear in *Justice League of America*, *New Teen Titans*, and any number of specials and annuals.

35. The Bat-bible is an unpublished document. The version cited here was forwarded by Dennis O'Neil in September 2010. Although the document concludes "January 1989," references to storylines such as "No Man's Land" (March-November 1999) indicate that it has been updated on several occasions to incorporate continuity additions and changes. Furthermore, O'Neil explained that versions had existed as early as 1986.

36. In the Bat-bible, Dennis O'Neil explains why the hero never kills his adversaries: "The trauma which created his obsession also generated in him a reverence for that most basic of values, the sacredness of human life."

37. Other guidelines from the Bat-bible that the more recent adaptations have incorporated, but Burton's films did not, include: the character is in his "early 30s"; the dark coloring of his costume "allows him to blend into shadows, a technique he learned from Japanese ninja"; and "he has experimented, and continues to experiment, with various types of body armor. He's unsatisfied with any he's tried; either they impede movement or they're too light to be effective." These elements have all appeared in the more in-continuity *Batman Begins* and its sequels.

38. The script for "The Man Who Falls" was added to later versions of the Bat-bible by O'Neil's assistant, Scott Peterson, indicating that the editorial staff considered it canonical.

39. The importance of the comics cited by Goyer and Nolan was reinforced in the promotion of *Batman Begins*, as "The Man Who Falls" was collected, alongside segments of *The Long Halloween* and *Batman: Year One*, in a miniature trade paperback that was included in the Deluxe Edition DVD of *Batman Begins*.

40. *The Dark Knight* alludes to a number of gritty television police procedurals. For instance, Lieutenant Gordon, like Lieutenant Cedric Daniels in *The Wire*, is the hard-working head of a major case unit, surrounded by incompetence and corruption. Furthermore, Gordon's colleagues are played by actors who have previously played police officers in *NYPD*

Blue (Ron Dean), *Without a Trace* (Monique Gabriela Curnen), and *Law and Order* (Keith Szarabajka).

41. Many commentators have picked up on Nolan's penchant for complex narratives, with *New York Press* critic Armond White chastising the director for continuing "the intellectual squalor popularized in his pseudo-existential hit Memento" ("Knight to Remember") in *Batman Begins* and *The Dark Knight*.

42. Online fans celebrated early images of *Batman Begins* for its perceived comic book fidelity, which distanced it from previous adaptations. For instance, an entry on *Dtheatre* about the new Bat-suit prompted one commentator to write, "It appears the Batman Begins film is following the graphic accounts illustrated in 'Year One.' I applaud the authorities behind this film for a noble attempt to capture the ominous terror of the Dark-Knight" (A random shemp), while another commentator observed, "So this movie is really doing what comics did and I'm happy with that. Bout time WB did a Batman movie right" (Silent_Azn_86).

43. *Superman Returns* eschewed the fidelity displayed by many modern comic book adaptations and served as a remake/sequel to Richard Donner's 1978 film, which itself had questionable fidelity, and was largely out-of-sync with the comic books by 2006. Although *Superman Returns* achieved blockbuster status, it was considered to have underperformed.

Chapter 4

1. Francis Lacassin proposes a further list of filmmakers who are fans of comics: "It is no accident that such film-makers as Federico Fellini, Alain Resnais, Chris Marker, Jacques Rivette, Jean-Luc Godard, Ado Kyrou, Claude Chabrol, Jacques Rozier, Boileau-Narcejac, Claude Lelouch, Jean-Paul Savignac, and Remo Forlani, not to mention television people, are assiduous readers of comic strips" (11).

2. When interviewed for this study, Mark Waid argued that comics have influenced the sustained narratives of television shows: "The impact seems to have been the idea you can create a universe around your show, the idea that you have a continued narrative. The mythology around primetime drama shows like *Lost* are very comic book, and very much what we've been doing for years."

3. Like McCloud, Sabin, and Eisner, Thierry Groensteen treats comics as a language in *The System of Comics*, adding, "that is to say, not as a historical, sociological, or economic phenomena, which it is also, but as an original ensemble of productive mechanisms of meaning" (2).

4. Duncan and Smith define the "panel" accordingly: "The process of encapsulation involves selecting certain moments of prime action from the imagined story and encapsulating, or enclosing, renderings of those moments in a discrete space (a unit of comic book communication that is called a panel, irrespective of whether or not there are actual panel borders)" (131).

5. Groensteen also describes how comic book panels enjoy a measure of autonomy, "whatever its contents (iconic, plastic, verbal) and the complexity that it eventually shows, the panel is an entity that leads to general manipulations. One can take it, for example, in order to enlarge it and create a seriegraph; one can also move it" (25).

6. Groensteen, like Eisner, also characterizes panel transitions as the punctuation of the comic language: "The panel frame plays an analogous role to that of punctuation marks in language (here comprised of the elementary sign that is the blank white space that separates

two words), these signs that divide, within a *continuum*, the pertinent units, thus allowing—or facilitating—the comprehension of the text" (43).

7. Lacassin observed that the language of comics and film are quite similar in their reliance on montage, "In both, the language is composed of a succession of 'shots,' (that is to say, images with variable framing) in a syntactical arrangement or *montage*" (11).

8. The thumbnail process testifies to the importance of layout in comics. In this preproduction stage, the creator will draft (and often redraft) the layout of the page in a smaller version (a thumbnail) in order to identify the optimum layout for storytelling and aesthetics. Artist Mark Buckingham notes, "If a reader is looking at a page and doesn't know where they are going, then it has failed as a comic book. It's become abstract art" (DeFalco *Comic Creators on Spider-Man* 222).

9. George Bluestone suggests that "the novel has three tenses; the film has only one" (48). Decades later, Brian McFarlane would make the same argument, noting that "even when film resorts to flashback to make us aware that the action depicted is meant to be read as happening in the past, there is nothing intrinsic to the image at any given moment to make us think, Ah, this is occurring at some anterior time. Once the filmgoer is transported to this past time, every action in the narrative seems to be happening with the same degree of presentness as the actions pertaining to the sequences set at the later date" ("Film and Literature" 21).

10. It is important to note that in the original publication of *The Amazing Spider-Man* #33, the two pages covering Spider-Man's escape from the debris were separated by advertisements for *Fantastic Four* #47 and *Marvel Collector's Item Classics* #1.

11. On the *Sin City* DVD commentary, director Robert Rodriguez describes using camera tilts to emulate the vertical panels of the graphic novel.

12. Suture was "perceived to be the effect of certain filmic codes that stitched the spectator into the film text" (Hayward 382).

13. The six IMAX sequences as listed on the DVD release of *The Dark Knight* are: "Prologue," "Hong Kong," "Armored Car Chase," "Lamborghini Crash," "Prewitt Building," and "Final Montage." Each of these sequences takes place on or within a cityscape of tall buildings.

14. *Box Office Mojo* reporter Scott Holleran commented that *Hulk* director Ang Lee got "carried away" with his attempts to approximate the source and that the multiple shot style was "distracting."

15. The nature and accuracy of representation is a central theme in *American Splendor*. This interest becomes particularly prominent in the sequences in which the real-life Harvey Pekar (who narrates the film) interacts with the many fictionalized versions of himself on page, stage, and screen.

16. *Showcase* #4 featured the first appearance of the Silver Age Flash, and is often credited with reigniting interest in superhero comics.

17. As noted in *The Marvel Vault*, the Italian film director Federico Fellini visited the Marvel Comics offices in the 1960s (Thomas and Sanderson 97). The director's interest in comics also led him to collaborate with artist Milo Manara on the 1990 graphic novel *Trip to Tulum*.

18. Celebrated comic book artist Geoff Darrow provided further concept art for *The Matrix*.

19. On its release, reviewers of *The Matrix* remarked on its comic book lineage, with Ray Conlogue of the *Globe and Mail* claiming, "For those who have been waiting for movies to catch up with the graphic possibilities of comic books, wait no longer: The Matrix is among us."

20. In addition to comic books, bullet-time was also influenced by the wirework of Hong Kong action films, as well as the traditional application of slow motion to cinema. *Fist of*

Legend (Chan 1994) fight choreographer Yuen Woo-ping was hired for *The Matrix*, with the film's success popularizing wirework sequences in Hollywood cinema. This technique became a key component of bullet-time, as the characters were contorted into the most exaggerated poses during these near-frozen moments. Furthermore, *The Matrix* digitally upgraded slow motion, which was recognized as early as 1933 by Rudolf Arnheim as creating "new movements . . . [that] have a curious gliding, floating character of their own" (116).

21. Writing before the development of bullet-time, Harvey suggested that when "filmmakers employ [slow motion], they almost seem to be tampering with the nature of the medium by prolonging time unnaturally. And what would seem unnatural in film seems quite at home in a comic strip" (176). Yet theorists as early as Rudolf Arnheim (116) and Walter Benjamin ("Mechanical Reproduction" 806) have suggested that slow motion is not unnatural in film but can create new movements, a contention supported by the bullet-time practiced in comic book adaptations and many modern films.

22. Michele Pierson predicted the integration of digital effects into the film narrative, writing in 1999 that "computer-generated special effects have ceased to figure in these films as objects of contemplation and wonder" (175).

23. In this near-frozen *tableau vivant* from *The Matrix Reloaded*, the spectator is confronted with five competing locus points of information: The hero, Neo, jumps clear of his attackers (Detail 1), with one assailant following him (Detail 2). A second assailant removes a trident from the wall (Detail 3), while a third runs across the banister (Detail 4). The final attacker, who Neo previously pinned to the wall, works his way free (Detail 5).

24. Many comic book fans who praised *The Dark Knight* criticized Christian Bale's interpretation of the hero's voice. This criticism was echoed by Bordwell, who suggests that Bale's vocal characterization was "over-underplayed as a hoarse bark" ("Superheroes for Sale").

25. It is worth noting that not all comics contain speech balloons. For instance, in December 2001 many Marvel Comics titles did not use speech balloons as part of the cross-title exercise, *'Nuff Said.*

26. The unique comic book fonts of creators such as Dave Gibbons, Brian Bolland, and many other artists are available for sale at the website *Comicbookfonts.com.*

27. It should be acknowledged that many theatrically screened silent films had musical accompaniments, but they were not synched directly with the film.

28. In describing the "graphic maneuvering" employed by comics, Harvey writes, "Style is the most illusive of the lot: it is the visual result of an individual artist's use of the entire arsenal of graphic devices available, including the very tools of the craft. An artist's style can be identified by describing the way he draws certain objects (shoes, hands, lips) or how he uses a brush or pen (thin lines, thick lines; sketchy or labored or detailed). Some artists display an individual style in the way they arrange panels on a page. But describing style is about as far as criticism can legitimately go. Style is the mark of the maker. It is peculiar to the individual artist. And finally, style is too individual a matter to provide a basis for evaluation" (152).

29. Describing his approach to filming *Dick Tracy*, cinematographer Vittorio Storaro said, "We were trying to use elements from the original Chester Gould drawings. One of the elements is that the story is usually told in vignette, so what we tried to do is never move the camera at all. *Never.* Try to make everything work into the frame" (D. Hughes 54). An early attempt to mirror the economic design of comics' static panels, deemed "prosaic" by comic

creator Stephen R. Bissette, was *Barbarella*. Bissette notes, "[The filmmakers] assume that the two-dimensional aspect of the comic book page, was somehow inherently characteristic of comics, and as a result . . . will set up very flat two-dimensional stagings . . . and assuming that keeping it static is typical of comics. . . . It's not" ("From Fumetti to Film").

30. During the opening sequence of *Unbreakable*, the camera is largely stationary and there are no cuts, instead the screen is spatialized with many different points of interest. Hence, within the one shot, the spectator can see that this scene is taking place in the reflection of a mirror (Detail 1), focuses on a mother who has just given birth (Detail 2) and a doctor concerned about the child's condition (Detail 3). In the background are gossiping shop assistants (Detail 4) and police looking for any signs of impropriety (Detail 5). All these details can be effectively and efficiently rendered without any need to edit.

31. *The Incredible Hulk* director Louis Letterier's remake of the 1981 film *Clash of the Titans* (2010) has been described as a "comic book war-of-the-gods fantasy" by *Entertainment Weekly* reporter Jeff Jensen, who also compares the film to comic book adaptation *Thor*. Thus, the film has been positioned within the comic book movie genre by key components of the inter-textual relay.

32. The role of the inker is colorfully addressed in *Chasing Amy* (Smith 1997). In the film, the protagonists are two comic book co-creators. The artist, Holden, is held in high regard by his peers and fans, while the inker, Banky, is dismissed as a "tracer," simply going over the lines of another artist's work. When asked by a fan in the film's opening, "So basically, you just trace?", Banky responds, "It's not tracing. I add depth and shading to give the image more definition. Only then does the drawing truly take shape."

33. As graphiation becomes more central to the constructed mise-en-scène of comic book adaptations, techniques such as inking now find parallels in filmmaking. For instance, Joe Harman, the computer graphics supervisor on *The Spirit*, noted, "There are a lot of areas where a wall might fall off completely black, but we never let anything be completely black. A matte painter will actually paint full detail brick [and] then we bring it down [in brightness] because . . . a subtle variation in the blacks can actually show up and the viewer can tell that it's inked, we call it inked out" ("Green World").

34. Speaking on the *Batman & Robin* DVD commentary, director Joel Schumacher suggests that "comic books usually rely on a very small color palette . . . and a lot of it are primary colors, so we tried to give you that feeling."

35. Noting the importance of color pops, Batman writer Dennis O'Neil remarked, "The colorist can be part of the storytelling process. If the vase in the corner is going to be very important to the story, they will color the panel in such a way to subtly emphasize that vase without a little arrow pointing to it saying, 'important clue.' The very best colorists think in those terms" (Pearson and Uricchio 26).

36. *Pleasantville* (Ross 1998) was the first feature to employ digital color grading, with *O Brother Where Art Thou?* (Coen brothers 2000) the first film to have a digital intermediate that was entirely color corrected. John Belton estimated in 2007 that 70 percent of major studio productions go through the process (58), while Prince believes that digital color "brings the medium closer to the kind of fine-grain aesthetic control that painters have long enjoyed" ("Filmic Artifacts" 28).

37. Colorist Bob Sharen notes that distinctive color pops are no longer necessary in comics: "As long as the colorist is aware of providing a contrasting background for [the] sake of clarity

. . . the costume colors don't matter that much. Hue and value contrast will make almost any character 'pop' in a given panel" (Duncan and Smith 142).

38. While only *Sin City* and *300* have been directly adapted from Frank Miller's work, *Daredevil* (Steven Johnson 2003), *The Dark Knight Trilogy*, and *The Wolverine* (Mangold 2013) are indebted to his contribution to these long-standing characters.

39. Deborah Del Prete, producer of *The Spirit*, noted the effect that digital technologies had on comic book film adaptations: "In previous comic book movies you got the story, but a key part of comics is the work of artists, and that was missing . . . with *Sin City* and *300* you finally got the artist's work up there on the screen" (Vaz 63). *Sin City* director Robert Rodriguez regularly suggested that his film was Miller's work on screen: "Instead of an adaptation of *Sin City*, we could just translate it, the way you drew it, right to the screen" (*Sin City* DVD commentary).

40. *The Spirit* cinematographer Bill Pope said of the film, "There are silhouetted people and silhouetted backgrounds or there are edge-lit people and sketchy backgrounds, they're trying to draw your eye to the main event and suggest the world beyond the same way that Frank suggests everything" ("Green World"). Similarly, Jim Bissell, production designer of *300* said, "Well, *300*, the graphic novel, is the departing point for us in terms of the look of the film" (*300* Webisodes), while the film's costume designer, Michael Wilkinson, used the term "Frank Miller-esque" when describing his work (*300* Webisodes).

41. Ian Gordon notes an early use of plewds in the *Life* cartoon "The Benefits of an Extended Repertoire" (Franklin Morris Howarth 1892): "Exaggerated sweat beads became a standard means of displaying anxiety in comic strips, and the credit for them belongs to [F. M.] Howarth" (23).

42. To educate novice readers, the hero's Spider-sense was explained seventeen times in *The Amazing Spider-Man* #45–57. Each reference was a combination of text and image. Not all of these thirteen issues (a yearly run) contained a reference, while others contained two. But with seventeen references over the course of the year, the reader was given ample opportunity to decipher this code.

43. Comic book adaptation *X2* introduced the superpowered teleporter Nightcrawler. Past screen interpretations of teleportation simply had the character disappear and reappear, but Nightcrawler's ability was conveyed through a blue mist, much like the comic. Similarly, the invisible woman of *Fantastic Four* was far from the first invisible character to (dis)appear on screen, but unlike *Hollow Man* (Verhoeven 2000), the superhero's abilities were denoted by a blue/green hue.

44. Mark Waid's criticism of some digital comics alludes to the "motion comic"—a transmedia initiative that adds minimal animation to original comic art. A *Watchmen* motion comic was released online and on DVD in 2009 to coincide with the film adaptation. However, the perceived gains of the motion comic served to diminish the form's specificity. For instance, the use of sound and motion obliterated the limitless discourse-time of the source. Being neither comic nor cartoon, the motion comic becomes an unnecessary byproduct of media convergence, and as Scott McCloud pointed out, when discussing a CD-ROM precursor to motion comics, "when it comes to time-based immersion, the art of film already does a better job than any tricked-up comic can" (*Reinventing Comics* 210).

45. One of the many densely packed shots from the opening credits of *Watchmen* reworks the *Life* magazine photo "V-J Day in Times Square." The shot presents the superhero,

Silhouette, kissing a nurse (Detail 1) as a sailor walks by in the background (Detail 2) and crowds cheer (Detail 3), with the iconic moment captured by a photographer (Detail 4).

Chapter 5

1. Of the Coen Brothers' 1987 comedy *Raising Arizona*, Bordwell and Thompson note, "high-speed tracking shots combine with distorting wide-angle close-ups to create comic-book exaggerations" (*Film Art* 467); reviewer Mike Scott suggested that Guy Ritchie's *Sherlock Holmes* (2009) gave audiences a "comic-book peek inside 221B Baker Street"; and screenwriter William Goldman suggested films as diverse as *Gunga Din* (Stevens 1939) and *The Deer Hunter* (Cimino 1978) had comic book qualities (151–52).

2. Martyn Pedler is one of many scholars who believes that the overlap between comics and cinema is stronger and more fertile than comics' links with other media: "In superhero adventures, action is everything. If superheroes cannot seem to be successfully translated into prose, their 'action comics' certainly share common ground with contemporary action cinema" ("The Fastest Man Alive" 251).

3. When discussing *Batman & Robin*, director Joel Schumacher suggested that "a lot of the angles are very much inspired by comic books, what we call 'Dutching,' where you take the camera and put it at an angle" (*Batman & Robin* DVD commentary).

4. David Bordwell also identifies how framing conventions have moved freely between comics and cinema: "Steep high and low angles, familiar in 1940s noir films, were picked up in comics, which in turn re-influenced movies" ("Superheroes for Sale").

5. When *Citizen Kane* was being developed, comics were at the height of their popularity, with sales doubling from ten to twenty million during 1941–44. Additionally, comic strips were identified in a Gallup poll of newspaper reader interests from 1930 as "the most frequently read part of newspapers" (Gordon 81).

6. Citing the deep-focus photography of *The Magnificent Ambersons* (Welles 1942), Bazin contends that Welles's "refusal to break up the action, to analyse the dramatic field in time, is a positive action the results of which are far superior to anything that could be achieved by the classical cut" (*What Is Cinema?* 34). Depth of field in comics serves a similar function, displaying an entire event in one (usually larger) panel, rather than using several smaller panels to convey the same meaning.

7. In a further example of the active relay between the comic and film languages, many comic creators cite *Citizen Kane* as an inspiration. This development was fictionalized in *The Amazing Adventures of Kavalier and Clay*, where the comic book creators attend the premiere of *Citizen Kane*. The pair meet the director, who claims that he never misses their comic, *The Escapist*. After seeing the film, Kavalier and Clay conclude, that in "its inextricable braiding of image and narrative—*Citizen Kane* was like a comic book" (362), and aspire to create work of comparable depth and style.

8. Michael Cohen notes how the use of a diopter lens in *Dick Tracy* (Beatty 1990) achieves the contrast in figure size that Lee describes: "The diopter lens allows the foreground and background characters and objects to be displayed in sharp focus, presenting a striking juxtaposition that defies the reality of their spatial position, and heightens their compositional

proximity . . . Warren Beatty's choice to use the diopter lens in *Dick Tracy* is the choice to move away from the language of 'cinema' towards the language of 'comics'" (34).

9. The deep-focus photography in the second White House scene from *X2* was accomplished using a Frazier lens, which was introduced in the late 1990s to enable filmmakers to achieve quality depth of field photography in minutes, rather than the hours it would have taken with traditional equipment ("Australian Invention Dazzles Hollywood"). This innovation allowed filmmakers to efficiently achieve the exaggerated depth of field typical of mainstream comics.

10. Filmmaker Joel Schumacher noted of the exaggerated performances that populated his comic book movies: "This scene will not win the award for under-acting, but hey it's a comic book" (*Batman & Robin* DVD commentary).

11. Another comic book hero convention in *Unbreakable* is the hero's name, David Dunn. Many superheroes have alliteration in their names, such as Peter Parker (Spider-Man), Matt Murdock (Daredevil), and Bruce Banner (the Hulk).

12. Many commentators have noted how the advertisers that targeted comic book readers often exploited the wish fulfillment aspect of the superhero. The most famous example of this was the Charles Atlas advertisement, "The Insult that Made a Man out of Mac," that ran for decades in comic books beginning in 1940. In the advertisement, told in comic book panels, a wimp is humiliated in front of his girlfriend by a "big bully." The wimp follows Atlas's "dynamic tension" exercises and returns as a "real man," punching the bully and getting the girl. It has been noted by Jeffrey A. Brown that these ads "revolve around the male daydream that, if we could just find the right word, the right experimental drug, the right radioactive waste, then we too might instantly become paragons of masculinity" ("Comic Book Masculinity" 32), with many others offering similar readings of the advertisement (Bukatman *Matters of Gravity* 60; Scott "Red, White, and Blue" 334).

Appendix

1. "Comic Book Adaptation—Movies at the Box Office," *Box Office Mojo*, IMDB, 30 Jul. 2014. http://www.boxofficemojo.com/genres/chart/?view=main&sort=date&order=DESC&pagenum =2&id=comicbookadaptation.htm.

WORKS CITED

Aberdeen, J. A. "Charlie Chaplin: Hollywood Renegade." *Welcome to Cobbles.com*, n.d. http://www.cobbles.com/simpp_archive/charlie-chaplin_biography.htm.

Abrams, J. J., Damon Lindelof, and Jeffrey Lieber. *Lost*. ABC, 22 Sept. 2004.

"Action Comics Superman Debut Copy Sells for $2.16m." *BBC News*, 12 Jan. 2011. http://www.bbc.com/news/entertainment-arts-15978677.

Adaptation. Dir. Spike Jonze. Perf. Nicolas Cage and Meryl Streep. Columbia Pictures, 2002.

Adler, Adam, prod. *The Cube*. ITV, 22 Aug. 2009.

Adventures in Babysitting. Dir. Chris Columbus. Perf. Elisabeth Shue and Vincent D'Onofrio. Buena Vista Pictures, 1987.

The Adventures of Tintin: The Secret of the Unicorn. Dir. Steven Spielberg. Perf. Jamie Bell and Andy Serkis. Paramount Pictures, 2012.

"Advertise with Us." *Comic Collector Live*, n.d. http://www.comiccollectorlive.com/.

Agent Carter. Dir. Louis D'Esposito. Perf. Hayley Atwell and Bradley Whitford. Marvel Studios, 2013.

Ahmed, Samira. "Spiderman Cuts His Ties." *Channel 4*, 19 June 2008. http://www.channel4.com/news/articles/arts_entertainment/film_tv/spiderman cuts his ties/1361467.

Ahrens, Jörn, and Arno Meteling. *Comics and the City: Urban Space in Print, Picture, and Sequence*. New York: Continuum, 2010.

Alice in Wonderland. Dir. Tim Burton. Perf. Johnny Depp and Mia Wasikowska. Walt Disney Pictures, 2010.

Aliens. Dir. James Cameron. Perf. Sigourney Weaver, Carrie Henn, and Michael Biehn. 20th Century Fox, 1986.

Ally Sloper. Dir. George Albert Smith. George Albert Smith Films, 1898.

Alter, Nora. "Movies, Anti-Climaxes, and Disenchantments." In *American Cinema of the 2000s: Themes and Variations*, edited by Timothy Corrigan, 19–39. New Brunswick, NJ: Rutgers Univeristy Press, 2012.

Althusser, Louis. *Lenin and Philosophy, and Other Essays*. New York: Monthly Review, 1972.

Altitude. Dir. Kaare Andrews. Perf. Mike Dopud, Jessica Lowndes, and Julianna Guill. Anchor Bay Entertainment, 2010.

Altman, Rick. "Cinema and Genre." In *The Oxford History of World Cinema*, edited by Geoffrey Nowell-Smith, 276–85. Oxford: Oxford University Press, 1996.

———. *Film/Genre*. London: BFI Publications, 1999.

———. "A Semantic/Syntactic Approach to Film Genre." In *Film Theory and Criticism: Introductory Readings*, edited by Leo Braudy and Marshall Cohen, 680–90. New York: Oxford University Press, 2004.

Alvin and the Chipmunks. Dir. Tim Hill. Perf. Jason Lee and David Cross. 20th Century Fox, 2007.

The Amazing Spider-Man. Dir. Marc Webb. Perf. Andrew Garfield and Emma Stone. Columbia Pictures, 2012. [DVD Commentary from 2012 edition].

"The Amazing Spider-Man—Face of the Fan." *Face Of The Fan Home*, n.d. http://www .faceofthefan.com/TheAmazingSpider-Man/.

The Amazing Spider-Man 2. Dir. Marc Webb. Perf. Andrew Garfield, Emma Stone, and Jamie Foxx. Columbia Pictures, 2014.

Ambrose, Tom. "LXG: The Extraordinary Truth." *Empire*, Mar. 2008: 119–25.

An American in Paris. Dir. Vincente Minnelli. Perf. Gene Kelly, Leslie Caron, and Oscar Levant. MGM/United Artists, 1951.

American Splendor. Dir. Shari Springer Berman and Robert Pulcini. Perf. Paul Giamatti and Hope Davis. HBO Films, 2003.

"America's 10 Greatest Films in 10 Classic Genres." *American Film Institute*, n.d. http://www.afi .com/10top10/.

Anderegg, Michael. "Welles/Shakespeare/Film: An Overview." In *Film Adaptation*, edited by James Naremore, 154–67. New Brunswick, NJ: Rutgers University Press, 2000.

Anderson, Nate. "Tim Berners-Lee on Web 2.0." *Ars Technica*, 2 Sept. 2006. http://arstechnica .com/business/2006/09/7650/.

Andrew, Dudley. *Concepts in Film Theory.* Oxford: Oxford University Press, 1984.

———. "The Economies of Adaptation." In *True to the Spirit: Film Adaptation and the Question of Fidelity*, edited by Colin MacCabe, Rick Warner, and Kathleen Murray, 27–39. Oxford: Oxford University Press, 2011.

Andrews, Kaare, and Jose Villarrubia. *Spider-Man: Reign.* New York: Marvel Comics, 2007.

Annie. Dir. John Huston. Perf. Aileen Quinn and Albert Finney. Columbia Pictures, 1982.

Aperlo, Peter. *Watchmen: The Film Companion.* London: Titan, 2009.

"Are New Comics a Good Investment?" *Comic Book Secrets*, 27 Nov. 2007. http://www.comic booksecrets.com/theblog/comic-book-picks/are-new-comics-a-good-investment/.

Armstrong, Stephen. "Giving Comics a Kick up the Backside." *Sunday Times (London)*, 21 Mar. 2010, Culture sec.: 11.

Arnheim, Rudolf. *Film as Art.* Berkeley: University of California, 1957.

Arnold, Andrew D. "The Most Serious Comix Pt. 2—." *Time*, 5 Feb. 2002. http://www.time.com/ time/columnist/arnold/article/0,9565,198966,00.html.

Arrant, Chris. "Catching up with Kaare." *Newsarama*, 15 Sept. 2004. http://forum.newsarama .com/showthread.php?s=&threadid=18068.

Art School Confidential. Dir. Terry Zwigoff. Perf. John Malkovich, Max Minghella, and Sophia Myles. Sony Pictures Classics, 2006.

"Association of Adaptation Studies." *Association Of Adaptation Studies*, n.d. http://www.adapta tion.uk.com/.

The A-Team. Dir. Joe Carnahan. Perf. Liam Neeson and Bradley Cooper. 20th Century Fox, 2010.

Atkinson, Paul. "The Time of Heroes Narrative, Progress, and Eternity in Miracleman." In *The Contemporary Comic Book Superhero*, edited by Angela Ndalianis, 44–63. New York: Routledge, 2009.

Works Cited

Austen, Jane. *Pride and Prejudice: A Novel: In Three Volumes.* London: Printed for T. Egerton, Military Library, Whitehall, 1813.

"Australian Invention Dazzles Hollywood—Jim Frazier." *World Intellectual Property Organization*, n.d. http://www.wipo.int/ipadvantage/en/details.jsp?id=2546.

Avatar. Dir. James Cameron. Perf. Sam Worthington, Zoe Saldana, and Stephen Lang. 20th Century Fox, 2009.

The Avengers. Dir. Joss Whedon. Perf. Robert Downey, Jr., Chris Evans, and Chris Hemsworth. Marvel Studios, 2012.

Avengers: Age of Ultron. Dir. Joss Whedon. Perf. Robert Downey, Jr., Chris Evans, and Mark Ruffalo. Marvel Studios, 2015.

The Aviator. Dir. Martin Scorsese. Perf. Leonardo DiCaprio. Warner Bros. Pictures, 2004.

Bacon-Smith, Camille, and Tyrone Yarbrough. "Batman: The Ethnography." In *The Many Lives of the Batman: Critical Approaches to a Superhero and His Media*, edited by Roberta E. Pearson and William Uricchio, 90–116. New York: Routledge, 1991.

"Bacterial Growth and Multiplication." *Home of CELLS Alive!*, n.d. http://www.cellsalive.com/ecoli.htm.

Baetens, Jan. "Revealing Traces: A New Theory of Graphic Enunciation." In *The Language of Comics: Word and Image*, edited by Robin Varnum and Christina T. Gibbons, 145–55. Jackson: University Press of Mississippi, 2001.

Bails, Jerry G. *The Guidebook to Comics Fandom.* Glendale: Bails and Spicer, 1965.

Bainbridge, Jason. "I Am New York—Spider-Man, New York City and the Marvel Universe." In *Comics and the City: Urban Space in Print, Picture, and Sequence*, edited by Jörn Ahrens and Arno Meteling, 163–79. New York: Continuum, 2010.

Bainbridge, Jason. "'Worlds Within Worlds' The Role of Superheroes in the Marvel and DC Universes." In *The Contemporary Comic Book Superhero*, edited by Angela Ndalianis, 64–85. New York: Routledge, 2009.

Bakhtin, Mikhail M., and Michael Holquist. *The Dialogic Imagination: Four Essays.* Austin: University of Texas, 1981.

The Band Wagon. Dir. Vincente Minnelli. Perf. Fred Astaire, Cyd Charisse, and Oscar Levant. MGM, 1953.

Barbarella. Dir. Roger Vadim. Perf. Jane Fonda. Paramount Pictures, 1968.

Barker, Martin, and Kate Brooks. *Knowing Audiences: Judge Dredd, Its Friends, Fans, and Foes.* Luton, Bedfordshire, UK: University of Luton, 1998.

Barker, Martin, and Ernest Mathijs. *Watching The Lord of the Rings: Tolkien's World Audiences.* New York: Peter Lang, 2008.

Barker, Martin, Ernest Mathijs, and Alberto Trobia. "Our Methodological Challenges and Solutions." In *Watching The Lord of the Rings: Tolkien's World Audiences*, edited by Martin Barker and Ernest Mathijs, 213–40. New York: Peter Lang, 2008.

Barsam, Richard Meran. *Nonfiction Film: A Critical History.* Bloomington: Indiana University Press, 1992.

Batman. Dir. Lambert Hillyer. Perf. Lewis Wilson, Douglas Croft, and J. Carrol Naish. Columbia Pictures, 1943.

Batman. Dir. Leslie H. Martinson. Perf. Adam West and Burt Ward. 20th Century Fox, 1966.

Batman. Dir. Tim Burton. Perf. Michael Keaton, Jack Nicholson, Kim Basinger, Billy Dee Williams, and Jack Palance. Warner Bros. Pictures, 1989.

Batman & Robin. Dir. Joel Schumacher. Perf. George Clooney, Arnold Schwarzenegger, and Chris O'Donnell. Warner Bros. Pictures, 1997. [DVD Commentary from 2005 edition].

Batman Begins. Dir. Christopher Nolan. Perf. Christian Bale, Michael Caine, Liam Neeson, and Katie Holmes. Warner Brothers, 2005.

Batman Documentary—1989. YouTube, 15 May 2007. http://www.youtube.com/watch?v=wCt V7huBBCA.

Batman Forever. Dir. Joel Schumacher. Perf. Val Kilmer, Tommy Lee Jones, and Jim Carrey. Warner Bros. Pictures, 1995. [DVD Commentary from 2005 edition].

Batman Returns. Dir. Tim Burton. Perf. Michael Keaton, Danny DeVito, and Michelle Pfeiffer. Warner Bros. Pictures, 1992. [DVD Commentary from 2005 edition].

Baudrillard, Jean. "The Spirit of Terrorism." *Le Monde*, 2 Nov. 2001: n. pag.

Bazin, André. "Adaptation, or the Cinema as Digest." 1948. In *Film Adaptation*, edited by James Naremore, 19–27. New Brunswick, NJ: Rutgers University Press, 2000.

———. "The Ontology of the Photographic Image." Translated by Hugh Gray. *Film Quarterly* 13.4 (1960): 4–9.

———. *What Is Cinema?* Translated by Hugh Gray. Berkeley: University of California, 1967.

"Be 1 of 300" (supplementary material on DVD release of *300*). Warner Home Video, 2007.

Beaty, Bart. "Comic Studies: Fifty Years After Film Studies." *Cinema Journal* 50.3 (2011): 106–10.

Becker, Richard A. "The Crisis of Confidence in Comics Adaptations: Why Comics Are So Rarely Faithfully Adapted to the Big Screen." *International Journal of Comic Art* 11.1 (2009): 436–56.

Becoming Jane. Dir. Julian Jarrold. Perf. Anne Hathaway and James McAvoy. Mirmax Films, 2007.

Beetlejuice. Dir. Tim Burton. Perf. Michael Keaton, Geena Davis, and Alec Baldwin. Warner Bros. Pictures, 1988.

Behind Enemy Lines. Dir. John Moore. Perf. Owen Wilson and Gene Hackman. 20th Century Fox, 2001.

Belton, John. "Painting by the Numbers: The Digital Intermediate." *Film Quarterly* 61.3 (2008): 58–65.

Ben Hur. Dir. William Wyler. Perf. Charlton Heston, Jack Hawkins, Stephen Boyd, and Haya Harareet. Metro-Goldwyn-Mayer, 1959.

Bendis, Brian Michael. *Fortune and Glory: A True Hollywood Comic Book Story*. Portland, OR: Oni, 2000.

Benjamin, Walter. *Illuminations*. Edited by Hannah Arendt. Translated by Harry Zohn. New York: Harcourt, Brace & World, 1968.

———. "The Work of Art in the Age of Mechanical Reproduction." In *Film Theory and Criticism: Introductory Readings*, edited by Leo Braudy and Marshall Cohen, 791–811. New York: Oxford University Press, 2004.

Berlanti, Gret, Marc Marc Guggenheim, and Andrew Kreisberg. "Pilot." *Arrow*. CW, 10 Oct. 2012.

Beronä, David A. "'Pictures Speak in Comics without Words: Pictorial Principles in the Work of Milt Gross, Hendrik Dorgathen, Eric Drooker, and Peter Kuper." In *The Language of*

Comics: Word and Image, edited by Robin Varnum and Christina T. Gibbons, 19–39. Jackson: University Press of Mississippi, 2001.

Berton, John A., Jr. "Film Theory for the Digital World: Connecting the Masters to the New Digital Cinema." *Leonardo* 3. Supplemental (1990): 5–11.

Beverly Hills Cop. Dir. Martin Brest. Perf. Eddie Murphy. Paramount Pictures, 1984.

Birkenstein, Jeff, Anna Froula, and Karen Randell. *Reframing 9/11: Film, Popular Culture and the "War on Terror."* New York: Continuum, 2010.

Black Hawk Down. Dir. Ridley Scott. Perf. Josh Hartnet and Eric Bana. Columbia Pictures, 2001.

Blackhawk. Dir. Spencer Gordon Bennet and Fred F. Sears. Perf. Kirk Alyn, Carol Forman, and John Crawford. Columbia Pictures, 1952.

Blackmore, Tim. "The Dark Knight of Democracy." *Journal of American Culture* 14 (1991): 37–56.

Blackwell, Anna, and Catherine P. Han. "Seventh Annual Association of Adaptation Studies Conference, University of York, York, 27–28th September, 2012." *Adaptation* 6.1 (2013): 132–38.

Blade. Dir. Stephen Norrington. Perf. Wesley Snipes and Stephen Dorff. New Line Cinema, 1998.

Blade: Trinity. Dir. David S. Goyer. Perf. Wesley Snipes, Kris Kristofferson, Jessica Biel, and Ryan Reynolds. New Line Cinema, 2004.

Blade II. Dir. Guillermo Del Toro. Perf. Wesley Snipes, Kris Kristofferson, and Ron Perlman. New Line Cinema, 2002.

Blazing Saddles. Dir. Mel Brooks. Perf. Cleavon Little and Gene Wilder. Warner Bros. Pictures, 1974.

Blue Is the Warmest Color. Dir. Abdellatif Kechiche. Perf. Adèle Exarchopoulos and Léa Seydoux. Wild Bunch, 2013.

Bluestone, George. *Novels into Film*. Baltimore: Johns Hopkins, 1957.

Boichel, Bill. "Batman: Commodity as Myth." In *The Many Lives of the Batman: Critical Approaches to a Superhero and His Media*, edited by Roberta E. Pearson and William Uricchio, 4–17. New York: Routledge, 1991.

Bolter, Jay David, and Richard A. Grusin. *Remediation: Understanding New Media*. Cambridge, MA: MIT, 1999.

Boole Williams, Whitney, and Edward Allen Bernero. "In Their Own Words." *Third Watch*. NBC, 15 Oct. 2001.

"Booze, Broads and Guns: The Props Of *Sin City*" (supplementary material on DVD release of *Frank Miller's Sin City: Recut & Extended*). Miramax Home Entertainment, 2007.

Borat: Cultural Learnings of America for Make Benefit Glorious Nation of Kazakhstan. Dir. Larry Charles. Perf. Sacha Baron Cohen and Ken Davitian. 20th Century Fox, 2006.

Bordwell, David. "Superheroes for Sale." *Observations on Film Art*, 16 Aug. 2008. http://www.davidbordwell.net/blog/2008/08/16/superheroes-for-sale/.

Bordwell, David, and Kristin Thompson. *Film Art: An Introduction*. 8th ed. New York: Mcgraw-Hill College, 2008.

———. *Minding Movies: Observations on the Art, Craft, and Business of Filmmaking*. Chicago: University of Chicago, 2011.

Boucher, Geoff. "'Watchmen' Sales Soar, What Does Alan Moore think?" *Hero Complex*. *Los Angeles Times*, 15 Aug. 2008. http://herocomplex.latimes.com/uncategorized/watchmen-sales/.

Bould, Mark. *Film Noir: From Berlin to Sin City*. London: Wallflower, 2005.

À Bout De Souffle. Dir. Jean-Luc Godard. Perf. Jean-Paul Belmondo and Jean Seberg. Les Films Georges De Beauregard, S.N.C., 1960.

Bowles, Scott. "Films, Actors, Thousands of Fans Ready to Roll at Comic-Con." *USA Today*, 22 July 2009. http://www.usatoday.com/life/movies/news/2009-07-21-comic-con_N.htm.

Brabner, Joyce, Harvey Pekar, and Frank Stack. *Our Cancer Year*. New York: Four Walls Eight Windows, 1994.

Braudy, Leo. *The World in a Frame: What We See in Films*. Chicago: University of Chicago, 2002.

Braund, Simon. "Ask the Boss #3." *Empire*, Dec. 2010: 92–95.

Brevoort, Tom. Personal interview, 17 Mar. 2012.

Brodesser, Claude. "Marvel Faces Rivalry from Catwoman and Co." *Variety*, 13 July 2003. http://variety.com/2003/film/news/marvel-faces-rivalry-from-catwoman-co-1117889165/.

Brodesser, Claude, and Michael Fleming. "The 'Die Hard' Is Cast for Scribe Richardson." *Variety*, 26 July 2004. http://variety.com/2004/film/news/the-die-hard-is-cast-for-scribe-richardson-1117908291/.

Broeske, Pat H. "Reshooting down the Rumors." *Entertainment Weekly*, 6 June 1997. http://www.ew.com/ew/article/0,,20610393_288247,00.html.

Brook, Tom. "Superhero Summer." *BBC World News Front Page*, 2008. http://www.bbcworldnews.com/Pages/ProgrammeFeature.aspx?id=41&FeatureID=901.

Brooker, Will. "Batman: One Life, Many Faces." In *Adaptations: From Text to Screen, Screen to Text*, edited by Deborah Cartmell and Imelda Whelehan, 185–98. London: Routledge, 1999.

———. *Batman Unmasked: Analyzing a Cultural Icon*. New York: Continuum, 2000.

———. *Hunting the Dark Knight: Twenty-First Century Batman*. London: I. B. Tauris, 2012.

———. *Using the Force: Creativity, Community, and Star Wars Fans*. New York: Continuum, 2002.

Brown, Jeffrey A. "Comic Book Fandom and Cultural Capital." *Journal of Popular Culture* 30.4 (1997): 13–31.

———. "Comic Book Masculinity and the New Black Superhero." *African American Review* 33.1 (1999): 25–42.

Brown, Lyn Mikel, Sharon Lamb, and Mark B. Tappan. *Packaging Boyhood: Saving Our Sons from Superheroes, Slackers, and Other Media Stereotypes*. New York: St. Martin's, 2009.

Bruce Gentry. Dir. Spencer Gordon Bennet and Thomas Carr. Perf. Tom Neal, Judy Clark, and Ralph Hodges. Columbia Pictures, 1949.

Buchanan, Judith. "Ben Hur 50 Years On." *4th International Association of Adaptation Studies Conference*.

Buckland, Warren. "A Close Encounter with Raiders of the Lost Ark: Notes on Narrative Aspects of the New Hollywood Blockbuster." In *Contemporary Hollywood Cinema*, edited by Steve Neale and Murray Smith, 166–77. London: Routledge, 1998.

"Building The Batmobile" (supplementary material on DVD release of *Batman*). Warner Bros. Home Entertainment, 2005.

Bukatman, Scott. *Matters of Gravity: Special Effects and Supermen in the 20th Century*. Durham, NC: Duke University Press, 2003.

———. *The Poetics of Slumberland: Animated Spirits and the Animating Spirit*. Berkeley: University of California, 2012.

———. "Secret Identity Politics." In *The Contemporary Comic Book Superhero*, edited by Angela Ndalianis, 109–25. New York: Routledge, 2009.

———. "Why I Hate Superhero Movies." *Cinema Journal* 50.3 (2011): 118–22.

Bullock, Saxon. "Bat to Basics." *Hotdog*, July 2003: n. pag.

Bunch, Sonny. "Gotham City's War on Terror." *Washington Times*, 18 July 2008: n. pag.

Burke, Liam, ed. *Fan Phenomena: Batman*. Bristol: Intellect, 2013.

Burke, Liam. "4th International Association of Adaptation Studies Conference, BFI Southbank, 24–25 September 2009." *Adaptation* 3.1 (2010): 53–59.

———. "Special Effect: Have Film Adaptations Changed Mainstream Comics?" *Scan: Journal of Media Arts Culture* 9.1 (2012): n. pag.

———. *Superhero Movies*. Harpenden: Pocket Essentials, 2008.

———. "'Superman in Green': An Audience Study of Comic-Book Film Adaptations Thor and Green Lantern." *Participations: Journal of Audience & Reception Studies* 9.2 (2012): 97–119.

Burton, Tim, and Mark Salisbury. *Burton on Burton*. London: Faber and Faber, 2006.

Buscombe, Edward. "The Western." In *The Oxford History of World Cinema*, edited by Geoffrey Nowell-Smith, 286–93. Oxford: Oxford University Press, 1996.

The Cabinet of Dr. Caligari. Dir. Robert Wiene. Perf. Conrad Veidt and Werner Krauss. Decla-Bioscop, 1920.

Cahir, Linda Costanzo. *Literature into Film: Theory and Practical Approaches*. Jefferson, NC: McFarland & Co., 2006.

Cain, James M. *Mildred Pierce*. New York: Knopf, 1941.

Canemaker, John. *Winsor Mccay: His Life and Art*. New York: H. N. Abrams, 2005.

"CapedWonder: Superman Imagery. Christopher Reeve Superman Photos, Images, Movies, Videos and More!" *CapedWonder Superman Imagery Christopher Reeve Superman Photos Images Movies Videos and More*, n.d. http://www.capedwonder.com/.

Captain America: The First Avenger. Dir. Joe Johnston. Perf. Chris Evans, Hayley Atwell, and Hugo Weaving. Marvel Studios, 2011.

Captain America: The Winter Soldier. Dir. Anthony Russo and Joe Russo. Perf. Chris Evans, Scarlett Johansson, and Sebastian Stan. Marvel Studios, 2014.

Captain Video: Master of the Stratosphere. Dir. Spencer Gordon Bennet and Wallace Grissell. Perf. Judd Holdren, Larry Stewart, and George Eldredge. Columbia Pictures, 1951.

Cardwell, Sarah. *Adaptation Revisited: Television and the Classic Novel*. Manchester: Manchester University Press, 2002.

Carrier, David. *The Aesthetics of Comics*. University Park: Pennsylvania State University Press, 2000.

Cars. Dir. John Lasseter and Joe Ranft. Perf. Owen Wilson, Paul Newman, and Bonnie Hunt. Buena Vista Pictures, 2006.

Carter, Bill. "Plot Twists Paid Off for 'Friends.'" *New York Times*, 18 Feb. 2002. http://www.nytimes.com/2002/02/18/arts/television/18FRIE.html?pagewanted=1&pagewanted=print?pagewanted=all.

Cartmell, Deborah. "Introduction." In *Adaptations: From Text to Screen, Screen to Text*, edited by Deborah Cartmell and Imelda Whelehan, 23–28 and 143–45. London: Routledge, 1999.

Cartmell, Deborah, Timothy Corrigan, and Imelda Whelehan. "Introduction to Adaptation." *Adaptation* 1.1 (2008): 1–4.

Cartmell, Deborah, and Imelda Whelehan. *Screen Adaptation: Impure Cinema*. Houndmills, Basingstoke, Hampshire, England: Palgrave Macmillan, 2010.

The Cat in the Hat. Dir. Bo Welch. Perf. Mike Myers, Alec Baldwin, and Kelly Preston. Universal Pictures, 2003.

Catwoman. Dir. Pitof. Perf. Halle Berry and Sharon Stone. Warner Bros. Pictures, 2004.

Cawelti, John. "Chinatown and Generic Transformation in Recent American Films." In *Film Genre Reader III*, edited by Barry Keith Grant, 243–61. Austin, TX: University of Texas, 2003.

CBGXtra.com., n.d. http://www.cbgxtra.com/.

Chabon, Michael. *The Amazing Adventures of Kavalier and Clay: A Novel*. New York: Random House, 2000.

Chang, Justin, and Peter Debruge. "Does 'Man of Steel' Exploit Disasters Like 9/11?" *Variety*, 17 June 2013. http://variety.com/2013/film/news/does-man-of-steel-exploit-disasters-like-911-1200497860/.

Chase, Alisia. "Three Modes of Description: The Problem of Costume in The Watchmen." Proc. of 4th International Association of Adaptation Studies Conference, BFI Southbank, London. N.p.: n.d., n. pag.

Chasing Amy. Dir. Kevin Smith. Perf. Ben Affleck, Joey Lauren Adams, and Jason Lee. View Askew Productions, 1997.

Chatman, Seymour. "What Novels Can Do That Films Can't (And Vice Versa)." *Critical Inquiry* 7.1 (1980): 121–40.

Chisholm, John. "Checkmate." *Smallville*. CW, 9 Apr. 2010.

Chrisafis, Angelique. "Spider-Man Seizes the Under-12s." *Guardian.co.uk*, 30 Aug. 2002. http://www.guardian.co.uk/media/2002/aug/30/filmnews.filmcensorship.

Christiansen, Hans-Christian. "Comics and Film: A Narrative Perspective." In *Comics & Culture: Analytical and Theoretical Approaches to Comics*, edited by Hans-Christian Christiansen and Anne Magnussen, 107–21. Copenhagen, Denmark: Museum Tusculanum, University of Copenhagen, 2000.

Christophe. "Un Arroseur Public." *Le Petit Français Illustré*, 3 Aug. 1889: n. pag.

"Christopher Nolan: 'Dark Knight Rises' Isn't Political." *Rolling Stone*, 20 July 2012. http://www.rollingstone.com/movies/news/christopher-nolan-dark-knight-rises-isn-t-political-20120720

The Chronicles of Narnia. Dir. Andrew Adamson. Perf. Tilda Swinton, Georgie Henley, and Skandar Keynes. Buena Vista Pictures, 2005.

Citizen Kane. Dir. Orson Welles. Perf. Orson Welles, Joseph Cotten, and Dorothy Comingore. RKO Radio Pictures, 1941.

Claremont, Chris. *X-Men 2: A Novelization*. New York: Del Rey/Ballantine Publishing Group, 2003.

Claremont, Chris, and Zak Penn. *X-Men: The Official Game*. N.p.: Activision, 2006.

Clash of the Titans. Dir. Louis Leterrier. Perf. Sam Worthington, Gemma Arterton, and Liam Neeson. Warner Bros. Pictures, 2010.

Clayton, James. "Comic Creators Kick Ass." *Den of Geek*, 16 Aug. 2013. http://www.denofgeek .com/movies/kick-ass-2/26900/the-james-clayton-column-comic-creators-kick-ass.

Cloverfield. Dir. Matt Reeves. Perf. Lizzy Caplan, Jessica Lucas, and T. J. Miller. Paramount Pictures, 2008.

Clowes, Daniel. *Ghost World*. Seattle, WA: Fantagraphics, 1997.

A Cock and Bull Story. Dir. Michael Winterbottom. Perf. Steve Coogan and Rob Brydon. Redbus Film Distribution, 2005.

Cohen, Keith. "Eisenstein's Subversive Adaptation." In *The Classic American Novel and the Movies*, edited by Gerald Peary and Roger Shatzkin, 239–57. New York: Ungar, 1977.

———. *Film and Fiction: The Dynamics of Exchange*. New Haven: Yale University Press, 1979.

Cohen, Michael. "Dick Tracy: In Pursuit of a Comic Book Aesthetic." In *Film and Comic Books*, edited by Ian Gordon, Mark Jancovich, and Matthew P. McAllister, 13–36. Jackson: University Press of Mississippi, 2007.

Coleman, Earle J. "The Funnies, the Movies and Aesthetics." *Journal of Popular Culture* 18.4 (1985): 89–100.

Collateral Damage. Dir. Andrew Davis. Perf. Arnold Schwarzenegger. Warner Bros. Pictures, 2002.

Collins, Jim. "Batman: The Movies, Narrative: The Hyperconscious." In *The Many Lives of the Batman: Critical Approaches to a Superhero and His Media*, edited by Roberta E. Pearson and William Uricchio, 164–81. New York: Routledge, 1991.

Comic Book Confidential. Dir. Ron Mann. Perf. Will Eisner, Robert Crumb, and Frank Miller. Cinecom Pictures, 1988. Videocassette.

Comic Book Fonts! Comicraft, n.d. http://www.comicbookfonts.com/index.html?sid=0001OCl hutjmhlUwXU59662.

"Comic Book Movie Season." *British Film Institute*, n.d. http://www.bfi.org.uk/whatson/ bfi_southbank/summer_holidays/young_people/comicbook_movies_film_season.

"Comic Book Sales Figures for July 2008." *Comics Chronicles: A Resource for Comics Research*, n.d. http://www.comichron.com/monthlycomicssales/2008/2008-07.html.

ComicBookMovie.com. n.d. http://www.comicbookmovie.com/.

"Comics and Superheroes" (supplementary material on DVD release of *Unbreakable*). Touchstone Home Video, 2000.

Commando. Dir. Mark L. Lester. Perf. Arnold Schwarzenegger. 20th Century Fox, 1985.

Comolli, Jean-Luc, and Paul Narboni. "Cinema/Ideology/Criticism." Translated by Susan Bennett. *Screen* 12.1 (1971): 27–36.

Comtois, Pierre. *Marvel Comics in the 1960s: An Issue by Issue Field Guide to a Pop Culture Phenomenon*. Raleigh: TwoMorrows, 2009.

Conlogue, Ray. "Matrix a Retro-stylish Disguise for Comic Book Fun." Review of *The Matrix*. *Globe and Mail (Toronto)*, 31 Mar. 1999: n. pag.

Connor, J. D. "The Persistence of Fidelity: Adaptation Theory Today." *M/C Journal* 10.2 (2007): n. pag.

Constandinides, Costas. "Para-adaptation: Or How I Learned to Stop Worrying and Love Convergence Culture." *Adaptation* Advanced Access (2012): 1–15.

Constantine. Dir. Lawrence Francis. Perf. Keanu Reeves and Rachel Weisz. Warner Bros. Pictures, 2005.

Coogan, Peter. *The Secret Origin of the Superhero: The Origin and Evolution of the Superhero Genre in America*. Austin: MonkeyBrain, 2002.

Corrigan, Timothy. "Adaptations, Obstructions, and Refractions: The Prophecies of André Bazin." 4th International Association of Adaptation Studies Conference. BFI Southbank, London, 25 Sept. 2009.

———. "Literature on Screen, a History: In the Gap." In *The Cambridge Companion to Literature on Screen*, edited by Deborah Cartmell and Imelda Whelehan, 29–44. Cambridge: Cambridge University Press, 2007.

"Costumes" (supplementary material on Blu-ray release of *The Amazing Spider-Man*). Sony Pictures Home Entertainment, 2012.

Couch, Chris. "The Publication and Formats of Comics, Graphic Novels, and Tankobon." *Image & Narrative* 1 (2000): n. pag. http://www.imageandnarrative.be/narratology/chriscouch.htm.

Cousins, Mark. *The Story of Film*. London: Pavilion, 2004.

The Covered Wagon. Dir. James Cruze. Perf. J. Warren Kerrigan and Lois Wilson. Paramount Pictures, 1923.

Cowboys & Aliens. Dir. Jon Favreau. Perf. Daniel Craig and Harrison Ford. Universal Pictures, 2011.

Cowtrout. "David Hayter Has a Letter for You about Watchmen!" *Ain't It Cool News*, 12 Mar. 2009. http://www.aintitcool.com/talkback_display/40409#comment_2553793.

Creating a Sustainable Irish Film and Television Sector. Rep. Irish Film Board, 29 June 2007.

Creeber, Glen. "DIGITAL THEORY: Theorizing New Media." In *Digital Cultures*, edited by Royston Martin and Glen Creeber, 11–22. Maidenhead: Open University Press, 2009.

Creepshow. Dir. George A. Romero. Perf. Ted Danson, Stephen King, and Ed Harris. Universal Studios, 1982.

Crocker, Jonathan. "Another Bullet in the Head for the Game-adap Genre." Review of *Max Payne*. *Total Film*, 10 Nov. 2008: 52.

Crocker, Jonathan, Jane Crowther, Ellie Genower, Jamie Russell, Mark Salisbury, Joe Utichi, and Josh Winning. "Ultimate Comic-Book Movie Preview." *Total Film*, Oct. 2010: 81–107.

Cronin, Brian. "The 75 Most Memorable Moments in DC Comics History #75-1." *Comic Book Resources*, 21 Aug. 2010. http://goodcomics.comicbookresources.com/2010/08/21/the-75-most-memorable-moments-in-dc-comics-history-75-1/

Crouching Tiger, Hidden Dragon. Dir. Ang Lee. Perf. Michelle Yeoh and Chow Yun-fat. Sony Picture Classics, 2000.

The Crow. Dir. Alex Proyas. Perf. Brandon Lee and Michael Wincott. Mirmax Films, 1994.

Danger: Diabolik! Dir. Mario Bava. Perf. John Phillip Law and Melissa Mell. Paramount Pictures, 1968.

Darabont, Frank. "Days Gone Bye." *The Walking Dead*. AMC, 31 Oct. 2010.

Daredevil. Dir. Mark Steven Johnson. Perf. Ben Affleck, Jennifer Garner and Colin Farrell. 20th Century Fox, 2003.

The Dark Knight. Dir. Christopher Nolan. Perf. Christian Bale, Heath Ledger, Aaron Eckhart, and Michael Caine. Warner Bros. Pictures, 2008.

The Dark Knight Rises. Dir. Christopher Nolan. Perf. Christian Bale, Anne Hathaway, and Tom Hardy. Warner Bros. Pictures, 2012.

Darkman. Dir. Sam Raimi. Perf. Liam Neeson. Universal Pictures, 1990.

Darley, Andrew. *Visual Digital Culture: Surface Play and Spectacle in New Media Genres*. London: Routledge, 2000.

David, Peter, Christos Gage, and Sean Chen. *The Road to The Avengers*. New York: Marvel, 2012.

Davis, Erik. "'The Avengers' Set for July, 2011!" *Cinematical*, 5 May 2008. http://www.cinematical.com/2008/05/05/the-avengers-set-for-july-2011/.

De Semlyen, Nick. "Fight Club." *Empire*, June 2008: 64–72.

Dean, Jonathan. "Comic-Book Movies." *Total Film*, Mar. 2009: 66–98.

Death Wish. Dir. Michael Winner. Perf. Charles Bronson. Paramount Pictures, 1974.

DeBona, Guerric. "Dickens, the Depression, and MGM's David Copperfield." In *Film Adaptation*, edited by James Naremore, 106–28. New Brunswick, NJ: Rutgers University Press, 2000.

The Deer Hunter. Dir. Michael Cimino. Perf. Robert De Niro, Christopher Walken, and John Savage. Universal Pictures, 1978.

DeFalco, Tom. *Comics Creators on Fantastic Four*. London: Titan, 2005.

———. *Comics Creators on Spider-Man*. London: Titan, 2004.

———. *Comics Creators on X-Men*. London: Titan, 2006.

DeKnight, Steven S. "Kill Them All." *Spartacus: Blood and Sand*. Starz, 16 Apr. 2010.

"Deleted Scenes" (supplementary material on DVD release of *Scott Pilgrim vs. The World*). Universal Pictures, 2010.

Denby, David. Review of *The Dark Knight*. *New Yorker*, 28 June 2008: n. pag.

Denison, Rayna. "It's a Bird! It's a Plane! No, It's DVD!" In *Film and Comic Books*, edited by Ian Gordon, Mark Jancovich, and Matthew P. McAllister, 160–79. Jackson: University Press of Mississippi, 2007.

Dennis, Everette E. Preface. *Images That Injure: Pictorial Stereotypes in the Media*. Edited by Susan Dente Ross and Paul Martin Lester. Santa Barbara, CA: Praeger, 2011, N. pag.

Desmond, John M., and Peter Hawkes. *Adaptation: Studying Film and Literature*. Boston, MA: McGraw-Hill, 2006.

Devil's Doorway. Dir. Anthony Mann. Perf. Robert Taylor and Louis Calhern. MGM, 1950.

Dick Tracy. Dir. Warren Beatty. Perf. Warren Beatty and Al Pacino. Touchstone Pictures, 1990.

Dickens, Charles. *Great Expectations*. London: Chapman & Hall, 1861.

Die Hard. Dir. John McTiernan. Perf. Bruce Willis. 20th Century Fox, 1988.

Die Hard 2: Die Harder. Dir. Renny Harlin. Perf. Bruce Willis, Bonnie Bedelia, and William Atherton. 20th Century Fox, 1990.

Die Hard 4.0. Dir. Len Wiseman. Perf. Bruce Willis. 20th Century Fox, 2007. US title *Live Free or Die Hard*.

Dini, Paul. "Heart of Ice." *Batman: The Animated Series*, 7 Sept. 1992.

Dini, Paul, and Chip Kidd. *Batman: Animated*. Harper Collins: New York, 1998.

Dirty Harry. Dir. Don Siegel. Perf. Clint Eastwood. Warner Bros. Pictures, 1971.

"Disney to Acquire Marvel Entertainment." *Marvel.com*, 31 Aug. 2009. http://marvel.com/news/comics/2009/8/31/9360/disney_to_acquire_marvel_entertainment.

Divergent. Dir. Neil Burger. Perf. Shailene Woodley, Theo James, and Zoe Kravitz. Summit Entertainment, 2014.

Dixon, Wheeler W. "Something Lost—Film after 9/11." In *Film and Television after 9/11*, 1–28. Carbondale: Southern Illinois University Press, 2004.

Doherty, Thomas. "The Death of Film Criticism." *Chronicle of Higher Education*, 28 Feb. 2010. http://chronicle.com/article/The-Death-of-Film-Criticism/64352/.

Dr. No. Dir. Terence Young. Perf. Sean Connery. United Artists, 1962.

Dr. Seuss' How the Grinch Stole Christmas. Dir. Ron Howard. Perf. Jim Carrey. Universal Pictures, 2000.

Dream of a Rarebit Fiend. Dir. Edwin S. Porter and Wallace McCutcheon. Perf. Jack Brawn. Edison Manufacturing Company, 1906.

Dredd. Dir. Pete Travis. Perf. Karl Urban and Olivia Thirlby. DNA Films, 2012.

Dries, Caroline. "Action." *Smallville.* CW, 25 Oct. 2007.

Dubose, Mike S. "Holding Out for a Hero: Reaganism, Comic Book Vigilantes and Captain America." *Journal of Popular Culture* 40.6 (2007): 915–35.

Dumbo. Prod. Walt Disney. Perf. Edward Brophy and Herman Bing. RKO Radio Pictures, 1941.

Duncan, Randy, and Matthew J. Smith. *The Power of Comics: History, Form and Culture.* New York: Continuum International Group, 2009.

Dwyer, Michael. "Truly Payneful." *Irish Times (Dublin)*, 13 Nov. 2008, The Ticket ed.: 13.

Dyer, Richard. *The Matter of Images: Essays on Representations.* 2nd ed. London: Routledge, 1993.

Early Cinema—Primitives And Pioneers. Dir. Louis Lumière and George Méliès. BFI Video, 2005.

Easy Riders, Raging Bulls. Dir. Kenneth Bowser. Perf. William H. Macy. BBC, 2003.

Ebert, Roger. Review of *Dick Tracy. Chicago Sun-Times*, 15 June 1990: n. pag. http://www.rogere bert.com/reviews/dick-tracy-1990.

———. Review of *Hulk. Chicago Sun-Times*, 20 June 2003: n. pag. http://www.rogerebert.com/reviews/hulk-2003.

———. Review of *MirrorMask. Chicago Sun-Times*, 30 Sept. 2005: n. pag. http://www.rogere bert.com/reviews/mirrormask-2005.

———. Review of *Watchmen. Chicago Sun-Times*, 4 Mar. 2009: n. pag. http://www.rogerebert .com/reviews/watchmen-2009.

———. Review of *X-Men. Chicago Sun-Times*, 14 July 2000: n. pag. http://www.rogerebert.com/reviews/x-men-2000.

Ecke, Jochen. "Spatializing the Movie Screen: How Mainstream Cinema Is Catching Up on the Formal Potentialities of the Comic Book Page." In *Comics as a Nexus of Cultures: Essays on the Interplay of Media, Disciplines and International Perspectives*, edited by Mark Berninger, Jochen Ecke, and Gideon Haberkorn, 7–20. Jefferson, NC: McFarland & Co., 2010.

Eco, Umberto. "The Myth of Superman." *Diacritics* 2.1 (1972): 14–22.

Edgerton, Samuel Y., Jr. "The American Super-hero Comic Strip: True Descendant of Italian Renaissance Art." *Children's Literature Association Quarterly* 9.1 (1984): 30–33.

Eisenstein, Sergei. "Dickens, Griffith, and Ourselves [Dickens, Griffith, and Film Today]." 1980. In *Film Theory and Criticism: Introductory Readings*, edited by Leo Braudy and Marshall Cohen, 436–44. New York: Oxford University Press, 2004.

Eisner, Will. *Comics & Sequential Art*. Tamarac, FL: Poorhouse, 1985.

———. *A Contract with God: And Other Tenement Stories*. New York: Baronet, 1978.

———. *Graphic Storytelling and Visual Narrative*. Tamarac, FL: Poorhouse, 1996.

———. "Phil Seuling." In *Will Eisner's Shop Talk*, 283–306. Milwaukie, OR: Dark Horse Comics, 2001.

Eisner, Will, Frank Miller, and Charles Brownstein. *Eisner/Miller: A One-on-one Interview*. Milwaukie, OR: Dark Horse, 2005.

Elektra. Dir. Rob Bowman. Perf. Jennifer Garner, Goran Višnjić, and Terrence Stamp. 20th Century Fox, 2005.

Ellin, Doug, and Julian Farino. "I Love You Too." *Entourage*. HBO, 31 July 2005.

Elliott, Kamilla. *Rethinking the Novel/Film Debate*. Cambridge, United Kingdom: Cambridge University Press, 2003.

Ellis, Warren, and Cully Hamner. *Red*. La Jolla, CA: Wildstorm, 2009.

Emerson, Jim. "How 'Star Wars' Shook the World." *MSN Movies: Movie Listings, Showtimes, Movie Reviews, Trailers, Movie Clips, DVD and More*, n.d. http://movies.msn.com/movies/starwars_2/.

Ender's Game. Dir. Gavin Hood. Perf. Asa Butterfield, Harrison Ford, and Hailee Steinfeld. Summit Entertainment, 2013.

Ennis, Garth. *The Punisher Max Vol. 1*. New York: Marvel Comics, 2004.

Ennis, Garth, and Steve Dillon. *Preacher, Book One*. New York: Vertigo, 2013.

Ennis, Garth, and Darick Robertson. *The Boys*. Runnemede, NJ: Dynamite Entertainment, 2010.

Escape Plan. Dir. Mikael Håfström. Perf. Sylvester Stallone and Arnold Schwarzenegger. Summit Entertainment, 2013.

Evans, Alex. "Superman Is the Faultline: Fissures in the Monomythic Man of Steel." In *Reframing 9/11: Film, Popular Culture and the "War on Terror*," edited by Jeff Birkenstein, Anna Froula, and Karen Randell, 117–26. New York: Continuum, 2010.

Everett, Anna. "Movies and Spectacle in a Political Year." In *American Cinema of the 2000s: Themes and Variations*, edited by Timothy Corrigan, 104–24. New Brunswick, NJ: Rutgers University Press, 2012.

Fantasia 2000. Dir. Pixote Hunt, Hendel Butoy, and Eric Goldberg. Perf. James Levine. Walt Disney Pictures, 1999.

Fantastic Four. Dir. Tim Story. Perf. Ioan Gruffud, Jessica Alba, Chris Evans, and Michael Chiklis. 20th Century Fox, 2005.

Fantastic Four: Rise of the Silver Surfer. Dir. Tim Story. Perf. Ioan Gruffudd, Jessica Alba, and Chris Evans. 20th Century Fox, 2007.

"Fashion 360." *MTV Photo Gallery*, 31 May 2009. http://www.mtv.com/photos/2009-mtv-movie-awards-fashion-360/1611667/3945724/photo.jhtml#3945724.

Fast & Furious. Dir. Justin Lin. Perf. Vin Diesel and Paul Walker. Universal Pictures, 2009.

Feiffer, Jules. *The Great Comic Book Heroes*. Seattle, WA: Fantagraphics, 2003.

Field, Syd. *Screenplay: The Foundations of Screenwriting*. New York, NY: Delta Trade Paperbacks, 2005.

"15 Minute Flick School" (supplementary material on DVD release of *Frank Miller's Sin City: Recut & Extended*). Miramax Home Entertainment, 2007.

Finding Nemo. Dir. Andrew Stanton and Lee Unkrich. Perf. Albert Brooks and Ellen DeGeneres. Walt Disney Pictures, 2003.

Fingeroth, Danny. *Superman on the Couch: What Superheroes Really Tell Us About Ourselves and Our Society*. New York: Continuum, 2005.

First Blood. Dir. Ted Kotcheff. Perf. Sylvester Stallone. Orion Pictures Corporation, 1982.

Fist of Legend. Dir. Gordon Chan. Perf. Jet Li. Golden Harvest, 1994.

Flanagan, Martin. "Teen Trajectories in Spider-Man and Ghost World." In *Film and Comic Books*, edited by Ian Gordon, Mark Jancovich, and Matthew P. McAllister, 137–59. Jackson: University Press of Mississippi, 2007.

Fleming, Mike. "New 'Spider-Man' Andrew Garfield." *Deadline.com*, 1 July 2010. http://www .deadline.com/2010/07/spider-mans-choice-of-andrew-garfield-latest-in-several-unpre dictable-turns-to-reawaken-tired-franchise.

Focillon, Henri. *The Life of Forms in Art*. New York: Wittenborn, Schultz, 1948.

"Follow the White Rabbit" (supplementary material on DVD release of *The Matrix*). Warner Bros. Home Entertainment, 1999.

48 Hrs. Dir. Walter Hill. Perf. Eddie Murphy and Nick Nolte. Paramount Pictures, 1982.

Fox, Gardner, Bill Finger, and Bob Kane. "Batman Versus the Vampire Part One." 2005. In *The Batman Chronicles*, vol. 31, 39–49. New York: Detective Comics, 1939.

Franich, Darren. "Samuel L. Jackson's next Comic Book Movie: 'The Secret Service'" *Entertainment Weekly*, 2 Aug. 2013. http://insidemovies.ew.com/2013/08/02/ secret-service-samuel-l-jackson/.

"Frank Miller Tapes" (supplementary material on DVD release of *300*). Warner Home Video, 2007.

Frankenstein Meets the Wolf Man. Dir. Roy William Neil. Perf. Lon Chaney, Jr. and Bela Lugosi. Universal Pictures, 1943.

Freddy vs. Jason. Dir. Ronny Yu. Perf. Robert Englund and Ken Kirzinger. New Line Cinema, 2003.

"Freeze Frame" (supplementary material on DVD release of *Batman & Robin*). Warner Bros. Home Entertainment, 2005.

French, Sean. *The Terminator*. London: British Film Institute, 1996.

Friday the 13th. Dir. Sean S. Cunningham. Perf. Betsy Palmer and Adrienne King. Paramount Pictures, 1980.

Friedberg, Anne. *The Virtual Window: From Alberti to Microsoft*. Cambridge: MIT, 2006.

Fritz, Ben. "Net Heads Finally Get Some Respect." *Variety*, 11 Apr. 2004. http://www.variety. com/article/VR1117903071.html?categoryid=1009&cs=1&query=%27Net+heads+finally+ge t+some+respect.

———. "Warner Bros.' 'Green Lantern' Marketing Campaign Delayed by Special-effects Work." *Los Angeles Times*, 29 Mar. 2011. http://latimesblogs.latimes.com/entertainmentnews-buzz/2011/03/warners-green-lantern-marketing-campaign-delayed-by-effects-work.html.

"From Asgard to Earth" (supplementary material on Blu-ray release of *Thor*). Paramount Studios, 2011.

"From Fumetti to Film" (supplementary material on DVD release of *Danger: Diabolik*). Paramount Home Entertainment, 2007.

From Hell. Dir. Albert Hughes and Allen Hughes. Perf. Johnny Depp, Heather Graham, and Robbie Coltraine. 20th Century Fox, 2001.

Frost/Nixon. Dir. Ron Howard. Perf. Frank Langella and Michael Sheen. Universal Pictures, 2008.

Frosty. "Exclusive Zack Snyder Video Interview Backstage at Saturn Awards." *Collider*, 26 June 2008. http://www.collider.com/entertainment/news/article.asp/aid/8331/tcid/1.

Gaiman, Neil. *The Sandman*. New York: Vertigo, 2010.

Gallagher, Tag. "Shoot-Out at the Genre Corral: Problems in the "Evolution" of the Western." In *Film Genre Reader III*, edited by Barry Keith Grant, 262–76. Austin, TX: University of Texas, 2003.

Gallen, Joel, prod. *America: A Tribute to Heroes*. ABC, CBS, Fox and NBC, 21 Sept. 2001.

Garfield, Simon. "Batman Versus Hollywood." *Time Out*, July 1989: 54.

Garfield: The Movie. Dir. Peter Hewitt. Perf. Bill Murray. 20th Century Fox Home Entertainment, 2004.

Garret, Frank. "The League of Extraordinary Gentleman: A Reboot Fan Cast." *ComicBook-Movie.com*, 22 Sept. 2010. http://www.comicbookmovie.com/fansites/TheUndertow/news/?a=22924.

Gelder, Ken. "Jane Campion: Limits of Literary Cinema." In *Adaptations: From Text to Screen, Screen to Text*, edited by Deborah Cartmell and Imelda Whelehan, 157–71. London: Routledge, 1999.

"Genesis of the Bat: A Look at the Dark Knight's Incarnation and Influences on the Film" (supplementary material on DVD release of *Batman Begins Two-Disc Deluxe Edition*). Warner Home Video, 2005.

Genette, Gérard. *Palimpsests: Literature in the Second Degree*. Lincoln: University of Nebraska, 1997.

"Genre Index." *Box Office Results for Movies by Genre—Comic Book Adaptation*, n.d. http://www.boxofficemojo.com/genres/chart/?id=comicbookadaptation.htm.

Gent, George. "N.B.C. Schedules Changes in Fall." *New York Times*, 21 Feb. 1968: 95.

Genter, Robert. "With Great Power Comes Great Responsibility: Cold War Culture and the Birth of Marvel Comics." *Journal of Popular Culture* 40.6 (2007): 953–78.

Geuens, Jean-Pierre. "The Digital World Picture." *Film Quarterly* 55.4 (2002): 16–27.

Ghost Rider. Dir. Mark Steven Johnson. Perf. Nicolas Cage, Eva Mendes, and Peter Fonda. Columbia Pictures, 2007.

Ghost World. Dir. Terry Zwigoff. Perf. Thora Brich, Scarlett Johansson, and Steve Buscemi. United Artists, 2001.

G.I. Joe: Rise of the Cobra. Dir. Stephen Sommers. Perf. Channing Tatum, Marlon Wayans, and Dennis Quaid. Paramount Pictures, 2009.

Gibbs, Ed. "Occupy Gotham." *Sydney Morning Herald*, 21 July 2012. http://www.smh.com.au/entertainment/movies/occupy-gotham-20120721-22gjd.html.

Giddings, Robert, Keith Selby, and Chris Wensley. *Screening the Novel: Theory and Practice of Literary Dramatization*. London: Palgrave Macmillan, 1990.

Gigli. Dir. Martin Brest. Perf. Ben Affleck and Jennifer Lopez. Columbia Pictures, 2003.

Gladiator. Dir. Ridley Scott. Perf. Russell Crowe, Joaquin Phoenix, and Connie Nielsen. DreamWorks Pictures, 2000.

Glitter. Dir. Vondie Curtis-Hall. Perf. Mariah Carey. 20th Century Fox, 2001.

The Glutton's Nightmare. Dir. Percy Stow. Hepworth, 1901.

Godzilla. Dir. Gareth Edwards. Perf. Aaron Taylor-Johnson, Bryan Cranston, and Elizabeth Olsen. Warner Bros. Pictures, 2014.

Goldberg, Evan. Personal interview, 24 Apr. 2008.

Goldman, William. *Adventures in the Screen Trade: A Personal View of Hollywood and Screenwriting*. New York: Warner, 1983.

Gombrich, E. H. *Art and Illusion: A Study in the Psychology of Pictorial Representation*. New York: Pantheon, 1960.

Gordon, Ian. *Comic Strips and Consumer Culture, 1890–1945*. Washington, DC: Smithsonian Institution, 1998.

Gordon, Ian, Mark Jancovich, and Matthew P. McAllister, eds. *Film and Comic Books*. Jackson: University Press of Mississippi, 2007.

Gough, Alfred, and Miles Millar. "Pilot." *Smallville*. WB, 16 Oct. 2001.

Gough, Kerry. "Translation Creativity and Alien Econ(c)omics: From Hollywood Blockbuster to Dark Horse Comic Book." In *Film and Comic Books*, edited by Ian Gordon, Mark Jancovich, and Matthew P. McAllister, 37–63. Jackson: University Press of Mississippi, 2007.

Goulart, Ron. *Comic Book Encyclopedia: The Ultimate Guide to Characters, Graphic Novels, Writers, and Artists in the Comic Book Universe*. New York: HarperEntertainment, 2004.

Grant, Barry Keith. *Film Genre: From Iconography to Ideology*. London: Wallflower, 2006.

Graser, Marc. "Marvel's Hiring Writers." *Variety*, 26 Mar. 2009. http://www.variety.com/article/VR1118001734.html?categoryid=13&cs=1.

Gravett, Paul. *Graphic Novels: Stories to Change Your Life*. New York: Aurum, 2005.

———. *1001 Comics You Must Read Before You Die*. New York: Universe, 2011.

Gray, Brandon. "'Borat' Bombards the Top Spot." *Box Office Mojo*, 6 Nov. 2006. http://boxofficemojo.com/news/?id=2194.

———. "'Daredevil' Hits Box Office Bullseye." *Box Office Mojo*, 18 Feb. 2003. http://www.boxofficemojo.com/news/?id=1237.

———. "Moviegoers Living in 'Sin City.'" *Box Office Mojo*, 4 Apr. 2005. http://www.boxofficemojo.com/news/?id=1772.

———. "Spider-Man 3 Soars into Record Books." *Box Office Mojo*, 7 May 2007. http://www.boxofficemojo.com/news/?id=2308&p=.htm.

———. "'Superman Returns' Solid If Unspectacular." *Box Office Mojo*, 5 July 2006. http://boxofficemojo.com/news/?id=2106.

———. "Weekend Briefing: 'Expendables,' 'Eat Pray Love,' 'Scott Pilgrim' Locked and Loaded." *Box Office Mojo*, 14 Aug. 2010. http://www.boxofficemojo.com/news/?id=2886.

———. "Weekend Report: Witch Blasts Off, Watchmen Burns Out." *Box Office Mojo*, 16 Mar. 2009. http://boxofficemojo.com/news/?id=2563.

———. "'X2' Unites 3,741 Theaters in Record Bow." *Box Office Mojo*, 1 May 2003. http://www.boxofficemojo.com/news/?id=1239&p=.htm.

Gray, Jonathan. *Show Sold Separately: Promos, Spoilers, and Other Media Paratexts*. New York: New York University Press, 2010.

Gray, Jonathan, Cornel Sandvoss, and C. Lee Harrington, eds. *Fandom: Identities and Communities in a Mediated World*. New York: New York University Press, 2007.

The Great Train Robbery. Prod. Edwin S. Porter. By Edwin S. Porter and James Blair Smith. Perf. J. D. Barnes and Gilbert M. Anderson. Edison Manufacturing Co., 1903.

The Green Hornet. Dir. Michel Gondry. Perf. Seth Rogen and Jay Chou. Sony, 2011.

Green Lantern. Dir. Martin Campbell. Perf. Ryan Reynolds, Mark Strong, Peter Sarsgaard, and Blake Lively. Warner Bros. Pictures, 2011.

"Green Lantern Story Details And Casting Update." *Latino Review*, 16 Sept. 2008. http://www.latinoreview.com/news/green-lantern-story-details-and-casting-update-5395 September 16.

"Green Lantern's Light" (supplementary material on Blu-ray release of *Green Lantern*). Warner Home Video, 2011.

"Green World" (supplementary material on DVD release of *The Spirit*). Lions Gate Home Entertainment, 2009.

Grevioux, Kevin. Personal interview, 16 Mar. 2012.

Griffith, James John. *Adaptations as Imitations: Films from Novels*. Newark: University of Delaware, 1997.

Groensteen, Thierry. *The System of Comics*. Translated by Bart Beaty and Nick Nguyen. Jackson: University Press of Mississippi, 2007.

Grossman, Lev. "Movies: The Art of War." *Time*, 2 Mar. 2007. http://content.time.com/time/magazine/article/0,9171,1595241,00.html.

Gumnaam. Dir. Raja Nawathe. Perf. Manoj Kumar and Nanda. Prithvi Pictures, 1965.

The Gunfighter. Dir. Henry King. Perf. Gregory Peck and Helen Westcott. 20th Century Fox, 1950.

Gunga Din. Dir. George Stevens. Perf. Cary Grant, Victor McLaglen, and Douglas Fairbanks, Jr. RKO Radio Pictures, 1939.

Gunning, Tom. "The Cinema of Attractions: Early Film, Its Spectator, and the Avant-Garde." In *Early Cinema: Space, Frame, Narrative*, edited by Thomas Elsaesser and Adam Barker, 56. London: BFI Publishing, 1990.

———. "Literary Appropriation and Translation in Early Cinema." In *True to the Spirit: Film Adaptation and the Question of Fidelity*, edited by Colin MacCabe, Rick Warner, and Kathleen Murray, 41–57. Oxford: Oxford University Press, 2011.

Gustines, George Gene. "The Battle Outside Raging, Superheroes Dive In." *New York Times*, 20 Feb. 2006. http://www.nytimes.com/2006/02/20/arts/design/20marv.html?ex=1298091600&en=f07499ccod5co31b&ei=5090.

The Guys. By Anne Nelson. New York City, The Flea Theater, 17 Jan. 2002.

Hagley, Annika, and Michael Harrison. "Fighting the Battles We Never Could: The Avengers and Post-September 11 American Political Identities." *PS: Political Science & Politics* 47.1 (2014): 120–24.

Hall, Rich. "How The West Was Lost." *How the West Was Lost*. BBC 4, 14 June 2008.

Halloween. Dir. John Carpenter. Perf. Jamie Lee Curtis. Compass International Pictures, 1978.

Halloween H2o. Dir. Steve Miner. Perf. Jamie Lee Curtis, Adam Arkin, and Michelle Williams. Miramax Films, 1998.

Hancock. Dir. Peter Berg. Perf. Will Smith, Charlize Theron, and Jason Bateman. Columbia Pictures, 2008.

Hansen, Miriam. "Early Cinema, Late Cinema: Transformation of the Public Sphere." In *Viewing Positions: Ways of Seeing Film*, edited by Linda Williams, 134–52. New Brunswick, NJ: Rutgers University Press, 1995.

Happy Hooligan. Dir. J. Stewart Blackton. Edison Manufacturing Company, 1900.

Hark, Ian Rae. "The Wrath of the Original Cast: Translating Embodied Television Characters to Other Media." In *Adaptations: From Text to Screen, Screen to Text*, edited by Deborah Cartmell and Imelda Whelehan, 172–84. London: Routledge, 1999.

Harlow, John. "Spider-Man Tobey Maguire Spins Deal for Fatherhood." *Sunday Times*, 14 Sept. 2008. http://entertainment.timesonline.co.uk/tol/arts_and_entertainment/film/article4749016.ece.

Harmon, Jim, and Donald F. Glut. *Great Movie Serials: Their Sound and Fury*. New York: Doubleday, 1972.

Harry Potter and the Sorcerer's Stone. Dir. Chris Columbus. Perf. Daniel Radcliffe, Rupert Grint, and Emma Watson. Warner Bros. Pictures, 2001.

Harvey, Robert C. *The Art of the Comic Book: An Aesthetic History*. Jackson: University Press of Mississippi, 1996.

Harwood, Ronald, and David Nicholas Wilkinson. *Ronald Harwood's Adaptations from Other Works into Films*. Isleworth: Guerilla, 2007.

Hatfield, Charles. *Alternative Comics: An Emerging Literature*. Jackson: University Press of Mississippi, 2005.

Hayden, Erik. "Ben Affleck as Batman: Negative Backlash on Twitter, Petition Launched to Drop Actor." *Hollywood Reporter*, 23 Aug. 2013. http://www.hollywoodreporter.com/heat-vision/ben-affleck-as-batman-negative-613619.

Hayter, David. "David Hayter Pens Open Letter to Watchmen Fans Comments." *Rotten Tomatoes*, 11 Mar. 2009. http://ie.rottentomatoes.com/m/watchmen/news/1801535/comments/david_hayter_pens_open_letter_to_watchmen_fans.

Hayward, Susan. *Cinema Studies: The Key Concepts*. London: Routledge, 2000.

Heaven's Gate. Dir. Michael Cimino. Perf. Kris Kristofferson and Christopher Walken. United Artists, 1980.

Heer, Jeet, and Kent Worcester. *A Comics Studies Reader*. Jackson: University Press of Mississippi, 2009.

Hellboy. Dir. Guillermo del Toro. Perf. Ron Perlman, Selma Blair, and Doug Jones. Universal Pictures, 2004.

Hellboy II: The Golden Army. Dir. Guillermo del Toro. Perf. Ron Perlman, Selma Blair, and Doug Jones. Universal Pictures, 2008.

"Heroes" (supplementary material on DVD release of *Batman Forever*). Warner Home Video, 2005.

Hewitt, Chris, Helen O'Hara, and Jeff Goldsmith. "Superhero Special." *Empire*, Nov. 2006: 77–105.

High Noon. Dir. Fred Zinnemann. Perf. Gary Cooper and Grace Kelly. United Artists, 1952.

Highmore, Ben. *Cityscapes: Cultural Readings in the Material and Symbolic City*. New York: Palgrave Macmillan, 2005.

Hight, Craig. "American Splendor: Translating Comic Autobiography into Drama-documentary." In *Film and Comic Books*, edited by Ian Gordon, Mark Jancovich, and Matthew P. McAllister, 180–98. Jackson: University Press of Mississippi, 2007.

Hill, Sefton. *Batman: Arkham City*. N.p.: Rocksteady Studios, 2011.

Hills, Matt. *Fan Cultures*. London: Routledge, 2002.

———. "Fiske's 'textual Productivity' and Digital Fandom: Web 2.0 Democratization versus

Fan Distinction?" *Participations: Journal of Audience & Reception Studies* 10.1 (2013): 130–53.

A History of Violence. Dir. David Cronenberg. Perf. Viggo Mortensen, Maria Bello, and Ed Harris. New Line Cinema, 2005.

The Hitcher. Dir. Dave Meyers. Perf. Sean Bean, Sophia Bush, and Zachary Knighton. Rogue Pictures, 2007.

Hodgman, John. "Righteousness in Tights." *New York Times*, 24 Apr. 2005: n. pag. http://www .nytimes.com/2005/04/24/books/review/24HODGMAN.html?pagewanted=all.

Holleran, Scott. "The Introspective Hulk." *Box Office Mojo*, 20 June 2003: n. pag. http://www .boxofficemojo.com/reviews/?id=60&p=.htm.

Hollow Man. Dir. Paul Verhoeven. Perf. Kevin Bacon and Elisabeth Shue. Columbia Pictures, 2000.

Hollywoodland. Dir. Alan Coulter. Perf. Adrien Brody, Diane Lane, and Ben Affleck. Focus Features, 2006.

Holmlund, Chris. *Impossible Bodies: Femininity and Masculinity at the Movies*. London: Routledge, 2002.

Honeycutt, Kirk. Review of *The League of Extraordinary Gentlemen*. *Hollywood Reporter*, 10 July 2003: n. pag.

"How It Went Down: Convincing Frank Miller to Make the Film" (supplementary material on DVD release of *Frank Miller's Sin City: Recut & Extended*). Miramax Home Entertainment, 2007.

Howard the Duck. Dir. Willard Huyck. Perf. Lea Thompson, Jeffrey Jones, and Tim Robbins. Universal Pictures, 1986.

Howe, Sean. *Marvel Comics: The Untold Story*. New York: Harper, 2012.

Hughes, David. *Comic Book Movies*. London: Virgin, 2003.

Hughes, Jamie A. "'Who Watches the Watchmen?': Ideology and 'Real World' Superheroes." *Journal of Popular Culture* 39.4 (2006): 546–57.

Hughes, Kathleen A. "Batman Fans Fear The Joke's on Them in Hollywood Epic." *Wall Street Journal*, 29 Nov. 1988: 1.

Hulk. Dir. Ang Lee. Perf. Eric Bana, Jennifer Connelly, and Nick Nolte. Universal Pictures, 2003. [DVD Commentary from 2003 edition].

The Hunger Games. Dir. Gary Ross. Perf. Jennifer Lawrence, Josh Hutcherson, and Liam Hemsworth. Lionsgate, 2012.

The Hunger Games: Catching Fire. Dir. Francis Lawrence. Perf. Jennifer Lawrence, Josh Hutcherson, and Liam Hemsworth. Lionsgate, 2013.

Hutcheon, Linda. *A Theory of Adaptation*. New York: Routledge, 2006.

Huver, Scott. "Jon Favreau on the Iron Man Franchise!" *SuperHeroHype*, 12 Sept. 2008. http:// www.superherohype.com/features/articles/97449-jon-favreau-on-the-iron-man-franchise.

"I am Iron Man" (supplementary material on DVD release of *Iron Man*). Paramount Pictures, 2008.

I, Frankenstein. Dir. Stuart Beattie. Perf. Aaron Eckhart and Yvonne Strahovski. Lionsgate, 2014.

I Know What You Did Last Summer. Dir. Jim Gillespie. Perf. Jennifer Love Hewitt, Sarah Michelle Gellar, and Ryan Phillippe. Columbia Pictures, 1997.

The Incredible Hulk. Dir. Louis Leterrier. Perf. Edward Norton, Liv Tyler, and Tim Roth. Universal Pictures, 2008. [DVD Commentary from 2008 edition].

The Incredibles. Dir. Brad Bird. Perf. Craig T. Nelson, Holly Hunter, and Samuel L. Jackson. Pixar, 2004. [DVD Commentary from 2005 edition].

Independence Day. Dir. Roland Emmerich. Perf. Will Smith, Bill Pullman, and Jeff Goldblum. 20th Century Fox, 1996.

Indiana Jones and the Last Crusade. Dir. Steven Spielberg. Perf. Harrison Ford and Sean Connery. Paramount Pictures, 1989.

Inge, M. Thomas. *Comics as Culture*. Jackson: University Press of Mississippi, 1990.

Ioannidou, Elisavet. "Adapting Superhero Comics for the Big Screen: Subculture for the Masses." *Adaptation* 6.2 (2013): 230–38.

The Iron Horse. Dir. John Ford. Perf. George O'Brien and Madge Bellamy. William Fox, 1924.

Iron Man. Dir. Jon Favreau. Perf. Robert Downey, Jr., Terrence Howard, Jeff Bridges, and Gwyneth Paltrow. Paramount Pictures, 2008.

Iron Man 2. Dir. Jon Favreau. Perf. Robert Downey, Jr., Gwyneth Paltrow, Mickey Rourke, and Samuel L. Jackson. Paramount Pictures, 2010.

Iron Man 3. Dir. Shane Black. Perf. Robert Downey, Jr., Gwyneth Paltrow, Guy Pearce, and Ben Kingsley. Marvel Studios, 2013.

Item 47. Dir. Louis D'Esposito. Perf. Jesse Bradford and Lizzy Caplan. Marvel Studios, 2012.

Jameson, Fredric. "Afterword." In *True to the Spirit: Film Adaptation and the Question of Fidelity*, edited by Colin MacCabe, Rick Warner, and Kathleen Murray, 215–33. Oxford: Oxford University Press, 2011.

Järvilehto, Petri. *Max Payne*. N.p.: Remedy Entertainment, 2001.

Jason X. Dir. James Isaac. Perf. Lexa Doig, Lisa Ryder, and Chuck Campbell. New Line Cinema, 2001.

Jaws. Dir. Steven Spielberg. Perf. Roy Scheider, Richard Dreyfuss, and Robert Shaw. Universal Pictures, 1975.

Jay and Silent Bob Strike Back. Dir. Kevin Smith. Perf. Jason Mewes, Kevin Smith, Ben Affleck, and Jason Lee. Dimension Films, 2001.

Jenkins, Henry. "Captain America Sheds His Mighty Tears." In *Terror, Culture, Politics: Rethinking 9/11*, edited by Daniel J. Sherman and Terry Nardin, 69-102. Bloomington: Indiana University Press, 2006.

———. "Comics and Convergence Part One." *Confessions of an Aca-Fan: The Official Weblog of Henry Jenkins*, 18 Aug. 2006. http://www.henryjenkins.org/2006/08/comics_and_conver gence.html.

———. *Convergence Culture: Where Old and New Media Collide*. New York: New York University Press, 2006.

———. *Fans, Bloggers, and Gamers: Exploring Participatory Culture*. New York: New York University Press, 2006.

———. "'Just Men in Tights' Rewriting Silver Age Comics in an Era of Multiplicity." In *The Contemporary Comic Book Superhero*, edited by Angela Ndalianis, 16–43. New York: Routledge, 2009.

———. *Textual Poachers: Television Fans & Participatory Culture*. New York: Routledge, 1992.

———. "The Tomorrow That Never Was: Retrofuturism in the Comics of Dean Motter." In *Comics and the City: Urban Space in Print, Picture, and Sequence*, edited by Jörn Ahrens and Arno Meteling, 63–83. New York: Continuum, 2010.

Works Cited

Jenkins, Henry, and David Bordwell. "The Aesthetics of Transmedia: In Response to David Bordwell (Part One)." Weblog post. *Confessions of an Aca-Fan: The Official Weblog of Henry Jenkins*, 10 Sept. 2010. http://henryjenkins.org/2009/09/the_aesthetics_of_transmedia_i.html.

———. "The Aesthetics of Transmedia: In Response to David Bordwell (Part Two)." Weblog post. *Confessions of an Aca-Fan: The Official Weblog of Henry Jenkins*, 13 Sept. 2010. http://henryjenkins.org/2009/09/the_aesthetics_of_transmedia_i_1.html.

———. "The Aesthetics of Transmedia: In Response to David Bordwell (Part Three)." Weblog post. *Confessions of an Aca-Fan: The Official Weblog of Henry Jenkins*, 16 Sept. 2010. http://henryjenkins.org/2009/09/the_aesthetics_of_transmedia_i_2.html.

Jensen, Jeff. "'Thor' Trailer Hits the Web. Watch and Opine!" *Entertainment Weekly*, 11 Dec. 2010. http://insidemovies.ew.com/2010/12/11/thor-trailer-hits-the-web-watch-and-opine/comment-page-2/.

Johnson, Derek. "Will the Real Wolverine Please Stand Up?" In *Film and Comic Books*, edited by Ian Gordon, Mark Jancovich, and Matthew P. McAllister, 64–85. Jackson: University Press of Mississippi, 2007.

Jonah Hex. Dir. Jimmy Hayward. Perf. Josh Brolin and Megan Fox. Warner Bros. Pictures, 2010.

Jones, Gerard, and Will Jacobs. *The Comic Book Heroes: The First History of Modern Comic Books from the Silver Age to the Present*. 2nd ed. California: Prima Publications, 1997.

Jones, Matthew T. "Fiend on Film: Edwin S. Porter's Adaptation of Dreams of the Rarebit Fiend." *International Journal of Comic Art* 8.1 (2006): 388–411 [1–15].

Josie and the Pussycats. Dir. Harry Elfont and Deborah Kaplan. Perf. Rachael Leigh Cook, Tara Reid, and Rosario Dawson. Universal Pictures, 2001.

"The Journey to *Tintin*" (supplementary material on Blu-ray release of *The Adventures of Tintin*). Paramount Pictures, 2011.

Judge Dredd. Dir. Danny Cannon. Perf. Sylvester Stallone. Buena Vista Pictures, 1995.

Jumper. Dir. Doug Liman. Perf. Hayden Christensen, Samuel L. Jackson, and Jamie Bell. 20th Century Fox, 2008. [DVD Commentary from 2008 edition].

Jurassic Park. Dir. Steven Spielberg. Perf. Sam Neill, Laura Dern, and Jeff Goldblum. Amblin Entertainment, 1993.

"Just Desserts: The Making of Creepshow" (supplementary material on DVD release of *Creepshow*). Warner Bros. Home Entertainment, 2007.

Kannenberg, Gene, Jr. "Charles Atlas: The Ad That Made an Icon Out of Mac." *Daryl Cagle's Professional Cartoonists Index*, n.d. http://cagle.msnbc.com/hogan/features/atlas.asp.

Karasik, Paul, David Mazzucchelli, and Paul Auster. *City of Glass*. New York: Picador, 2004.

Karnick, Kristine Brunovska, and Henry Jenkins. *Classical Hollywood Comedy*. New York: Routledge, 1995.

Kelly, Joe. Personal interview, 17 Mar. 2012.

Kelly, Joe, Doug Mahnke, and Lee Bermejo. "What's So Funny About Truth, Justice & the American Way?" *Action Comics*. 775th ed. DC Comics: March 2001.

Khordoc, Catherine. "The Comic Book's Soundtrack: Visual Sound Effects in Asterix." In *The Language of Comics: Word and Image*, edited by Robin Varnum and Christina T. Gibbons, 156–73. Jackson: University Press of Mississippi, 2001.

Kick-Ass. Dir. Matthew Vaughn. Perf. Aaron Johnson, Nicolas Cage, and Mark Strong. Lionsgate, 2010.

Kick-Ass 2. Dir. Jeff Wadlow. Perf. Aaron Taylor-Johnson, Christopher Mintz-Plasse, and Chloë Grace Moretz. Universal Pictures, 2013.

King, Geoff. *New Hollywood Cinema: An Introduction*. New York: Columbia University Press, 2002.

King Kong. Dir. Merian C. Cooper and Ernest B. Schoedsack. Perf. Fay Wray, Robert Armstrong, and Bruce Cabot. Radio Pictures, 1933.

King Kong vs. Godzilla. Dir. Ishirō Honda. Perf. Tadao Takashima and Kenji Sahara. Toho, 1962.

Kingsman: The Secret Service. Dir. Matthew Vaughn. Perf. Colin Firth, Michael Caine, and Samuel L. Jackson. 20th Century Fox, 2015.

Kirchoff, Jeffrey, S.J. "Beyond Remediation: Comic Book Captions and Silent Film Intertitles as the Same Genre." *Studies in Comics* 3.1 (2012): 25–45.

Kirkland, Boyd, dir. "Beware the Gray Ghost." *Batman: The Animated Series*. Fox, 4 Nov. 1992.

Kirkland, Mark, dir. "Treehouse of Horror VIII." *The Simpsons*. Fox, 26 Oct. 1997.

Kirkman, Robert, and Tony Moore. *The Walking Dead*. Orange, CA: Image Comics, 2005.

Kitses, Jim. "Authorship and Genre: Notes on the Western." In *The Western Reader*, edited by Jim Kitses and Gregg Rickman, 57–68. New York: Limelight Editions, 1998.

———. *Horizons West*. New ed. London: BFI, 2004.

Kitses, Jim, and Gregg Rickman. *The Western Reader*. New York: Limelight Editions, 1998.

Klavan, Andrew. "What Bush and Batman Have in Common." *Wall Street Journal*, 25 July 2008. http://online.wsj.com/public/article_print/SB121694247343482821.html.

Klein, Alan M. *Little Big Men: Bodybuilding Subculture and Gender Construction*. Albany: State University of New York, 1993.

Klein, Michael, and Gillian Parker. *The English Novel and the Movies*. New York: Ungar, 1981.

Klock, Geoff. *How to Read Superhero Comics and Why*. New York: Continuum, 2002.

Knowles, Harry. "From 300 Trailer Comes One Helluva Rorshach [*sic*] First Look at WATCHMEN?" *Ain't It Cool News*, 9 Mar. 2007. http://www.aintitcool.com/node/31814.

———. "THE INCREDIBLE HULK Smashes Harry's Brain into Undulating Geek Neurons Firing on the Possibilities Ahead of Us!" *Ain't It Cool News*, 5 June 2008. http://www.aintitcool.com/node/36973.

———. "So Bryan Singer Just Called regarding Matthew Vaughn's X-MEN: FIRST CLASS . . . I'm Quite Excited Now." *Ain't It Cool News*, 20 Aug. 2010. http://www.aintitcool.com/node/46217.

———. "TITANIC Review." *Ain't It Cool News*, 17 Dec. 1997. http://www.aintitcool.com/node/1718.

Köhler, Wolfgang. *Gestalt Psychology*. New York: H. Liveright, 1929.

Kozinets, Robert V. *Netnography: Doing Ethnographic Research Online*. Los Angeles, CA: SAGE, 2010.

Kring, Tim. "Genesis." *Heroes*. NBC, 25 Sept. 2006.

Kristeva, Julia. *Desire in Language: A Semiotic Approach to Literature and Art*. New York: Columbia University Press, 1980.

Kunzle, David. *The History of the Comic Strip: The 19th Century*. Berkeley: University of California, 1990.

Lacassin, Francis. "The Comic Strip and Film Language." *Film Quarterly* 26.1 (1972): 11–23.

L'Age D'or. Dir. Luis Buñuel. Perf. Gaston Modot, Lya Lys, and Max Ernst. Cornith Films, 1930.

L'Amour, Beau. "Hopalong Cassidy Novels by Louis L'Amour." *Hopalong Cassidy Novels by Louis L'Amour*, 2010. http://www.louislamour.com/novels/hopalong4byLouis.htm.

Landesman, Cosmo. Review of *The Dark Knight. Sunday Times (London)*, 27 July 2008, Culture sec.: n. pag.

Landon, Brooks. *The Aesthetics of Ambivalence: Rethinking Science Fiction Film in the Age of Electronic (re)production*. Westport, CT: Greenwood, 1992.

Langford, Barry. *Film Genre: Hollywood and Beyond*. Edinburgh: Edinburgh University Press, 2005.

L'Arroseur Arrosé. Dir. Louis Lumière. Perf. François Clerc and Benoît Duval. 1895.

LaSalle, Mick. "Life in the Big Sleazy City Comes Alive in All Colors." *San Francisco Chronicle*, 1 Apr. 2005, sec. E:1.

Lawrence, John Shelton, and Robert Jewett. *The Myth of the American Superhero*. Grand Rapids, MI: W. B. Eerdmans, 2002.

"Lawsuit Filed by Spider-Man Creator." *BBC News*, 13 Nov. 2002. http://news.bbc.co.uk/2/hi/entertainment/2458083.stm.

The League of Extraordinary Gentlemen. Dir. Stephen Norrington. Perf. Sean Connery, Shane West, and Jason Flemyng. 20th Century Fox, 2003. [DVD Commentary from 2003 edition].

Leary, Denis, and Peter Tolan. "Guts." *Rescue Me*. FX, 7 June 2004.

Lee, Stan. Telephone interview, 25 Nov. 2007.

———. "TheRealStanLee." Weblog comment. *Twitter*, 22 Aug. 2010. https://twitter.com/TheReal StanLee.

Lee, Stan, and John Buscema. *How to Draw Comics the Marvel Way*. New York: Simon and Schuster, 1978.

Lee, Stan, and Jack Kirby. *Fantastic Four*. Vol. 3. New York: Marvel Comics, 1961.

Lefèvre, Pascal. "Incompatible Visual Ontologies: The Problematic Adaptation of Drawn Images." In *Film and Comic Books*, edited by Ian Gordon, Mark Jancovich, and Matthew P. McAllister, 1–12. Jackson: University Press of Mississippi, 2007.

Leitch, Thomas. "Adaptation, the Genre." *Adaptation* 1.2 (2008): 106–20.

———. "Adaptation Studies at a Crossroads." *Adaptation* 1.1 (2008): 63–77.

———. *Film Adaptation and Its Discontents: From Gone with the Wind to The Passion of the Christ*. Baltimore, MD: Johns Hopkins University Press, 2007.

———. "Twice-Told Tales: Disavowal and the Rhetoric of the Remake." In *Dead Ringers: The Remake in Theory and Practice*, edited by Jennifer Forrest and Leonard R. Koos, 37–62. Albany: State University of New York, 2002.

Leonard, John. "The Wish of James M. Cain." *New York Times*, 2 Mar. 1969, Book Review ed.: 2.

Lesnick, Silas. "New The Amazing Spider-Man 2 Photos Show Off Mary Jane and the New Costume." *Superhero Hype*, 26 Feb. 2013. http://www.superherohype.com/news/175241-new-the-amazing-spider-man-2-photos-show-off-mary-jane-and-the-new-costume.

Lethal Weapon. Dir. Richard Donner. Perf. Mel Gibson and Danny Glover. Warner Bros. Pictures, 1987.

Lévi-Strauss, Claude. *Structural Anthropology*. New York: Basic, 1963.

Levitz, Paul. Telephone interview, 21 Aug. 2012.

Lévy, Pierre. *Collective Intelligence: Mankind's Emerging World in Cyberspace.* New York: Plenum Trade, 1997.

Lichtenfeld, Eric. "Excelsior!: March of the Superheroes." In *Action Speaks Louder: Violence, Spectacle, and the American Action Movie*, 286–331. Westport, CT: Praeger, 2007.

Lipton, James. "Hugh Jackman." *Inside the Actors Studio.* Bravo, 7 Mar. 2004.

Little Big Man. Dir. Arthur Penn. Perf. Dustin Hoffman and Faye Dunaway. National General, 1970.

Loeb, Jeph, and Tim Sale. *Batman: The Long Halloween.* New York, NY: DC Comics, 1998.

"Look Out! Here Comes Spider-Man Week!" *New York Daily News*, 1 Apr. 2007. http://www.nydailynews.com/entertainment/tv-movies/spider-man-week-article-1.211670.

The Lord of the Rings: The Fellowship of the Ring. Dir. Peter Jackson. Perf. Elijah Wood, Ian McKellen, and Viggo Mortensen. New Line Cinema, 2001.

The Lord of the Rings: The Return of the King. Dir. Peter Jackson. Perf. Elijah Wood and Viggo Mortensen. New Line Cinema, 2003.

Lorre, Chuck, and Bill Prady. "The Pilot." *The Big Bang Theory.* CBS, 24 Sept. 2007.

The Losers. Dir. Sylvain White. Perf. Jeffrey Dean Morgan, Zoe Saldana, and Chris Evans. Warner Bros. Pictures, 2010.

Loucks, Jonathan. "Getting Away with Homage." In *True to the Spirit: Film Adaptation and the Question of Fidelity*, edited by Colin MacCabe, Rick Warner, and Kathleen Murray, 143–55. Oxford: Oxford University Press, 2011.

Lowry, Brian. "Beware the Comic-Con False Positive." *Variety*, 14 July 2009. http://variety.com/2009/film/news/beware-the-comic-con-false-positive-1118005970/.

Lukow, Gregory, and Steven Ricci. "The 'Audience' Goes 'Public': Inter-Textuality, Genre and the Responsibilities of Film Literacy." *On Film* 12 (1984): 29–36.

Lunenfeld, Peter. *The Digital Dialectic: New Essays on New Media.* Cambridge, MA: MIT, 1999.

MacCabe, Colin. "Adaptation." Lecture, Moore Institute, NUI Galway, Galway, 27 May 2010.

MacCabe, Colin, Rick Warner, and Kathleen Murray. *True to the Spirit: Film Adaptation and the Question of Fidelity.* Oxford: Oxford University Press, 2011.

MacDonald, Heidi. "Inside the Superboy Copyright Decision." *Publishers Weekly*, 11 Apr. 2006: n. pag.

"The Magic Behind the Cape" (supplementary material on DVD release of *Superman: The Movie*). Warner Home Video, 2001.

The Magnificent Ambersons. Dir. Orson Welles. Perf. Joseph Cotten, Dolores Costello, and Anne Baxter. RKO Radio Pictures, 1942.

"Making the Amazing" (supplementary material on DVD release of *Spider-Man 2*). Sony Pictures Home Entertainment, 2004.

"Making of Daredevil" (supplementary material on DVD release of *Daredevil*). 20th Century Fox Home Video, 2003.

"The Making of Hulk" (supplementary material on DVD release of *Hulk*). 20th Century Fox Home Entertainment. 2003.

The Making of Superman: The Movie. Dir. Iain Johnstone. Perf. Ernie Anderson and Christopher Reeve. Dovemead Films, 1980.

"Making of *300*" (supplementary material on DVD release of *300*). Warner Home Video, 2007.

Malloy, Elizabeth. "Charting Comic-Con's Hulk-like Growth." *San Diego Daily Transcript*, 18 Apr. 2008. http://www.sddt.com/Hospitality/article.cfm?SourceCode=20080418tbe.

Malphurs, Ryan. "The Media's Frontier Construction of President George W. Bush." *Journal of American Culture* 31.2 (2008): 185–201.

Maltby, Richard. "'To Prevent the Prevalent Type of Book': Censorship and Adaptation in Hollywood, 1924–1934." In *Film Adaptation*, edited by James Naremore, 79–105. New Brunswick, NJ: Rutgers University Press, 2000.

Man of Steel. Dir. Zack Snyder. Perf. Henry Cavill, Amy Adams, and Michael Shannon. Warner Bros. Pictures, 2013.

The Man Who Laughs. Dir. Paul Leni. Perf. Mary Philbin, Conrad Veidt, and Brandon Hurst. Universal Pictures, 1928.

Manara, Milo, Federico Fellini, and Vincenzo Mollica. *Trip to Tulum: From a Script for a Film Idea*. New York: Catalan Communications, 1990.

Manovich, Lev. *Language of New Media*. Cambridge, MA: MIT, 2002.

Marmaduke. Dir. Tom Dey. Perf. Owen Wilson. 20th Century Fox, 2010.

Marotta, David. "With Great Characters Come Great Stock Returns." *Moneynews*, 3 Aug. 2007. http://www.moneynews.com/DavidMarotta/Great-Stock-Returns/2007/08/03/id/324526.

Marshall, Rick. "Christian Bale's Batman Voice Was 'Over The Top,' Says 'Arkham Asylum' Actor Kevin Conroy," *MTV.com*, 31 Aug. 2009. http://splashpage.mtv.com/2009/08/31/christian-bales-dark-knight-voice-was-over-the-top-says-batman-arkham-asylum-actor-kevin-conroy/.

———. "DC Entertainment President Talks Comics, Movies and Creators-And How The Recent Changes Will Affect Them." *MTV.com*, 11 Sept. 2009. http://splashpage.mtv.com/2009/09/11/exclusive-dc-entertainment-president-talks-comics-movies-and-creators%E2%80%94and-how-the-new-environment-will-affect-them/

Mary Poppins. Dir. Robert Stevenson. Perf. Julie Andrews, Dick Van Dyke, David Tomlinson, and Glynis Johns. Buena Vista Distribution Co., 1964.

The Mask. Dir. Chuck Russell. Perf. Jim Carrey, Peter Riegert, and Cameron Diaz. New Line Cinema, 1994.

Mason, Jeff. *9-11 Emergency Relief*. Gainesville, FL: Alternative Comics, 2002.

Mathews, Jack. "People Not Machines: Human Stories Will Be The Most Special Effect In The Movies Of 2002." *New York Daily News*, 30 Dec. 2001. http://www.nydailynews.com/people-machines-human-stories-special-effect-movies-2002-article-1.936706.

The Matrix. Dir. Andy Wachowski and Larry Wachowski. Perf. Keanu Reeves and Laurence Fishburne. Warner Bros. Pictures, 1999.

The Matrix Reloaded. Dir. Andy Wachowski and Larry Wachowski. Perf. Keanu Reeves, Carrie-Anne Moss, and Laurence Fishburne. Warner Bros. Pictures, 2003.

The Matrix Revisited. Dir. Josh Oreck. Perf. The Wachowskis, Joel Silver, and Keanu Reeves. Warner Home Video, 2001.

Max Payne. Dir. John Moore. Perf. Mark Wahlberg, Mila Kunis, Beau Bridges, and Ludacris. 20th Century Fox, 2008.

McBride, Joseph. *What Ever Happened to Orson Welles?: A Portrait of an Independent Career*. Lexington, KY: University of Kentucky, 2006.

McCarthy, Todd. "X2." *Variety*, 28 Apr. 2003: n. pag.

McCay, Winsor. *Dreams of the Rarebit Fiend*. New York: Dover Publications, 1973.

McCay, Winsor, and Ulrich Merkl. *The Complete Dream of the Rarebit Fiend: (1904–1913)*. Hohenstein-Ernstthal: Merkl, 2007.

McClintock, Pamela, and Anne Thompson. "Spielberg, Jackson Team for Tintin." *Variety*, 14 May 2007. http://variety.com/2007/film/news/spielberg-jackson-team-for-tintin-1117 964927/.

McCloud, Scott. *Making Comics: Storytelling Secrets of Comics, Manga and Graphic Novels*. New York: Harper, 2006.

———. *Reinventing Comics*. New York: Perennial, 2000.

———. *Understanding Comics: The Invisible Art*. New York: HarperPerennial, 1994.

McFarlane, Brian. *Novel to Film: An Introduction to the Theory of Adaptation*. Oxford: Clarendon, 1996.

———. "Reading Film and Literature." In *The Cambridge Companion to Literature on Screen*, edited by Deborah Cartmell and Imelda Whelehan, 15–28. Cambridge: Cambridge University Press, 2007.

McLaughlin, Jeff. *Comics as Philosophy*. Jackson: University Press of Mississippi, 2005.

McLuhan, Marshall. *Understanding Media: The Extensions of Man*. New York: McGraw-Hill, 1964.

McQ. Dir. John Sturges. Perf. John Wayne. Warner Bros. Pictures, 1974.

Medhurst, Andy. "Batman, Deviance and Camp." In *The Many Lives of the Batman: Critical Approaches to a Superhero and His Media*, edited by Roberta E. Pearson and William Uricchio, 149–63. New York: Routledge, 1991.

Meehan, Eileen. "Holy Commodity Fetish, Batman!: The Political Economy of a Commercial Intertext." In *The Many Lives of the Batman: Critical Approaches to a Superhero and His Media*, edited by Roberta E. Pearson and William Uricchio, 47–65. New York: Routledge, 1991.

Meet the Spartans. Dir. Jason Friedberg and Aaron Seltzer. Perf. Sean Maguire, Carmen Electra, and Ken Davitian. 20th Century Fox, 2008.

Melnick, Jeffrey Paul. *9/11 Culture: America under Construction*. Chichester, West Sussex, UK: Wiley-Blackwell, 2009.

Memento. Dir. Christopher Nolan. Perf. Guy Pearce, Carrie-Anne Moss, and Joe Pantoliano. Summit Entertainment, 2000.

Men in Black. Dir. Barry Sonnenfeld. Perf. Will Smith and Tommy Lee Jones. Columbia Pictures, 1997.

Mendelson, Scott. "20 Years Later, How Batman Changed the Movie Business." *Open Salon*, 24 June 2009. http://open.salon.com/blog/scott_mendelson/2009/06/24/20_years_later_ how_batman_changed_the_movie_business.

Mendryk, Harry. "Evolution of Kirby Krackle." *Jack Kirby Museum*, 3 Sept. 2011. http://kirbymu seum.org/blogs/simonandkirby/archives/3997.

Meteling, Arno. "A Tale of Two Cities: Politics and Superheroics in Starman and Ex Machina." In *Comics and the City: Urban Space in Print, Picture, and Sequence*, edited by Jörn Ahrens and Arno Meteling, 133–49. New York: Continuum, 2010.

Metz, Christian. "Film Language." 1974. In *Film Theory and Criticism: Introductory Readings*, edited by Leo Braudy and Marshall Cohen, 65–86. New York: Oxford University Press, 2004.

Milch, David. "Deadwood." *Deadwood*. HBO, 21 Apr. 2004.

Milch, David, and Steven Bocho. "Pilot." *NYPD Blue*. ABC, 21 Sept. 1993.

Millar, Mark, and J. G. Jones. *Wanted*. Los Angeles, CA: Top Cow Productions, 2007.

Millar, Mark, and Steve McNiven. *Civil War: A Marvel Comics Event*. New York, NY: Marvel Publishing, 2007.

Millar, Mark, and John Romita, Jr. *Kick-Ass*. New York, NY: Marvel Pub., 2010.

Miller, Frank. *Sin City: The Big Fat Kill*. Milwaukie, OR: Dark Horse, 2010.

———. *Sin City: The Hard Goodbye*. Milwaukie, OR: Dark Horse, 2005.

———. *Sin City: That Yellow Bastard*. Milvaukie, OR: Dark Horse Comics, 1996.

Miller, Frank, Klaus Janson, and Lynn Varley. *The Dark Knight Returns*. London: Titan, 1997.

Miller, Frank, and David Mazzucchelli. *Batman: Year One*. Milano: R.C.S. Rizzoli Periodici, 1988.

Miller, Frank, and Lynn Varley. *300*. Milwaukie, OR: Dark Horse Comics, 1999.

———. "Glory." *300*, July 1998: n. pag.

The Miller and the Sweep. Dir. George Albert Smith. 1897.

"Miller on Miller" (supplementary material on DVD release of *Frank Miller's Sin City: Recut & Extended*). Miramax Home Entertainment, 2007.

MirrorMask. Dir. Dave McKean. Perf. Stephanie Leonidas, Rob Brydon, and Gina McKee. Jim Henson Pictures, 2005.

Mission: Impossible. Dir. Brian De Palma. Perf. Tom Cruise. Paramount Pictures, 1996.

Moench, Doug, Chuck Dixon, and Alan Grant. *Batman: Knightfall*. New York, NY: DC Comics, 2012.

Moodie, Alison. "'I'm Bummed': Shailene Woodley on Her Mary Jane Role Getting Cut from The Amazing Spider-Man 2." *Mail Online*, 19 June 2013. http://www.dailymail.co.uk/tvshow biz/article-2344672/Shailene-Woodley-Mary-Jane-role-getting-cut-The-Amazing-Spider -Man-2.html.

Moore, Alan, and Brian Bolland. *Batman: The Killing Joke*. London: Titan, 1988.

Moore, Alan, and Eddie Campbell. *From Hell: Being a Melodrama in Sixteen Parts*. Marietta, GA: Top Shelf Productions, 2006.

Moore, Alan, and Dave Gibbons. *Watchmen*. New York: DC Comics, 1987.

Moore, Alan, and David Lloyd. *V for Vendetta*. London: Titan, 1990.

Moore, Alan, and Kevin O'Neill. *The League of Extraordinary Gentlemen*. La Jolla, CA: America's Best Comics, 2000.

Moore, Alan, J. H. Williams, and Mick Gray. *Promethea*. La Jolla, CA: America's Best Comics, 2000.

Moore, Michael Ryan. "Adaptation and New Media." *Adaptation* 3.2 (2010): 179–92.

Moriarty. "AICN EXCLUSIVE! X3 Script Review! Plus An Open Letter To Tom Rothman And Fox Stockholders!!" *Ain't It Cool News*, 15 June 2007. http://www.aintitcool.com/node/20443.

Morris, Nigel. "Movies and Crisis." In *American Cinema of the 2000s: Themes and Variations*, edited by Timothy Corrigan, 147–71. New Brunswick, NJ: Rutgers University Press, 2012.

Morrison, Grant. *Supergods: Our World in the Age of the Superhero*. London: Jonathan Cape, 2011.

Morrison, Grant, Tony S. Daniel, and Guy Major. *Batman R.I.P.* New York: DC Comics, 2009.

Morrison, Grant, Chris Sprouse, Frazer Irving, and Yanick Paquette. *Batman: The Return of Bruce Wayne*. New York: DC Comics, 2011.

Morton, Drew. "Godard's Comic Strip Mise-en-Scène." *Senses of Cinema* 53 (Dec. 2009): n. pag.

Mount, Harry. "Holy Propaganda! Batman Is Tackling Osama Bin Laden." *Telegraph*, 15 Feb. 2006. http://www.telegraph.co.uk/news/worldnews/northamerica/usa/1510556/Holy-propaganda-Batman-is-tackling-Osama-bin-Laden.html.

Moyo, Last. "Digital Democracy: Enhancing the Public Sphere." In *Digital Cultures*, edited by Glen Creeber and Royston Martin, 139–56. Maidenhead: Open University Press, 2009.

Mr. Mom. Dir. Stan Dragoti. Perf. Michael Keaton and Teri Garr. 20th Century Fox, 1983.

Mumpower, David. "Top 12 Film Industry Stories of 2008: #11 Writers' Strike Impact Not So Horrible." *Box Office Prophets*, 7 Jan. 2009. http://www.boxofficeprophets.com/column/index.cfm?columnID=11207.

Murphie, Andrew, and John Potts. *Culture and Technology*. New York: Palgrave Macmillan, 2003.

Murray, Kathleen. "To Have and Have Not." In *True to the Spirit: Film Adaptation and the Question of Fidelity*, edited by Colin MacCabe, Rick Warner, and Kathleen Murray, 91–113. Oxford: Oxford University Press, 2011.

Musser, Charles. "Program Notes by Film Historian Charles Musser." In *The Movies Begin Volume Three: Experimentation and Discovery*. New York: Kino on Video, 2002, n. pag.

The Mutant Watch. Dir. Thomas C. Grane. Perf. Bruce Davidson and Bryan Singer. 20th Century Fox, 2000.

Mutt and Jeff and the Country Judge. Prod. David Horsley. Perf. Sam D. Drane and Gus Alexander. Nestor Film Company, 1911.

Mutt and Jeff and the Dog Catchers. Prod. David Horsley. Perf. Sam D. Drane and Gus Alexander. Nestor Film Company, 1911.

My Darling Clementine. Dir. John Ford. Perf. Henry Fonda, Victor Mature, and Linda Darnell. 20th Century Fox, 1946.

My Super Ex-Girlfriend. Dir. Ivan Reitman. Perf. Luke Wilson and Uma Thurman. 20th Century Fox, 2006.

Mystery Men. Dir. Kinka Usher. Perf. Hank Azaria, Claire Forlani, and Janeane Garofalo. Universal Pictures, 1999.

Naremore, James. "Acting in Cinema." In *The Cinema Book*, edited by Pam Cook, 114–18. 3rd ed. Annapolis: British Film Institute, 2007.

———. "Introduction: Film and the Reign of Adaptation.'" In *Film Adaptation*, 1–18. New Brunswick, NJ: Rutgers University Press, 2000.

Nathan, Ian. Review of *Watchmen*. *Empire*, n.d.: n. pag. http://www.empireonline.com/reviews/reviewcomplete.asp?DVDID=118154.

Ndalianis, Angela. "Comic Book Superheroes: An Introduction." In *The Contemporary Comic Book Superhero*, edited by Angela Ndalianis, 3–15. New York: Routledge, 2009.

———. "The Frenzy of the Visible in Comic Book Worlds." *Animation* 4.3 (2009): 237–48.

———. "Why Comics Studies?" *Cinema Journal* 50.3 (2011): 113–17.

Neale, Steve. *Genre and Hollywood*. London: Routledge, 2000.

———. "Questions of Genre." *Screen* 31.1 (1990): 45–66.

Need for Speed. Dir. Scott Waugh. Perf. Aaron Paul, Dominic Cooper, and Imogen Poots. Touchstone Pictures, 2014.

New Nightmare. Dir. Wes Craven. Perf. Robert Englund and Heather Langenkamp. New Line Cinema, 1994.

Newman, Kim. Review of *Batman Begins*. *Empire*, July 2005: n. pag. http://www.empireonline .com/reviews/review.asp?DVDID=11299.

A Nightmare on Elm Street. Dir. Wes Craven. Perf. John Saxon, Ronee Blakley, Heather Langen- kamp, Johnny Depp, Robert Englund, and Jsu Garcia. New Line Cinema, 1984.

Nightwatching. Dir. Peter Greenaway. Perf. Martin Freeman. ContentFilm International, 2007.

Niles, Steve. Personal interview, 16 Mar. 2012.

Niles, Steve, Ben Templesmith, and Robbie Robbins. *30 Days of Night*. San Diego, CA: Idea & Design Works, LLC, 2003.

9-11: Artists Respond. Milwaukie, OR: Dark Horse Comics, 2002.

9-11: The World's Finest Comic Book Writers and Artists Tell Stories to Remember. New York, NY: DC Comics, 2002.

No Country for Old Men. Dir. Joel Coen and Ethan Coen. Perf. Tommy Lee Jones and Javier Bardem. Miramax, 2007.

O Brother Where Art Thou? Dir. Joel Coen and Ethan Coen. Perf. George Clooney, John Tur- turro, and Tim Blake Nelson. Momentum Pictures, 2000.

Oblivion. Dir. Joseph Kosinski. Perf. Tom Cruise, Olga Kurylenko, and Andrea Riseborough. Universal Pictures, 2013.

O'Hara, Helen. "Zack Snyder Talks Watchmen." *Empire: Film Reviews, Movie News and Inter- views*, 14 Nov. 2008. http://www.empireonline.com/news/story.asp?NID=23670.

Oldboy. Dir. Chan-wook Park. Perf. Choi Min-sik, Yoo Ji-tae, and Kang Hye-jung. Show East, 2003.

O'Malley, Bryan Lee. *Scott Pilgrim's Precious Little Life*. Portland, OR: Oni, 2004.

O'Neil, Dennis. "Bat-bible." Email to the author, 23 Sept. 2010.

———. *Bat-bible*. N.p.: Unpublished, 25 Sept. 2010. DOC.

O'Neil, Dennis, and Dick Giordano. "The Man Who Falls." In *Secret Origins of the World's Greatest Super-Heroes*, edited by Mark Waid and Roy Thomas, n. pag. New York, NY: DC Comics, 1989.

Otterbourg, Sam. "Yo, Bruce Wayne, I'm Really Happy for You and I'ma Let You Finish, but Green Arrow Had One of the Best Rebirths of All Time." Weblog post. *Flash Facts: Studies in Superheroics*, 19 May 2010. http://studiesinsuperheroics.blogspot.com.au/2010/05/yo -bruce-wayne-im-really-happy-for-you.html.

Outcault, Richard F. "Feudal Pride in Hogan's Alley." *Truth*, 2 June 1894: 4.

"Outfitting a Hero" (supplementary material on Blu-ray release of *Captain America: The First Avenger*). Paramount Studios, 2011.

Packer, Sharon. *Superheroes and Superegos: Analyzing the Minds behind the Masks*. Santa Bar- bara: Praeger/ABC-CLIO, 2010.

Parody, Claire. "Franchising/Adaptation." *Adaptation* 4.2 (2011): 210–18.

Parsons, Patrick. "Batman and His Audience: The Dialectic of Culture." In *The Many Lives of the Batman: Critical Approaches to a Superhero and His Media*, edited by Roberta E. Pearson and William Uricchio, 66–89. New York: Routledge, 1991.

Pasko, Martin. *The DC Vault: A Museum-in-a-book Featuring Rare Collectibles from the DC Universe*. Philadelphia: Running, 2008.

Pearson, Roberta E., and William Uricchio. *The Many Lives of the Batman: Critical Approaches to a Superhero and His Media*. New York: Routledge, 1991.

——. "Notes from the Batcave: An Interview with Dennis O'Neil." In *The Many Lives of the Batman: Critical Approaches to a Superhero and His Media,* edited by Roberta E. Pearson and William Uricchio, 18–32. New York: Routledge, 1991.

Pedler, Martyn. "The Fastest Man Alive: Stasis and Speed in Contemporary Superhero Comics." *Animation* 4.3 (2009): 249–63.

——. "Morrison's Muscle Mystery Versus Everyday Reality . . . and Other Parallel Worlds!" In *The Contemporary Comic Book Superhero,* edited by Angela Ndalianis, 250–69. New York: Routledge, 2009.

Pekar, Harvey, and R. Crumb. *American Splendor Presents Bob & Harv's Comics.* New York: Four Walls Eight Windows, 1996.

Percy Jackson and the Lightning Thief. Dir. Chris Columbus. Perf. Logan Lerman, Brandon T. Jackson, and Alexandra Daddario. 20th Century Fox, 2010.

Perenson, Melissa J. "Bat Seat Driver." *Film Review,* July 1997: 32–40.

Perry, David. *Enter the Matrix.* Computer software. N.p.: Warner Bros. Interactive Entertainment, 2003.

Perry, Spencer. "Mary Jane Won't Appear in The Amazing Spider-Man 2, Role Pushed to Third Film." *Superhero Hype,* 19 June 2013. http://www.superherohype.com/news/177605-mary-jane-wont-appear-in-the-amazing-spider-man-2-role-pushed-to-third-film.

Persepolis. Dir. Marjane Satrapi and Vincent Paronnaud. Perf. Chiara Mastroianni and Catherine Deneuve. Sony Pictures Classics, 2008.

A Personal Journey with Martin Scorsese Through American Movies. Dir. Martin Scorsese and Michael Henry Wilson. Perf. Martin Scorsese. British Film Institute, 1995.

Petersen, Robert. "The Acoustics of Manga." In *A Comics Studies Reader,* edited by Jeet Heer and Kent Worcester, 163–71. Jackson: University Press of Mississippi, 2009.

The Phantom. Dir. Simon Wincer. Perf. Billy Zane. Paramount Pictures, 1996.

The Piano. Dir. Jane Campion. Perf. Holly Hunter, Harvey Keitel, Sam Neill, and Anna Paquin. Miramax Films, 1993.

Pierson, Michele. "CGI Effects in Hollywood Science-fiction Cinema 1989–95: The Wonder Years." *Screen* 40.2 (1999): 158–76.

Pietrzak-Franger, Monika. "Fifth International Association of Adaptation Studies Conference, The Centre for British Studies, Berlin, 30 September to 1 October 2010." *Adaptation* 4.1 (2011): 108–15.

Pirates of the Caribbean: Dead Man's Chest. Dir. Gore Verbinski. Perf. Johnny Depp and Keira Knightley. Walt Disney Pictures, 2006.

Pleasantville. Dir. Gary Ross. Perf. Tobey Maguire, William H. Macy, and Joan Allen. New Line Cinema, 1998.

Plumb, Ali. "Nic Cage Talks Tim Burton's Superman Lives." *Empireonline.com,* 19 July 2013. http://www.empireonline.com/news/story.asp?NID=38155.

Polan, Dana. "Movies, A Nation and New Identities." In *American Cinema of the 2000s: Themes and Variations,* edited by Timothy Corrigan, 216–37. New Brunswick, NJ: Rutgers Universisty Press, 2012.

The Polar Express. Dir. Robert Zemeckis. Perf. Tom Hanks. Warner Bros. Pictures, 2004.

Popeye. Dir. Robert Altman. Perf. Robin Williams and Shelley Duvall. Paramount Pictures, 1980.

Predator. Dir. John McTiernan. Perf. Arnold Schwarzenegger, Carl Weathers, and Bill Duke. 20th Century Fox, 1987.

Primorac, Antonija. "Sixth Annual Association of Adaptation Studies Conference, Yeni Yüzyıl University, Istanbul, 29–30 September 2011." *Adaptation* 5.1 (2012): 129–35.

Prince of Persia: The Sands of Time. Dir. Mike Newell. Perf. Jake Gyllenhaal, Gemma Arterton, and Ben Kingsley. Walt Disney Pictures, 2010.

Prince, Stephen. "The Discourse of Pictures: Iconicity and Film Studies." *Film Quarterly* 47.1 (1993): 16–28.

———. "The Emergence of Filmic Artifacts: Cinema and Cinematography in the Digital Era." *Film Quarterly* 57.3 (2004): 24–33.

———. "True Lies: Perceptual Realism, Digital Images, and Film Theory." *Film Quarterly* 49.3 (1996): 27–37.

Proctor, William. "Dark Knight Triumphant: Fandom, Hegemony and the Rebirth of Batman on Film." In *Fan Phenomena: Batman*, edited by Liam Burke, 154–65. Bristol: Intellect, 2013.

———. "'Holy Crap, More Star Wars! More Star Wars? What If They're Crap?': Disney, Lucasfilm and Star Wars Online Fandom in the 21st Century." *Participations: Journal of Audience & Reception Studies* 10.1 (2013): 198–224.

Propp, Vladimir. *Morphology of the Folktale*. Austin: University of Texas, 1968.

Psycho. Dir. Alfred Hitchcock. Perf. Janet Leigh and Anthony Perkins. Paramount Pictures, 1960.

Psycho. Dir. Gus Van Sant. Perf. Anne Heche and Vince Vaughan. Universal Pictures, 1998.

Psycho II. Dir. Richard Franklin. Perf. Anthony Perkins, Vera Miles, and Robert Loggia. Universal Pictures, 1983.

Psycho III. Dir. Anthony Perkins. Perf. Anthony Perkins, Diana Scarwid, and Jeff Fahey. Universal Pictures, 1986.

The Public Enemy. Dir. William Augustus Wellman. Perf. James Cagney and Jean Harlow. Warner Bros. Pictures, 1931.

The Punisher. Dir. Mark Goldblatt. Perf. Dolph Lundgren and Louis Gossett, Jr. New World Pictures, 1989.

The Punisher. Dir. Jonathan Hensleigh. Perf. Thomas Jane and John Travolta. Lionsgate, 2004.

Punisher: War Zone. Dir. Lexi Alexander. Perf. Ray Stevenson, Dominic West, and Julie Benz. Lionsgate, 2008. [DVD Commentary from 2009 edition].

Push. Dir. Paul McGuigan. Perf. Chris Evans and Dakota Fanning. Summit Entertainment, 2009.

Pustz, Matthew. *Comic Book Culture: Fanboys and True Believers*. Jackson: University Press of Mississippi, 1999.

Radish, Christina. "Composer Hans Zimmer Talks About Crowd Sourcing Chants for the Score of THE DARK KNIGHT RISES." *Collider*, 9 Dec. 2011. http://collider.com/hans-zimmer-dark-knight-rises-interview/.

Rae, Neil, and Jonathan Gray. "When Gen-X Met The X-Men: Retextualizing Comic Book Film Reception." In *Film and Comic Books*, edited by Ian Gordon, Mark Jancovich, and Matthew P. McAllister, 86–100. Jackson: University Press of Mississippi, 2007.

Raiders of the Lost Ark. Dir. Steven Spielberg. Perf. Harrison Ford. Paramount Pictures, 1981.

Raising Arizona. Dir. Joel Coen and Ethan Coen. Perf. Nicolas Cage and Holly Hunter. 20th Century Fox, 1987.

Ramachandran, V. S., and E. M. Hubbard. "Synaesthesia: A Window into Perception, Thought and Language." *Journal of Consciousness Studies* 8.12 (2001): 3–34.

Rambo. Dir. Sylvester Stallone. Perf. Sylvester Stallone, Julie Benz, and Paul Schulze. Millennium Films, 2008.

Rambo: First Blood Part II. Dir. George P. Cosmatos. Perf. Sylvester Stallone. TriStar Pictures, 1985.

Raw, Laurence. "Does Not Incorporate New Developments in Adaptation Theory." *Amazon .com: True to the Spirit: Film Adaptation and the Question of Fidelity (9780195374674): Colin MacCabe, Kathleen Murray, Rick Warner: Books*, 22 Nov. 2011. http://www.amazon.com/ True-Spirit-Adaptation-Question-Fidelity/dp/0195374673.

Ray, Robert B. "The Field of "Literature and Film." In *Film Adaptation*, edited by James Naremore, 38–53. New Brunswick, NJ: Rutgers University Press, 2000.

Red. Dir. Robert Schwentke. Perf. Bruce Willis, Morgan Freeman, and John Malkovich. Summit Entertainment, 2010.

Regalado, Aldo J. "Unbreakable and the Limits of Transgression." In *Film and Comic Books*, edited by Ian Gordon, Mark Jancovich, and Matthew P. McAllister, 116–36. Jackson: University Press of Mississippi, 2007.

Rehak, Bob. "Movies, 'Shock and Awe,' and the Blockbuster." In *American Cinema of the 2000s: Themes and Variations*, edited by Timothy Corrigan, 83–103. New Brunswick, NJ: Rutgers University Press, 2012.

Reinhard, Carrie Lynn. "Comics Aren't Film and Other Vicey Verses." Proc. of Comics Arts Conference, San Diego. N.p.: 2007, n. pag.

Resident Evil. Dir. Paul W. S. Anderson. Perf. Milla Jovovich, Michelle Rodriguez, and Eric Mabius. Constantin Film, 2002.

Rêve à La Lune. Dir. Gaston Velle. Perf. Ferdinand Zecca. Pathé, 1905.

Reynolds, Paul. "Declining Use of 'War on Terror.'" *BBC News*, 17 Apr. 2007. http://news.bbc .co.uk/2/hi/uk_news/politics/6562709.stm.

Reynolds, Richard. *Super Heroes: A Modern Mythology*. Jackson: University Press of Mississippi, 1992.

Rich, Joshua. "'Hulk': An 'Incredible' Weekend Win." *Entertainment Weekly*, 16 June 2008. http:// www.ew.com/ew/article/0,,20206822,00.html.

Rickman, Lance. "Bande Dessinée and the Cinematograph: Visual Narrative in 1895." *European Comic Art* 1.1 (2008): 1–20.

Riddick. Dir. David Twohy. Perf. Vin Diesel and Katee Sackhoff. Universal Pictures, 2013.

Riddle Me This: Why Is Batman Forever. Dir. John Pattyson and Michael Meadows. Perf. Chris O'Donnell. Warner Bros., 1995.

R.I.P.D. Dir. Robert Schwentke. Perf. Jeff Bridges and Ryan Reynolds. Universal Pictures, 2013.

"Rite of Passage" (supplementary material on Blu-ray release of *The Amazing Spider-Man*). Sony Pictures Home Entertainment, 2012.

Road to Perdition. Dir. Sam Mendes. Perf. Tom Hanks, Jude Law, and Paul Newman. DreamWorks Pictures, 2002.

Robertson, Barbara. "The Colorists." *CGSociety: Society of Digital Artists*, 1 May 2006. http:// features.cgsociety.org/story_custom.php?story_id=3549.

RoboCop. Dir. Paul Verhoeven. Perf. Peter Weller and Nancy Allen. Orion Pictures Corporation, 1987.

The Rocketeer. Dir. Joe Johnston. Perf. Billy Campbell and Jennifer Connelly. Walt Disney Pictures, 1991.

RocknRolla. Dir. Guy Ritchie. Perf. Gerard Butler and Mark Strong. Warner Bros. Pictures, 2008.

Rockoff, Adam. *Going to Pieces: The Rise and Fall of the Slasher Film, 1978–1986*. Jefferson, NC: McFarland & Co., 2002.

Roddenberry, Gene, prod. "Where No Man Has Gone Before." *Star Trek*. NBC, 22 Sept. 1966.

Rodowick, D. N. "Dr. Strange Media; Or, How I Learned to Stop Worrying and Love Film Theory." *PMLA* 116.5 (2001): 1396–404.

Rogen, Seth, and Evan Goldberg. "Homer the Whopper." *The Simpsons*. Dir. Lance Kramer. Fox, 27 Sept. 2009.

Rogers, Vaneta. "Newsarama.com: The COMIC BOOK MOVIE Decade—And Beyond." *Newsarama*, 4 Feb. 2010. http://www.newsarama.com/film/Comic-Movie-Decade-100204 .html.

Rope. Dir. Alfred Hitchcock. Perf. James Stewart. Warner Bros. Pictures, 1948.

Rosenbaum, Jon H., and Peter C. Sederberg. "Vigilantism: An Analysis of Establishment Violence." *Comparative Politics* 6.4 (1974): 541–70.

Rosenbaum, Jonathan. "Two Forms of Adaptation: Housekeeping and Naked Lunch." In *Film Adaptation*, edited by James Naremore, 206–20. New Brunswick, NJ: Rutgers University Press, 2000.

Rosenberg, Adam. "NYCC: Shyamalan's 'Unbreakable.'" *Comic Book Resources*, 13 Oct. 2010. http://www.comicbookresources.com/?page=article&id=28868.

Rosenberg, Scott Mitchell. Personal interview, 16 Mar. 2012.

Rosenberg, Scott Mitchell, Andrew Foley, Luciano Lima, and Fred Van Lente. *Cowboys & Aliens*. New York: It, 2011.

Ross, Susan Dente. Introduction. In *Images That Injure: Pictorial Stereotypes in the Media*, edited by Susan Dente Ross and Paul Martin Lester, 1–4. Santa Barbara, CA: Praeger, 2011.

Rossen, Jake. *Superman vs. Hollywood: How Fiendish Producers, Devious Directors, and Warring Writers Grounded an American Icon*. Chicago, IL: Chicago Review, 2008.

Rossman, Margaret. "The Passive Case: How Warner Bros. Employed Viral Marketing and Alternate Reality Gaming to Bring Fandom Back Into the Culture Industry." In *Fan Phenomena: Batman*, edited by Liam Burke, 68–77. Chicago: University Of Chicago Press, 2013.

Russell, Vanessa. "The Mild-Mannered Reporter: How Clark Kent Surpassed Superman." In *The Contemporary Comic Book Superhero*, edited by Angela Ndalianis, 216–32. New York: Routledge, 2009.

Russian Ark. Dir. Aleksandr Sokurov. Perf. Sergei Dontsov. Wellspring Media, 2002.

Ryan, Marie-Louise. "The Modes of Narrativity and Their Visual Metaphors." *Style* 26.3 (1992): 368–87.

Sabin, Roger. *Comics, Comix & Graphic Novels: A History of Graphic Novels*. London: Phaidon, 1996.

Sadlier, Darlene J. "The Politics of Adaptation: How Tasty Was My Little Frenchman." In *Film Adaptation*, edited by James Naremore, 190–205. New Brunswick, NJ: Rutgers University Press, 2000.

Sadoul, Georges. "Lumière—The Last Interview." *Sight and Sound*, Summer 1948: n. pag.

Said, S. F. "The Misfits of Zwigoff." *Sight and Sound*, Aug. 2000: 21–22.

Salisbury, Mark. "X-Men." *Total Film*, Aug. 2000: 44–54.

Sansweet, Stephen J., and Peter Vilmur. *The Star Wars Vault: A Scrapbook of 30 Years of Rare Removable Memorabilia*. New York: Harper Entertainment, 2007.

Saraceni, Mario. *The Language of Comics*. London: Routledge, 2003.

Sarris, Andrew. "Ang Lee's Angst-Ridden Hulk: The Not-So-Jolly Green Giant." *New York Observer*, 7 July 2003: n. pag. http://observer.com/2003/07/ang-lees-angstridden-hulk-the-notsojolly-green-giant/.

———. "Notes on the Auteur Theory." In *Film Theory and Criticism: Introductory Readings*, edited by Leo Braudy and Marshall Cohen, 561–65. 6th ed. New York: Oxford University Press, 2004.

Scary Movie. Dir. Keenan Ivory Wayans. Perf. Anna Faris and Marlon Wayans. Dimension Films, 2000.

Schaefer, Sandy. "First Look At '300 Prequel Comic Book." *ScreenRant*, 2010. http://screenrant.com/300-prequel-comic-book-xerxes-sandy-62930/.

Schatz, Thomas. "Film Genre and the Genre Film." In *Film Theory and Criticism: Introductory Readings*, edited by Leo Braudy and Marshall Cohen, 691–702. 6th ed. New York: Oxford University Press, 2004.

———. *The Genius of the System: Hollywood Filmmaking in the Studio Era*. New York: Pantheon, 1988.

———. *Hollywood Genres: Formulas, Filmmaking, and the Studio System*. Philadelphia: Temple University Press, 1981.

———. "Hollywood: The Triumph of the Studio System." In *The Oxford History of World Cinema*, edited by Geoffrey Nowell-Smith, 220–34. Oxford: Oxford Univeristy Press, 1996.

———. "Movies and a Hollywood Too Big to Fail." In *American Cinema of the 2000s: Themes and Variations*, edited by Timothy Corrigan, 194–215. New Brunswick, NJ: Rutgers University Press, 2012.

Schelly, Bill. *Sense of Wonder: A Life in Comic Fandom*. Raleigh: TwoMorrows, 2001.

Schindler's List. Dir. Steven Spielberg. Perf. Liam Neeson, Ben Kingsley, and Ralph Fiennes. Universal Pictures, 1993.

Schneider, Steven Jay. "Architectural Nostalgia and the New York City Skyline on Film." In *Film and Television after 9/11*, edited by Wheeler W. Dixon, 29–41. Carbondale: Southern Illinois University Press, 2004.

Schuker, Lauren A. E. "Warner Bets on Fewer, Bigger Movies." *Wall Street Journal*, 22 Aug. 2008. http://online.wsj.com/news/articles/SB121936107614461929.

Schwarzbaum, Lisa. Review of *Mirrormask*. *Entertainment Weekly*, 28 Sept. 2005: n. pag. http://www.ew.com/ew/article/0,,1114678,00.html.

Scooby-Doo. Dir. Raja Gosnell. Perf. Freddie Prinze, Jr., Sarah Michelle Gellar, and Matthew Lillard. Warner Bros. Pictures, 2002.

Scott, A. O. "How Many Superheroes Does It Take to Tire a Genre?" *New York Times*, 24 July 2008: n. pag. http://www.nytimes.com/2008/07/24/movies/24supe.html.

Scott, Cord. "Written in Red, White, and Blue: A Comparison of Comic Book Propaganda from World War II and September 11." *Journal of Popular Culture* 40.2 (2007): 325–43.

Scott, Mike. "'Sherlock Holmes,' or the Case of Style over Substance." *Times-Picayune*, 25 Dec. 2009: n. pag. http://www.nola.com/movies/index.ssf/2009/12/sherlock_holmes_or_the_case_of.html.

Scott Pilgrim vs. The World. Dir. Edgar Wright. Perf. Michael Cera, Chris Evans, and Brandon Routh. Universal Pictures, 2010.

Scream. Dir. Wes Craven. Perf. Neve Campbell, David Arquette, and Courtney Cox. Dimension Films, 1996.

"Scream 2009." *Spike.com*, n.d. http://www.spike.com/event/scream.

The Searchers. Dir. John Ford. Perf. John Wayne and Jeffrey Hunter. Warner Bros. Pictures, 1956.

Semple, Lorenzo, Jr. "Hi Diddle Riddle." *Batman*. ABC, 12 Jan. 1966.

Serpico. Dir. Sidney Lumet. Perf. Al Pacino. Paramount Pictures, 1973.

Seymour, Gene. "On the Field of This Battle, War Is Swell." *Newsday*, 9 Mar. 2007: n. pag.

The Shadow. Dir. Russell Mulcahy. Perf. Alec Baldwin. Universal Pictures, 1994.

"Shadows of the Bat: The Cinematic Saga of the Dark Knight, Part 2" (supplementary material on DVD release of *Batman*). Warner Home Video, 2007.

Shakespeare, William. *Hamlet*. London: Methuen, 1982.

Shaner, Timothy. *The Art of "X-Men 2."* London: Titan, 2003.

Shankar, Naren. "Family Affair." *CSI: Crime Scene Investigation*. CBS, 24 Sept. 2009.

Sharrett, Christopher. "Batman and the Twilight of the Idols: An Interview with Frank Miller." In *The Many Lives of the Batman: Critical Approaches to a Superhero and His Media*, edited by Roberta E. Pearson and William Uricchio, 33–46. New York: Routledge, 1991.

Shaw, Chris. "The Film Classification Debate." *Culture Northern Ireland*, n.d. http://www.culturenorthernireland.org/article.aspx?art_id=2354&cmd=print.

Sherlock Holmes. Dir. Guy Ritchie. Perf. Robert Downey, Jr., and Jude Law. Warner Bros. Pictures, 2009.

Shoard, Catherine. "Dark Knight Rises: Fancy a Capitalist Caped Crusader as Your Superhero?" *Guardian*, 17 July 2012. http://www.theguardian.com/film/filmblog/2012/jul/17/dark-knight-rises-capitalist-superhero.

Shrek. Dir. Andrew Adamson and Vicky Jenson. Perf. Mike Myers and Cameron Diaz. Dreamworks Pictures, 2001.

Simon, David. "The Target." *The Wire*. HBO, 2 June 2002.

Simpson, David. *9/11: The Culture of Commemoration*. Chicago: University of Chicago, 2006.

Sin City. Dir. Robert Rodriguez. Perf. Mickey Rourke, Bruce Willis, and Jessica Alba. Dimension Films, 2005. [DVD Commentary from 2007 edition].

Sinfield, Alan. *Faultlines: Cultural Materialism and the Politics of Dissident Reading*. Berkeley: University of California, 1992.

Singin' in the Rain. Dir. Gene Kelly and Stanley Donen. Perf. Gene Kelly, Donald O'Connor, and Debbie Reynolds. MGM, 1952.

Sirota, David. "Batman Hates the 99 Percent." *Salon*, 19 July 2010. http://www.salon.com/2012/07/18/batman_hates_the_99_percent/.

Sky Captain and the World of Tomorrow. Dir. Kerry Conran. Perf. Jude Law, Gwyneth Paltrow, and Angelina Jolie. Paramount Pictures, 2004.

Sliney, Will. "The Comic Book Film Adaptation." Email to the author, 12 Mar. 2014.

"Slo-Mo" (supplementary material on Blu-ray release of *Dredd*). Icon Home Entertainment, 2013.

Smith, Anne K. "Marvel Entertainment: Super Hero Stock?" *Washington Post*, 15 May 2008. http://www.washingtonpost.com/wp-dyn/content/article/2008/05/15/AR2008051501267 .html.

Smith, Ben. "A Noun, a Verb, and 9/11 . . ." *Politico.com*, 30 Oct. 2007. http://www.politico.com/ blogs/bensmith/1007/A_noun_a_verb_and_911.html.

Smith, Dina. "Movies and the Art of Living Dangerously." In *American Cinema of the 2000s: Themes and Variations*, edited by Timothy Corrigan, 172–93. New Brunswick, NJ: Rutgers University Press, 2012.

Smith, Greg M. "It Ain't Easy Studying Comics." *Cinema Journal* 50.3 (2011): 110-12.

The Smurfs. Dir. Raja Gosnell. Perf. Hank Azaria, Neil Patrick Harris, and Jayma Mays. Sony Pictures Animation, 2011.

Snakes on a Plane. Dir. David R. Ellis. Perf. Samuel L. Jackson and Julianna Margulies. New Line Cinema, 2006.

Snickars, Pelle, and Patrick Vonderau. *The YouTube Reader*. Stockholm: National Library of Sweden, 2009.

Sobchack, Vivian Carol. *Screening Space: The American Science Fiction Film*. New York: Ungar, 1987.

Soda Jerks. Dir. Charles R. Bower and Bud Fischer. 1925.

Solomon, Charles. *The Art of the Animated Image: An Anthology*. Los Angeles, CA: American Film Institute, 1987.

Somigli, Luca. "Superhero with a Thousand Faces: Visual Narratives on Film and Paper." In *Play It Again, Sam: Retakes on Remakes*, edited by Andrew Horton and Stuart Y. McDougal, 279–94. Berkeley: University of California, 1998.

Sorlin, Pierre. "Godard: Lo Schermo Come Fascicolo a Fumetti." Proc. of XV International Film Studies Conference, Italy, Udine. N.p.: 2008, n. pag.

Sparrow, Andrew. "Dark Knight: MPs Criticise Batman Film's 12A Certificate." *Guardian.co.uk.*, 5 Aug. 2008. http://www.guardian.co.uk/politics/2008/aug/05/politicsandthearts.

Spawn. Dir. Mark A. Z. Dippé. Perf. John Leguizamo, Michael Jai White, and Martin Sheen. New Line Cinema, 1997.

Speed Racer. Dir. Andy Wachowski and Larry Wachowski. Perf. Emile Hirsch, Christina Ricci, and Matthew Fox. Warner Bros. Pictures, 2008.

Sperling, Nicole. "Next 'Spider-Man' Film Will Be a Gritty, Contemporary Reboot of the Franchise." *Entertainment Weekly*, 11 Jan. 2010. http://hollywoodinsider.ew.com/2010/01/11/ spider-man-reboot/.

Spider-Man. Dir. Sam Raimi. Perf. Tobey Maguire and Willem Dafoe. Columbia Pictures, 2002.

Spider-Man 2. Dir. Sam Raimi. Perf. Tobey Maguire, Kirsten Dunst, and Alfred Molina. Columbia Pictures, 2004.

Spider-Man 3. Dir. Sam Raimi. Perf. Tobey Maguire, Kirsten Dunst, and James Franco. Columbia Pictures, 2007.

Spider-Man: Turn Off the Dark. By Bono, Edge, Julie Taymor, Glen Berger, and Roberto Aguirre-Sacasa. Foxwoods Theatre, New York, 27 Nov. 2013.

Spiegelman, Art. *In the Shadow of No Towers*. New York: Pantheon, 2004.

———. *Maus I: A Survivor's Tale: My Father Bleeds History*. New York: Pantheon, 1986.

———. "Picturing a Glassy-eyed Private I." In *City of Glass*, by Paul Karasik, David Mazzuc-chelli, and Paul Auster. Bath: Faber and Faber, 2005: n. pag.

Spines, Christine. "Exclusive: Fox Chairman Says Leaked 'Wolverine' Is an 'Unfinished Version' and 'a Complete Misrepresentation of the Film.'" *Entertainment Weekly*, 3 Apr. 2009. http://insidemovies.ew.com/2009/04/03/exclusive-fox-c/.

———. "'Wolverine' Tracking Data: Interest in the Film Remains High, Despite Internet Leak." *Entertainment Weekly*, 13 Apr. 2009. http://insidemovies.ew.com/2009/04/13/wolverine-disas/.

The Spirit. Dir. Frank Miller. Perf. Gabriel Macht and Eva Mendes. Lionsgate, 2008. [DVD Commentary from 2009 edition].

Stagecoach. Dir. John Ford. Perf. Claire Trevor, John Wayne, and Andy Devine. United Artists, 1939.

Stam, Robert. "Beyond Fidelity: The Dialogics of Adaptation." In *Film Adaptation*, edited by James Naremore, 54–78. New Brunswick, NJ: Rutgers University Press, 2000.

———. *Film Theory: An Introduction*. Malden, MA: Blackwell, 2000.

———. "Introduction: The Theory and Practice of Adaptation." In *Literature and Film: A Guide to the Theory and Practice of Film Adaptation*, edited by Alessandra Raengo and Robert Stam, 1–52. Malden, MA: Blackwell, 2005.

Stam, Robert, and Alessandra Raengo. *Literature and Film: A Guide to the Theory and Practice of Film Adaptation*. Malden, MA: Blackwell, 2005.

Star Wars. Dir. George Lucas. Perf. Mark Hamill, Harrison Ford, Carrie Fisher, Peter Cushing, Alec Guinness, and Anthony Daniels. 20th Century Fox, 1977.

Star Wars: The Phantom Menace. Dir. George Lucas. Perf. Liam Neeson, Ewan McGregor, and Natalie Portman. 20th Century Fox, 1999.

Steranko, James. *The Steranko History of Comics*. Vol. 2. Pennsylvania: Supergraphics, 1972. [DVD Commentary from 2004 edition].

Studio Briefing. "Parents Cautioned About Taking Small Kids To See Spider-Man." *Internet Movie Database*, 7 May 2002. http://www.imdb.com/news/ni0095040/.

Stuever, Hank. "A Dead-Letters Day: Comic Books End Printed Mail Columns As Fans Turn to Web." *Washington Post*, 10 Dec. 2002, sec. C: 1.

Sunrise: A Song of Two Humans. Dir. F. W. Murnau. Perf. George O'Brien and Janet Gaynor. Eureka Entertainment, 1927. [DVD Commentary from 2004 edition].

Super. Dir. James Gunn. Perf. Rainn Wilson, Ellen Page, and Liv Tyler. IFC Films, 2010.

"Superfans and Batmaniacs." *Newsweek*, 15 Feb. 1965: 89.

Superhero Movie. Dir. Craig Mazin. Perf. Drake Bell, Sara Paxton, Christopher McDonald, and Kevin Hart. Metro-Goldwyn-Mayer, 2008.

Superman. Dir. Spencer Gordon Bennet and Thomas Carr. Perf. Kirk Alyn and Noel Neill. Columbia Pictures, 1948.

Superman II. Dir. Richard Lester. Perf. Christopher Reeve, Terrence Stamp, and Gene Hackman. Warner Bros. Pictures, 1980.

Superman IV: The Quest for Peace. Dir. Sidney J. Furie. Perf. Christopher Reeve, Gene Hackman, and Jackie Cooper. Cannon Films, 1987.

Superman: The Movie. Dir. Richard Donner. Perf. Christopher Reeve and Marlon Brando. Warner Bros. Pictures, 1978.

Superman Returns. Dir. Bryan Singer. Perf. Brandon Routh, Kate Bosworth, and Kevin Spacey. Warner Bros. Pictures, 2006.

Superman vs. The Elite. Dir. Michael Change. By Joe Kelly. Perf. George Newbern and Pauley Perrette. Warner Home Video, 2012.

Surrogates. Dir. Jonathan Mostow. Perf. Bruce Willis. Touchstone Pictures, 2009.

Sutton, Damian. "The DreamWorks Effect: Studying the Ideology of Production Design." *Screen* 45.4 (2004): 383–90.

Swordfish. Dir. Dominic Sena. Perf. Hugh Jackman, Halle Berry, and John Travolta. Universal Pictures, 2001.

Takacs, Stacy. "The Contemporary Politics of the Western Form: Bush, Saving Jessica Lynch, and Deadwood." In *Reframing 9/11: Film, Popular Culture and the "War on Terror,"* edited by Jeff Birkenstein, Anna Froula, and Karen Randell, 153–66. New York: Continuum, 2010.

"Taking Flight: The Development of Superman" (supplementary material on DVD release of *Superman: The Movie*). Warner Home Video, 2001.

Tamara Drewe. Dir. Stephen Frears. Perf. Gemma Arterton, Dominic Cooper, and Luke Evans. Ruby Films, 2010.

Tappan, Mark. "Superheroes and the Media." *"Packaging Boyhood,"* 18 Aug. 2010. http://packag ingboyhood.com.

Taxi Driver. Dir. Martin Scorsese. Perf. Robert De Niro, Jodie Foster, Albert Brooks, Harvey Keitel, and Cybill Shepherd. Columbia Pictures Presents, 1976.

Taylor, Todd. "If He Catches You, You're Through: Coyotes and Visual Ethos." In *The Language of Comics: Word and Image*, edited by Robin Varnum and Christina T. Gibbons, 40–59. Jackson: University Press of Mississippi, 2001.

Teenage Mutant Ninja Turtles. Dir. Steve Barron. Perf. Judith Hoag, Elias Koteas, and Raymond Serra. New Line Cinema, 1990.

"10 Lessons Learned From the $1.5 Billion AVENGERS Movie." *Newsarama*, 2 May 2012. http:// www.newsarama.com/15542-10-lessons-learned-from-the-1-5-billion-avengers-movie.html.

The Texas Chainsaw Massacre. Dir. Marcus Nispel. Perf. Jessica Biel, Jonathan Tucker, and Erica Leerhsen. New Line Cinema, 2003.

Theatrical Market Statistics. Rep. Motion Picture Association of America, 21 Mar. 2013. http:// www.mpaa.org/wp-content/uploads/2014/03/2012-Theatrical-Market-Statistics-Report .pdf.

There Will Be Blood. Dir. Paul Thomas Anderson. Perf. Daniel Day-Lewis, Paul Dano, Kevin J. O'Connor, Ciarán Hinds, and Dillon Freasier. Paramount Vantage, 2007.

30 Days of Night. Dir. David Slade. Perf. Josh Hartnett and Melissa George. Sony Pictures, 2007.

Thomas, Roy, and Peter Sanderson. *The Marvel Vault*. Philadelphia: Running, 2007.

Thompson, Anne. "Filmmakers Intent on Producing New Comic-book Movies." *Sun-Sentinel (Fort Lauderdale)*, 26 Aug. 1986: n. pag.

Thompson, Don. "OK. Axis, Here We Come!" In *All in Color for a Dime*, edited by Richard A. Lupoff and Don Thompson, 110–29. New Rochelle, NY: Arlington House, 1970.

Thompson, Kristin. *The Frodo Franchise: The Lord of the Rings and Modern Hollywood*. Berkeley: University of California, 2007.

Thompson, Luke Y. "Comic-Con Move From San Diego To Anaheim Or LA? (Hell No! We Won't Go!)" *Deadline*, 8 May 2010. http://www.deadline.com/2010/05/ comic-con-move-from-san-diego-to-anaheim-or-la-hell-no-we-wont-go/.

Thor. Dir. Kenneth Branagh. Perf. Chris Hemsworth and Natalie Portman. Paramount Pictures, 2011. [Blu-Ray Commentary from 2011 edition].

Thor: The Dark World. Dir. Alan Taylor. Perf. Chris Hemsworth and Natalie Portman. Marvel Studios, 2013.

300. Dir. Zack Snyder. Perf. Gerard Butler, Michael Fassbender, and Dominic West. Warner Bros. Pictures, 2007. [DVD Commentary from 2007 edition].

300: Rise of an Empire. Dir. Noam Murro. Perf. Sullivan Stapleton, Eva Green, and Lena Headey. Warner Bros. Pictures, 2014.

The 300 Spartans. Dir. Rudolph Maté. Perf. Richard Egan, Ralph Richardson, and Diane Baker. 20th Century Fox, 1962.

"300 Spartans—Fact or Fiction?" (supplementary material on DVD release of *300*). Warner Home Video, 2007.

"300 Webisodes" (supplementary material on DVD release of *300*). Warner Home Video, 2007.

Tilley, Carol L. "Seducing the Innocent: Fredric Wertham and the Falsifications That Helped Condemn Comics." *Information and Culture: A Journal of History* 47.4 (2012): 383–413.

Time Code. Dir. Mike Figgis. Perf. Holly Hunter, Saffron Burrows, and Stellan Skarsgård. Screen Gems, 2000.

Toh, Justine. "The Tools and Toys of (the) War (on Terror): Consumer Desire, Military Fetish, and Regime Change in Batman Begins." In *Reframing 9/11: Film, Popular Culture and the "War on Terror,"* edited by Jeff Birkenstein, Anna Froula, and Karen Randell, 127–40. New York: Continuum, 2010.

Tolkien, J. R. R. *The Lord of the Rings*. Boston: Houghton Mifflin, 1954.

Transformers: Revenge of the Fallen. Dir. Michael Bay. Perf. Shia LeBouf, Megan Fox, and John Turturro. DreamWorks Pictures, 2009.

True Lies. Dir. James Cameron. Perf. Arnold Schwarzenegger and Jamie Lee Curtis. 20th Century Fox, 1994.

Tucker, Ken. "Caped Fears." *Entertainment Weekly*, 16 June 2000. http://www.ew.com/ew/article/0,,276435,00.html.

Tudor, Andrew. *Theories of Film*. New York: Viking, 1974.

Tuthill, Matt. "Man of Steel: How Henry Cavill Got Superhero-Shredded." *Muscle & Fitness*, n.d. http://www.muscleandfitness.com/news-and-features/athletes-and-celebrities/man-steel-henry-cavill.

21. Dir. Robert Luketic. Perf. Jim Sturgess and Kevin Spacey. Columbia Pictures, 2008.

Twilight. Dir. Catherine Hardwicke. Perf. Kristen Stewart and Robert Pattinson. Summit Entertainment, 2008.

Unbreakable. Dir. M. Night Shyamalan. Perf. Bruce Willis, Samuel L. Jackson, and Robin Wright Penn. Touchstone Pictures, 2000.

"Uncanny Suspects" (supplementary material on DVD release of *X-Men 1.5*). 20th Century Fox Home Entertainment, 2003.

Underworld. Dir. Len Wiseman. Perf. Kate Beckinsale, Scott Speedman, and Michael Sheen. Sony Pictures Entertainment, 2003.

"The Unique Style of Editing the Hulk" (supplementary material on DVD release of *Hulk*). 20th Century Fox Home Entertainment, 2003.

Up. Dir. Pete Docter. Perf. Ed Asner, Christopher Plummer, and Jordan Nagai. Pixar, 2009.

Urban Legend. Dir. Jamie Blanks. Perf. Jared Leto, Alicia Witt, and Rebecca Gayheart. TriStar Pictures, 1998.

Uricchio, William. "The Batman's Gotham City™: Story, Ideology, Performance." In *Comics and the City: Urban Space in Print, Picture, and Sequence,* edited by Jörn Ahrens and Arno Meteling, 119–33. New York: Continuum, 2010.

Uslan, Michael E. Telephone interview, 15 Aug. 2012.

V for Vendetta. Dir. James McTeigue. Perf. Natalie Portman, Hugo Weaving, and Stephen Fry. Warner Bros. Pictures, 2005.

Valentine. Dir. Jamie Blanks. Perf. David Boreanaz and Denise Richards. Warner Bros. Pictures, 2001.

Valluri, Gautman. "The Death of the Dutch Angle." *BrokenProjector.com,* 24 July 2007. http://www.brokenprojector.com.

Varnum, Robin, and Christina T. Gibbons. *The Language of Comics: Word and Image.* Jackson: University Press of Mississippi, 2001.

Vaughan, Brian K., and Tony Harris. *Ex Machina.* La Jolla, CA: WildStorm Productions/DC Comics, 2007.

Vaughan, Brian K., and Fiona Staples. *Saga.* Berkeley, CA: Image Comics, 2012.

Vaz, Mark Cotta. *The Spirit: The Movie Visual Companion.* London: Titan Book, 2008.

Vineyard, Jennifer. "Alan Moore: The Last Angry Man." *Movies on MTV.com,* n.d. http://www.mtv.com/shared/movies/interviews/m/moore_alan_060315/.

———. "How To Reboot The Superman Movie Franchise—Comic Writers Chime In." *Splash Page,* 8 Nov. 2008. http://splashpage.mtv.com/2008/08/11/how-to-reboot-the-superman-movie-franchise-comic-writers-chime-in/.

"Visual Effect" (supplementary material on DVD release of *Star Wars: The Phantom Menace*). 20th Century Fox Home Video, 2001.

"The Visual Effects of X-Men" (supplementary material on DVD release of *X-Men 1.5*). 20th Century Fox Home Entertainment, 2003.

"Visualising Gotham: The Production Design of Batman" (supplementary material on DVD release of *Batman*). Warner Bros. Home Entertainment, 2005.

Vogel, Harold L. *Entertainment Industry Economics: A Guide for Financial Analysis.* 7th ed. Cambridge: Cambridge University Press, 2007.

Von Riedemann, Dominic. "Cars 2 Announced: Disney/Pixar Film Will Come to Theatres in 2011." *Suite101.com,* 6 Mar. 2008. http://hollywood-animated-films.suite101.com/article.cfm/cars_2_announced.

Wagner, Geoffrey Atheling. *The Novel and the Cinema.* Rutherford, NJ: Fairleigh Dickinson University Press, 1975.

Waid, Mark. Personal interview, 17 Mar. 2012.

Waid, Mark, and Leinil Francis Yu. *Superman: Birthright.* New York: DC Comics, 2004.

Waid, Mark, and Alex Ross. *Kingdom Come.* New York: DC Comics, 2008.

Wakeman, Gregory. "5 Bullettime Fight Scenes That Ripped Off The Matrix." *Screen Junkies,* 30 July 2013. http://www.screenjunkies.com/tag/bullet-time-sequences-inspired-by-the-matrix/.

Walker, Michael. *The Movie Book of Film Noir.* Edited by Ian Cameron. London: Cassell Illustrated, 1994.

Walker, Mort. *The Lexicon of Comicana*. New York: Backinprint.com, 2000.

Wall-E. Dir. Andrew Stanton. Perf. Ben Burtt, Elissa Knight, and Jeff Garlin. Pixar, 2008.

Waller, Gregory A. "Rambo: Getting to Win This Time." In *From Hanoi to Hollywood: The Vietnam War in American Film*, edited by Linda Dittmar and Gene Michaud, 113–28. New Brunswick, NJ: Rutgers University Press, 1990.

Wanted. Dir. Timur Bekmambetov. Perf. James McAvoy, Angelina Jolie, and Morgan Freeman. Spyglass Entertainment, 2008.

War of the Worlds. Dir. Steven Spielberg. Perf. Tom Cruise, Dakota Fanning, Miranda Otto, and Justin Chatwin. Paramount Pictures, 2005.

Ward, Kate. "21 Worst Comic-Book Movies." *Entertainment Weekly*, 18 May 2011. http://www.ew.com/ew/gallery/0,,20186843_20558036,00.html.

"Warner Bros. Press notes." *Thedarkknight.warnerbros.com*. http://thedarkknight.warnerbros.com/dvdsite/event/index.html.

The Warriors Ultimate Director's Cut. Dir. Walter Hill. Perf. Michael Beck and James Remar. Paramount Pictures, 2006.

Watchmen. Dir. Zack Snyder. Perf. Patrick Wilson, Jackie Earle Haley, and Billy Crudup. Warner Bros. Pictures, 2009.

"Weaving the Web" (supplementary material on DVD release of *Spider-Man*). Columbia Tristar Home Entertainment, 2002.

Weiner, Rex. "WWW.H'W'D.TICKED." *Variety*, 29 July 1997. http://www.variety.com/article/VR1116675713.html?categoryid=1009&cs=1.

Weiner, Stephen. *The 101 Best Graphic Novels*. New York: NBM, 2005.

Weird Science. Dir. John Hughes. Perf. Anthony Michael Hall and Kelly LeBrock. Universal Pictures, 1985.

Welland, Jonah. "'300' Post-Game: One-on-One with Zack Snyder." *Comic Book Resources*, 14 Mar. 2007. http://www.comicbookresources.com/?page=article&old=1&id=9982.

Wells, Paul. *Animation: Genre and Authorship*. London: Wallflower, 2002.

Wertham, Fredric. *Seduction of the Innocent*. New York: Rinehart, 1954.

———. *The World of Fanzines: A Special Form of Communication*. Carbondale: Southern Illinois University Press, 1973.

"What is Bullet-time?" (supplementary material on DVD release of *The Matrix*). Warner Bros. Home Entertainment, 1999.

Whedon, Joss, Jed Whedon, and Maurissa Tancharoen. "Pilot." *Agents of S.H.I.E.L.D.* ABC, 24 Sept. 2013.

Whelehan, Imelda. "Adaptations: The Contemporary Dilemmas." In *Adaptations: From Text to Screen, Screen to Text*, edited by Deborah Cartmell and Imelda Whelehan, 3–20. London: Routledge, 1999.

White, Armond. "Knight to Remember." *New York Press*, 23 July 2008: n. pag. http://nypress.com/knight-to-remember/.

White, James. "Thor Teaser Poster Released." *Empireonline.com*, 10 Dec. 2010. http://www.empireonline.com/news/story.asp?NID=29700.

Whitmore, Sean, and Brandon Hanvey. "Hayter-ade." *ComicCritics.com: A Webcomic about Comics*, 20 Mar. 2009. http://comiccritics.com/2009/03/20/hayter-ade/.

"Who Were the Spartans?" (supplementary material on DVD release of *300*). Warner Home Video, 2007.

"'Who's Watching the Watchmen? Everybody.'" *TodayShow.com*, 8 Mar. 2009. http://www.msnbc.msn.com/id/29584644/.

Williams, Linda Ruth. "Movies, Smart Films, and Dumb Stories." In *American Cinema of the 2000s: Themes and Variations*, edited by Timothy Corrigan, 40–60. New Brunswick, NJ: Rutgers University Press, 2012.

Williamson, Catherine. "'Draped Crusaders': Disrobing Gender in The Mark of Zorro." *Cinema Journal* 36.2 (1997): 3–16.

Willingham, Bill. *Fables*. New York: DC Comics, 2002.

Willis, Sharon. "Movies and Melancholy." In *American Cinema of the 2000s: Themes and Variations*, edited by Timothy Corrigan, 61–82. New Brunswick, NJ: Rutgers University Press, 2012.

Wilonksy, Robert. "The Brave and the Bold." *SF Weekly (San Francisco)*, 3 Oct. 2001, Arts sec.: 1.

Winchester '73. Dir. Anthony Mann. Perf. James Stewart and Shelly Winters. Universal International, 1950.

Wind(up)bird. "BATMAN BEGINS: New Pics of the Batsuit!" Weblog post. *Dtheatre*, 28 July 2004. http://www.dtheatre.com/read.php?sid=2543.

Winsor McCay: The Famous Cartoonist of the N.Y. Herald and His Moving Comics. Dir. J. Stuart Blackton and Winsor McCay. Perf. Winsor McCay. 1911.

Winston, Brian. *Media Technology and Society: A History: From the Telegraph to the Internet*. London: Routledge, 1998.

Winters Keegan, Rebecca. "Graphic Novels Are Hollywood's Newest Gold Mine." *Time*, 19 June 2008. http://www.time.com/time/magazine/article/0,9171,1816487,00.html#ixzz0qphIjjuu.

"Wired: The Visual Effects of Iron Man" (supplementary material on DVD release of *Iron Man*). Paramount Pictures, 2008.

Witek, Joseph. *Comic Books as History: The Narrative Art of Jack Jackson, Art Spiegelman, and Harvey Pekar*. Jackson: University Press of Mississippi, 1989.

———. "From Genre to Medium: Comics and Contemporary American Culture." In *Rejuvenating the Humanities*, edited by Ray B. Browne and Marshall William Fishwick, 71–79. Bowling Green, OH: Bowling Green State University Popular Press, 1992.

Wolf, Thomas. "Reading Reconsidered." *Harvard Educational Review* 47 (1977): 411–29.

The Wolverine. Dir. James Mangold. Perf. Hugh Jackman, Tao Okamoto, and Rila Fukushima. 20th Century Fox, 2013.

Wood, Aylish. "Timespaces in Spectacular Cinema: Crossing the Great Divide of Spectacle versus Narrative." *Screen* 43.4 (2002): 370–86.

Worcester, Kent. "New York City, 9/11, and Comics." *Radical History Review* 2011.111 (2011): 139–54.

World Trade Center. Dir. Oliver Stone. Perf. Nicolas Cage and Michael Peña. Paramount Pictures, 2006.

Wright, Bradford W. *Comic Book Nation: The Transformation of Youth Culture in America*. Baltimore: Johns Hopkins University Press, 2003.

Wright, Jarrell D. "Shades of Horror." In *True to the Spirit: Film Adaptation and the Question of Fidelity*, edited by Colin MacCabe, Rick Warner, and Kathleen Murray, 173–93. Oxford: Oxford University Press, 2011.

"X-Factor: The Look of the X-Men" (supplementary material on DVD release of *X-Men 1.5*). 20th Century Fox Home Entertainment, 2003.

X-Men. Dir. Bryan Singer. Perf. Patrick Stewart, Hugh Jackman, and Halle Berry. 20th Century Fox, 2000.

X-Men: Days of Future Past. Dir. Bryan Singer. Perf. Hugh Jackman, James McAvoy, and Michael Fassbender. 20th Century Fox, 2014.

X-Men: First Class. Dir. Matthew Vaughn. Perf. James McAvoy, Michael Fassbender, and Jennifer Lawrence. 20th Century Fox, 2011.

X-Men: The Last Stand. Dir. Brett Ratner. Perf. Patrick Stewart, Hugh Jackman, and Halle Berry. 20th Century Fox, 2006.

X-Men Legends. N.p.: Activision, 2005.

X-Men Origins: Wolverine. Dir. Gavin Hood. Perf. Hugh Jackman, Liev Schreiber, and Danny Huston. 20th Century Fox, 2009.

"X-Men: Production Scrapbook" (supplementary material on DVD release of *X-Men 1.5*). 20th Century Fox Home Entertainment, 2003.

X2. Dir. Bryan Singer. Perf. Patrick Stewart, Hugh Jackman, and Halle Berry. 20th Century Fox, 2003.

Zakarian, Jordan. "The Insane Destruction That The Final 'Man Of Steel' Battle Would Do To NYC, By The Numbers." *BuzzFeed*, 17 June 2013. http://www.buzzfeed.com/jordanzakarin/man-of-steel-destruction-death-analysis.

Žižek, Slavoj. "Welcome to the Desert of the Real!" *South Atlantic Quarterly* 101.2 (2002): 385–89.

Zoolander. Dir. Ben Stiller. Perf. Ben Stiller and Owen Wilson. Paramount Pictures, 2001.

Zuckerman, Ed. "Prescription for Death." *Law & Order*. NBC, 13 Sept. 1990.

INDEX

Page numbers in **bold** indicate an illustration.